Heterologies

Theory and History of Literature
Edited by Wlad Godzich and Jochen Schulte-Sasse

Heterologies
Discourse on the Other

Michel de Certeau

Translated by Brian Massumi
Foreword by Wlad Godzich

Theory and History of Literature, Volume 17

 University of Minnesota Press
Minneapolis
London

The University of Minnesota Press is grateful for assistance to translation and publication of this book by the Georges Lurcy Charitable and Educational Trust, New York, and for translation support provided by the French Ministry of Culture and Communication.

Michel de Certeau gratefully acknowledges the assistance of Luce Giard, who revised the translation under his supervision.

Published by the University of Minnesota Press
2037 University Avenue Southeast, Minneapolis, MN 55455-3092
Printed in the United States of America on acid-free paper

Third printing, 1993

Library of Congress Cataloging-in-Publication Data

Certeau, Michel de.
  Heterologies: discourse on the other.

  (Theory and history of literature; v. 17)
  Collection of essays, some previously published, translated from the French.
  Includes bibliographical references and index.
  1. Literature—Philosophy—Addresses, essays, lectures. I. Title. II. Series.
PN45.C4 1985   801   85-16457
ISBN 0-8166-1403-2
ISBN 0-8166-1404-0 (pbk.)

Chapter 1, "Psychoanalysis and Its History," was originally published as "Histoire et psychanalyse," in *La nouvelle histoire*, ed. J. Le Goff, R. Chartier, J. Revel (Paris: Retz, 1978), pp. 477–487, and is reprinted with permission of the publisher. Chapter 8, "The Beauty of the Dead: Nisard," first appeared as "La beauté du mort" (chapter 3), in *La culture au pluriel*, 2nd ed., series 10/18 (Paris: U.G.E., 1980), pp. 49–80, and is reproduced with permission of Christian Bourgois.

Contents

IV. OTHERS' HISTORIES

V. CONCLUSION

Foreword
The Further Possibility of Knowledge
Wlad Godzich

Michel de Certeau is the author of nearly a score of books that range in subject matter from theology and history of religions to anthropology and that include theoretical reflections on the writing of history as well as contributions to contemporary cultural criticism, literary theory, and the analysis of everyday life. In his case, this is not merely an indication of a profusion of intellectual interests but rather the proper and legitimate exercise of certifiably acquired knowledge: he has received advanced training in theology, history, the study of comparative religions, psychoanalysis, and anthropology. He has taught in all these fields at major universities in France and in the Americas, and is currently dividing his time between the University of California at Los Angeles, where he teaches literature, and Paris, where, in addition to his teaching and research duties, he is active in a number of collective endeavors, not the least of which is the journal *Traverses*, a very stimulating pluridisciplinary publication of the design center at Beaubourg.

The present volume provides ample evidence of this wide range of activity, and its title, though perhaps not altogether euphonious in English, is further indication that the author not only is aware of this but intends it. *Heterology* is a term that has come to designate a philosophical countertradition that, in shorthand, could be described as being deeply suspicious of the Parmenidean principle of the identity of thought and being. Although de Certeau does not make overt reference to the themes and motifs of this tradition, his choice of title, significantly pluralized, places him among those who have reacted against the modern forms of this prejudice, that is, against the mainstream of speculative

vii

philosophy which finds the Parmenidean principle embodied in the inexorable workings of the Hegelian dialectic as it paves the way for the Spirit's conquest of the world. De Certeau's line of attack upon this problem is of interest to all who are concerned with the present state, and the further possibilities, of knowledge, for it is the very organization of knowledge, in its present dependence (albeit a generally unconscious one) upon the Hegelian model, that figures at the center of his preoccupations.

I

Most members of the countervailing tradition—Nietzsche, Heidegger, Bataille, Blanchot, Derrida—have been mainly concerned with either the ontological or the epistemolgial questions that any critique of the Hegelian position inevitably raises. De Certeau tends to stay away from these aspects of the matter in order to explore other, seemingly less momentous, features, primarily of a discursive order. In the process he shows quite conclusively how pervasive, and nefarious, the Parmenidean model is across what we like to call the disciplines, and by what means we may work around it. In contrast, then, to the tradition of which he is a part, de Certeau has clear practical aims. There is thus something very atheoretical about his endeavor, not because of any opposition to theory as such, but because the old construction of the opposition of theory and practice is part of the speculative edifice that de Certeau no longer finds hospitable or, perhaps more accurately, affordable. It exacts too high a price for the amenities that it provides. But this atheoretical stance does not make for an absence of theory in what he writes, as the reader will quickly discover. It simply makes for a different positioning of the theoretical, one that strikes me as quite novel.

De Certeau relegates to the background the epistemological questions that have recently figured so prominently in our discussions as he conducts his reflection on the present organization of knowledge. This reflection leads him to pay special attention to the question of the Other, a question that figures as a leitmotif in many of the current discussions of knowledge, whether they originate in epistemological concerns or not. This is not the place for an exhaustive historical analysis of the emergence of this issue in contemporary reflections, but it may be useful to recall two somewhat different areas in which it has imposed itself on our consciousnesses far beyond any theoretical concern that we may have: the conception of the subject as the organizer and sense-maker of lived experience, and the challenge posed to forms of Western thought by the liberation movements of the past forty years. Both of these have contributed to a sense of fragmentation that is widespread in our culture and that has been diversely theorized in recent years.

fragmentate of self/knowledge

II

The first may be usefully approached through the process of social abstraction, of which de Certeau, in his multifarious guises, would appear to be a prime example. This process, whose nature was recognized in the Enlightenment—the period during which it achieved nearly universal extension in the industrializing countries—cleaves the subject and disrupts other entities, such as the family, in order to tailor it to the needs of production. There results an internal division of the subject between the kind of self that one needs to be in certain situations, generally linked to one's means of livelihood, and the kind of self that one is in other settings. The individual no longer feels his or her self to be a whole, but rather a series of diverse zones, subject to differing constraints, frequently of an irreconcilable sort. The paradigmatic, though extreme, example here is of the Nazi executioner who carries out his orders cold-bloodedly (if he is not the one who gives them) but sheds tears of most exquisite sensitivity at the performance of a Beethoven quartet. The results of this process of social abstraction have been thematized in literature, with varying degrees of pathos, as the fragmentation of the self; they have also constituted the psychological ground of French existentialism. Most contemporary theory, save for those strands of it that retain some connection to Marxist perspectives, has generally accepted this fragmentation and has sought to ground it either ontologically or psychologically. In fact, it has tended to focus its efforts on bringing theories of the subject in line with this experience. And, since the fundamental effect of this experience is to create a sense of powerlessness with respect to one's ability to direct or control larger historical processes, history as a dimension of human practice has borne the brunt of these efforts. Notions of desire or even of the aleatory have been put forward in its stead.

It would be tempting to see Michel de Certeau's rather large range of pursuits as an instance of this process of social abstraction in the intellectual field. This field does not so readily admit of this process, however. Our present organization of knowledge may very well share with other forms of the division of labor a commitment to the efficiency of performance, but, rightly or wrongly, it conceives itself more properly as an allocation of competences that are appropriate to their object, an object that is no longer defined as a given of the world but is a construct of the theoretical and methodological traditions of each discipline. The disciplinary outlook, in other words, permits each discipline to function as if the problem of fragmentation did not arise since the concepts that it mobilizes and the operations it performs are adequate, if not isomorphic, to its object —an elegant variant of the Parmenidean principle of the identity of thought and being. This may well account for the blindness of the disciplinary perspective to the problem of fragmentation: it is constitutive of that perspective.

In such a context, the reach of de Certeau's activities is bound to be seen as excessive, and his attitude as extravagant, unless it can be construed as one of the reminders that the disciplines do not really constitute wholly autonomous domains but are part of a larger whole. To be sure, there have been ample periodic reminders of the fact that the disciplines do not, and properly cannot, close up upon themselves, but these very reminders serve more as boundary markers than as attempts to open up the disciplines. The same may be said of the persistent yet unfruitful efforts to establish interdisciplinary approaches over the past thirty years. And, of course, there have been claims of primacy of position made on behalf of certain disciplines or specific approaches, most significantly the Husserlian one for phenomenology, and, more recently, the rather widespread one for the more scholastic conceptions of semiotics. But de Certeau's approach seeks neither to affirm some evanescent unity nor to play the role of the protector of the integrity of the present configuration of knowledge. His attitude is more scandalous in that he seeks to exacerbate the fragmentation by deliberately uncovering the ways in which the various disciplinary enterprises rely upon models and paradigms borrowed from each other, and never less so than when they proclaim their independence, so that the mutual relation of the disciplines is never one of autonomy or of heteronomy, but some sort of complicated set of textual relations that needs to be unraveled in each instance—a task that Michel de Certeau accomplishes with maestria in several of the chapters of this book. His is a challenge to the present organization of knowledge, a challenge that is attentive to the dimension of crisis throughout this area.

III

In retrospect, it should have been obvious at the time that the great sociopolitical upheavals of the late fifties and sixties, especially those regrouped under the names of decolonization and liberation movements, would have a major impact on the ways of knowledge. This impact, though it had begun to occur almost immediately, has not, for the most part, been recognized for a variety of reasons, the strongest of which is the imperviousness of the branches of knowledge—as an organic conception of the disciplines likes to call them—to phenomena that "fall" outside their predefined scope and, at a more general level, our reluctance to see a relationship so global in reach—between the epistemology of knowledge and the liberation of people—a relationship that we are not properly able to theorize. Yet there is no need for a belief in the totalizability of social phenomena, nor is it necessary to have a fully articulated theory of the cross-determinations of economic, social, political, psychological, and epistemological phenomena, to take note of such an impact. In what follows, I will try to briefly sketch the main lines of the evolving form of impact.

Decolonization, as we know, has been a multifaceted process that does not lend itself to facile generalization. Yet it may be apprehended at the discursive level as a tense interaction of the older liberal discourse (gnawed from within by its reliance upon late eighteenth-century conceptions of the role of nations as both agents of history and containers of lower forms of agency) and the Marxist one, an interaction particularly visible in the cultural movement called French existentialism. The ideology of universalism common to the two discourses can be the means of enslavement—instrumental reason in the service of rapacity unrestrained in the laissez-faire market of liberalism or the even greater omnipotence of the hypostasized state—or it can be emancipatory. This is the famous dialectic of the Enlightenment that requires the vigilance of intellectuals to ensure that the positive project of modernism prevails over its less savory alter ego, in Habermas's self-assumed historical task, so noble yet so difficult to carry out. For a Sartre, e.g., the struggles of the colonized were just and deserved the support of all individuals of conscience because of the legitimacy of their claim to universal rights. A similar attitude prevailed in liberal circles in the American civil-rights movement. But when the latter evolved in the direction of Black Power, that is, toward the rejection of the ideology of universalism, and began to put forth a claim of particularism, liberal support vanished, and indeed changed into outright hostility, since the universalism that constituted the core of its ideological stance presupposes the eradication of particularisms.

Be that as it may, decolonization was followed by a reterritorialization that became rapidly conceptualized through notions of core and periphery, in which the former colonial powers together with other economically dominant nations constitute the core whereas the former colonies form the periphery. The latter admits of measurement in relation to the core as an index of its degree of development, where it is of course implicit that the core's own development is normative and somehow "natural." Such an approach requires that one distinguish circles, if not outright peripheries, within the core as well and that ultimately some center be located, even if it means that national and regional boundaries must be ignored. Part of the present broader economic crisis certainly seems to have to do with the determination of such a new center.

Again, in retrospect, it is apparent that, of all the poststructuralisms, deconstruction is the one that has reacted critically to this development—what we know as neocolonialism—by doggedly revealing the fact that there never is anything "natural" or "inevitable" or to be taken for granted in the setting up of center and periphery. It is always the result of specific and discernible operations: rhetorical ones in texts, power ones in the broader social area; though there may well be a gain in describing the latter in terms of the subtle analytics of textual operations. This would explain, among other things, the difficult relationship of deconstruction to the previous forms of emancipatory discourses, especially the institutionalized Marxist one: the neocolonialism of center and periphery is practiced as much if not more by the Soviet Union as it is by the Western powers, whether the old colonial empires or the new neocolonial ones. Structuralism, for its part, shared in the operative conceptualization of neocolonialism by elevating the notion of function, or, more precisely, of efficiency, to the highest. It is more efficient to structure in terms of center and periphery. In Gramscian terms, structuralism, by which I mean the international movement called French Structuralism, thus would correspond to the position of the organic intellectual formation, whereas the poststructuralisms would represent an emancipatory response to the hegemony of neocolonialism. The relation of deconstruction to structuralism becomes clearer in the process.

There is another movement that challenges our thought even further: the wars of liberation against neocolonialism that differ from the earlier colonialist ones in that they are not waged from a position of nation—something that is understandable to liberalism—or of class—as Marxism would prefer it—but from settings or entities that have not been thought out within the framework of Western tradition. Such will remain the enduring significance of the Cuban Revolution, which can be usefully contrasted in this respect to the Algerian War of national independence. Such are the characteristics of the complex struggles being waged in parts of Africa and in Central America, though they differ markedly from each other. Whatever views one may hold with respect to these struggles, one must acknowledge that they are part of a series of challenges to the dominant forms and organizations of knowledge among us. The response to these new liberation struggles is telling. There is relatively little attempt to understand them in their specificity; it is easier to impose upon them the bipolarity that is so constitutive a part of structuralism: there will not be one center with its periphery but two antagonistic centers with their own peripheries, with flashpoints at the boundaries.

As in the case of the fragmented subject, the historical dimension is again ignored: historical forces are taken to be no more than acts of willfulness, perhaps of an irrational form, which it is then easy to attribute to "terrorists." Not only does such a reformulation ignore the specificity of the political movements at hand, but, as de Certeau shows in the case of the struggles of the autochthonous peoples of the Americas, it deprives them of a ground from which to make their claims. But, as daily headlines make clear, such a ground is being found, though we tend to experience the resulting claims as disruptions to our patterns of perception, and we find ourselves in a position of bewilderment that makes us easy prey to manipulations of all sorts. We do not know, often enough, what the values that we hold require of us in front of phenomena that strike us as other.

IV

*But also,
Rousseau, Eden.
etc.*

Thesis

Western thought has always thematized the other as a threat to be reduced, as a potential same-to-be, a yet-not-same. The paradigmatic conception here is that of the quest in romances of chivalry in which the adventurous knight leaves Arthur's court—the realm of the known—to encounter some form of otherness, a domain in which the courtly values of the Arthurian world do not prevail. The quest is brought to an end when this alien domain is brought within the hegemonic sway of the Arthurian world: the other has been reduced to (more of) the same. The quest has shown that the other is amenable to being reduced to the status of the same. And, in those few instances where the errant knight—Lohengrin, for example—does find a form of otherness that he prefers to the realm of the same from which he came, this otherness is interpreted—by contemporary critics as much as by medieval writers—as the realm of the dead, for it is ideologically inconceivable that there should exist an otherness of the same ontological status as the same, without there being immediately mounted an effort at its appropriation.

Again, we may be unable to provide a satisfactory theorization of the link between epistemology and broader forms of social practice, but it is clear that the hegemonic impulse thematized in the chivalric quest was a fact of culture and that its failure in the political realm—witness the case of the wars upon Islam (the Crusades)—in no way invalidated its hold in other areas, especially in the practice of knowledge, as Edward Said has convincingly shown. Politically, the West may have had to grudgingly accept the existence of the Islamic otherness, but in the realm of knowledge it acknowledged no such possibility.

This hegemonic tendency of the cognitive realm is not the exclusive purview of traditional disciplines. It permeates the writings of even the most theoretically daring thinkers, as is evident in the case of Michel Foucault. Foucault conceived of himself as the surveyor of these very hegemonic modes of cognition, as someone who would describe their systematicity and their hold. Though he labeled his enterprise an archaeology, he paid scant attention to the ways in which these hegemonic modes of cognition did establish themselves and to the means by which they managed to maintain their grasp. In fact, his own concern with the hegemonic forced him to discard with a ruthlessness equal to that of what he was describing any practices, discursive or otherwise, that sought to maintain any autonomy with respect to these hegemonic behemoths. This led to the famous problem of his inability to articulate the movement, or the shift, from one hegemonic mode of cognition to another. De Certeau, by contrast, is attentive to precisely this constitutive moment, even in Foucault's own case, to the interplay of "emergent" and "residual" forces as Raymond Williams usefully calls them, that is, to the impulses, the enabling conditions, for living in relation to these hegemonic forces. That is why he is always concerned with

*dC compared
to Foucault.*

practices and discourses—and the distinction between these two is not ontological as far as he is concerned—that are either on the wane or in the making, or that even do not quite manage to constitute themselves. Foucault's descriptions present a vast machinery of power; de Certeau's pit individual or small-group efforts against this machinery as a mode of interaction that constitutes the lived experience of these people. He is, therefore, more attentive to the actual working of power as well as to the tactics, strategies, and ruses that the neutralization of such vast power requires.

V

We have seen, however, that not all forms of otherness allow themselves to be subsumed into sameness, and indeed, there has been growing recognition of this fact within Western thought itself. One discipline that has been existentially concerned with this realization is anthropology, especially among its American practitioners. The wrenching experience of the Vietnam War, in which anthropologists saw the findings of their fieldwork mobilized to accomplish the destruction of the cultures, if not the annihilation of the peoples, whom they had studied, has led anthropologists to question their role, and by extension, that of knowledge, in the spread of hegemony. The debates at the annual meetings of the American Anthropological Association during the late sixties and seventies failed to produce a solution, for the problem far exceeds the conjunctural dimension in which it was generally considered.

Significantly, though, the proposed solutions sought to correct the perceived vulnerability of the epistemological with an injection of the ethical. Otherness, thematized as cultural diversity, not only calls for the respect that the anthropologist is expected to grant it, but in a self-reflexive gesture, is further expected to relativize the position of the anthropologist. As Clifford Geertz succinctly puts it:

> To see ourselves as others see us can be eye-opening. To see others as sharing a nature with ourselves is the merest decency. But it is from the far more difficult achievement of seeing ourselves amongst others, as a local example of the forms human life has locally taken, a case among cases, a world among worlds, that the largeness of mind, without which objectivity is self-congratulation and tolerance a sham, comes. If interpretive anthropology has any general office in the world it is to keep reteaching this fugitive truth.

In this rather remarkable concluding paragraph to the introduction of his *Local Knowledge*, Geertz articulates the main tenets of a newly emerging conception of knowledge, a conception that one finds working its way into some of the theses of Jean François Lyotard's *The Postmodern Condition* as well. Knowledge must surrender its global pretensions. Its reach is always limited to its loci and condition of emergence, what Geertz calls the local and Lyotard, the pagan (from the Latin *pagus*, enclosed field). It must not serve as an instrument of domination; in fact, it must renounce mastery as such. Its relations with others must be governed, for Geertz at least, by ethical considerations. The language of tolerance, objectivity, sham, and fugitive truth here is a subtle mixture of religious discourse and Enlightenment rationalism.

This "fugitive truth" is a bitter pill to swallow for the rationalism that is, properly speaking, the heir to gnosticism, because it puts into question the latter's progressive legitimation against a notion of truth that is somehow beyond the immediate purview of reason. Against the notion that salvation originates in faith (*pistis*), gnosticism has always held that it is the result of knowledge (*gnosis*) and that error or false knowledge are the causes of perdition. Yet gnosticism did not stand alone but rather as a rationalist instrument of support of revealed truth, and this is in Judaism, Christianity, and later in Islam. But its support was qualified and limited to the extent that the gnostic held that reason was sufficient to reach the truths of religion. In the Christian West, a giant step toward the acceptance of the gnostic position was made in Aquinas's famous assertion that nothing in faith is contrary to reason and its corollary that reason is a proper avenue to the realm of the truths of faith—a significant extension of the Anselmian *fides quaerens intellectum* position. The gnostic viewpoint was given legitimacy. It achieved supremacy with the Cartesian reversal of the relationship of faith and reason in relation to truth: henceforth the belief in God and the truths that he dispenses would be subject to the prior operations of reason. And this reason, it turns out, can be quite constraining: I discover the truth through the free exercise of my own reason; therefore I cannot refuse this truth; I must adopt it, as must all who are equally rational. The gnostic viewpoint far surpasses the uncertainties of faith because it rests on the certitudes of rationality. The reason of the Enlightenment is fundamentally gnostic, and, since it seeks to replace the vagaries of faith with the certitudes of rationality, it is logical that it should attempt to assert its hegemony. To sin against faith is to sin against a God whose designs are at best tortuous or visible "in a glass darkly," but, in any case, in need of mediation. But to sin against reason is a matter of easy demonstration and therefore calls for immediate correction in all the meanings of this term. If the shift in our conception of knowledge, articulated by Geertz, does represent more than a passing aberration, we may well come to see modernity as the period when the gnostic claim to be able to account rationally for all truths has held sway and the period that is currently beginning as one that seeks to distance itself from this gnostic domination.

The most consistent denouncer of the gnostic position in our day has been the French philosopher and Talmudic scholar Emmanuel Lévinas, who, in a work that spans nearly fifty years, has rigorously argued for a notion of truth that is at considerable odds with the dominant rationalist one, a notion that relies upon the category—or, more accurately within the Lévinasian framework, upon the lived experience—of the other. Against a notion of the truth as the instrument of a mastery being exercised by the knower over areas of the unknown as he or she brings them within the fold of the same, Lévinas argues that there is a form of truth that is totally alien to me, that I do not discover within myself, but that calls on me from beyond me, and it requires me to leave the realms of the known and of the same in order to settle in a land that is under its rule. Here the knower sets out on an adventure of uncertain outcome, and the instruments that he or she brings may well be inappropriate to the tasks that will arise. Reason will play a role, but it will be a secondary one; it can only come into play once the primary fact of the irruption of the other has been experienced. And this other is not a threat to be reduced or an object that I give myself to know in my capacity as knowing subject, but that which constitutes me as an ethical being: in my originary encounter I discover my responsibility for the existence of this other, a responsibility that will lie at the root of all my subsequent ethical decisions. Knowledge and its operations are subordinated to this initial ethical moment, for the responsibility that I then experience is the very ground of my response-ability, that is, my capacity to communicate with others and with myself in noncoercive ways. Reason can now deploy itself in the field that has been opened up by the relation I have to the other. It is a reason chastised, not likely to seek hegemonic control, for were it to do so it would have to do violence to my self as the self that is in this relation of response-ability to the other.

VI

Lévinas's position provides philosophical and theoretical underpinnings for a more epistemologically oriented position such as that of Geertz. It is significant that there is currently quite a vogue of interest in his work and that it is beginning to reshape the attitudes and positions of established critics. Tzvetan Todorov, for example, reads the encounter between the Europeans and the autochthonous inhabitants of the New World through Lévinasian lenses, and he interprets Bakhtin's notion of dialogue similarly. Yet this position, and the uses to which it is being put in literary criticism, raise considerable questions perhaps best formulated by Edward Said in his *The World, the Text and the Critic.*

Said is concerned with the emergence of this new conception of knowledge for it signals to him the abandonment of the secular position of the intellectual and a return to what he sees as religious criticism practiced by clerics who are not capable of, or even really interested in, maintaining a truly critical position. The reliance upon an almighty form of reason provided a solution to the human need for certainty, and in Kant's famous phrase, it gave rise to the Idea of a consensus of all free and rational consciousnesses, thus establishing a sense of group solidarity and of communal belonging—features that Said believes to constitute fundamental human needs. But he finds that increasingly these needs are being addressed through the religious dimension rather than through the secular one, and he takes the present concern with the other as an instance of this phenomenon. In the conclusion to his book, which really ought to be cited in toto, he sees the return of religion in the theories and practices of criticism that put forward notions of unthinkability, undecidability, and paradox, as well as in those that make direct appeal to "magic, divine ordinance, or sacred texts." Further, he sees evidence of it even in those theoretical approaches that one would presume to be immune, such as Marxism, feminism, and psychoanalysis, for in much of their current practice, these "stress the private and hermetic over the public and social."

For the organization and the practice of knowledge, the results are "unpleasant to contemplate. There is an increase in the number of fixed special languages, many of them impenetrable, deliberately obscure, willfully illogical. . . . Instead of discrimination and evaluation, we have an intensified division of intellectual labor." The critical dimension of criticism is rapidly eroding as the critic, evincing the same sort of belief as the neoconservative in the mystical workings of the marketplace, renounces the responsibilities of the intellectual in order to "become a cleric in the worst sense of the word."

These are serious charges, and they deserve a much more detailed examination than I can give them here. As my own earlier characterization of the problematic condition of the practice and organization of knowledge ought to indicate, I share Said's concerns and accept large parts of his diagnosis. I am struck, however, by the fact that Said is unable to overcome, or to reinscribe, the problem that he so ably describes, and must content himself with a general appeal for a more secular criticism. His predicament, it seems to me, comes from the fact that he has not sufficiently examined the ground of the present return to religion, a ground that I shall attempt to make more explicit by returning to my earlier assertion about the Hegelian form of our present organization of knowledge. I will also claim that Michel de Certeau's handling of these issues may well get us out of Said's predicament.

Said's stated preference for a form of criticism that openly assumes a social and political responsibility as well as his distaste for certain forms of philosophical theorizing leads him to construe the problem of the organization of knowledge in sociological terms that, to me, already partake of the problem he seeks to address. Quite rightly, Said brings to the fore of his considerations the role that the institutionalization of knowledge has played. Describing this institutionalization through the passage of filiation to affiliation, he is able to show how forms of authority are instituted and used to create a sense of caste among those who are so affiliated. Curiously enough, though, Said does not seem to recognize in this pattern the accomplishment of a project that is properly Hegelian in origin, a project that already foresees all the other features of the present situation. Of course, it has become commonplace to assert that this project has failed and thus suggest that it no longer need concern us, yet a closer examination of the organization of knowledge may well lead us to reconsider this widespread belief.

It will be recalled that Hegel proposed a global interpretation of history that focuses on the status of knowledge. Roughly speaking, this interpretation runs as follows: history is over because knowledge has become absolute. Rationality is the absolute becoming of the spirit in history, the stages of history marking the progressive development of the spirit as it invests ever more of the world. It is generally forgotten, however, that this development and the manner of its investment proceed through institutionalized forms, so that another way of describing history is to record the progressive institutionalization of rationality until it becomes absolute in the ultimate institution, the Hegelian State, at which point history comes to an end. It was Hegel's ambition to thematize the entire narrative of Western rationality, a project that has been widely discussed and generally rejected. But it was as much his ambition to announce its ultimate accomplishment in history, that is, in the institutions through which rationality would henceforth exercise its hold over all of reality and the modes of cognition we bring to bear upon it. And this second aspect of the project has received less attention since it must have seemed that the ascertained failure of the first would take care of the second, and since Hegel himself devoted more attention to the first, which he considered a historical precondition of the second. Yet the very multiplication of disciplines, their autonomization, the rise of the specialized languages that Said rightly deplores, the shunting away of the historical dimension toward ever more remote corners—all of these provide ample evidence of the fact that the present organization of knowledge has aligned itself upon the Hegelian conception, though mostly without any direct knowledge of it. Perhaps the best index of that alignment is the suspicion, if not the outright hostility, with which any questioning of the fundamental mechanism of this organization, namely the Hegelian dialectic identified for all practical purposes with rationality itself—though never under its proper name—is greeted within the boundaries of these institutionalized forms of knowledge.

This is where the heterological countertradition comes in. It has focused, as I indicated earlier, on the epistemological dimension of the problem. But the strategies available to it are limited: either it must deconstruct the epistemology from within, a rather arduous task that constantly runs the risk of becoming one more specialized language on the verge of institutionalization or, as the fate of deconstruction in American universities demonstrates, a new system of affiliation, in Said's terms; or it must critique this epistemology from the outside, and then it runs the risk of relying upon the ethical and the figure of the other and its possible religious overtones. In other words, the two strategies require that one position oneself with respect to the central Hegelian claim of the end of history. The second strategy relies directly upon the consensual perception that history has not come to an end, and seeks to anchor the epistemological in something other than the spirit's own deployment. History is thus retained, and one remains agnostic with respect to the outcome of the Hegelian prediction, but at a cost that Said is right to see as unbearable since it reestablishes the dominance of the religious over the rational which Hegel himself found to prevail prior to the advent of absolute knowledge.

It is against the discomforts of this "solution," as much as against the problem itself, that the first, and more properly heterological, strategy has evolved. It begins by granting, for the sake of the argument as it were, the Hegelian thesis on the end of history; then it proceeds to unravel the institutional claims of rationality, showing that the institutionalization that presently prevails does not correspond to the Hegelian principle of the deployment of the spirit that alone could properly justify it. But this strategy does not seek to establish in an oblique way what the other strategy already takes for granted, namely that history has not come to an end; rather it seeks to show that indeed a certain kind of history may well have come to an end but that this ending does not exhaust history. If anything, this strategy, as pursued in some of Derrida's, and especially Paul de Man's, writings, may allow us to finally come to grasps with history.

In his rightful anguish, Said allows himself to be caught on a ground that fails to distinguish between these two strategies. He desires the historical dimension but not at the price that the second strategy exacts, for its construct of the historical as sacred or transcendent is precisely the kind of history that he seeks to avoid; yet he cannot accept the tortuous way in which the first strategy proceeds to the historical, drawing justification from the fact that indeed it does not seem to attain it.

But in Michel de Certeau's work, it is attained. The heterological countertradition has shown that the particular vulnerability of the Hegelian claims lies in their inability to articulate the dependence of knowledge upon language. Although Hegel took great pains, in the narrative part of his project, to show that the progressive development of the spirit, and the concomitant rise of absolute knowledge, consisted primarily in their liberation from material forms (hence the appropriateness of the Idealist label), he was blind to the materiality of language, going so far as to state that the language of poetry had achieved such a liberation. The heterological tradition, focusing upon epistemological issues, has sought in the ontological dimension the reasons for this particular resistance of language, frequently granting a privileged status to literature as the linguistic practice in which this resistance is most easily apparent in the form of a complex nondialectical interplay of the representational and the nonrepresentational.

De Certeau, for his part, has preferred to avoid a ground that is rather uncertain since literature is first and foremost an institutional determination, and thus to seek to ground it ontologically may well amount to no more than shoring up the institution at the very moment when its vulnerability becomes apparent. The quality that is recognized in literature, he seems to think, does not come from the fact that it is a special mode of language, but rather from the fact that it is a part of language, a mode of language use, that is a discourse. Unlike language, which, as an object of knowledge, is a construct of philosophers and linguists, discourses constitute forms of actual social interaction and practice. As such, they are not irrational, but they are subject to the pulls and pressures of the situations in which they are used as well as to the weights of their own tradition. They must always handle the complex interplay of that which is of the order of representation and the nonrepresentable part which is just as much constitutive of them, their own other. And because of this dual nature, they are not really disciplines—these operate within the realm of representation which is thematized by Hegel as the investment of the real by the spirit; they are logics, that is, they have a coherence *sui generis*, one that needs to be rigorously and thoroughly described in each instance. For de Certeau, the most important role in the constitution of that logic is reserved for the complex, and properly textual, play of the other with the more overt, representational part of the discourse, hence his designation of his project as *heterologies*. This other, which forces discourses to take the meandering appearance that they have, is not a magical or a transcendental entity; it is the discourse's mode of relation to its own historicity in the moment of its utterance.

In my earlier reference to the gnostic conception of rationality, I indicated the moral power of this rationality, which could claim hegemonic domination because of the universalism of its assertions. Such a claim is inherent in the Hegelian conception of rationality, of course, to the extent that it represents the development of the spirit. But it is also inherent, though less overtly explicit, in the institutions of rationality, including the disciplines—though the emergence of the expert as a major figure of authority in our culture shows that such claims are societally acknowledged and even receive legal sanction. This gnostic conception of rationality, and its Hegelian institutional implementation, remove human beings from the sphere of history as practice, since history is conceived of then as the inexorable process of rationality's own rational development. Here are to be found further causes of the sense of loss of historical agency that accompany the fragmentation of the self characteristic of social abstraction and reasons for the bewilderment that marks our inability to comprehend historical processes that exceed those of our institutionalized knowledge. De Certeau's conception of discourse, so different from Foucault's hegemonic one, recovers an agential dimension for us inasmuch as it recognizes that discursive activity is a form of social activity, an activity in which we attempt to apply the roles of the discourses that we assume. These may not be heroic roles, but they place us much more squarely in front of our responsibility as historical actors.

Part I
The Return of the
Repressed in Psychoanalysis

Chapter 1
Psychoanalysis and Its History

The process upon which psychoanalysis is based lies at the heart of Freud's discoveries—the return of the repressed. This "mechanism" is linked to a certain conception of time and memory, according to which consciousness is both the deceptive *mask* and the operative *trace* of events that organize the present. If the past (that which took place during, and took the form of, a decisive moment in the course of a crisis) is *repressed*, it *returns* in the present from which it was excluded, but does so surreptitiously. One of Freud's favorite examples is a figuration of this detour-return, which constitutes the ruse of history: Hamlet's father returns after his murder, but in the form of a phantom, in another scene, and it is only then that he becomes the law his son obeys.

Two Strategies of Time

There is an "uncanniness" about this past that a present occupant has expelled (or thinks it has) in an effort to take its place. The dead haunt the living. The past: it "re-bites" [*il re-mord*] (it is a secret and repeated biting).[1] History is "cannibalistic," and memory becomes the closed arena of conflict between two contradictory operations: forgetting, which is not something passive, a loss, but an action directed against the past; and the mnemic trace, the return of what was forgotten, in other words, an action by a past that is now forced to disguise itself. More generally speaking, any autonomous order is founded upon what it eliminates; it produces a "residue" condemned to be forgotten. But what was excluded re-infiltrates the place of its origin—now the present's "clean" [*propre*] place. It resurfaces, it troubles, it turns the present's feeling of being "at home" into an illusion, it lurks—this "wild," this "ob-scene," this "filth," this "resistance" of "superstition"—within the walls of the residence, and, behind the back of the owner (the *ego*), or over its objections, it inscribes there the law of the other.

Historiography, on the other hand, is based on a clean break between the past and the present. It is the product of relations of knowledge and power linking two supposedly distinct domains: on one hand, there is the present (scientific, professional, social) place of work, the technical and conceptual apparatus of *inquiry* and interpretation, and the operation of describing and/or explaining; on the other hand, there are the places (museums, archives, libraries) where the materials forming the object of this research are kept and, secondarily, set off in time, there are the past systems or *events* to which these materials give analysis access. There is a boundary line separating the present institution (which fabricates representations) from past or distant regions (which historiographical representations bring into play).

Even though historiography postulates a continuity (a genealogy), a solidarity (an affiliation), and a complicity (a sympathy) between its agents and its objects, it nevertheless distinguishes a *difference* between them, a difference established out of principle by a will to objectivity. The space it organizes is divided and hierarchical. That space has an "own" [*un propre*] (the present of this historiography) and an "other" (the "past" under study). The dividing line between them affects both the practice (the research apparatus distinguishes itself from the material it treats), and the enactment in writing (the discourse of interpretative knowledge subjugates the known, cited, represented past).

Psychoanalysis and historiography thus have two different ways of distributing the *space of memory*. They conceive of the relation between the past and present differently. Psychoanalysis recognizes the past *in* the present; historiography places them one *beside* the other. Psychoanalysis treats the relation as one of imbrication (one in the place of the other), of repetition (one reproduces the other in another form), of the equivocal and of the *quiproquo* (What "takes the place" of what? Everywhere, there are games of masking, reversal, and ambiguity). Historiography conceives the relation as one of succession (one after the other), correlation (greater or lesser proximities), cause and effect (one follows from the other), and disjunction (either one or the other, but not both at the same time).

Two strategies of *time* thus confront one another. They do, however, develop in the context of analogous problems: to find principles and criteria to serve as guides to follow in attempting to understand the differences, or guarantee the continuities, between the organization of the actual and the formations of the past; to give the past explanatory value and/or make the present capable of explaining the past; to relate the representations of the past or present to the conditions which determined their production; to elaborate (how? where?) different ways of thinking, and by so doing overcome violence (the conflicts and contingencies of history), including the violence of thought itself; to define and construct a narrative, which is for both disciplines the favored form of elucidating discourse. In order to determine the possibilities and limitations of the renewal of historiography promised by its encounter with psychoanalysis, we will survey the interrelations and debates between these two strategies since the time of Freud (1856-1939).

Freud and History

Freud's method of "elucidation" (*Aufklärung*) is supported by two pillars he built and considered equally fundamental and founding: *The Interpretation of Dreams* (1900) and *Totem and Taboo* (1912-1913). Of the second, he said in 1914, "I have made an attempt to deal with problems of social anthropology in the light of analysis; this line of investigation leads directly to the origins of the most important institutions of our civilization, of the structure of the state, of morality and religion, and, moreover, of the prohibition against incest and of conscience."[2] His method is enacted on two scenes, one individual and the other collective. It takes, in turn, the (biographical) form of "case histories" (the "*Krankengeschichten*," 1905-1918)[3] and the (global) form of the "historical novel" (*Moses and Monotheism*, 1939: the original title specifies that the subject is the relation of a single man—"der Mann Moses"—to the historical configuration of Jewish monotheism).[4]

Freud's forays into historiography are semi-surgical operations which display a certain number of characteristics:

1. He invalidates the break between individual psychology and collective psychology.

2. He thinks of the "pathological" as a region where the structural modes of functioning of human experience become intensified and display themselves. Accordingly, the distinction between normality and abnormality is only phenomenal; fundamentally, it has no scientific relevance.

3. He identifies the relation of historicity to *crises* which organize and displace it. He reveals, in decisive events (of a relational and conflictual nature, originally genealogical and sexual), the sites where psychic *structures* are constituted. Therapeutic confirmations allow him to orient his analyses in three directions: a) the search for determining factors in the life of the adult which are linked to "primitive scenes" experienced by the child, and which presuppose

that the child (that epigone, until then kept on the sidelines) plays a central role in the story; b) the necessity of postulating a genealogical violence at the origin of peoples (a struggle between the father and the son), the repression of which is the work of tradition (it hides the corpse), but whose repetitive effects are nevertheless identifiable across their successive camouflages (there are traces left behind); c) the assurance of finding in any discourse "small fragments of truth" ("*Stükchen Wahrheit*")[5]—splinters and debris relative to those decisive moments—the forgetting of which organizes itself into psychosociological systems and the remembrance of which creates possibilities of change for the present state.

4. He alters the historiographical "genre" of writing by introducing the need for the analyst to *mark his place* (his affective, imaginary, and symbolic place). He makes this explicitness the condition of possibility of a form of lucidity, and thus substitutes for "objective" discourse (a discourse that aims to express the real) a discourse that adopts the form of a "fiction" (if by "fiction" we understand a text that openly declares its relation to the singular place of its production).

Curiously, some of the subsequent avatars of the psychoanalytic tradition and its applications totally reverse these positions. A few instructive examples will suffice. Freudianism, for one thing, was reduced to individual psychology and biography. It was either boxed into the category of the "pathological" (for example, *economic* and *social* history left an unexplained, abnormal "residue," in the areas of sorcery and Nazism, which was abandoned to psychoanalysis). Or, to take another example, where Freud found displacements of representations linked to primal conflicts, there was an assumption that all-prevailing and stable "symbols" or "archetypes" lurked somewhere beneath the phenomena. In the same way, the subject's division between the pleasure principle (*Eros*) and the law of the other (*Thanatos*)—for Freud an insurmountable division which, from *Beyond the Pleasure Principle* (1920) to *Civilization and its Discontents* (1930), he defined in terms of the alienation of need by society and the constitutive frustration of desires—was "forgotten" by therapies whose goal was to "integrate" the ego into society. Perhaps these inheritors "betrayed" Freud in both senses of the term: they deflected his thought and unveiled it. Their actions conform to the theory of tradition Freud presented in *Moses and Monotheism*, according to which tradition inverts and conceals precisely what it claims to reproduce, and does so in its name. Leaving that aside, it is necessary to review at least two of Freud's positions that are more directly relevant to history. A discussion of two essential texts will be enough for an outline.

1. In *Group Psychology and the Analysis of the Ego* (1921; written on Gustave Le Bon's *The Crowd: A Study of the Popular Mind*), Freud firmly holds that "the relation of an individual to his parents and to his brothers and sisters, to the object of his love, and to his physician—in fact all the relations which have

hitherto been the chief subject of psychoanalytic research—may claim to be considered as social phenomena."[6] They are only distinguishable from the phenomena treated by collective psychology by a "numerical consideration" that is irrelevant from the point of view of the psychic structures involved. The constitution of the subject through its relation to other (parents, etc.) and to language, postulates from the beginning a social life composed of various formations that are progressively larger in scale, but follow identical laws. Freud thus feels authorized to take his analytical apparatus across the lines dividing the established disciplines, which apportion psychic phenomena among themselves according to a distinction (between "individual" and "collective") that Freud challenges and wishes to transform.

2. These already constituted domains are also distinguished from one another by the particular techniques each has adopted. Freud was not equally competent in all of them, which does not, at least theoretically, place in question the object of study that psychoanalysis, like any other science, chose for itself. His first studies were on eels (1877) and crayfish (1882). He was a psychiatric doctor. He effected the psychoanalytic "conversion" using the materials and methods that specialty provided for him. Afterward, beginning in 1907 (when Freud was 51), he extended it to the study of literary texts;[7] still later, beginning in 1910 (in relation to "primal words" and Leonardo da Vinci), he further extended it to ethnology and history.[8] But as the preface to *Totem and Taboo* (1913)—the book marking the second moment in the psychoanalytic *conquista*—makes clear, when it comes to ethnology he no longer has "a sufficient grasp of the material that awaits ("harrenden") (psychoanalytic) treatment."[9] Though constructed and verifiable within the bounds of a particular field, his theory was not meant to be anchored there; it was, rather, destined to renew other fields, in relation to which Freud himself nonetheless lacked the necessary elements for first-hand information and technical control. The material (*Materiel*) originating in these foreign realms, culled by their respective explorers, is for Freud both what the analyst "lacks" and what is "missed" by a (Freudian) theoretical treatment capable of "harmonizing" the "diversity" of facts and throwing "a ray of light into this obscurity."[10] Freud calls these domains "quarries," or "treasures" to be exploited. He works them, devouring the texts of Smith, Wundt, Crawley, Frazer, and others, as well as documents from the seventeenth century, scholarly studies of the Bible, etc.—but all without the professional "security" his home territory affords him.

When a theoretical point of view is extended beyond the field within which it was elaborated, where it remains subject to a system of verification, does it not, as Canguilhem said, cross the line between scientific "theories" and scientific "*ideologies*"? That is frequently the case. Freud himself at times had doubts about the status of his socio-historical research, and toward the end of his life he claimed with irony that he wrote them as a hobby, while smoking his pipe. He was admitting a crack of ambiguity in his analytic edifice. It is up to his posterity to accept the theoretical challenge this admission represents. In history, Freud was a pioneer, but not a practitioner, in spite of his passion for collecting "antiquities" and the breadth of his readings in the field, begun in adolescence. In addition to a coherent corpus of verifiable, theoretical hypotheses, he injected into historiography the suspense of a detective story ("Who killed Harry?") and the uncanniness of a fantasy novel (there is a ghost in the house). He reintroduced mythic conflicts into a scientific system. He brought back the sorcery in knowledge, taking it even to the offices of the historians, who seem to assume that the past is already neatly ordered, piecemeal, sitting on the archive shelves. A seriousness [*un sérieux*] of history appears, bringing all its dangers with it. A half century after Michelet, Freud observes that the dead are in fact "beginning to speak."[11] But they are not speaking through the "medium" of the historian-wizard, as Michelet believed: *it is speaking [ça parle]* in the work and in the silences of the historian, but without his knowledge. These voices—whose disappearance every historian posits, which he replaces with his writing—"re-bite" [*re-mordent*] the space from which they were excluded; they continue to speak in the text/tomb that erudition erects in their place.

Traditions

Freud, in his 1919 preface to Theodor Reik's *Ritual* (Reik believed *Totem and Taboo* to be "the most important book of its kind . . . the standard illustration of what psychoanalysis can perform in the sphere of the [human] sciences"), surveyed psychoanalytic research since the appearance of *Die Bedeutung der Psychoanalyse für die Geisteswissenschaften* (1913), by Otto Rank and Hanns Sachs: "Mythology and the history of literature and religion appear to furnish the most easily accessible material." He praises Reik, whose book he says represents the first volume in the "Psychology of Religions." "He keeps steadily in view the relationship between pre-historic man and primitive man of today, as well as the connection between cultural activities and neurotic substitute formations." This constitutes a declaration of victory in the battle to "submit the prehistoric and ethnological material . . . to psychoanalytic elaboration."[12] It is the first success scored by the "attempted invasions by psychoanalysis."[13]

These three domains ("*mythology* and the history of *literature* and *religion*") were already a preoccupation of the Wednesday night meetings at Freud's office (beginning in 1902), and the discussions continued in the Psychoanalytic Society of Vienna (founded in 1908).[14] In the beginning, Rank (the group's secretary), Adler, Federn, Sachs, Schilder, Steiner, and others (with Reik, Tausk, and Lou Andreas-Salomé joining in later) treated questions concerning incest, symbolism, myth, Wagner, Nietzsche, etc. These "applications" of psychoanalysis

the psychological process represents a complex superstructure founded on physi-
ological processes to which it is subordinated."[19] Luriia developed this point of
view. But, beginning in 1930, Soviet criticism made an about-face. Vnukov, in
a 1933 article on "Psychoanalysis" in the Soviet *Medical Encyclopaedia*,
attacked psychoanalysis' "pretentions" of "having the right to solve problems
of vast cultural and historical significance" when it is "inherent to bourgeois
democracy." Under Stalinism, which by decision of the Communist Party
(1936) limited psychology to conscious and practical reason, Freudianism was
accused of being ultra-individualist (cf. the article "Freudianism" in the *Bolshaia Entsiklopediia*, 1935), and was held to be totally false because it could not
"understand psychic processes and needs as the product of social and historical
development" (the article "Psychoanalysis," in the *Bolshaia Entsiklopediia*,
1940, by Luriia, who followed the political tide).[20] The "pseudo-science" of
psychoanalysis, dismissed as "American" and "reactionary" (1948), is thus
excluded from historiography by Soviet history; only de-Stalinization was to
moderate the excommunication.

In the United States, Freud, who (with Jung and Ferenczi) was invited to visit
in 1909, felt he was finally seeing psychoanalysis receive the academic conse-
cration that it had been refused in Austria. The "cause" made rapid progress
there. Two psychoanalytic associations were founded in the spring of 1911.
Americans such as Kardiner,[21] and even masters like Frink, went to study in
Vienna. Aided by the authority of James Jackson Putnam (Harvard), Freudianism set down roots, taking on a new, "Made in USA" configuration in a country
where the experimental positivism of psychiatric neurology existed side by side
with the spiritual "soul healing" of the Emmanuel Movement (organized to
combat the "American nervousness") and the enchanting psychological systems
of William James and Bergson.[22] The adoption of Viennese methodology left
intact the American confidence in the resourcefulness of the ego, and in society's
ability to integrate individuals while guaranteeing their "self-expression." This
attitude is still evident fifty years later in the work of Norman O. Brown, whose
refusal of all repression has the style of a "revival."[23]

The privileged position accorded to personal history was not so much a desire
to reduce psychoanalysis to individual therapy, as it was a reflection of a certain
type of society. Thus, Erik Erikson's subtle biographies present us with the half-
political, half-religious, *social* model of the pioneer who, freed from the law of
the father, overcomes the tension between rebellion and submission.[24] Psychoanalysis was reflected in the mirrors of a USA mythology; its departures from
Freud were due first of all to a restructuring of the psychoanalytic inheritance
according to the demands of a particular national experience. The relation of
these texts to history cannot be gauged simply by their author's (insufficient)
knowledge of the archives, but has to do with the fact that they symbolize an
American historicity (even if they were not consciously thought of in those

terms). So biography prospered. It has given rise to a series of theoretical examinations,[25] as well as to courses and colloquia.

Gradually, however, the range of investigation extended to include family genealogies and community structures,[26] a result of convergences between the history of kinship systems, an anthropology of the Oedipus complex, and the generalization of the Freudian "family romance." This widening of perspective is historically the product of the more anthropologically oriented psychoanalysis of the first associations (in Vienna, Berlin, Frankfort, and Hungary), which was carried into exile in the United States. For example, from 1938 on, the extensive investigations of Geza Róheim (whose work began in Hungary near Ferenczi) were completed in the United States; the new direction they were to take for a time, in a departure from the work of the traditional groups, was to confront the Nazi question.

American psychoanalysis was overdetermined in its early stages by the experience of émigrés, particularly Jewish and German, who were fleeing from Nazism. Beginning in 1942, research institutes began to mobilize analysis around the question of popular opinion and the case of Hitler: Erikson, Jahoda, Ackerman, Bettelheim, and others delivered papers on the subject. As Adorno put it: "the essence of history" was disclosed at Auschwitz.[27] With Reich, Fromm, Adorno, Marcuse (who became interested in Freud only after his arrival in the United States), Horkheimer, etc., all of whom were refugees, similar questions had been under discussion since 1931. For all of them, though admittedly in different modes, to analyze historicity was to analyze the relation between reason and Nazi violence; in particular, in the Marxist context, it was to analyze the failure of the most highly evolved proletariat of Europe—and thus the failure of *revolution* itself—in the face of fascism. Critical reflection looked toward psychoanalysis for aid. Examples are: Reich's "politico-psychological" analysis, which saw in fascism "an expression of the irrational character structure of the average man," and, in particular, of religious and/or political forms of the "need for authority";[28] Fromm's symbolic analysis, which, in its attempt to escape social alienation, took recourse in a kind of pietist anthropology;[29] Marcuse's battle against the technocratic "over-repression" of the libido in our society, where "anonymity" makes Freud's "conflict model" of the struggle between father and son irrelevant, etc.[30] Mourning for a revolution—a tragedy of history—haunted these diagnostics without a therapy. Only Reich (who passed through Marx and Freud and traversed the USA and the USSR, everywhere rejected) chose to attempt an impossible biological mutation of man, and he pursued his dream into insanity.

In France, a triple obstacle closed the door on Freud, especially to the sociopolitical aspect of his work: the powerful leadership of the Paris School of psychology and psychiatry (Charcot, Clairambault, Janet, Ribot) had nothing to learn from foreigners, since it had already, definitively, outlined the realm of the serious [*le sérieux*] within the individual; a moralizing tradition condemned Freudian "pansexualism"; linguistic and cultural resistance—nationalist and chauvinist during and after the war—rejected a Germanic influence considered to be too excessive, obscure, and "Wagnerian." Moreover, apart from Marie Bonaparte, there was for a long time no disciple of Freud's based in France (Freud himself only spent a few hours in Paris, in 1938); the Psychoanalytic Society of Paris was not founded until 1926. There were no close historical ties between Paris and Vienna. The introduction of psychoanalysis in France was originally the work of men of letters (the first favorable article was written by Albert Thibaudet[31]); André Breton (who was not taken seriously by Freud), Jules Romains, André Gide, Jacques Rivière, Pierre-Jean Jouve, etc., became interested before the psychiatrists did (today the situation is the same in the United States with Lacan). The French scientific establishment became gradually familiar with the Freudian corpus, which finally made it to France (in the form of dispersed and fragmentary translations); but it was removed from its original context (which was long misunderstood). The texts of Freud have been the object of interpretations and disputes, up to (and including) the revolutionary "return to Freud" undertaken by Jacques Lacan, which precipitated a rupture within the Psychoanalytic Society of Paris and the Paris Institute of Psychoanalysis (Nacht), leading in 1953 to the formation of the French Psychoanalytic Society (Lacan, Lagache), and later the Freudian School of Paris (1964-1980; Lacan). But nothing, or next to nothing, in these traditions was done to explain the strange silence that reigns in France on the subject of the (German) Occupation—those rejected years, that period that is too dangerously close not to be "forgotten" even by psychoanalysis.

Historiography, which has become intensely professional, was completely under the sway of economic, culturalist methodologies, some of Marxist inspiration. Apart from a few important studies (George Devereux, Alain Besançon)[32] that remained marginal to the discipline, it took the shock of May 1968 for the *ethno-historical* works of Freud—along with Marcuse, Reich, etc.—to be considered relevant and to gain theoretical influence on analyses of psychiatric institutions, law, the "medical order," history, and the psychoanalytic associations themselves. Filling the vacuum left by the philosophies of consciousness (Sartre, etc.)—and, since 1968, advancing as structuralism receded—psychoanalysis in France, by introducing the question of the subject, has caused fissures to form in all the human sciences, and even in their vulgate. In this all-directional expansionism, the variants can be thought of as falling into two camps, both allied with very old philosophical traditions. One, anthropological in form, is historically the return of a quasi-ontology; its aim is to constitute a domain of knowledge which would link the present ego to symbols which supposedly underlie all human experience. The second, in defining the subject, begins at the point where the institution of language is articulated upon the biological organism; its final form is the one given it by Lacan in his most remarkable (and most historio-graphical) seminar (1959–1960): an "Ethics of Psychoanalysis."

Displacements and Perspectives

In 1971, the International Congress of Psychoanalysis was held in Vienna for the first time. A return to origins. Nearly 3,000 analysts gathered at the apart-ment/museum on Berggassestrasse and filed past the crimson furniture of the lost master, past his couch and his curios. The Western world was assembled there; a Marxist pilgrimage would have gathered the Eastern world together, on that same German soil, the interface of the empires. In Vienna, the silence of the place, analogous to the silence of the Freudian corpus,[33] caused a crowd to speak. But only the ovation given Anna Freud, the daughter of the founder, could drown out the dissonant rumblings, which were simultaneously a testi-mony to Freud's international success and the dismemberment of his work—as in *Totem and Taboo*—by the horde of its inheritors. Psychoanalysis had become history. It would be a part of it from then on. And its relationship to historiog-raphy would be altered by that fact. There are presently, following the displace-ments that have taken place, three major orientations in psychoanalysis:

A History of Psychoanalysis

The psychoanalysis of the founders treated history as a region to be con-quered. Today, history has become the relation of psychoanalysis to itself, of its origin to its subsequent developments, of its theories to its institutions, of transference to filiations, etc. Of course, inscribing personal destinies within a more general genealogy still has some relevance; for example, there is relevance in examining Freud's connections to the Moravian Jewish tradition, which was marked by Sabbateanism,[34] or in recognizing Lacan's links to Surrealism, or to an entire current of Christian thinking which substitutes the *logos* for the lost body. But a psychoanalysis of history must adopt an inward orientation, accept-ing the necessary work of elucidating the meaning of the gaps in the theory on the following points: a) the relations of transference and the conflictual ones upon which analytic discourse is constructed, b) the functioning of Freudian associations or schools, for example their forms of licensure and the nature of the power inherent in "holding" the position of analyst, and c) the possibilities of establishing analytic procedures within psychiatric institutions, where psy-choanalysis, after emerging from its offices dedicated to a privileged clientele, would come into contact with the administrative alliances of politics and ther-apy, as well as the popular murmur of madness.

In this respect, the experiences of the La Borde clinic opens a new chapter in psychoanalytic history. It is no longer a question of "applying" psychoanaly-sis, but of bringing to light a "revolutionary subjectivity," of "grasping the point of *rupture* where political economy and libidinal economy *are finally one and the same.*"[35]

A Self-Critical Biography

The psychoanalytic interest in biography dates to its very inception: topics of the "Wednesday meetings" included studies of Lenau, Wedekind, Jean-Paul, K. F. Meyer, Kleist, Leonardo da Vinci. That interest remains central. Biography is the *self-critique* of liberal, bourgeois society, based on the primary unit that society created. The individual—the central epistemological and historical figure of the modern Western world, the foundation of capitalist economy and democratic politics—becomes the stage upon which the certitudes of its creators and beneficiaries (the clientele of cures, or the heroes of historiography) finally come undone. Freud's work, though born of the *Aufklärung*, reverses the act that founded enlightened consciousness—Kant's assertion of the rights and obligations of that consciousness: "freedom" and full responsibility, autonomous knowledge, and the possibility for a man to progress at a "steady pace" and escape his "tutelage."[36] The response of psychoanalysis to Kant was to send the adult back to its infantile "tutelage," to send knowledge back to the instinctual mechanisms determining it, freedom back to the law of the unconscious, and progress back to originating events.

Psychoanalytic biography effects a reversal at the place delimited by an ambition, and affirms an erosion of its own postulates. Working from within, it dismantles—like the mysticism of the sixteenth and seventeenth centuries in the context of a *received* religious tradition—the historical and social figure that is the standard unit of the system within which Freudianism developed. Even if social pressures can lead it to encomiums in defense of the individual, psychoanalytic biography is in principle a form of self-critique, and its narrativity is an anti-mythic force, like *Don Quixote* in the Spain of the *hidalgos*. It remains to be seen what new and different form (which will no longer have to be "biographical") this machinery heralds, or is now preparing for us.

A History of Nature

In taking the individual back to the something other (or unconscious) which determines it without its knowledge, psychoanalysis returned to the symbolic configurations articulated by social practices in traditional civilizations. The dream, fable, myth—these discourses, excluded by enlightened reason, became the site where the critique of bourgeois and technological society developed. Admittedly, the theologians of Freudianism rushed to transform these languages into positivities. But that is not the point. Freudian critique, since it takes the myths and rites repressed by reason and analyzes them as symbolic formations, may now *seem* like an anthropology. But, in fact, it initiated something that could be called a new history of "nature" which introduced into historicity:

a) The persistence and lingering action of the *irrational*, the violence at work inside scientificity and theory itself.

b) A dynamics of *nature* (drives, affects, the libido) conjoined with language—in opposition to the ideologies of history which privilege the relations among people and reduce nature to a passive terrain permanently open to social or scientific conquest.

c) The relevance of *pleasure* (orgasmic, festive, etc.), which was repressed by the incredibly ascetic ethic of progress; the subversive influence of the pleasure principle has infiltrated our cultural system.

These issues, sown in the field of historiography, are already bearing fruit; they are not necessarily the signs of a psychoanalytic affiliation, but they do signal a Freudian debt and Freudian tasks.

Further Reading

The following list of basic studies in the field is meant to supplement the works cited in the notes. Many of the books mentioned contain detailed bibliographies on the various themes they treat.

Barbu, Zevedi. *Problems of Historical Psychology*. New York: Grove Press, 1969.

Besançon, Alain. *Histoire et expérience du moi*. Paris: Flammarion, 1975.

Besançon, Alain, ed. *L'Histoire psychanalytique: Une anthologie*. Paris: Mouton, 1974.

de Certeau, Michel. *L'écriture de l'histoire*. Paris: Gallimard, 1975.

Dupront, A. "L'histoire après Freud," *Revue de l'enseignement supérieur*, no. 44–45 (1969).

Friedländer, S. *Histoire et psychanalyse*. Paris: Seuil, 1975.

Horkheimer, Max. "Geschichte und Psychologie," in *Zeischrift fur Socialforschung*, Vol. 1, no. 1–2, 1932.

Mazlish, Bruce. "Clio on the Couch," *Encounter*, Vol. 31, no. 3 (1968).

Mazlish, Bruce, ed. *Psychoanalysis and History*. New York: Grosset and Dunlop, 1971.

Meyerhoff, H. "On Psychoanalysis and History," *Psychoanalysis and Psychoanalytic Review*, Vol. 42, no. 2 (1962).

Strout, Cushing. "Ego Psychology and the Historian," *History and Theory*, Vol. 7, no. 3 (1968).

Wehler, Hans-Ulrich, ed. *Geschichte und Psychoanalyse*. Cologne: Kiepenheuer, Witsch, 1971.

Weinstein, F. and Platt, G. "History and Theory: The Question of Psychoanalysis," *The Journal of Interdisciplinary History*, Vol. 2, no. 4 (1972).

Wolman, Benjamin. *The Psychoanalytic Interpretation of History*. New York: Basic Books, 1971.

Chapter 2
The Freudian Novel:
History and Literature

What is the impact of Freudianism on the configuration which for three centuries has governed the relationship between history and literature? These "disciplines" are distributed today among institutions (professional associations, university departments) which manage them and insure them against accidents. Certainly the divorce of history from literature is a process that involves very old events and is too long to be recounted here. Already apparent in the seventeenth century,[1] legalized in the eighteenth century as a result of the split between the "humanities" and the "sciences," the break was institutionalized in the nineteenth century by the academic establishment. At the foundations of this split is the boundary which the positive sciences established between the "objective" and the imaginary, that is to say between that which they controlled and the "remainder."

This distinction has been subject to revision. In this case as in many others, literature has played a pioneering role. The fantasy novel[2] serves as an example of this, as Todorov showed. Freudianism, which evinces some aspects of the fantasy novel, participates in this re-evaluation. It makes new relationships possible, as it redefines the terms of the relationship. Taking Freud as a point of departure, it is this problem of boundaries that I would like to examine. This problem raises the question of a redistribution of epistemological terrain. Ultimately it concerns writing and its relationship to the institution.

I will state my argument without delay: literature is the theoretic discourse of the historical process. It creates the non-topos where the effective operations of a society attain a formalization. Far from envisioning literature as the expression of a referential, it would be necessary to recognize here the analogue of that which for a long time mathematics has been for the exact sciences: a "logical" discourse of history, the "fiction" which allows it to be thought.[3]

Historical Preliminaries

Two prerequisites must be considered before any examination of Freud's analysis concerning the difficult relations between literature and history. On the one hand, Freud assumed that through a new practice of language, his method could transform the whole field of humanities. But he tested the effectiveness of his arguments only in a special branch of knowledge, psychiatry, and he was unable to test his method technically on matters on which he was "not competent," as he said.[4] Freudianism risks its future in this distance between the global aspect of its theory and the local aspect of its testing ground. Freud's "essays" on literature and history only provide a framework of hypotheses, concepts, and rules for the purpose of future research work to be done outside the very field where psychoanalysis was "scientifically" formulated.

On the other hand, it would be an illusion to make reference to Freudianism as to a single united theory: when, in 1971, for the first time since Freud's death, the International Psychoanalytical Congress took place in Vienna, the supposed unity between schools and trends present there had, for its only expression, the silent unoccupied apartment in Berggassestrasse (a family vault with decorative curios) and the roaring ovation given to the departed's daughter, Anna Freud (a name supported by a genealogical *quid pro quo*). To these two marks of absence, an empty place and a displaced name, we could add a third mark, the monument erected in the *Gesammelte Werke* edition. While quarreling as to which of them should supervise every volume of this edition, the followers remind us of the argument developed in *Totem and Taboo*: the "horde" of heirs tear the corpse after the father's death; it might also remind us of the thesis in *Moses and Monotheism*, on the "tradition" which reverses the founder's thought while keeping his name devotedly.

From India to California, from Georgia to Argentina, Freudianism is now broken into pieces as much as Marxism itself. Great professional institutions constituted to defend Freudianism against the transformations of time gave it up to the disseminating work of history, i.e., to its partition into different cultures, nations, classes, professions, and generations. They hastened the decomposition of the very corpus by which they profited. To refuse to acknowledge the fact would be equal to the turning of the theory into an ideology and/or a fetish. At present there is no way of being "well placed" such that it might secure the right interpretation of Freud. This essay too must be situated somewhere within the dissemination of Freudianism, as an essay inspired and (now that we have to mourn the Ecole Freudienne de Paris) posited on the borderline of the school of Lacan. Historian by profession, and member of this school since its founding, I am not better placed to speak on Freud or to speak for one of his representatives. Every institution gives a position. It does not give legitimation.

Two prerequisites are to be remembered: on the one hand, some general arguments built on particular experiences only; on the other hand, a special interpretation of these arguments. That localization designates a historicity. Before becoming a subject for discourse, history includes and locates the analysis, the former constituting an unavoidable prerequisite for the latter. Any theory of history is entangled in a labyrinth of conjunctures and relations which it does not keep under control. It is a "literature" overlooked by the subject matter it deals with.

From "Scientificity" to the Novel

In his *Studies on Hysteria* (1895), Freud, "being trained," he says, "to local diagnosis and to electrodiagnosis," is rather ironically surprised that his "histories of ill ones" (*Krankengeschichte*) read like novels (*Novellen*) and that they are devoid of the serious character of scientificity (*Wissenschaftlichkeit*). This happens to him as would a sickness. His manner of treating hysteria transforms his manner of writing. It is a metamorphosis of discourse: "The fact is that local diagnosis and electrical reactions lead nowhere in the study of hysteria, whereas a detailed description (*Darstellung*) of mental processes such as we are accustomed to find in the works of poets (*Dichter*) enables me, with the use of a few psychological formulas, to obtain at least some kind of insight into the course of that affection."[5] Displacement toward the poetic or novelistic genre. Psychoanalytic conversion is a conversion to literature. This movement duplicates itself with a call to "poets and novelists" who "know, of heaven and earth, more than our scholarly knowledge would dream of": "the novelist has always preceded the scientist."[6]

The orientation is a stable one. It does not stop projecting itself until the last work, *Moses and Monotheism* (1939), referred to as a "novel," as Freud wrote it to Arnold Zweig.[7] Setting aside pedagogical treatises, analytic discourse has as its form that which can be called, in a Freudian term, "theoretic fiction."[8]

Curiously, as Freud was nourished by the scientific *Aufklärung* of the nineteenth century and though he passionately wished for his work to be recognized as the "*sérieux*" of the Viennese academic model, he seems to be caught off guard by his own discovery. He is drawn back by this discovery to the motherland, the *Muttererde*, of which he wrote to Arnold Zweig that unlike all other civilizations which created sciences (the Egyptian, the Greek, etc.), ancient Palestine had "made up only religions, sacred and outlandish stories," in short, fictions.[9] Indeed, the Freudian discourse is the fiction which comes back to the realm of scientificity, not only insofar as it is the object of the analysis, but insofar as it is the form. The novelistic mode becomes theoretic writing. Biblical form, the literary gesture by which the conflict of the Covenant is articulated, that is to say the historical proceedings between Yahweh and his people, seems to reformulate (from a distance) psychiatric knowledge to make it the discourse of the transferential process between analyst and patient. In unearthing the relationships which are haunting the connection between knowledge and its object, Freud betrays the scientific norm. He rediscovers the literary genre which was, in the Bible, the "theoretical" discourse of this relationship. In addition, as Lacan remarked, Freud is one of the only modern authors capable of creating myths,[10] which means, at least, capable of creating novels with a theoretic function.

Whatever the possible apparition of this great biblical ghost in the Freudian corpus may be, it remains that the importance given to historicity is here precisely that which leads back to a novelistic form, even to a poetic art. In this connection, three aspects concern the literary narrative.

1. For Freud, the "novel" is defined as the conjunction in a single text of, on the one hand, "the symptoms of the illness" (*Krankheitssymptome*), in other words, a semiology based on the identification of pathological structures and, on the other hand, "the history of the suffering" (*Leidensgeschichte*), in other words, a series of related events which intervene and alter the structural model.[11] To adopt the style of the novel is to abandon the "case study" as it was presented and practiced by Charcot in his Tuesday sessions (*ses Mardis*). These latter consisted of "observations," that is to say coherent charts or pictures, composed by noting the facts relevant to a synchronic model of an illness. In Freud's writing, the pathological structure becomes the framework where events are produced but not integrated—events nonetheless decisive from the viewpoint of the illness's development. In this perspective, Charcot's "tableau" or chart is transformed into a "novel." The text which appears to lack "scientific authenticity" is rather the effect of the serious treatment of the dialogic function integral to the cure. In short, no historicity without novel.

2. Freud is himself involved in the relation with his interlocutor. The most rigorous part of his writing, his case analyses, narrate unexpected transformations of his positions produced by the "suffering" of his patients. For the purpose of a first approximation, let us assert that Freud's "position" is represented in his text by the model which serves as a theoretic framework to his selection and interpretation of the material presented by the patient. This is a pathological configuration, the system of an illness. The novel results from those differences

which the suffering of the other introduces into this framework. These differences mark theoretical deficits and narrative events simultaneously in the text. These two values, one relative to the model and the other relative to the narrative, have, however, the same signification: the theoretic deficit defines the event of the narration. From this viewpoint, the novel instances the relationship which theory maintains with the event-triggered apparition of its limits.

In effect, the disturbances that the "suffering" of the other introduces into the system of "illness" also attain something that is beyond the analyst's knowledge. In response to the patient there are "affects" and reminiscences of every sort. Freud considers these reactions "memorable" (*denkwürdig*). In his discourse they mark a divergence between his historic place (an unconscious) and his scientific position (a knowledge). The dialogue brings to the surface a "disturbing familiarity" in the analyst himself. The "recognition" of this internal alteration defines precisely that which separates the psychoanalytic "novel" from the psychiatric "chart." In removing thus a part of its "*sérieux*" from the scientific model, the Freudian narrative inscribes there a hidden historicity of the analyst and a reciprocal mutation of the interlocutors. It is a sculpture of events, previously unknown, in the structural framework of knowledge.

3. Conversely, Freud's way of looking at his own writing instructs as to the reading of other documents. It allows us to consider any narrative as a relationship between a structure and some events, that is to say between a system (be it explicit or not) and its alteration by an otherness. In this case, the literary work is not reducible to the "*sérieux*" of a structural model imposed by a conception of scientificity. Nor would one be able to reduce it in those happenstances of reading (affective or reminiscent) which fantasy or erudition multiply indefinitely. The literary work will appear rather as a setting of historical alterations within a formal framework. Moreover, there is a continuity between Freud's manner of listening to a patient, his manner of interpreting a document (literary or other), and his manner of writing. There is no essential break between these three operations. The "novel" in this sense can characterize at once the utterances of a patient, a literary work, and the psychoanalytic discourse itself.

A Tragedy and a Rhetoric of History

Although Freudian interpretation takes the form of a novel, it remains nonetheless historical. Let us give to the term "historical" the definition that will serve as a point of departure: by "historical" we intend the analysis which considers its materials as effects of symptoms (economic, social, political, ideological, etc.) and which aims at elucidating the temporal operations (causality, intersection, inversion, coalescence, etc.) which were able to produce such effects. A postulate of production and a spotting of its chronological processes specify a history-related problematic. Such a problematic characterizes the Freudian reuse of models borrowed especially from two regions of literature which have been clearly set out since Aristotle[12]: tragedy and rhetoric. An exchange symptomatic of the psychoanalytic ambiguity: its models are literary ones but transformed by their injection into a historical terrain; they no longer belong to either one.

A. *Tragedy in Freud's work.* Freudian analysis adopts as its system of explanation the structuration of psychic phenomena through the positing of three agencies (*Instanz*): the Ego (*Ich*), the Id (*Es*), and the Superego (*Über-Ich*). The psychic machine echoes a theatrical model. It is constituted in the manner of a Greek tragedy and in that of Shakespearian drama, from which we know that Freud drew structures of thought, categories of analysis and authoritative quotations. Non-human "role-players" (here, Freudian "principles," and there, Greek gods) form a configuration of roles which respond to one another by their opposition; from the beginning of the play, they set forth in synchronic fashion the stages through which the name-bestowing hero (the "I" for Freud, King Lear or Hamlet for Shakespeare) will pass in order to find himself at the end in the inverse of his original position.[13] At the beginning, an order of agencies yields in topographical form, the "moments" which will unfold in diachronic form with successive displacement of the "hero." Every play or story is the progressive transformation of a spatial order into a temporal series. The psychic apparatus and its function are built on this "literary" model of theater.

The Freudian apparatus, however, distinguishes itself in two ways from the model it borrows from tragedy. First, it locates forces which articulate the effective psychic course, and not only the personas of a play. It is a matter of representation, but one which explains the events. Although it is a dramatic model, its function is historic.

Moreover, if one accepts the formalization of Georges Dumézil, in which there is, from myth to novel, a reproduction of the same structures and the same function in spite of the discontinuity marked by the transformation of the cosmological scene into a psychological scene,[14] Freud's procedure operates inversely. He initiates a return to myth from the novel. He remains generally in an intermediate zone, the "entre-deux" of tragedy (which functioned in Greek civilization as a historicization of myth). Freudian depsychologization, which turns the novel toward the myth, stops where mythification would deprive the narrative of historicity. Situated between novel and myth, because the former tells of an unfolding and the latter sets out structures, the psychoanalytic machine thus offers the model of tragedy to the historical interpretation of documents.

B. *Freudian rhetoric.* The historicization of literary models appears even more clearly in the sector of the processes of production. These "mechanisms" have as their characteristic to "displace," to "disfigure," to "disguise," in short, to be "deformations" (*Entstellungen*). In Freud's analytic practice from the *Interpretation of Dreams* (1980) onward, the operations which order representation by articulation through the psychic system are in effect rhetorical:

metaphors, metonymics, synecdoches, paranomasia, etc. Here again, literature provides the model. But Freud finds these "rhetorical" figures in a "literary" ghetto where a conception of scientificity had enclosed them. He frees them from that ghetto. He restores their historical pertinence, recognizing in them a network of operations which produce manifestations relative to the other (from Oedipus and castration to transference). Hence, rhetoric constitutes the terrain (unduly restrained to that which has become "literature") where formal figures are elaborated from another logic than that of accepted scientificity. These processes do not come from the rationality of Aufklärung, which privileges analogy, coherence, identity, and reproduction. They correspond to all the alterations, inversions, equivocations, or deformations inherent when playing on circumstances (chance) and with the locus defining identification (the masks) in one's relationship to the other (relating to chances and masks). Maybe it is also possible to recognize in this renaissance of rhetoric in Freud's work a return of a logic often encountered in the Semitic and Jewish tradition of formal "stories," of linguistic play and of "parabolic" displacements.

To use one of Freud's terms, the literary work thus becomes "a mine" where one stocks the historical tactics relative to circumstances; tactics characterized by the "deformations" which they bring about in a social and/or linguistic system. The literary text is like a game. With its sets of rules and surprises, a game is a somewhat theoretic space where the formalities of social strategies can be explained on a terrain protected from the pressure of action and from the opaque complexity of daily struggle. In the same way, the literary text, which is also a game, delineates an equally theoretic space, protected as is a laboratory, where the artful practices of social interaction are formulated, separated, combined, and tested. It is the field where a logic of the other is exercised, the same logic that the sciences rejected to the extent to which they practiced a logic of the same.[15]

Freud first used the dream to rearticulate these "literary" procedures in the realm of psychic and social reality. Perhaps he used the dream as a Trojan horse to historicize rhetoric and to reintroduce it into the citadel of science. In doing so, he makes the literary text into the deployment of formal operations which organize historical effectiveness. He gives it, or rather, he returns to it, the status of a theoretic fiction in which the logical models necessary for any historical "explanation" are recognized and produced.

The Anti-Individualist Biography

After considering the literary form of analysis (the novel) and its conceptual apparatus (a system of tragedy and rhetorical procedures), one can consider its major substance: the case history. Inherited from psychiatry, this privileged object ultimately defines the discipline: psychoanalysis, one might say, is biography. Indeed, interest in biographical study dates to the beginning of Freudianism. In the "Wednesday sessions" (related to Charcot's Tuesdays?), even before the founding of the International Association, "cases" were examined: Jean-Paul, H. Kleist, N. Lenau, Leonardo da Vinci, K. F. Meyer, F. Wedekind, etc. This first interest was growing on and on among the Freudians (although, for example, it is nearly absent in the work of Lacan). It is a question, moreover, of literary authors in most cases. Already, in this fairly classic dimension, biography introduces historicity into literature. But the innovation of Freudianism consists in its use of biography as a means of destroying the individualism posited by a modern and contemporary psychology. With this tool, it undermines the postulate of liberal and bourgeois society. It undoes it. It substitutes another history in returning, as we have seen, to the system of tragedy.

Elaborated in the sixteenth and the seventeenth centuries individualism served as a social base and as the epistemological foundation of a capitalist economy and democratic politic.[16] It hands over its technical and mythic postulate to the rational management of a society supposedly constituted of productive and autonomous entities. Individualism is the historical trope for occidental modernity. The author's psychology is no more than a variant of this system. If *Robinson Crusoe* is the mythic novel of this postulate, Freudianism takes this heritage from its birthplace as a social given. But it does not accept it any longer as its postulate. To the contrary, Freudianism dismantles individualism. It destroys its truth-seemingness.

One comparison will demonstrate the essential. In 1784 Kant enumerated the rights and the obligations of an enlightened consciousness: "a full liberty" and responsibility, an autonomy of knowledge, a "move" which enables man to "transcend his minority."[17] This ethic of progress depends upon the postulate of individualism. A century later, Freud reverses one by one all the Kantian affirmations. In his analysis, the "adult" appears to be defined by his "minority"; knowledge, by desire mechanisms; liberty, by the law of the unconscious; progress, by originary events.

Thus, his biographical novels would be for the individualist ethic that conquered the modern bourgeoisie, what Cervantes' Don Quixote was to the Spanish *Hidalguía* at the beginning of the seventeenth century. The figure which organizes the practices of a society becomes the stage for its critical reversal. Once again the figure defines the place of its disappearance. It is no longer anything but the place of its other—a mask. This critical procedure is typically Freudian. When "scientificity" creates a place for itself by eliminating what does not conform to it, Freudian analysis perceives the alterity haunting and without being aware, determining this appropriation; it demonstrates the contradictory games which occur in the same place, between the manifest and the hidden; it diagnoses the ambiguity and the plurality of this very place. Also, the figure is a novelistic one from this viewpoint. The parallel with *Don Quixote* is neither a coincidence nor an exception.

The same type of criticism aims at another "fundamental" unity whose formation is furthermore historically linked to that of individualism: national unity. For Freud, as for Marx, the nation is only a decor. It is the belated fusion (*Verschmelzung*) of constituant parts where the antinomy soon reappears in other forms (*Wiederherstellungen*).[18] Here also, Freudian analysis takes up accepted historical unity (for example, the Jewish nation) in order to find in it the superficial union (a *Verlötung*) of opposing forces and the evidence of their resurgence. Like "biographical" criticism of individualism, this "sociopolitical" criticism of the idea of national unity has as its literary form the "historical novel," *Moses and Monotheism*. The historical novel does not institute its own unities, as would a scientific discipline. The fictive character of its subject surfaces as it evinces the contradictions which determine it. This operation does not take place without evoking the theoretic process and the literary form which Karl Marx employed in *Der achtzehnte Brumaire* to demystify political representation, rejecting the Hegelian conception of integration of the social totality. For Freud, the nation and the individual are equal disguises for a struggle, a dismemberment (*Zerfall*), which always returns to the scene from which it is erased; and the novel is the theoretic instrument of this analysis.

A Stylistics of Affects

The affect (*Affekt*) also reappears in the Freudian discourse. It is the elementary form of drive. From the *Studies on Hysteria*, the affect furnishes a basis for the "economic" analysis of psychic mechanism. Although it is most often autonomous in its relationship to representational operations, it is submitted to the generating mechanisms of pathological figures: its "conversions" produce hysteria; its "displacements," obsession; its transformations, neurosis; etc. It plays a more and more decisive role in Freud's analytic practice. But these refinements of the theory do not allow us to forget a massive phenomenon: affects are the form which the return of the passions take in Freud's work.

Indeed, the destiny of passions is strange. After having been considered by the ancient medical or philosophical theories (until Spinoza, Locke, or Hume)[19] as determining movements whose composition organized social life, they were forgotten by the productivist economy of the nineteenth century, or rejected into the sphere of literature. The study of passions thus became a literary specialization in the nineteenth century; it no longer belonged to political philosophy or economy. With Freud, this feature having been eliminated from science reappears in an economical discourse. A remarkable fact, in its own perspective, Freudianism simultaneously returns relevancy to passions, to rhetoric, and to literature. Indeed they have something in common, both having been excluded together from positivist scientificity.

This return takes effect in Freud's work by means of the detour of the unconscious. In reality, this deviation is first the description, or if one prefers, the clinical observation of that which nineteenth century epistemology had made of passions, exiling them from legitimate discourse of social "reason," deporting them to the region of the trivial (*"pas sérieux"*) which is literature, reducing them to psychological deviations from order; in short, rendering the passions marginal. Indeed, this epistemological rejection is the reason pronounced by a productivist bourgeoise for an ethical excommunication. The affects which Freud classified according to his own conception of the psychic apparatus are recovered where the passions had been discarded in a recent upset, among the refuse of rationality and cast out morality. Nevertheless these "blind" movements, lacking a technical language, determine the economy of social relationships, from this place of rejection, and to a greater degree as they are more repressed.

Freud restores their legitimacy in scientific discourse which obviously transports this discourse to the side of the novel. His analyses of affects concern literature and history in two more specific ways.

1. The manifestation of the revivification of the affect is the condition necessary so that a patient's memories might have a therapeutic value and so that the analyst's interpretation might have theoretic value. Also, the cure's technique includes an awakening in the patient of the affect dissimulated by representation; the cure fails if it does not accomplish this, unless this failure be the indication of a psychosis. At the same time, in the cure which he conducts or in the text he writes, Freud, as psychoanalyst, takes care to "confess," as he says, his affective reaction to the person or document he analyses: he is troubled by Dora, frightened by Michelangelo's Moses, irritated by the Biblical Yahweh, etc. With this golden rule, every psychoanalytic treatment directly contradicts a first norm, a constituent part of scientific discourse, which argues that the truth of the utterance be independent of the speaking subject. Freud's assumption, the inverse of this norm, is that the speaking subject's place is decisive in a conflicting network of abreactions and that it is specified by the affect. This allows reintroduction of that which the objective utterance hides: its historicity—that which stuctured relationships, and that which changes them. To make this historicity reappear is the condition of analytic elucidation and of its operativeness.

This method exerts and elucidates language as an intersubjective practice. By doing so, it renders analytic discourse a fiction, in other words, a discourse where the particular nature of its speaker, essentially his affectivity, makes an impression. Hence, it is no longer scientific; "it is literature," so to speak. From the Freudian viewpoint this common *doxa* is true, but it has a positive value. The two factions use the same strategy, only reversing it: if positivism rejects the discourse of subjectivity as non-scientific, psychoanalysis considers "blind," or pathogenic, the positivism which disfigures subjective discourse. What the former condemns, the latter advances. However, psychoanalysis takes up the definition given to fiction as being a knowledge jeopardized and wounded by its otherness (the affect, etc.) or a statement that the speaking subject's utterance deprives of its "*sérieux*." In the analytic field, this discourse is effective because it is "touched" or wounded by the affect. The diminution of "*sérieux*" allows it to spring into operation. This is the theoretic status of the novel.

2. To admit the affect is also to re-learn a language "forgotten" by scientific rationality and repressed by social norms. Rooted in sexual differences and in early childhood stages, this language still circulates, disguised in dreams, in legends, and in myths. In demonstrating at the same time their fundamental signification and their proximity to his own discourse, Freud knows that, as novelists and poets used to do, "he dared to take the side of antiquity and of popular superstition against the ostracism of the positive sciences."[20] Ultimately it is André Breton, however, this "trivial" admirer, who best recognized the unity of these analyses and who seized the occasion they offered to found an original and transgressive language on the return to affectivity.[21] He foresaw what would remain of Freud: a theory which makes literature itself appear as a different logic.

"The novelist has always preceded the scientist!" Certainly Freud was not very grateful for having been so lucidly "unveiled." He was also a professor. After all, he took seriously the "*sérieux*." But literature is equally composed of works which, by losing their scientific reality, reveal in their fall, and thanks to time's devaluation of their technical "*sérieux*," a different logic which supported them all along, this one "literary." Breton saw in advance, in Freudian texts, what they would be transformed into by their scientific "death."

Emile Benveniste stressed that, linguistically, the operations identified by Freud in relation to what happens in dream, myth, or surrealist poetry, correspond to the "stylistic processes of discourse."[22] This is a decisive indication. Style concerns the enunciation or the *elocution* of ancient rhetoric. In the text it is the trace of its place of production. It refers to a theory of affects and their representations. There is a stylistic in Freud's writing. It does not send us back to a classification, however pioneering, such as the one Bally built on a psychological nomenclature of affects.[23] In following the play of affects between their disguises and their confessions, Freud's stylistics analyze in effect the modalization of utterance by speech acts; it founds a "linguistics of speech"[24] which gives us in terms which are today conceivable an equivalent of the ancient theory of passions.

The Poem and/or the Institution

The analyst's and patient's languages belong to the same problematic. Ultimately they both originate in the study, central to Freud, of "the construction and transformation of legends" (*die Bildung und Umgestaltung von Sagen*), and this, to the extent that Freud refers to his own narration as "fiction" or "novel," and calls "legends" (but also "fictions") those languages which deny their status as fictions in order to imply (or to make one believe) that they speak of the real. Their common pre-determination by the same process of "construction" is an essential element in Freud's interpretative system. The Freudian discourse does not protect itself from the mechanism which it uncovers in its "objects." It is not exempt as it would be if it occupied the privileged position of an "observer." It elucidates an operation to which it is also subjected.

At least this is true in principle. In fact, Freud's work contains two very different kinds of texts. The first category practices theory, the second category expounds upon it, like the knowledge of the teacher. The "Lessons," "Contributions," "Abrégé," etc., belong to this second category. While psychoanalytic discourse is itself subjected to the transformations and deformations it treats in the first texts, in the second texts it is assured an authoritative place in the name of the psychoanalytic and social institutions which support it. A double game can be ascertained from the beginning. This game developed within Freudianism provoking an oscillation between what one might call "analytic" moments and "didactic" moments. The history of psychoanalysis is built on this alternation between "transferential" elucidations and pedagogical "coups de force." As in Freud's work, the analytic sessions are interrupted by dogmatic statements.

At the center of this oscillation there is a strategic point: the position of the analyst as "a subject supposed to have knowledge." Theory insists on the "supposed" knowledge of the analyst which refers back to the "nothing" of knowledge and to the demystifying reciprocity in the relationship of one to another. But the practice is often dependent on the accredited "knowledge" of the affiliation and on the proper name of the institution. The inverse is also true: the "exposé" can take advantage of an authority which practice reduces to nothing. Freud's position grows out of this ambivalence. As concerns his disciples, how does Freud handle (or receive) the status of "a subject supposed to have knowledge"? The reference to Freud functions sometimes as does the relationship to an analyst, sometimes as the relationship to a teacher. This reference puts into question the definition of discourse, which is at times "writing," at times "institution."

This question can be clarified by returning to what Freud calls "the writing of history" (*Geschichtsschreibung*),[25] a nodal point for relationships between literature and history. For Freud, "the writing of history" is produced from events of which nothing remains: it "takes their place." Historically, writing is excluded from that which it discusses and nevertheless it is a "cannibalistic discourse." It "takes the place" of the history lost to it. For Freud, the writing process combines "biblical" fiction, which establishes at the beginning of writing a separation or an exile, and Greco-Roman "fiction," the conceivable order, the logos, to return to the original and consuming violence of Cronos-Saturn. All proceeds as if writing had taken from time the double characteristic of loss of place (the exile) and of devouring life (cannibalism). It is as though the writing process were the interminable movement and the insatiable hunger of the body of the letter. In any case, there is present in the process of writing itself a duality which allows it to work (as well as the analyst) at times as a cast-off excluded from reality, an illusion of knowledge, a dejection of science, and at times as a voracious authority and a dominating institution. This duality is not only attributable to the manner in which writing is used, as though it were a blemish caused by a second operation, a transgression of history, from which writing itself would be undamaged. There is no first innocence, not even in the writing process. Duplicity governs production (not just exploitation), although pedagogy privileges and reinforces the cannibalism of discourse.

Discourse credits itself with an authority which tends to compensate the reality from which it is exiled. If this discourse's assertion is to speak in the name of that of which it is deprived, it is because it is separated from it. At first glance the authority appears to cover the loss and then, to avail itself of this loss to exercise power. This authority is the prestigious substitute which plays with something it does not possess and which receives its effectiveness by promising something it will not deliver. But in fact it is the institution which fills the "nothing" of knowledge with this authority. This institution is the articulating force between authority and nothingness. Hence, the institutional machine affects and guarantees the partly magical operation which substitutes authority for this nothingness.

It is necessary to confront Freud's manner of writing with these general notions: to compare what he says to what he does, his theory of writing to his practice of writing. In a decisive moment of Freud's project, he designates, in *Moses and Monotheism*,[26] the nothingness ("*rien*") on which "the writing of history" is constructed. This will serve as an example of Freud's manner of writing. By a device customary to Freud at important turning-points in his analyses, he ultimately authorizes his conception, not by proofs, but by the quotation which shapes his thought. It is a poem; that is writing where truth is supported by nothing other than writing's relationship to itself, its beauty. The authorizing poem is a fragment, one of Schiller's aphorisms:

> What will live of the poem's immortal
> must darken in this life[27]

This poetic theory of writing is put into practice by the Freudian text. It is its "demonstration" in the sense that one demonstrates the features of a car or a stove. The Freudian text "exercises" Schillerian thought, which posits the prerequisite of the death of the living for the birth of the poem to take place. To quote Schiller is to base one's work on a fiction which deprives itself of experimental referentiality. Far from supporting the discourse with a scientific authority, with a "good author," this return to the "literary" strips the "*sérieux*" from the discourse. It is a loss of knowledge. More than this, however, as for Freud, to lose cannot be dissociated from a wish to lose. The act of writing consists here, in effect, in throwing oneself into the nothingness ("*rien*") of the poem. In the same way that Schiller's poem states what the poem *is* (in this sense it is meta-discursive: the relationship of divine death to mortal birth is the model for the relationship between the disappearance of the referential and the production of each poem), the presence of Schiller's quote in the Freudian discourse functions in order that the latter might *do* or *become* what it *says* of writing (in this sense it is performative). Freud's theoretic production is permitted by a loss of knowledge while for Schiller poetic creation is permitted by a disappearance of being.

Yet, Schiller's poem functions also as an institution. It comes with this "function" in Freud's text to fill the gap of knowledge. It replaces, in Freud's own admission, that which historical information lacks. It intervenes in this loophole of the argumentation to the extent that the referred poem belongs to "classical" culture and was credited with literary value. (Freud is neither very original nor daring in his literary tastes: he limits himself to accepted writers.) The quotation legitimizes the Freudian text. In short, it renders it believable; it makes one believe. The function of the quote for Freud differs, then, from the function proper to Schiller's text. The poem assures its own credibility because it rests uniquely on the force of its form and because it is other, presented in the visibility of its unknowing ("*non-savoir*"). The Freudian text makes itself believable because of its dependence on the other—the reference to the other (to the "witness") always generates some credibility. Far from being poetic, the Freudian text is located in an analytic position where there is one "supposed to have knowledge": it renders itself credible in the name of the other. Here the other is the poem. During the cure it will be the unconscious: the analyst could say that the "other" which authorizes my discourse is in you, patients; I am expected to speak, to intervene in the name of this "nothing," your unconscious. For Freud, however, there is a continuity from the poem to the unconscious, were it not that the poem already responds to the unconscious and that in this respect psychoanalysts would be the substitutes for the poem, repeating it in the place where the poem has already spoken, substituting for it where it has become silent.

From this point of view, Freudian discourse again makes a poetic gesture, all the while institutionalizing this gesture. It thereby gains legitimation, while the poem is the text which nothing authorizes. This difference holds the psychoanalytic novel at the threshold of the poem. It fixes it in an economy of believing/ making believed which, in reproducing the poetic gesture, avails itself of it in a manner that is no longer poetic.

"Believing" in Writing

From the single mechanism of believing two different functions might follow: one more "exilic" (poetic), the other more "devouring" (analytic). Perhaps even better than Schiller's *Griechenlands*, an unfinished text by Mallarmé, a poem written on the theme *"épouser la notion,"* could specify this first function:

> And there need exist nothing for me to embrace it
> and believe in it totally
> Nothing—nothing.[28]

Mallarmé places himself in the same vein as Schiller. He identifies, however, precisely that which attaches writing to "nothing": a believing. In 1870, he spoke of a "Belief."[29] The poem is the trace of that belief: there need exist nothing for one to believe in it; nothing need remain of the thing in order for one to give credit to it, to write. Reciprocally, the poem makes one believe because there is nothing. When Mallarmé evokes "Beauty" in his letters to Casalis, he refers to the same construct as when he speaks of "Belief." He refers to that which no reality supports, to something which originates no longer in being. Belief is thus the movement born of and creator of a void. It is a beginning, a starting point. If the poem is not "legitimized," it legitimizes a different space; it is the nothingness of this space. It reveals the possibility of that other space in the very excess of what imposes itself. This gesture belongs equally to aesthetics and to ethics (the difference between the two is not so great, as the aesthetic is essentially the appearance or the form of ethics in the domain of language). This gesture rejects the authority of the fact. Its origin is not there. It transgresses the social convention which demands that the "real" be law. The poem opposes social conventions with its own nothingness—atopical, revolutionary, "poetic."

The project of historiography is the inverse of the poetic one. It consists of furnishing discourse with referentiality, to make it function as "expressive," to legitimize it by means of the "real," in short, to initiate discourse as that which is supposed to have knowledge. The law of historiography functions to obscure nothingness, to suppress the void, to fill the gap. The discourse must not appear separate from its referents. The absence or loss at the origin of its construct must not be unveiled. Literary history, for example, meticulously links the literary text to "realistic" (economic, social, psychological, ideological, etc.) structures.

The text would be the effect of these structures. Literary history's function is to tirelessly restore referentiality; it produces such referentiality and forces its recognition from the text. Literary history thus contrives the belief that the text articulates the real. In this fashion, it transforms the text into an institution, if we define the institution as the instrument which renders credible the adequation of discourse and reality by imposing its discourse as the law governing the real. Certainly literary history by itself would not be sufficient to produce this result. Each specific institution is supported, rather, by others in a network which constitutes the "web of belief."[30]

This consideration reintroduces the relationship of discourse to pedagogy and to the institution, two forms of the same structure: all institutions are pedagogical, and pedagogical discourse is always institutional. Historiography is in efect pedagogical: I will teach you, readers, something you do not know, and it is a law, written by reality itself. The historian teaches laws which supposedly have a real referent. But this capacity to institutionalize the texts he studies (chosen for their non-literary value or selected in such a way as to avoid their development toward "literary" autonomy in relation to the facts they are considered to signify) is the product of an accreditation to a profession or of a membership in a learned community. His position as a professor or member of an academic association brings to his discourse a double strength and this strength is represented within the discourse by the supposed link between the utterance and the facts to which it refers. "Realism," or the legitimation of discourse by its "references," originates with the author, the person legitimized by social credentials, and is transferred from the author to his text. The text is in turn authorized by its adherence to the events which it is believed to explicate or to signify. Contrary to all scientific tradition which postulates an autonomy of discourse in relation to its producer's position, the position has an epistemological effect on the text: social credentials play a decisive role in the definition of the discourse's status.

This is well recognized. The value of scientific statements today is relative to the hierarchy of laboratories which produce them. Their "*sérieux*" is valued in accordance with the position of their authors. In another field, Philippe Lejeune demonstrated that in the final analysis, the autobiographical genre is grounded not on the text itself, but on the conjunction between the author named by the text and his effective social place.[31] This argument can be generalized: the accreditation of the author by his historical place generates the legitimation of the text by its referent. Reciprocally, an attitude of docility toward the norms of a community (learned or not) assures the possibility of the text's "conformity" to the facts. Here, one does not believe in writing, but in the institution which determines its function. The text's relationship to a place gives the form and guarantee of that place to the supposed knowledge of the text. The reality of this position renders credible the semblance of referentiality. Strip the title of professor from the author of a historical study and he is no longer anything but a novelist.

Freud has an acute awareness of this instability. He is lucid. He knows that when he crosses beyond the terrain of the profession which authorizes him, he falls into the novel. But his discovery precisely exiles him from the land of the "*sérieux*." Cleverly, he maneuvers between the "nothing" of writing and the "authority" that the institution furnishes the text. At times he confesses himself to be a novelist, a way of marking his sensitivity to what he knows of the semblance the institution adds to the text. At times he prevails upon his academic position as professor and works to remain "Master" of "his community." He works at it all the more as, like Felix the Cat, his project carries him outside the validated ground of the psychiatric profession. He needs to assure a surplus of institutional force in the place where it is lacking in his discourse so that it might be supposed to have knowledge. He is not able to renounce (this would be a Mallarmean mourning) a place which credits the semblance of referentiality, rather he chooses it because he knows that without it he would only be a novelist. The more he perceives a dangerous kinship and a disquieting resemblance between his discourse and ancient legends, the more he institutes and restores from day to day an institutional place which authorizes this discourse in the eyes of his followers and posterity.

The great myths which Freud creates, from *Totem and Taboo* to *Moses and Monotheism*, evince their ambivalence, their fictive character (nothing found there is truly historical), and the affirmation that they have a relationship to the real (they provide the form that historical movement must present). In fact, the second aspect is sustained by institutional practice ("it works," therefore it is real), just as in exact science laboratories the formalism of utterances (they are also fictions) has as its counterpoint and prerequisite the political power of institutions. Freud, however, cannot give this articulation the clarity which permitted the growth of institutional power to scientific institutions. He works in two fields at once. He mixes them. In addition, he elaborates myths as though fiction were describing what "must have" happened.

To conclude, Freud's "authoritarism" is the effect of a lucidity parallel to that of Mallarmé. But, in conformity to what he himself analyzed in fetishism (relative to a missing referent), he cannot be content with this "nothing," or what he already "knows." Without illusion concerning the realism of "positive science," he finds a solution in the institution which controls the function of a "supposed knowledge," a knowledge relative to what remains irreducible in the question of the other.

From this point of view, one might wonder what would remain of the "realism" of the unconscious itself, without the institution which supports its truth-seemingness. R. Castel said that the institution is the unconscious of psychoanalysis. He referred to what psychoanalysis represses as it denies its own institutions. But Castel could also be understood in the sense that the psycho-analytic institution gives credit to the reality of the unconscious and that, short of this, it would be nothing other than a hypothetical space, the framework a theory erects to allow further elaboration, like Thomas More's Utopian Island. Without the institution that represents the other, the effect of the real disappears. Only the formal network organized by writing is left behind, there "nothing" remains of what this writing concerns. Deprived of its institutionalization, the unconscious is only the new paradigm furnishing theoretic space to the novel, to tragedy, to rhetoric, and to Freud's stylistic.

Psychoanalysts have shown even more determination than their founder in the defense of the institution (or in turning the founding work into an institution) which guarantees credibility for "supposed knowledge." In order to benefit from this result, they pay a heavy tax to their association or school. Literature professors, however, do the same thing by a fatal consequence of their academic position when they attempt to demonstrate that literature "expresses" a time or an ideology, and when they try, thereby, to "explicate" a text by means of its referent. They historicize the text. They institutionalize it—although they often lack Freud's lucidity concerning the redoubtable character of literature. Un-aware of its danger, they manipulate it. In any case, the distinction is not made between literature and history. Rather, it is made between two ways of compre-hending the document: one, as "legitimized" by one institution; or another, as relative to "nothingness."

These two perspectives are not optional matters, as though one could choose between them. Undoubtedly there exist, from the work of certain "mystics" to Mallarmé, experiences of "nothingness" which give place to an exilic writing, a literary form (esthetic) of the "purely" ethical gesture of believing. This object-less "belief," however, is not the result of a decision. One "believes" thusly when one cannot do otherwise, when real grounds for belief are lacking. Life in a society requires belief of a very different sort. It is a belief whose artic-ulation is based upon the supposed knowledge guaranteed by institutions. This belief is rooted in the supporting associations which protect the question of the other from the folly of "nothingness." One must at least make a distinction between the delinquency of the literary "non-sérieux" and the normativity based on institutional credibility. One cannot be reduced to the other. It is permitted, though, to consider such a possibility. Without ideologically challenging the institutional historicity dominating the social function of writing and originating in the "cannibalistic" discourse of writing itself, it is possible to believe in writing, as did Mallarmé, precisely because, legitimized by "nothing," it legiti-mizes the other and ceaselessly begins.

Chapter 3
The Institution of Rot

During the night [. . .] *one* single *night, the lower God*
(Ariman) appeared [. . .] *his voice resounded in a mighty*
bass as if directly in front of my bedroom windows [. . .]
What *was spoken did not sound friendly by any means:*
everything seemed calculated to instill fright and terror in me
and the word "rotten *person"* (Luder) *was frequently heard—an*
expression quite common in the basic language (Grundsprache)
to denote a human being destined to be destroyed by God and to
feel God's power and wrath. Yet everything that was spoken was
genuine, *not phrases learnt by rote* [. . .] *For this reason any*
impression was not one of alarm and fear, but largely one of
admiration for the magnificent and the sublime: the effect on my
nerves was therefore beneficial, despite the insults contained in
the words [. . .]

—Daniel Paul Schreber, *Memoirs of My Nervous Illness*[1]

Don't write on the shitters, shit on writing.

—Graffiti in the bathroom of a Paris movie theater, 1977

Interspace: Psychoanalysis and Mysticism

I speak neither as an analyst nor as a mystic. I am accredited by neither of these two experiences, which have constituted, one after the other, inaccessible authorizations of discourse. To begin, I have only Saint-John Perse's Friday to invoke as my muse: the savage, transported to the kitchens of London, whose parlors his master Robinson Crusoe frequents, plays the soup spoiler and flirt.[2] Mysticism, especially, can only be dealt with from a distance, as a savage in the kitchen. Its discourse is produced on another scene. It is no more possible to conceptualize it than it is to dispense with it. Like Schreber's "basic language," it is "somewhat antiquated," "but nevertheless powerful."[3] It is like the phantom that returns to the stage.

The remoteness of this "basic" thing that returns in the form of mysticism, a hallucination of absences, is a mark of age, or a first death (the separation between its time and ours), and of a modesty to be retained (our distance from the place where this thing was written). The remoteness is also internal to me: I am divided by uncertainty when speaking of *that* [*ça*], of this relation between signifiers and an unknown, of this discourse, foreign yet near at hand, that is perhaps haunted by a maternal indeterminacy. This binds me even though I cannot believe to be in it, or what is worse, cannot pretend to have it. But after all, this is not unlike what psychoanalysis, along its borders and on its thresholds, tells to those who are determined not to *be a part of it* (of its institution), not to speak *from that place*, precisely because of what comes from it. There is thus, from the outset, a cleavage between the fact of being invested (captured?) in it, and the fact of not being there (neither in nor of that place).

It seems to me that Schreber's revelation, which is close to mysticism in so many respects, offers an approach to outlining the articulation between these two experiences, as well as their relation to the institution. In the course of that "unique night" in 1894, there rang forth a "mighty bass voice," not "friendly by any means," yet "beneficial" and "refreshing," and it said to the President: *Luder*, in other words, "harpy," "filth," "slut," or rather, since there is a certain familiarity to the insult, "*rotten* person." I propose to *meditate* upon this word, and that, according to Madame Guyon, means swallowing it. It appears in the interspace of mysticism and psychoanalysis, and demands attention even though it has nothing to justify it other than what it produces here and there: a "formula" that is heard, a "small fragment of truth"—a *splinter* of what?

A few global analogies can provide a framework, an admittedly fragile one, for Schreber's enactment of this *word* that is the archive of the subject (its corrupt document) and the saying of the subject's non-identity. I will mention only three points of convergence between psychoanalysis and mysticism. First, the distinction between a statement and a speech-act, a corpus and an act by the subject: that this distinction is central in Lacan does not alter the fact that it was precisely the mystic discourse of the sixteenth and seventeenth centuries that first established it.[4]

Second, Lacanian theory entertains relations of "separation" and "debt" with the mystics (Meister Eckhart, Hadewijch of Anvers, St. Teresa, Angelus Silesius, etc.); or, what amounts to the same thing, it rejects their goods, corpses of truths, and recognizes itself in the lack from which they received their name: something should be written about the return of these Christian phantoms at strategic points in analytic discourse, a movement that is homologous to the relation of "contestation" (*absprechen*) and "belonging" (*angehören*) that links the Freudian text to the Jewish tradition; something should be written about it—a zebrine patterning and labor of absences—to bide the time until what is written can be said in re-presentations of those strangers, who share responsibility for making Lacanian theory possible.[5]

Finally, in the mysticism of the sixteenth and seventeenth centuries, there is a desire analogous to that which Philippe Lévy discerned in Freud: a will to be done with, a death drive. With the mystics, a wish for loss is directed both toward the religious language in which the trace of their walk is imprinted and the course of their itinerary itself. Their voyages simultaneously create and destroy the paths they take. Or, more exactly, they take their course, but wish to lose the landscape and the way. Mysticism operates as a process whereby the objects of meaning vanish, beginning with God himself; it is as though the function of mysticism were to bring a religious *episteme* to a close and erase itself at the same time, to produce the night of the subject while marking the twilight of culture. It seems to me, in the context of our own time, that analytic trajectories have a similar historical function; they labor to expose the defection of a culture by its ("bourgeois") representatives, and through this diminishing of the signifying economy, they hollow out the place of an *other* that is the beyond of that which continues to support analytic critique. In this respect, mysticism and psychoanalysis presuppose—in the past in relation to "corrupt" Churches, today by way of "civilization and its discontents"—Schreber's feeling, so "perfectly clear" and intolerable, that, "in Hamlet's words, there is something rotten (*faul*) in the state of Denmark."[6]

This horizon of questions is not the subject I am addressing. It simply encircles the word *Luder*, which names the subject as a relation to the decomposition of the symbolic body, that identifying institution, and thus connotes a transformation in the status of the institution and in its mode of transmission.

Nomination: The Noble and the Rotten

Certain characteristics of the word Schreber heard are in consonance with the old mystic narratives, and are worthy of mention. First, there is a passage from sight to hearing. Sight blends into a voice-effect with the act of "perceiving speech" (*ich vernahm seine Sprache*), a "mighty bass voice" whose location, "in front of the window," is specifiable. The semi-blinding of the subject creates a void from which the word of the Other rings forth. Many of the auditory hallucinations that mark the path of mystic writings are like this. In fact, with Schreber, there is an inversion of content between the voice and sight. The voice assigns him a place that is the opposite of what he sees in God. The God whom he contemplates "in all His purity (*Reinheit*)" names him "rottenness." The oppositional terms symbolize within a rotten/pure, heard/seen structure. The word that condemns him to be annihilated (*zu vernichtenden*) comes during a spectacle offered by "God's omnipotence (*Allmacht*)." Speech nullifies the witness of glory. More exactly, this call to be carrion discloses the secret supporting the divine epiphany; Schreber carries its imprint (*Eindruck*), which is carved or written on his body as he stands in wonder before the "grandiose" and the "sublime." The decay of the subject, dictated by a voice, is the precondition for the theatrical institution of "omnipotence in all its purity." The basic language thus announces the *spoken* place at which the pure gold of a *shown* truth originates. In this respect, it converges with the knowledge that unfolds in mystical modes of narrative.

But this only concerns the content. The form of Schreber's experience is more important: it is one of nomination. The naming in question is one of a series in Schreber's career; it is an additional one and is doubtless one too many. The year before (1893), Schreber had been named president of the appeals court in Dresden, *Senatspräsident*. That nomination, a promotion to a task and an application of the subject (he was addressed as "Mister President"), is replaced by the one imposed by the voice of the God Ariman: "Your name is rottenness, *Luder*." A play of identities in the empty space left by the original name, which is foreclosed, *expired*.

Is this the empty center of initiatory ruptures? Name changes and beginnings by the name are to be found everywhere in the mystics' tradition. For example, John of the Cross (Juan de la Cruz) replaces Juan de Yepes, his family name. In these onomastic substitutions, the new appellation is presented as a program for being, a clear program that takes the place of an earlier, obscure one—it is any "proper" name imposing upon the subject the duty-to-be of the unknown that is the will of the other; it introduces, through a switch of fathers, a filiation of meaning to replace filiation by birth. From this angle, nomination is related to the family romance; it is an adoption into and by the noble family replacing the obscure one. In the case of Schreber, however "insulting" the name he received may be, it is still a sign that he has been adopted by the God Ariman, whom his "genuine" words and "expression of true feeling" brings close and renders "beneficial." To be called "rotten" or a "slut" is to be adopted by the noble family. This structure was operative in all religious "families" before it resurfaced in ideological, political, or psychoanalytic institutions.

The name imposed by the other is in addition authorized by nothing, and that is its special trait. "It signifies in itself something that refers first and foremost to signification as such."[7] The name is not authorized by any meaning; on the contrary, it authorizes signification, like a poem that is preceded by nothing and creates unlimited possibilities for meaning. But this occurs because the word *Luder* plays the role of that which cannot deceive. It compels belief more than it is believed. It has the status, Schreber says, of something veracious and authentic (*echt*). The basic language is here responding to a general necessity: "there has to be something somewhere that does not deceive"; science itself presupposes that "matter is not deceptive," so that even if we "deceive ourselves," at least "matter does not deceive us."[8] For Schreber, what guarantees the truth of all the rest and makes the interpretive proliferation of his discourse possible, as well as its slow metamorphosis into the body of a prostitute, is this name that he takes at its word, this signifier that comes from the other like a touch, this bass voice that affects his nerves and leaves an imprint on his body—a soothing effect produced by the "direct utterance of a real affectivity." Belief is founded upon the touch of a voice, which makes one believe that one is recognized, known, even loved. Here, it makes Schreber believe that it has finally established him somewhere, that it has fixed a place for him, that it has put an end to his drifting, that it has given him a place defined by the name by which it calls him.

Nomination does in effect assign him a place. It is a calling to be what it dictates: your name is *Luder*. The name performs. It does what it says. Schreber's nerves immediately begin to obey it. And that is only the beginning. He will "incarnate" his name by believing it; he would like, he says, "to hand over my body in the manner of a female harlot."[9]

He hands it over the instant he believes. He executes himself in every sense of the word. He makes himself the body of the signifier. But the word that is heard designates precisely this transformation. It is more than a splinter of meaning embedded in the flesh. It has the status of a concept because, in circumscribing the object of belief, it also articulates the *operation* of believing, which consists in passing from a nameless, disintegrating body—a "rottenness" that no longer has a name in any language—to a body "remade" for and by the name: a "harlot" formed according to the specifications of the signifier of the other. The signified of the word, which oscillates between decomposition and slut, designates the overall functioning of the signifier, or Schreber's effective relation to the law of the signifier. It expresses the precondition and the result of believing in the word, when this belief operates as identification or well-being.

This madness is not a particular madness. It is *general*. It is a part of any institution that assures a language of meaning, right or truth. The only odd thing about Schreber, the jurist, is that he knows its hard-to-take and "insulting" secret. He is not someone who can go on knowing nothing about it. The same is true for many mystics, who do not extend to others, whom they consider "Pharisees" or "abnormal," the "insult" of the evangelical word targeting the "rottenness" that is presupposed by the "fine appearance" (institutional and sepulchral) of truth and justice;[10] they know it is addressed to them; their mystical nights have also taught them what shrouding conditions the verisimilitude of God, what (immemorial) error and (analytic) defection of the body underlies the recognition of the Name, and what unveiling of decay is both the effect and the "reason" of the belief in a justification.[11]

From Torture to Confession

The positioning of the subject under the sign of refuse is the point where the institution of "true" discourse is imprinted. And this established discourse transmits itself by tirelessly producing, in "subjects," its condition of possibility, which is the "soothing" and moreover truthful confession that those subjects are no more than putrescence. To this sly law of the tradition-transmission of a noble doctrine can be added an extreme procedure that has always proliferated along the borders of institutions of truth and which, far from diminishing, like an archaeological phenomenon of history, constantly develops, becoming more and more of a "regular administrative practice," or a political "routine": torture.[12]

It is necessary to examine the hidden alliances between mysticism and torture. They share features that are in appearance accidental, or tied to particular events. For example, certain old ascetic techniques and contemporary torture practices coincide: as one example, the forms of sleep deprivation used by Suso, the Rhenish mystic, are very similar to those found in Greek or Brazilian prisons. Neither is it purely by chance that work on mysticism develops in totalitarian periods, as was the case in France during the occupation under the Vichy regime. This fact must be set in relation to the differences among the historical figures assumed by evangelical radicality in the seventeenth century: it was particularly "mystical" in the Catholic monarchies like Spain and France, and "prophetic" instead in the more democratic, reformed monarchies of England and Scandinavia.[13] These mystic experiences assume an acceptance of an "absolute" power that one should not, or can no longer, change, and which reflects back toward the subject interrogations of which it is capable of being neither the representation nor the object.

This leads us to a more fundamental feature. The goal of torture, in effect, is to produce acceptance of a State discourse, through the confession of putrescence. What the torturer in the end wants to extort from the victim he tortures is to reduce him to being no more than *that* [*ça*], rottenness, which is what the torturer himself is and knows that he is, but without avowing it. The victim must be the *voice* of the filth, everywhere denied, that everywhere supports the *representation* of the regime's "omnipotence," in other words, the "glorious image" of themselves the regime provides for its adherents through its recognition of them. The victim must therefore assume the position of the subject upon whom the theater of identifying power is performed.

But this voice is also muzzled in the darkness of the prison cell, discarded into the night of torment, the moment it confesses that which, in the subject, makes the epiphany of power possible. It is a disavowed avowal. The voice can only be the other, the enemy. It must be simultaneously heard and repressed: heard because in saying the putrescence of the subject it guarantees or reestablishes a "belonging"—in secret, so it does not compromise the image upon which the institution's power of assuring its adherents the privilege of being recognized is based. The voice is required, but only as a whisper in the back halls of the institution. A murmurous scream exacted by torture, which must create fear without creating a scandal, legitimizes the system without toppling it.

What makes the victim right for this operation is precisely that he comes from outside. He brings a confession that is necessary for the internal functioning of the institution, but can at the same time be exorcized as something pertaining to the adversary. It is also true that the victim is the enemy. The stranger to or rebel against the institution displays an ambition that is intolerable within it (except hypocritically): he assumes, in one way or another, that a discourse—either a political discourse (a revolutionary project), a religious one (a reformist intention), or even an analytical one ("free" expression)—has the power to remake the institution. In opposition to this claim to reconstruct the order of history from a base in "adversarial" speech, torture applies the law of the institution, which assigns speech the reverse role of being no more than a confession linked to adherence.

Once again, torture is the perfect example of an *initiation* into the reality of social practices.[14] Its effect is always to demystify discourse. It is the *passage* from what is *said* outside to what is *practiced* within. This transit, the moment during which the torturer must *produce* assent from an exteriority, therefore *betrays* the game of the institution, but in darkness, under cover of night. While utopian (revolutionary) projects assume that modes of saying have the ability to determine modes of power, or that the institution can become the visible articulation of a "truth" that has been spoken or will be spoken—while this kind of project preserves an "evangelical" structure—torture on the other hand restores the law of what effectively *happens*. The voice, in torture, is no longer "prophetic"; it no longer aims for the transgression of following a desire. A name, *Luder*, dictates to the subject what he must be in order for the institution to be, in order for him to believe what it shows of itself, in order for it to adopt and recognize him.

The torture victim is surprised; he finds himself before a law he did not expect. For in the end, no one demands that he declare true what he holds to be false. The institution does not rest on the recognition of a truth it displays on the outside and in theory (on the inside, who takes it to be true?), but on its adherents' recognition of *their own* filthiness. Therefore, the subject seized by the apparatus of torture is faced not with the value or horror of the system—a ground upon which he would stand strong—but with a rift and intimate rottenness—a ground of weakness for him. The revelation of his own filth, which is what torture tries to produce by degrading him, should be enough to deprive him, like his torturers and all the others, of his right to rebel. The machinery of humiliation, through this reversal of the situation and this reverse use of speech (which no longer places the institution in question, but rather the subject), hopes to force the victim to accept the name by which his torturers address him: *Luder.*

What is perverse about the confession procedure is that, no matter what, it is bound to hit the spot. Like Schreber isolated in the Sonnerstein mental hospital, the torture victim is deprived of the collective guarantees which ensure "normality"; he is abandoned to equipment that tears his body and unrelentingly works to prove to him that he is a betrayer, a coward, a pile of shit. He loses the alibi of the political, ideological, or social affiliations which in the past protected him against what the insulting name now teaches him about himself. Is this nomination not indeed the voice of what he is? "Yes, *that* [*ça*] is what I am, *Luder.*" What the name articulates in language is enough to make one forget past solidarities:[15] it is that "real" lurking behind a fragile self-possession and self-belonging. It is a mouth which opens to reveal what is rotten in the state of social relations or relations among militants. This thing that is pronounced and received is related to the hard-to-take revelation that mystic denuding and analytic elucidation adopt, in inverse modes but in the same solitude, as the beginning or principle of another voyage. We must inquire into what effects this confession has, what it enables the initiate to do, and what benefit an institution derives from such an enucleation.

There Is Some Other

Once he knows *that*, the torture victim may be annihilated, becoming the passive instrument of power; or he may allow himself any liberty, cynically exploiting his secret: these two figures exist among the agents of the system—those who verify the revelation by conforming to the name, and those who exploit it by covering it over with a different, fine-sounding name. However, another outlet is open which is not a resistance based upon the "purity" of militancy or the "majesty" of a cause, nor the game of the "rotten" within the institution of power. It is signaled in a movement that is neither denial [*dénégation*] nor perversion. It would be something to the effect of: "I am only *that* [*ça*], *but so what?*" Being rot does not necessarily lead the subject to identify with "that," or with an institution which "covers" it over. There is some real that survives this defection: a history, struggles, other subjects. It is perhaps even the case that the only thing real is what no longer seems liable to fix an identity or earn recognition for marchers.

Accounts by torture victims indicate the stage of breakdown at which their resistance intervenes. They "held up," they say, by maintaining (perhaps we should even say "enduring") the memory of comrades who, for their own part, were not "rotten"; by keeping in mind the struggle in which they were engaged, a struggle which survived their own "degradation" intact, and did not unburden them of it any more than it depended on it; by discerning still, through the din of their tortures, the silence of human anger and the genealogy of suffering that lay behind their birth, and from which they could no longer protect or expect anything; or by praying, in other words by assuming an otherness, God, from which neither aid nor justification was forthcoming, and to which they were of no use and could not offer their services—exactly what an old rabbi means when he says that praying is "talking to the wall." This resistance eludes the torturers because it is something ungraspable. It originates precisely in what eludes the victim himself, in what exists without him and allows him to elude the institution that takes him as its adopted son only through reducing him to *that* [*ça*], putrescence. Resistance such as this rests on *nothing* that could belong to him. It is a *no* preserved in him by what he does not have. Born of a recognized defection, it is the memory of a *real* that is no longer guaranteed by a Father.

The destruction of human dignity is also the beginning for the mystics—despite the fact that this corruption, which signs the subject and is often accompanied by the theatricalization of his body (wounds, infections, purulence, etc.), is unbearable for right-thinking commentators and is always disclaimed by "humanist" interpreters. In the words of Gottfried Benn,[16] the "stigmatized self" is the locus of breakdown and decomposition where "faith" arises. About this relation between contempt (you're nothing but rot) and faith (there is some other), we have a first indication in the form assumed by "pure love" for three or four generations of seventeenth century mystics: I love you no less for being damned. The subject does not stop looking toward the Orient from which he has been definitively separated, even after being rejected, cast away as waste. There is an outside—an *Out*—of what he *is*. But this moving, historical figure of faith conceived in terms of damnation is only a variant of the structure defined by Meister Eckhart with the concept of *Gelassenheit* (*gelâzenheit*): self-desertion based on the absolute (un-bound) of being, a "letting the Other be."[17]

Another example of this, of more classical inspiration (at least that is how it has come across in the written tradition that is all that remains of it), is to be found in the way in which St. John of the Cross characterizes the principle (nearly an *a priori*) that organizes the mystic voyage from start to finish. The principle of movement is "that which exceeds" (*aquello que excede*). It does not function as the presence and summation of all that is lacking. On the contrary, the excess and the unknown of an existence interface in every experience, just as in all knowing. Each stage arises out of the non-identity of the subject to the state in which he is. Perception, vision, ecstasy, deprivation, even putrescence, are one after the other cut off from a "that's not it [*ça*]," so that the discourse of St. John of the Cross constitutes an indefinite series of *not it, not it, not it*. The story he tells, as interminable as the events he classifies, in some way narrativizes the functioning of the signifier *God*, a source that introduces *always less* satisfaction and *always more* un-known in the subject's position. In short, what thus unfolds is the labor of what figures at the beginning of *The Ascent of Mount Carmel* as the postulate, or convention and rule of propriety (*conviene*), of an entire spiritual itinerary, to wit: *creer su ser*. Given the distinction between the verb *ser* (to be, ex-ist) and the verb *estar* (which is relative to a state), I translate this: to believe that there is some other.[18] In effect, for these mystics there is always some other, from which they in principle recover nothing. An other of no return. It ex-ists, nameless and unnaming.

Undoubtedly, the *there is some other* functioned on two registers which I am assuming we, unlike the mystics, can no longer hold to be identical. One is related to the role of the signifier, to a function of language: here, "God" is the meaningless fragment that breaks off all appropriation; it is the diamond splinter that restores an "always more" and an "always less' in relation to every act of knowledge and every pleasure. But the *there is* also expresses the meaning of Heidegger's *Es gibt*: "it gives." God in this case is the outside that is inside, the intimacy of Exteriority. It seems to me that the conjunction of these two functionings of the "there is some other," or of "God," was already problematical for the mystics. The certitude of the first often implies the verisimilitude of the second, or manages to hold it in suspense and make its uncertainty tolerable. However that may be, what I am able to conceive of it today (for reasons which I do not attribute to an anonymous and fictional contemporary *episteme* but to much more particular fixations which, moreover, place my "masculine" approach to the mystics in question) is from the perspective that takes mysticism as the "science of the mere probability of the other."[19] This science assigns the recognition of a named putrescence (a calling, like a vocation) the role of an opening onto the indefinite probability of the other.

Tradition by Rotting

In this triangular sketch of "rottenness," whose revelation was heard by Schreber, the mystics and torture victims, I am simply exhibiting regions—psychoanalytic, Christian, and political—where I have encountered an identical problem. This geography of haunted itineraries has perhaps only subjective coherence. In truth, both our questions and the places where they are found precede us. The question at hand concerns either the *utopia* which, since the Reformation and the *Aufklärung*, has enacted the will to remake (rotten) institutions using fictions of "purity" as models, or the *realism*, the hidden figure of cynicism, which authorizes power by its ability to give recognition—or a noble adoptive filiation—to adherents who have already been convinced they are filth. In the first instance, the institution is the putrescence that must be reformed by recourse to more originary innocence, freedom, and purity. In the second, rottenness is something originary that the institution makes it profitable to recognize, and at the same time covers up. The resultant modes of initiation and transmission differ from one another and place the subject in opposing positions in relation to power and knowledge.

Looking back on the three experiences I have outlined, I am led to wonder whether there are outcomes other than reform based on a fiction of purity (where theory effects a denial [*dénégation*], or conservatism based on an exploitation of putrescence (where the function of theory is to obscure its actual role). In the absence of a general reply to this question (there is none), I will limit myself to a few hypotheses concerning the features I have brought into focus.

President Schreber, whose name is rot, constructs a system *on the basis of* his degradation. He incarnates his name to become a filthy slut, or carrion—but the filth and whore of God, who "deals only with corpses,"[20] and is himself nothing more than a whore (*Hure*).[21] The end of the world haunting this "prophet" of the absence of the other, the catastrophe of the Last Judgment in whose abyss he disappears, comes to a halt before "the name of that which has no name."[22] "He rebuilds the world" upon this spoken place.[23] The genesis of a world on the foundation of a word. The production of a "delusional," fictional world on the basis of a genuine and authentic (*echt*) word. Schreber has to eliminate from the fiction he constructs any rifts into which universal disaster might seep. No nothing, no *nichts-denken* (thinking about nothing, conceiving nothingness) can be allowed to punch a hole in the corpus of his identity. He is at the last frontier—the putrescent—before total decomposition, and he can allow himself no rest and no absence, for *there is nothing other* than this discursive proliferation. In order to make this exhausting wager, he generates the *homogeneous*; he becomes a mother who loses nothing, and from within the network of divine rays he spins, he is able, in 1898, to consider himself "entitled to shit on the entire world."[24]

This discourse, which escapes the institution by substituting itself for it, can be likened to discourses that are termed spiritual, prophetic, or mystical, except that these often do not erect themselves upon so veridical a word. But this is not the case with the mystics of whom I spoke, to the extent that the *institution* itself *is the other* in relation to their delirium, and that is why the institution is relevant for them. In this context, there is no disappearance of the other, but an antimony between, on the one hand, nomination, the poem that is authorized by nothing, and, on the other hand, the institution, which tends to control, rework, and alter the poem, allowing only interpreted or corrupt versions to circulate. But the debate is narrower. It is a question of determining whether, in refusing to replace the institution with a delusion, the mystic is not actually in the position of aligning himself with it, and by conforming to it in this way, of eliminating the other and returning to the same.

Such is the game of the institution. It *lodges* rottenness at the same time as it designates it. It assigns it a place, but a circumscribed one, constituted as an internal secret: between us, you're nothing but a slut, you're only a subject who is *supposed* to know. By lodging this "rottenness" within itself, the institution takes charge of it, limiting it to a truth that is known and pronounced on the inside, while allowing another discourse on the outside, the noble discourse of its theoretical manifestation. A piece of grafitti in a movie theater in Paris offered readers a transgression rejected by the institution: "Don't write in the shitters, shit on writing." Schreber went from one of these deviancies to the other. But for the institutional system, to shit in the shitters inside is the precondition for theory on the outside. Inside, "old fart" is a friendly term expressing the truth of a sodality: it is only said to those who are just that. This institutional "intimacy" is the only thing that makes it possible to qualify for engaging publicly in the discourse of and on the Other.

To put it another way, the institution is not only the delusional epiphany of an ideal ego which makes it possible to produce believers. It is not only a set of processes which generate credibility by withdrawing what they promise to give. It is not only a relation between something *known* and something *kept silent*, which is the mode in which Freud interprets the sacerdotal institution: that it is designed to keep a known murder silent. The institution is in addition the assignation-localization of rottenness on the inside, which is what makes its discourse "grandiose"; it is a combination of the nocturnal *voice* which designates rotten people for itself, and the *manifestation* or "theory" of the sublime. This combination defines the relation to the master: call me *Luder*, so I can engage in your discourse. The transmission of knowledge takes the route of the rotten; tradition takes the route of a corruption that is recognized and allows the institution to remain the same.[25]

Thus, what goes on in the kitchen is quite different from what happens in the parlor. Perhaps the approach to take is rather the one temporarily traced in times past by St. Teresa and others, who wanted to join a *corrupt* order, and therefore sought from it neither their identity nor recognition, but only the alteration of their necessary delirium. This would be to find in the institution itself both the seriousness of a real, and the mockery of the truth it displays.

Chapter 4
Lacan:
An Ethics of Speech
Translated by Marie-Rose Logan

He speaks—to his patients, to the members of his School, to the seminar's audience, a bit everywhere. Such, he says, is his profession as an analyst. He turns this speaking into a way of withdrawing. It is the very act of his theory, the gesture which formulates this theory; it is also a lifetime's paradox. He attracts because he withdraws. Departures are scattered throughout his career: in 1953, he leaves the Societé de Paris; in 1963, the Association Psychanalytique Internationale; in 1980, the Ecole Freudienne de Paris, the "School" which was formed sixteen years earlier by the "act" which created it in the name of an aloneness: "I establish—just as alone as I have always been in my relationship to the psychoanalytic cause. . . . "[1] Even his strategies are inspired by a detachment which often excludes even his closest companions (a characteristic evidenced by Freud, who preferred what was distant, as if a separation created the analytic space). According to the legend (and not without reason), "Lacan" designates a rhetoric of withdrawal. This proper name cuts out the silhouette of a scandalous character: in the small world of intellectuals, this character disdains the social code which impels these intellectuals to run to the media in search of a wider presence; in the field of research, he violates the rule which bases the salability of knowledge upon the readability of its statements. What he sets forth

Copyright © Michel de Certeau. English translation copyright © Marie-Rose Logan. This chapter was originally published as "Lacan: une éthique de la parole," in Le débat, 22 (November 1982), pp. 54–69, and it first appeared in English as "Lacan: An Ethics of Speech," in Representation, 3 (1983), pp. 21–39.

he will not allow to be understood. His audience contravenes the apparent laws of publicity. He did not want that publicity. That all came upon him like a sickness; it seized him when he was over sixty. One does not start life over again at that age. In any case, this is not it. "I realized that what made up my path was the realm of *I want to know nothing about it*."[2] No compromise, neither on television nor in the good years at Vincennes nor during the series of lectures outside France. A coyness perhaps (for isn't this too a game?), this withdrawal is the violent gesture which constitutes his thought and which gives birth to all its brilliance. He grounds speech just as he theorizes about it and just as he upholds its act.

Lacan belongs to no one. He is not situated, not entrapped in his own discourse, where certain faithful think they hold him, not chained to an institution and to a genealogy, not even to his own. He speaks and is alone: both are aspects of the same battle. He is Other, as he signs in this final declaration of 1980: "If it should happen that I leave, you may say that it is only in order to be at last Other. One can be happy being Other like everybody else after a life spent, in spite of the Law, trying to be Other."[3] It happened. The passing figure has left. He never stopped leaving, replacing his body (physical body, doctrinal body, social body) by the inductive signifiers of a "speech" which is called "Lacan." Such a politics of substitution is completed just when he becomes "Other like everybody else." His name remains with the stormy School where it is embalmed, like Empedocles' sandals on the banks of the Etna.[4] The "writings" are but the sandals of this passing figure, the result of the withdrawal which upheld his speaking. I am not concerned here, then, with the tomb ("theoretical" or not) which a goup might raise for its own benefit by using these "writings"—the "good of the city" is the imperative from which Lacan withdraws.[5] I don't care to repeat the lesson, but rather to distinguish the act which turns his discourse into the ethics of a speech.

The Tragi-Comedy

I shall begin where it all ended: the last years of the Seminar. It was then said that the old man was declining. What ever happened to the Seminars of the old days, begun at the Sainte-Anne Hospital (1953), limited to a few analysts-students? There we were among our own kind. From the Freudian texts, the Master was carving the blocks of a psychoanalytic organon (Ego, psychoses, object, unconscious, transference; 1953–1964), before focusing on the question of the Other and on the corollary concepts of the "objet petit *a*" and the "crossed out subject" (1964–1974).[6] During this second period, things are already deteriorating. Into the hall of the Ecole Normale Supérieure, which provides a theater for the proceedings after 1964, the audience spreads, grows, overflows increasingly beyond control. The "proper" place, i.e., the Ecole, fills up with anybody and anything. But in 1968, the administration no longer puts up with the "dirtiness" which reigns, and uses the physical disorder as a pretext to banish the intellectual disorder. Once again, Lacan moves. He then must carry the crowd which plagues his speech. He leads it like the pied piper to the Pantheon (the land of the dead), but at the same time he seeks to restore "proper" places by rearranging the department of psychoanalysis (Vincennes), by establishing a "headquarters" of the School (69, rue Claude-Bernard), and by strengthening the initiatory procedures of membership (the "permit"). In a strategy responding to its broader appeal, the Lacanian apparatus, which formerly articulated a public speech on a discipline's silent labor, now undergoes a geographical mapping which sets in different places, on the one hand, a speech, devoted to the scientific "immorality" of a "free speech," and, on the other hand, the professional and didactic choice of a School set on a street: both elements carry the same label, "Lacan." The isolation and thus the visibility of the institutional conditions of analysis provoke, within the School itself, a series of surprises, destructive revisions and tensions which have continued to grow. Exposed, the power behind the "free speech" must nonetheless be itself taken in hand by the theory based upon it. But first, what happens to this speech dislocated from the professional circles . . . unleashed, released in the crowd?

This is the period of the "Borromean knots." With bits of string, the Master would produce a metatheory in terms of topology: a possibility. The demonstration is not conclusive, even if it puts into play the encounter of two polar extremities of language (the scriptuary statement of the most formal kind and the oral misunderstanding of the dialogue) and even if it offers a general theory of space for thinking out metonymy (a psychoanalytic and literary process more fundamental than metaphor). These two points are so intriguing that I, like many others, would like to believe in them; but the essential is not here. Lacan goes on to a theoretical rite: the slow erosion of conceptual content releases the theatrical act which built it. The gesture which reorganized the field of analytic practices and categories repeats itself, slowly freeing itself from the elements which it delineated and carrying only aphorisms and fragments, relics and seashells, the debris of the successive stages which guided its trajectory. All the work pursued through the thesis on *La Psychose paranoïaque* (1932), the "Discours de Rome" (1953), the Seminar (after 1953), the *Ecrits* (1966), and so on—all this work was needed so that the teaching, which emerged late, after years of practice, could end at last in a purified form which offers little more to grasp and which reduces the psychoanalytic exercise to its essence of being identically act and theater . . . a speech.

Serious people are kindly requested to stay away. In the depths of the revered Faculty of Law (1968–1980), there re-emerges the ancient alliance ("relatives in joking") between a wisdom beheaded of its knowledge and a curiosity not yet handicapped by power. Here nothing useful is produced; for the public, there is no required preparation, no entry fee, no permanent check. But the actor is at work. In this *commedia dell'arte*, where the art of the analyst takes the stage, a starring role is assumed by the speaking body, and especially by this body's throat. Coughing, slightly grumbling, clearing the throat—like tatoos on the process of phonation—punctuate the chain of words and indicate all their secret of being "for the other" and of producing for the listeners the effects of meaning, of the signified. The signifiers are all the more understood in so far as there is misunderstanding about what they designate. Another emblem of the speaking body, the sigh, introduces into the discourse something which troubles this body (the price of a pleasure?), which interrupts discourse (the time of another story), and which pulls back ("Are you still there?"). These corporal indicators bring speech to what they do not know. They reappear in the work of many Lacanians, and rightly so. These criteria of belonging are more trustworthy than a theoretical or clannish policy of exclusion. In the current confusion, their use must be extended, with the didactic strings remaining the Master's property.

In fact, this mimicry is only part of the repertory of a theatrical art which consists of the loss of the body in order to speak and which holds a place close to the art of Artaud. Like his "patient," the analyst lets his discourse recount that part of his story which "escapes" him and which "flushes" (like a hare is flushed) the Other, represented by all those anonymous and scattered listeners. But he also knows that the swarming of interpretations engendered in the crowd will never confer a meaning or an acceptable image upon the word games or ramblings received from the Other whom he does not know. And, indeed, he does not ask for this result. He is speaking for the Other, as one would speak in one's hat, fruitlessly. But he is speaking "thanks to" that iconoclastic crowd which shatters and disperses the image of himself, an image which he might expect to be sent back to him in return for what he brings about. As an analyst, he "expects" from this audience, he says, "nothing more than to be the object thanks to which what I teach is not self-analysis."[7] Otherwise, this theater would be reduced to a hysterization of the actor (assuming a body for the other); this process calls forth a paranoid interpretation by the listeners (a proliferation of signifieds born of the question, "What then does he want from us?"). He thus "operates" only insofar as the actor does not take pleasure in his public.[8] The analyst is dependent on listeners from whom, supposedly, he hopes to get neither his pleasure nor his own identity. By stepping back ("I want to know nothing of it"), he *holds* the difference separating the speaking (symbolic) from an identification (imaginary).

This exercise resembles a prayer to which and for which nothing would answer. A Midrash once said, "Praying is speaking to the wall."[9] Lacan turns speech into a conception close to this rabbinical austerity. The Other is there, but we can expect nothing from it except the desire which is produced by being deprived of it. Perhaps the sharpest expression of speech is to be found in one of those "formulas" which, in Lacanian language, appear to be quotations and fragments from an original discourse: "I am asking you to refuse what I am giving to you because that's not it."[10]

Speech as comedy: a "fundamental failure" of action in order to return to the desire which resides there, a ceaseless fading of the object, a scorn for knowledge, an ambiguity of meaning in witty words, mutual misunderstandings among the characters on stage. Lacan the actor pulls out all the gimmicks through which a theory of desire unfolds. The use of these classic tricks and the secret of the theory mold the same gestures and the same cuteness. What takes place there is something like the laugh provoked by the undefined misfiring of the action and of the things themselves. Such a smile appeared on the faces of gods who were not tricked. But, in order to become human, Lacan identifies himself with the "tragic dimension" of the "being-for-death." For him, the art of laughing is an art of dying. This art is constantly reborn from the impossibility which brought it forth. It is even haunted by a fury against those presences whose quiet stability hides their destiny of disappearing in order to nourish desire. One must die in order to speak, as one dies of pleasure, "finally Other." Sometimes the actor dies, sometimes he gargles. The "Lacanian mass" is a tragi-comedy which tells us exactly what it does: it speaks.

"The Artist Goes On"[11]

Speech, like dreams, would be an "act of homage to missed reality."[12] If we were to follow Lacanian speech from its theatrical conclusion back to is psychiatric beginnings, we would find that speech traces the history of a "style." In fact, this theory of the psychoanalytical act develops an aesthetics, if we understand this to mean that the signifiers "operate" by doing without the things which they seem to signify. My first thesis is: Lacan is first of all an exercise of literature (a literature which would know what it is). Maybe it is a scandal within the discipline, but why will literature always be labeled "not serious"? If we follow Lacan where he leads, toward a "speaking" [dire] whose nature is revealed by its analytical experience, he points toward the "truth" of literary practice.

Freud opened up this perspective as early as the *Studies on Hysteria* (1895), with a gesture which joined the discovery of psychoanalysis with the necessity of betraying scientific discourse and of moving into the camp of the "novelists" and "poets."[13] Throughout his life, he took models, conceptual figures and key examples from literature; the discipline he created remains colored by the "authority of the poet."[14] And "the poetics of Freud's work" constitutes the "first entry way into its meaning."[15] Far from forgetting this lesson, Lacan stresses it with research which, even in his early publications, probes into "style." Thus, even before his dissertation, in 1932, his study of a "schizography'' is directed toward defining, within pathological writing, the procedures "related to procedures uniformly present in poetic creation."[16] In 1933, Lacan's thesis opens onto "the problem of style," that is, onto a group of questions "forever unresolvable for an anthropology which is not freed from the naive realism of the object":[17] here begins his "literary" polemic against the object.

Except for Freud's writings (and especially the most "literary" among them, such as *The Science of Dreams, On Jokes and Their Relation to the Unconscious*, and the *Psychopathology of Everyday Life*), Lacan comments particularly on literary masterpieces: Sophocles, courtly poetry, Marguerite de Navarre, Shakespeare, Sade, Joyce. His discourse is punctuated with bits of poems (Eluard, Aragon, etc.) which implant in the language something which, in the absence of setting out a *said*, open up a *speaking* [*dire*]. Those links which attracted him to the Surrealist movement between the two wars (Breton, and others) refer back not only to the "literary" reception of Freud in France, but also to a theoretical alliance.[18] Moreover, Lacan adds rhetoric, dialectics (in the Aristotelian sense), grammar, and especially poetics to the Freudian list of "auxiliary sciences" (a list already including "literary history and criticism"), sciences which allow for the thinking-out of psychoanalysis.[19] This addition is characteristic: it signals, between literature and psychoanalysis, a crossroads which henceforth carries Lacan's name.

This coincidence is astonishing. For example, does not the relationship to the text remove from the analysis the entire relationship of analyst to analysand? Does one read a text as if it were lying on the couch? Indeed, Freud himself did not hesitate to cross this Rubicon again and again, from his analysis of Schreber, made exclusively on the basis of the text, to the examination of numerous literary, historical, and anthropological documents. Yet, these movements from cure to reading question the analytic "reception" of the literary work and, conversely, the passage from oral experience to the scriptuary production of the psychoanalyst himself. The writing is the result and the fiction of the oral relationship. At issue is, finally, the psychoanalytic tradition itself; for Lacan, this central question stands between Freud's texts (to which he calls us back) and the psychoanalytical disciples (whom he wishes to train). This question deals with how to *read* Freud. The interaction between Freudian readings and literary readings will bring forth, between them, the relationship of a voice to the text. The shifter of this interaction is the seminar (a "lectio" in the medieval sense of the term) through which the equivocal relation between two kinds of text mediates the oral relation between the Master and the disciples.

A questioning of precisely what Lacanian practice draws from the literary text brings out three elements. First, "literary" describes the return of the *voice* in the text. In the vocabulary of Jakobson, priority is given to the "poetic function," which "promotes the palpability of signs" and which seeks in them that which "sounds better."[20] This valorization of sound, the key to paranomases, alliterations, rhymes, and other phonic games, seeds an oral transgression through the semantic organization of the discourse, a transgression which displaces or cuts the articulated meanings and which renders the signifier autonomous in relation to the signified. This sonorous wave spreads across the syntactic landscape; it permeates it with leeways, charms, and meanderings of something unknown. The analyst's ear practices precisely on hearing the murmurs and the games of these other languages. It makes itself attentive to the poetics which is present in every discourse: these hidden voices, forgotten in the name of pragmatic and ideological interests, introduce into every statement of meaning the "difference" of the *act* which utters it. The signifiers dance within the text. Loosened from the signified, they multiply, in the gaps of the meaning, the rites of inquiry or response—but to which Other are they directed? From this point of view, "literary" is that language which makes something else heard than that which it says; conversely, psychoanalysis is a literary practice of language.

If the literary text displays the stirrings of the enunciative act in a system of statements, it also exhibits the procedures which articulate these two terms, that is, the diverse circuits which alter the statements by imprinting on them what the speaking subject wants of the other. At issue here is rhetoric, and no longer poetics. But this rhetoric could not be reduced to a descriptive catalogue of "manners" (or tropes) of ornamenting the discourse. It is rather (as already in *The Science of Dreams* or in *On Jokes*) the logic of "displacements" (*Verschiebungen*) and of "distortions" (*Entstellungen*) which the relationship to the other produces in language. Among these altering relationships, which are presented in a particular combination in each literary text and which contain a logic to be elucidated by a rhetoric, Lacan preferred the metaphor and the metonymy.[21] I wonder, however, if the metonymic "displacement" (or, as he translates, the "swerving") may have asserted itself for him as more fundamental insofar as the topology to which teaching of recent years refers would be a development of the spatial problematic suited to metonymy: Lacanian topology would then represent an effort to elaborate a new rhetoric in contemporary discourse and, more particularly, a "metonymic" logic. In any case, a "literary" question once again defines the way in which a psychoanalytic theory sets forth the formalities of its practices.

More broadly, through mutual misunderstandings induced by the "letter" (identified to the signifier), literature explores the realm within which the entire human journey unfolds—the realm of trickery. It works within this trickery; it traces there a "truth" which is not the opposite of error, but, within the lie itself, is the symbolization of the impossibility at play. Now it is striking that Lacan sees in one of Freud's most remarkable stagings—or rather he hears there—the Moses of psychoanalysis dedicating himself to leading his people. "Whatever it is, I must go there"—Where?—To the realm of trickery. . . . "There is the country where I lead my people,'' and this takes place ''through thirst for truth.''[22] Whoever goes into this region is a psychoanalyst, like that solitary being (a monk) who in past times ventured into the desert. But even there ''the artist always goes ahead'' and ''opens the way for him.''[23] Thus did Marguerite Duras, opening with Jacques Hold the ''field of the lie, immense but with iron limits,'' the ''kidnapping'' of Lol V. Stein. But where is Lol V. Stein? ''There she is naked. Who is there on the bed? Who, does she believe?''[24] The novel introduces ''this image of the self in which the Other clothes and dresses you, and which leaves you when you are stripped of it, to be what underneath?''[25] Lacan compliments Marguerite Duras for this lie, for ''proving to know, apart from me, what I teach''; in a unique instance, he invokes ''what (she) witnesses for me''—he quotes this voice—in order to authorize the ''support'' which he finds in her novel.[26]

With a different theoretical apparatus, the psychoanalyst proceeds in turn in the steps of the ''artists'' who went before. Is it astonishing that he has recourse, just like his ''sick patient,'' to the ''ever constant procedures of poetic creation''? Studies of Lacanian procedures themselves are, of course, now numerous; their wide range includes genres ranging from the polemics of serious linguistics to the jocularity of friendly stylistics.[27] It would be pointless to review these studies here. What is essential is to recognize in them the grouping of operations brought about in language by the ''speaking subject.'' These literary traits are a theory's gestures, its ways of going forward. They may outline the ''linguistics of speech'' which Roland Barthes believed still impossible and which constituted a ''new way of thinking.''[28] In any case, it appears impossible to reduce this linguistics to, or to measure it by, the linguistic systems from which it has constantly distinguished itself (''language is not the speaking subject''), while still borrowing concepts from these systems and nonetheless using them as metaphors.[29] Only an inversion of image, a mutual misunderstanding in itself quite revealing, can explain that Lacan appears as a ''psycholinguist'' on American posters. His very endeavor requires a questioning on the internal necessity which leads analytical speech to a poetic writing and which turns this experience into the elucidation of what constitutes the practice of literature.

The Lie and Its Truth

In order to join in the dance which brings together the lie and the truth (as once were the living and the dead), we must return to the psychoanalytic cure and proceed from there to the analytical discourse, which is ''the social link determined by the practice of an analysis.''[30] This practice starts out as a mutual trickery, a general postulate of a ''psychoanalytic'' cure, that is, one founded exclusively on the treatment of language. At the beginning, the analyst is ''presumed'' by his patients to ''know''; he functions as object of their belief. As for these patients, they expect from him what at heart they do not want to know (the secret of their "trouble"), and they instead want only an ear to hear their symptoms. This locus brings the "medical" relationship back to the status of an ordinary conversation, but, when the social codes respect, ad impose respect for, this game of trickery, the cure begins with the way in which the analyst separates himself from this respect.

What, then, is an analyst? Lacan answers that, "Whoever it may be," he is put in the position of "supposed knowledge," he has grasped and does not forget the state of this knowledge; thereafter, he becomes capable of "operating" with this hand of cards, if and only if he does not identify with this position and does not turn what is given to him into an object of pleasure. His formula would be: "there is only that," the lie, but it deceives my desire, "which is not that."

On his part, the analysand constantly keeps his concern for protecting the knowledge which he supposes resides in the other. He fears less being tricked than tricking his analyst. He arranges his admissions in order to preserve what he believes about the other: "If I had told it to you earlier, you would have believed. . . . " His narrative works at fostering and maintaining the belief which makes his interpretation possible. It is, after all, the patient who interprets. The analyst coughs slightly, mumbles "Hum, hum," says "Do you think so?" while the analysand wonders endlessly about the meaning of these clues. What trials am I undergoing? What does he want of me? What truths are hiding in this enigma? The patient is in the situation of a jealous person whose interpretations of the other proliferate. He formulates his tales. Then, what "returns" to him from his suppositions about the other is something else *in himself*; here is a part of his own "forgotten" story, about which he learns, little by little, that, constituted by relationships to others (parents and so on), it does not come from the analyst's knowledge. At last there is here *nothing* to believe, except that each person's historicity is founded on what the other makes believed. The locus of the supposed knowledge is but the stage on which the other's lack of knowledge plays. But here again, the ghost appears only if the analyst does not take the stage on his own account, if he does not take himself as the image of the self which is addressed to him, if he accepts the "abjection" of being merely the representative of what he knows not, and finally if he upholds the "vanity" of a discourse which takes its operativity from a fiction.[31]

This "abjection" is nonetheless an art. Like the tightrope walker whom Kant holds up as the paragon of the art of doing,[32] the analyst seeks, by imperceptible comments, to remain balanced between a corporeal presence (a fondness) supportive of the analysand's assertions and the necessary separation (Lacan refers even to a "disdain") which evokes or signals the ambiguity of these assertions. In Freud's words, it is a "matter of tact." This "tact" consists in drawing out from the other what is unknown. It is the art of slipping the gamble of words' meaning into their own chain so that the analysand unearths a signifier (a "small bit of truth'' in Freud's words), like a bone deposited by the past, from which he now fashions his speech, that is, the (ethical) act of upholding alone his desire in the very language of the trickery imposed on him by his history.

The fundamentals of this truth were set down by Lacan from 1936 onward in analyzing what he calls "the mirror stage." This childhood drama is not only, for him, a developmental stage (between six and eighteen months), but also an "exemplary function."[33] While the child has only bodily experiences, dispersed, consecutive, and changeable, he obtains from the mirror the image which makes him *one*, though in terms of a *fiction*. In a "flutter of jubilant activity" he discovers that he is *one* (a primordial form of the *self*), but this discovery occurs through that alienation which identifies him with what is *other* than him (a speculary image). The experience can be put into the formula, *I* am *that*. The *self* takes shape only in self-alienation. Its capture begins at birth. From this exemplary episode emerges the matrix of an "alienating identity" to be reaffirmed in secondary identifications. From its origins, this matrix sets the self up as the "discordance of the subject with its own reality," and it calls forth the workings of the negative ("it isn't that") through which the subject is marked off within the lie of its identity ("I am that").[34]

The movement from the "speculary self" to the "social self" by way of language renders the effects of this matrix more complex, but does not modify its structure. Here is not the place to trace stratification and intertwinings which have been the subject for many years of teaching. It is enough to say that by formulating the analytical experience on a theory of the subject, this matrix furnishes a password for the interpretation of two aesthetic ranges favored by Lacan: the iconic and the literary. This matrix makes it possible to examine anew the issues it raised: the images which awaken the "flutter of jubilant activity" of the child caught up by the appearance of his enigmatic identity; the literature which produces, with a text, the narcissistic scene of an interminable discordance; the myth itself, which makes "one" from a group (sym-bol) by giving it the fiction which presupposes and denies its social practices; and so on. In all these fields, the lie is the element in which its truth can emerge, the truth that the Other always institutes the subject by alienating it.

Freud's Return

In the matter of the relationship to the other, the manner in which Lacan refers back to Freud provides, as indeed it should, a model. "Return to Freud": such is Lacan's plan. By this return, Lacan aims at a *text* whose author he never knew. A dead man is there only through his discourse, just like Sophocles and Shakespeare, but the only dead man who truly counts is the father. The central role which Lacan gives to the "name of the father" and to the setting-up of the law through the father's death already indicates the weight of this reference—or gives this reference its weight.

Even more can be perceived on another scene, in the commentary where Lacan analyzes "the tragedy of desire" which constitutes, in his view, Shakespeare's *Hamlet* (a work haunted by the importance already given to it by Freud and by Freud's interpretation).[35] In this locus of the father, the ghost of Freud rears up at the same time as that of the king assassinated by those close to him. The law the king imposes demands the death of whoever reigns in his palace in his place. As Lacan emphasizes, Hamlet does not encounter a dead man in this ghost, but rather death itself, and the action he is commissioned to undertake can be accomplished only if it is fatal, an achievement of the being-for-death. Nonetheless, however determined Hamlet may be (he does not hesitate about the justice of the murder he must commit and he is entirely guided by it), he takes oblique paths, he "dawdles." This grace period, the length of a lifetime, is a time devoted to the mother. More precisely, he creates an interspace for the "interventions" to which, on the ghost's commands, Hamlet must respond, by precious words, literary conceits, slipped in between his mother and the love which binds her to the traitor Claudius:

> O, step between her and her fighting soul,
> Conceit in weakest bodies strongest works,
> Speak to her, Hamlet.[36]

Avenging me while waiting death, speak. Put "precious" words between her and the object with which she identifies. The commentator's voice adds, " '*Between her and her . . .* ': it's our work, that. '*Conceit in weakest bodies strongest works*': to the analyst is addressed this appeal."[37] By whom, if not by Freud; and to whom, if not to Lacan?

Is it appropriate to decipher what is said about Lacan through the discourse of Shakespeare? It would be fruitless, because the essential is spelled out in its entirety, literally, in the Shakespearean "dream." Yet, two corollaries allow us to specify the functioning of the name, on the one hand, and of Freud's work, on the other hand. The first such corollary deals with the intransigent unicity of the Freudian reference in Lacan's discourse. Why speak of a single reference? Where does this unique reference, among many others, come from? It is not enough merely to invoke the discipline which carries its founder's name. We know, after *Moses and Monotheism*, that the preservation of the name (*Name*) goes along with the betrayal of the "reality" (*Wesen*) which it designates, and that, by a customary exchange in traditions, this very "reality" returns under other names.[38] The history of the Freudian current tells us much about the correctness of the Freudian thesis, a history which is precisely what Lacan seeks to rethink. For him, the name of the lost one is unique, as, in monotheism, only the separated is *one*. Just as unique is the name of what psychoanalysts hate and seek to forget. Only the Other, this repressed, is the unique. Behind the work which consists, with the "conceits," in separating the fighting subject, the "fighting soul," from its alienating identifications and thereby reinstating the desire for the absent, there is in Lacan, just as in Hamlet, a fury alternately ironic and violent. This fury runs through the entire range of the discipline which spreads and prospers thanks to this loss. The leitmotif? Something is rotten in the state of Denmark. To avenge the father eliminated by his horde, Lacan turns Freud's name into the foreign signifier by which the unique returns, forever inseparable from death.

But in relation to the irreparability of this separation, what positive form will the interpretation of the Freudian work take? How can one remain "faithful" to Freud? This point is strategic for Lacan, whose first preoccupation was always to train analysts and thus to ensure the transmission of the analytic experience. He talked everywhere of "my teaching," and he tested its progress, its achievements, and the "remainder" which he held back as an impregnable future. But is not the very possibility of a conformity with Freud forbidden to whoever can lean only on someone absent? The debates engendered by this suspicion have led, in the Freudian School, to increasingly rigorous supervision (the institution always has to take the deficits of theory in hand). But the questioning also carries a theoretical response: the relationship to the absent already molds the Freudian discourse, so that the position in which Freud's departure leaves us reiterates what he elucidated in his writings and can then become the guide for their reading. In this respect, the *after*-Freud may be conceived as a return *of* Freud, and not only as a return *to* Freud. His texts do not designate a past to be rediscovered. They articulate what, in different scenes in the psychic structure, does not cease being the return to that Other which constitutes the subject as a relationship to an impossible object. According to this hypothesis, the "patients," like ghosts, still breathe what is articulated in Freudian discourse.

A Christian Archaeology

But what is, after all, this Other whose irreducible brilliance streaks through the entire work? "The Other is there precisely as it is recognized, but as it is not known."[39] "This Other [is] that I call here *the dark God*."[40] Such formulations, and a thousand others similar to them, like the analyst's apparatus, gradually bring the strange impression that the house is haunted by monotheism. This monotheism resides in the concepts scattered throughout the discourse, concepts whose theoretical (and/or mythical) promotion is most often marked by a capital letter: *the* Word [*Parole*] is articulated on *the* Other by *the* Name of the father, *the* Desire, *the* Truth, and so on. Repeated throughout is the monotheistic form of the capital letter singular, an index of something which, under the signifier of the Other, always amounts to the same.

All this is not something which Lacan would render hidden and mysterious. On the contrary, he reiterates that "there is a One" which is always the Other.[41] On condition that one "never have recourse to any substance" nor to "any being,"[42] "speaking [dire] brings God" and "as long as something will speak, the hypothesis God will be there."[43] Such a hypothesis, such a "song" (an expression of the mystics) does not come from a void. In Lacanian discourse, it has its history, its narratives, and its theoretical loci: it is Christian. Trailing its apparitions, one is impressed by the corpus which is there quoted and commented upon: Biblical and evangelical texts; theological texts (St. Paul, St. Augustine, Pascal, of course, and also authors of a theological inclination like Nygren and Rousselot); and especially mystical texts (Hadewijch of Antwerp, Master Eckhart, the *Imitation of Christ* or *Internal Consolation*, Luther, Theresa of Avila, Angelus Silesius, etc.). They punctuate the Lacanian space where they figure as *exordia* (where does it begin?) or as exits (where to end?). To this fundamental grillwork is added the central figure of the speaking analyst, "Master of truth,"[44] even "director of conscience,"[45] a "saint" who "wastes away,"[46] one whose speaking, devoted to the price which the body must pay for having access to the symbolic, is a speech structured like that of the person praying.

Certain indications point to an even more precise identification. Let us remember, for instance, the strange dedication introducing Lacan's thesis of 1932: "To the Reverend Father Marc-François Lacan, Benedictine of the Congregation of France, my brother in religion."[47] Lacan knows what he says. "Religion" here means the "religious congregation," and "brother in religion" points to a brotherhood based not on blood but on a common sharing in the Order. This statement, which is, like the "purloined letter," placed in the most obvious place and for this very reason obscured from view, highlights "Benedictine" characteristics which I had not before noted: Lacan's conception of the "master" (according to the rules which characterize "spiritual guidance"); the definition of a "work" which is essentially "speech" (like the Benedictine *opus Dei*); the practice of literature as an exercise of desire (in conformity with the monastic tradition of *lectio divina*);[48] and the very idea of a school of truth where membership is determined by an experience involving the subjects and where the *abbas* (elected) holds both the authority of discourse and the power of management. In Lacan's circle, the "monk" (*monos*) and the ascetic of the speech which he upholds (with humor, even with a ferocious irony found in monastic speech patterns), the founder of a "congregation" in a desert labeled as "worldly," all gather together the practitioners of a desire whose truth can liberate those alienated from their identity. Even the militancy of the spiritual warriors of other times (at war with which demons?) and even their rebellious freedom from public authorities are indices of the Freudian School of Paris.

No more than Freud does Lacan underestimate the religious belief to which he does not adhere. What can be done today with this weighty history, if one rejects giving the illusion of repressing it? The West has for three centuries been concerned with the question of what to do about the Other. Georges Bataille is a witness to this for Lacan himself, whose analysis concerns equally his relationship to Freud and his relationship to Christianity.

We know what value Freud placed upon allegiances likely to extend psychoanalysis to non-Jews. In this respect, under the figure of what Lacan would represent as "spiritual," does Christian history introduce into Freudian theory a gap narrower than under the "theological" figure so characteristic of Jung? What are the effects of Lacan's "spiritualism" on the Jewish tradition as articulated in Freud's work? It is probably too early (before the publication of all of Lacan's texts) and too daring to follow these celestial battles into sidelines of theory. If we consider only what touches on speech, an "archaeological" divergence still appears determinative. The Jewish tradition is rooted in the biological, familial, and social reality of a present and identifiable "body" distinguished from others by "election," a body persecuted through endless wanderings, a body transcended by Scriptures marking on it an unknowable sign. But Christianity received its form of being apart from its ethnic origin, with a break from its heredity. The "separation" giving rise to the Christian *Logos* has as an index the very loss of the body which should hold the place of all others, that of Jesus, so that the "evangelical" word, born of this disappearance, must itself take charge of the creation of ecclesiastical, doctrinal, or "glorious" bodies destined to be substitutes for the absent body. The word itself becomes the source of a "sacrament" in place of the body. Perhaps Christianity also receives, from its relationship to this absence, its way of rebelling against history in the name of the *Logos*—a style of "defiance" which hardly belongs to the Jewish tradition. The residue of this "detachment," through a defiance of the word and the trials which it brings against the "biological" element, can be used to gauge, in Lacan's theoretical, professional, and social determinations, the difference which a Christian history has introduced into Freudianism.

Such an archaeology emerges from Lacan's work only as it is transformed by what he does. The transformation consists in rethinking, in terms which are no longer those of the past, the return of religious history. This is the task for a theory. In Freud, it leads to *Moses and Monotheism*, a work he "simmered" for years ("after *Totem and Taboo*, he thought only about this story of Moses and the religion of his fathers").[49] To this masterwork, Lacan offered a counterpart in his *Ethique de la psychanalyse* (1959–1960) which he consistently held to be the strategic point of his teaching, the only seminar which he really wanted "to write."[50] These two confrontations gave birth to major works, but it is quite revealing that the first opened on to a theory of writing (the heart of the Freudian work), while the second produced an ethics of speech (the springboard of Lacanian thought).

A non-Freudian discourse, which held sway during the post-War years, shared in the genesis of the *Ethique*: Hegel's *Phenomenology of the Mind*. In Kojeve's commentaries (which profoundly marked the content and the style of the Seminar), in Koyré's or Hippolyte's analyses, Lacan founded the theoretical model of a historical development whose successive "figures" manifested the movement of absolute knowledge which ultimately emerges from its last positivity, religion. In his *Ethique*, he rethinks both the *Moses* and the *Phenomenology*. The original path he blazes between them favors ethical figures like Aristotle, St. Paul, poets of courtly love, Sade, Kant, and others, through whom a thought of desire is led through to the ambiguous relationships of reality and pleasure as Freud elucidated them. In limiting oneself to what concerns Christianity, one has access to ethics when, instead of identifying oneself with one's object, belief rejects the illusion and, thereby, speaks its truth. Ethics is the form of a belief removed from the alienating imagination where it would guarantee the real and shed into speech that which is said by the desire instituted by this lack. Like Beckett's Godot, the Other is not only the ghost of a God removed from the history where the passage of his believers remains nonetheless engraved, but also the general structure whose theory is made possible by the erasure of the religious positivity and by acceptance of its mournings.

Freudian analysis operates as the instrument which enables Lacan to localize, within an erotic or aesthetic framework, an ascetic practice for supporting a desire which cannot be identified with an act. Already for Kant, the categorical imperative does not deal with the possible: it is unconditional.[51] For Lacan, it is the very relationship to the impossible that determines an ethics. The ethics meets in man "this last request to be deprived of something of the real," or "this speaking essence" which weds him to death.[52] "The only thing of which one can be guilty," finally, "is having given in to one's desire." "There is no other good than that which can serve to pay the price for access to desire"—that which can only do so without "breaching not only every fear, but also all pity."[53] This ethical anarchism constitutes the way of taking the question of the subject seriously, a question inherent in the history of Christianity. In contrast, the commentary on Sophocles' *Antigone* sets forth an ethics based upon "the good of the city." Creon's morality, which in essence recalls that of Aristotle, always rests on a "morality of the master." It requires the sacrifice of desire for the benefit of the city. Every new power, however revolutionary it might be, repeats Creon's law: "Keep on working. . . . Let it be well understood that there is, in any event, no occasion to show the least bit of desire." This "morality of power," emphasizes "civil requirements," and repeats in a hundred ways whatever smashes speech: "As for desires, you will have to forget them."[54]

A Politics of Speech?

How, then, are we to understand the history of the School in which Lacan appeared, in turn, as Master of Truth, as Maffioso hatching his plots in the arcane circles of the "family," and as a dying Sardanapalus wiping out his seraglio? It is not a matter of meddling, once again, in the recent episodes (1980) which repeated, in a violent way, the tragi-comedy of the Pantheon within the Freudian School, nor of outlining, as an indiscreet and grotesque enterprise, the psychology of a character whose strong friendships, and even tender attachments, had their consequences in tricks and hatreds. One must instead analyze the politics to which this speech gives tricks and hatreds. One must instead analyze the politics to which this speech gives rise since, in the form of an institution, it is wrought within the game of power plays.

Its charter (1964) defined the School as "the organism in which a work must be accomplished—a work which, in the field opened by Freud, restores the cutting blade of the plough to its truth, which brings the original praxis which it instituted under the name of psychoanalysis back to its proper duty in our world and which, through assiduous criticism, denounces the deviations and compromises which slow its progress while degrading its work." An "added note," in specifically stating some procedural modalities, affirms, moreover, that "this charter holds as naught simple habits," that is, the legal apparatus of a *common* right, independent of the task which specifies a *particular* association.[55] In this superb exodus, a "spiritual" model is recognized, with its "monastic" archaeology. A challenge sets it up. From the start, it does not obey the law of possibility. To the "world" it opposes a "duty." Speech must create its own body, a body missing in the "world" in which the truth is misunderstood. The institution is thus a "School." It even has the very form of a teaching facility: speech must give birth to a body which it defines in its entirety. To return to the past which structures it, this "genesis" appears to be supported by a provocation of "Christian" style. While, in the "genesis" of the Jewish Bible, speech does not create, but instead *separates*, producing some distinction in the intial chaos and effecting thus an "analytical" distribution of space, in the Christian "genesis" of the New Testament, speech *gives birth* to a body, it is the word which becomes flesh, a *fiat*. It is from this difference that the Lacanian project already takes its bearing.

The School is characterized by its fascinating and haughty ambition to regulate all institutional actions upon the ethics of the speaking subject. It is the School of desire set up by an object which is never an "it." The School therefore functions in various ways. The relationship to the only Master always escapes being fixed. Through the groups or "cartels" are pursued, among four or five psychoanalysts, the processes of transference liberated from the dual relationship. The "permit," or initiation into the place of the analyst, to revive the terms already proposed by the charter, consists in testing and controlling the analytic style of the candidates. The meetings and the establishment of the "headquarters" aim at thwarting on stage and by public confrontation the tribal law of the sectarianism formed among colleagues of the same generation, or among "descendants" of the same analyst. Finally, the Seminars and the congresses extend the schooling of the members of the School (as if these theaters of knowledge served as an erudite and social alibi for the "alleged" knowledge of the analytical practice) and, in fact, make possible the symbolizing, in a tragicomic, theoretical, and quasi-choral speech, of the solitary asceticism of the daily exercise. Within, the School is thus the course of treatment insofar as it never "ends" and will never be ended until human energy is exhausted.

Viewed from the outside, the institution has a double function. On the one hand, it publicly "represents" the subject who is supposed to know (the institution is its address)—that is, it takes up socially the *belief* whose demystification is the precise goal of the cure. On the other hand, it provides legal accreditation (in the name of a profession and of a serious establishment) for the *price to be paid* for this access to the symbolic supposedly handled by analysis. These two functions uphold each other: a belief is founded on that which it takes away, it is reinforced by that which it withdraws and, finally, it works because one pays it.

All this was forcefully articulated and thought out. Why then the violence, the tensions, and ultimately the failure? Simply because history does not obey the speech that challenges it. Certainly the radical authoritarianism of the Lacanian truth struck the heart of a societal disease, of the pathogenic and uncritically accepted moment created by the substitution of the individual for the subject. It aggravated as much as it explained the problem. But the difficulties did not come from the outside. The success instead revealed a fundamental (founding) impracticability of the undertaking. Once beyond the threshold of the "primitive" intimacy among first participants of the same experience, once also the legitimacy which the School received by opposing itself to the ruling psychoanalytical Associations was lost (this opposition endowed the institution with the very function of speech and concealed its own problems from it), then the School of truth appeared for what it really was, an institution like the others, committed to debates concerning the "position" of the analysts, to the power plays among them and, also, a problem that is just as political, to their "fantasm of omnipotence." The activities at the University of Vincennes (1968), which required the confrontation with legal structures independent of the analytical experience, marked the beginning of a divisive reconsideration destined to bring the School out of its rootedness in speech, that is, out of itself. Practice and theory had to tear themselves away from the isolated double scene of the School and the couch. But how could we have dealt with these questions in the name of experience which had held "for naught" the legal means for their regulation?

The tactics remained: playing tricks with history; trying to betray history in order not to "give in to one's desire." These are Lacan's subtleties, founded on a radicalism of speech. From this point of view, Lacan is the anti-Machiavelli, if one recognizes the work of Machiavelli for what it is, an ethics of the "good of the city" and a theory of political ethics. What Lacan himself did not betray could end only in failure. His institutional adventure, this *trip* of his desire, must have itself terminated by this "failing": this is not that. Fundamentally, the retreat of 1980, as surprising as it was in its outcome, was inscribed in its ethics. It still "spoke" in separating itself from this love object, which became in turn an alienating identity. From there it reiterated, forty years later, the gesture which it called forth in 1946: "I have removed myself for many years from every resolution of expressing myself."[56]

In *Les petites annonces*, Catherine Rihoit recalls the following words of Lacan on Freud: "I think he missed the mark. Like me, in a very little time, everyone will have had his fill of psychoanalysis." Whatever is the future of the psychoanalytical institution, Lacan, by his "misfiring," will hold on to his speech. Like the texts which he did not cease to awaken, his writings, tortured, and broken in conceits, *concetti*, by this speech, keep this speech loud enough to be heard. But if it is true, according to Freud, that the tradition does not stop cheating on its founder, will Lacan still be heard in those places where one claims possession of his heritage and his name, or will he return under other names?

Part II
Representation Altered by the Subject
(Sixteenth and Seventeenth Centuries)

Chapter 5
Montaigne's "Of Cannibals":
The Savage "I"

We ought to have topographers . . .

—Montaigne, I, 31

If we are to believe Montaigne, what is near masks a foreignness. Therefore, the "ordinary" includes "facts just as wonderful as those that we go collecting in remote countries and centuries" (II, 12).[1] Take the well-known essay "Of Cannibals" (I, 31) as an example; let us assume that there are surprises in store for us in this familiar text. What Montaigne ponders in this essay is precisely the status of the strange: Who is "barbarian"? What is a "savage"? In short, what is the place of the other?

Topography

This line of questioning places into question both the text's power of composing and distributing places, its ability to be a narrative of space,[2] and the necessity for it to define its relation to what it treats, in other words, to construct a place of its own. The first aspect concerns the space of the other; the second, the space of the text. On the one hand, the text accomplishes a spatializing operation which results in the determination or displacement of the boundaries delimiting cultural fields (the familiar vs. the strange). In addition, it reworks the spatial divisions which underlie and organize a culture.[3] For these socio- or ethno-cultural boundaries to be changed, reinforced, or disrupted, a space of interplay is needed, one that establishes the text's difference, makes possible its operations and gives it "credibility" in the eyes of its readers, by distinguishing it both from the conditions within which it arose (the context) and from its object (the content). Montaigne's essay functions both as an *Index locorum* (a redistribution of cultural space) and as the affirmation of a place (a locus of utterance). These two aspects are only formally distinguishable, because it is in fact the text's reworking of space that simultaneously produces the space of the text.

Book IV of Herodotus' *Histories*, devoted to the Scythians, proceeds in the same manner; it is twice mentioned in the essay "Of Cannibals," and forms its fundamental precondition (in an "archaeological" history of the "Savage"). It combines a *representation of the other* (which places in opposition the Scythian nomad and the Athenian city-dweller, or the barbarian no-place and the Greek *oikoumenè*) and the fabrication and accreditation of the *text as witness of the other*. It is in describing the Scythians that Herodotus' text constructs a place of its own. By specifying the operations which produce a "barbarian" space as distinct from Greek space, he multiplies the utterative markings ("I saw," "I heard," etc.) and modalities (it is obvious, doubtful, inadmissible, etc.) which, with regard to the "marvels" recounted (the *thôma*), organize the place at which he would like to make himself heard and believed.[4] An image of the other and the place of the text are simultaneously produced.

Herodotus' book, while adopting the function of mediator, or knowledge (*histôr*, he who knows), between the Greek *logos* and its barbarian other, also develops as a play on mediators. At the level of the history the book recounts, the mediator is the Persian, who advances into Scythian territory before attacking the Greeks, and plays the role of third party and divulger for both sides. At the level of the production of a truth, or of historical verisimilitude, that is, at the level of the text's own production, the mediators are the witnesses, interpreters, legends, and documents—the sayings of others about the other—that Herodotus manipulates and modalizes, by means of a subtle, permanent practice of distancing, so as to distinguish from these sources his own "testimony," that interspace where the fiction is erected of a discourse, addressed to the Greeks, which treats both the Greek and the Barbarian, both one and the other.

"Of Cannibals" is inscribed within this heterological tradition, in which the discourse about the other is a means of constructing a discourse authorized by the other. It exhibits the same structural features as the fourth book of Herodotus, although it makes different use of them. From the heterological angle, it is more closely related to Montaigne's own "Apology for Raymond Sebond" (II, 12). These two essays arise from the same problematic: the circularity between the production of the Other and the production of the text. God and the cannibal, equally elusive, are assigned by the text the role of the Word in whose name its writing takes place—but also the role of a place constantly altered by the inaccessible (t)exterior [*hors-texte*] which authorizes that writing.

A Travel Account

The essay develops in three stages which give it the structure of a travel account.[5] First comes the outbound journey: the search for the strange, which is presumed to be different from the place assigned it in the beginning by the discourse of culture. This *a priori* of difference, the postulate of the voyage, results in a rhetoric of distance in travel accounts. It is illustrated by a series of surprises and intervals (monsters, storms, lapses of time, etc.) which at the same time substantiate the alterity of the savage, and empower the text to speak from elsewhere and command belief. Montaigne begins with the same initial postulate (the non-identity of the cannibal and his designation), but the approach is linguistic in form. It consists in establishing a distance from nearby representations: first, from common opinion (which talks about "barbarians" and "savages"), then from the ancient sources (Plato's Atlantis and the pseudo-Aristotle's island), and finally from contemporary information (the cosmography of the period, Thévet, etc.). Faced with these increasingly authoritative discourses, the essay only repeats: that's not it, that's not it. . . . The critique of proximities places both the savage and the narrator at a distance from our own lands.

Next comes a depiction of savage society, as seen by a "true" witness. Beyond words and systems of discourse, appears the savage "body," a beautiful and natural organicity balancing conjunction (a group "without division") and disjunction (war among men, different functions for each sex). As in Jean de Léry's *Histoire d'un voyage fait en la terre du Brésil* (1578), this "ethnological" depiction lies at the center, between the accounts of the outward journey and of the return. An ahistorical image, the picture of a new body, is framed by two histories (the departure and the return) that have the status of meta-discourses, since the narration speaks of itself in them. In travel accounts, this historical "frame" entertains a double relation to the picture it supports. On the one hand, the frame is necessary to assure the strangeness of the picture. On the other, it draws upon the representation for the possibility of transforming itself: the discourse that sets off in search of the other with the impossible task of saying the truth returns from afar with the authority to speak in the name of the other and command belief. This characteristic of (meta-discursive) history and (descriptive) depiction—their ability to mutually empower one another—is also found in Montaigne, but he treats it in his own fashion.

The picture of savage society is tied to travel accounts in another way. It is organized around two strategic questions, cannibalism and polygamy. These two cardinal differences bring into play savage society's relation to its exteriority (war) and to its interiority (marriage), as well as the status of men and that of women. Montaigne takes his place in a long tradition (which began before him and continued after) when he transforms these two "barbarities" into forms of "beauty" judged deserving of that name due to their utility to the social body. But he gives ethical standing to what in Jean de Léry, for example, appeared as an esthetic or technical beauty.

The third stage is the return voyage, the homecoming of the traveler-narrator. In the essay, it is the savage himself, originally absent from common representations, either ancient or cosmological, who returns in the text. As in Kagel's work (*Mare Nostrum*), he enters our languages and our lands. He comes with the narrative. Or rather, his words come progressively nearer through the "songs," "opinions," and "responses" he addresses in Rouen to interviewers close to the narrator, and then finally through what "he told me." The text reports his words, which figure as a ghost that has returned to our stage. The narrative becomes the saying of the other, or it *almost* becomes it, because the mediation of an interpreter (and his "stupidity"), the accidents of translation, and the tricks of memory maintain, as in Léry,[6] a *linguistic* boundary line between savage speech and travel writing.

Distancing, or the Defection of Discourse

The first stage recounts a series of disappearances. The cannibals slip away from the words and discourses that fix their place, just as, at the beginning of Book IV of Herodotus, the Scythians vanish from the successive locations where the Persian army attempts to catch them. They are not to be found where they are sought.[7] They are never *there*. Nomadism is not an attribute of the Scythian or the Cannibal: it is their very definition. What is foreign is that which escapes from a place.

From square one, the essay dissociates the name from the thing. This nominalist postulate, which also underlies the mystic discourse of the time, is firmly held to: "There is the name and the thing. The name is a sound which designates and signifies the thing; the name is not a part of substance, it is a piece attached to the thing that is foreign to and outside of it" (II, 16). What is foreign is first of all the "thing." It is never where the word is. The cannibal is only a variant of this general difference, but a typical one since he is supposed to demarcate a boundary line. Therefore when he sidesteps the identifications given him, he causes a disturbance that places the entire symbolic order in question. The global delimitation of "our" culture in relation to the savage concerns the entire gridding of the system that brushes up against the boundary and presupposes, as in the *Ars Memoriae*,[8] that there is a *place* for every *figure*. The cannibal is a figure on the fringe who leaves the premises, and in doing so jolts the entire topographical order of language.

This difference, running through all the codes like a fault line, is treated by the essay on two levels—that of the word ("barbarous," "savage"), the elementary unit of nomination, and that of discourse, seen as referential testimonies (ancient or contemporary). The identities formulated at these two levels are meant to define the position of the other in language. Montaigne, for his part, is only aware of them as "fictions" that derive from a place. For him, the statements are only "stories" related to their particular places of utterance. In short, they signify not the reality of which they speak, but the reality from which they depart, and which they disguise, the place of their enunciation [*élocution*].

This critique does not assume that the text signed by Montaigne has a guarantee of truth that authorizes it to judge the stories. The defection of names and discourses is due only to their coming together. They destroy one another as soon as they touch: a shattering of mirrors, the defection of images, one after the other.

On the level of the discourse, or of the witnesses, the text plays upon three major reference points: common opinion (*doxa*, which is also what has been passed down, verisimilitude, in other words the discourse of the other), the opinion of the Ancients (tradition), and the opinion of the Moderns (observation). The operation comprises three moments. First, "vulgar opinion," or "popular say," is impugned because it is devoid of the "reason" exhibited by the examples from antiquity (Pyrrhus, the Greeks, Philippus, etc.). Then the Ancients (Plato citing Solon who cited Egyptian priests, and Aristotle—if it is indeed he—citing the Carthaginians) are spurned in favor of information furnished by contemporary travelers and cosmographers. These Moderns, "clever people," are in the end themselves rejected on grounds of unreliability: they add things, spinning "stories," aimed at augmenting their status, which substitute a fictionalized global view for their partial observation.[9] We thus come back to the "simple" man in his capacity as a traveler (travel experience is what the Ancients were lacking in) and a faithful witness (reliability is what the Moderns lack). This craftsman of information becomes the pivot of the text.

Traversing the three authorities of discourse one after another, this critical traveling shot also describes, like a curve, the three conditions of testimony (reason, information, reliability), but they appear as exterior to one another: where one is present, the others are lacking. The series is one of disjunctions: reliability without reason, reason without knowledge, knowledge without reliability. It functions by the extraposition of parts whose conjunction would be necessary in that case. All that remains of the whole, which has been disseminated into particularities foreign to one another, is its form, an obsessive relic, a model repeated in the "inventions" of poetry, philosophy, and deceit: the totalizing schema exerts control over particular pieces of knowledge and takes their place. It gets to the point that "we embrace everything, but clasp only wind." The "simple" man, on the contrary, admits the particularity of his place and his experience; by virtue of this, he is already something of a savage.

The discourses rejected by the essay are presented as a series of positivities which, though made to go together (they are symbolic), become disconnected (they become dia-bolic) because a distance intervenes between them. The exteriority that compromises each one of them is the law of space itself. Placed under the sign of paradigmatic disjunction, this series composed of three disjointed elements aims for the impossible center point of the conjunction of those elements—the true witness. The saying of the thing. It is noteworthy that this "series" is structured as a *written* discourse: the written text, a *spatial* dissemination of elements destined for an impossible symbolization, dooms the unity it aims for (the thing, or meaning), as well as the unity it presupposes (the speaker), to inaccessibility (by the very fact of the exteriority of the graphs to one another).

The same procedure is repeated in the terrain of the name. It takes place in a landscape of tumultuous, mobile, vanishing things: Atlantis swallowed by the sea, the dislocated whole Italy/Sicily, the land of Gascony with its changing shores, the vacillating riverbed of the Dordogne, the elusive author hidden beneath the text credited to Aristotle. The boundaries of these bodies are uncertain, their reality in motion. How can borders distinguishing one from the other be determined? It is the task of nomination to fix a *locus proprius* for them, and to set limits for their drifting.

The difference formulated by the term "savage," which is equated with the division between land and water, is the act which in principle begins the genesis of a language of "culture." It was for that reason the object of a major contemporary debate.[10] In Montaigne's essay the whole, "barbarian and savage," has been *received* from the opinions of others as a *fact* of language, but it is torn apart by the work of the text just as the unity Italy-Sicily (*tellus una*) was "divided" by the work of the sea. This labor deploys the polysemous nature of the expression, undercutting the use commonly made of it (the savage, or the barbarian is the other); it uproots it from the social conventions defining it and restores its semantic mobility. Then "savage" drifts toward "natural" (as in "wild" fruits)[11] and takes as its opposite either an "artificiality" that alters nature, or "frivolity." Either way, this sliding gives the word "savage" a positive connotation. The signifier moves, it escapes and switches sides. The ferret is on the run.[12]

The word "barbarian," for its part, leaves behind its status as a noun (the Barbarians) to take on the value of an adjective (cruel, etc.). Montaigne's analysis lets the word run away, and is wary of not giving it another definition. But although it watches the uncertain essence of the word recede into the distance and declines to name *beings*, it still ponders the behaviors to which it could apply as a *predicate* (an adjective). It does this in three ways which gradually bring into evidence the inadequation of the word to its supposed referent: an ambivalence (cannibals are "barbarian" because of their "original naturalness"; Occidentals are barbarian because of their cruelty); a comparison (our ways are more barbarian than theirs); and an alternative (one of us has to be barbarian, us or them, and it's not them).

Thus, the name comes undone. It functions as an adjective in relation to places that have the value of undefined nouns. It bursts into pieces disseminated throughout space. It becomes dispersed in contradictory meanings, which are indifferently assignable to cases that used to be kept carefully separate: for example, "savage" remains over where it was, but with an inverted meaning, and "barbarian" comes our way, assigned to the very place from which it had been excluded. In this way, the place of the Cannibals is emptied—it becomes vacant and distant. Where are they? The first part of the essay places them out of reach.

The play on discourse and words that produces this distancing also produces the space of the text; but it does not found it upon an authority or truth of its own. The "outward journey" that generates this textual space has the form of a meta-discourse. It is a critique of language, carried out in the name of language and nothing else. It develops, in a fashion analogous to a textual critique, through a series of negative "tests" (as in popular stories or travel accounts) which constitute language in its relation to that which it is unable to appropriate, that is to say, in its relation to a (t)exterior [*un hors-texte*]. A linguistic labor thus produces the first figure of the other.

From the Body to Speech, or Cannibalistic Utterance

It is precisely as a (t)exterior [*hors-texte*], as an image, that the cannibal appears in the second part. After the critical journey through the languages which compel belief, now we get "to see" savage society. It offers present "experience" a more amazing reality than either the fictions of myth (the Golden Age) or the conceptions of philosophy (Plato's *Republic*). This depiction is introduced by a "simple" ("a simple, crude fellow") and familiar ("with me for a long time," "my man") character who constitutes the pivotal point of the text; it is he who allows it to pass from those eroded discourses to reliable speech. The text changes register. It proceeds, from this point on, in the name of someone's words: first, the word of the simple man, then that of the savage. There is a continuity between the two. What they have in common is that they are both reliable, sustained by bodies that have been put to the test—of travel (the eyewitness) or combat (the Cannibals)—and that they have not been altered by the ability of discourse to conceal particulars beneath the fiction of generality (the simple man "has not the stuff to build," and the Cannibals have "no knowledge of letters"). The man who "had lived ten or twelve years in that other world" is endowed with the same virtues as the savages. What they are over there, he is here.

The "illiterate" who lends his word the support of what his body has experienced and adds to it no "interpretation" has been around since the fourteenth century, in the form of the (anti-theological and mystical) figure of the *Idiotus*. It was made famous by the story from Strasbourg about the Friend of God, who was from Oberland, a wild region, and knew from his own experience more than any Doctor of Divinity, Tauler included.[13] The cannibal came to rest in the place occupied by the *Idiotus*, which for two centuries had been the only place that could authorize "new language." But the appearance of the cannibal in this emptied place—which, as the tradition itself suggests, was made possible by a critique of the established discourses—is announced by the eyewitness who "made the trip" and who, an illiterate prophet, avouches only what his body *has been through* and *seen*. Montaigne—unlike the mystic theologians of his day—does not use this cautious, yet fundamentally important, mediator between the Old World's *Idiotus* and the savage of the New only to point to a (qualitatively) different mode of speech in whose name discourses may be "reformed" and/or invented. Thanks to the anonymous Atlas who supports the mirror of savage society, he can give the representation a content serving as a metaphor for his own discourse.

The question may be asked as to why the text hides the literary sources at its basis beneath the authority of "simple" speech: these sources include Gomara,[14] Thévet,[15] probably Léry,[16] and not Las Casas,[17] etc. Not one reference is made to them.[18] To be sure, Montaigne's obliteration of his sources means that he adopts the "manner" of certain of the narratives he rejects (like Léry), which claim to speak only in the name of experience, while other narratives explicitly combine data received from the tradition with direct observation (as do maps, for that matter). Only an appeal to the senses (hearing, sight, touch, taste) and a link to the body (touched, carved, tested by experience) seem capable of bringing closer and guaranteeing, in a singular but indisputable fashion, the real that was lost by language. Proximity is thus necessary; for Montaigne, it takes the double form of the traveler and the private collection, both of which are his and in his home. In this context, conformity with what has appeared in books becomes irrelevant. It is a (fortunate) coincidence. By "forgetting" them and holding them at a distance, the text changes their status (even if today erudition is returning to the sources in the belief that it can explain the text). He displaces that which founds authority, though in spite of that he continues to repeat known facts and prior discourses, as is always the case.

Presenting itself throughout as an indirect discourse relating a saying that is "faithful" (though it gives no other reference than that),[19] Montaigne's depiction of savage society first offers a beautiful body "without divisions," unsplit by any trade, partition, hierarchy, or lie. The entire description is related to this body, it centers on it—a unified body ("they never saw one palsied, bleary-eyed, toothless, or bent with age") corresponding to the "Apollonian vision" of the savage, which was then competing, in travel accounts, with the diabolical figuration of the savage.[20] The presence of the body is affirmed—a tangible real (Montaigne "tasted" their cassava), and one that is visible (he can see their objects and ornaments in his own home). The body is there from the beginning, first in time (they are "men freshly issued forth from the gods," *viri a diis recentes*). A new discourse originates in it.

The somewhat Rabelaisian accumulation of details about the physical aspects of the prototype includes two exceptions which signal a turning point: the first has to do with the symbolic dwelling place of the dead (the worthy go to the East, where the New World is dawning, and the "damned" go to the West, where a world is coming to its end); the second has to do with the punishment of the "priests and prophets" who abuse language in speaking of the unknowable, and thus put it to the same use Western speakers do. These exceptions announce the essential theme of the essay's subsequent development: that the savage body obeys a law, the law of faithful and verifiable speech.

This is demonstrated in the analysis of the only two "articles" contained in the "ethical science" of the savages: "valor against the enemy and love for their wives." Cannibalism, because it is approached from the angle of the victim (the heroism of the vanquished) and not the perpetrator, brings to light an ethic of faithfulness in war; and polygamy, because it is seen from the point of view of service (the "solicitude" of the women), not masculine domination, similarly reveals a superior degree of conjugal fidelity. These two scandalous elements of supposedly barbarian society in fact constitute an *economy of speech*, in which the body is the price. A reversal of perspective transforms the solar body of the savage into a value sacrificed to speech. This is reminiscent of Donatello at the end of his life, when he shattered the Apollonian body he had invented himself, sculpting in its place the suffering of thought. The style changes as well. We pass from a bulimic nomenclature, a dictionary of the savage body, to carefully constructed, copious, and precise argumentation, in turn fervent and lyrical:

—Thesis: savage society is a body in the service of saying. It is the visible, palpable, verifiable *exemplum* which realizes before our eyes an ethic of speech.

—Demonstration: cannibalism is the climax of a variety of war that is motivated neither by conquest nor self-interest, but operates on the basis of a "challenge" to one's honor and a demand for "confession" under pain of death. "The gain of the victor is glory." As for polygamy, it assumes the height of unselfishness on the part of the women, who work together without jealousy in the service of their husband's "valor" and "virtue." In both cases, the value of speech is affirmed in the "loss" of self-interest and the "ruin" of one's own body. It is defined as a "triumphant loss." The cannibalistic community is founded upon this ethic. It draws its strength from it since a heroic faithfulness to speech is precisely what produces the unity and continuity of the social body: the ingested warrior nourishes his adversaries with the flesh of their own fore-fathers, and the women compete to reproduce with the most valiant men. The ethic of speech is also an economy.

—Illustration: in order to measure the virtue of cannibalism, comparison must be sought among the most heroic examples Greek courage has to offer (King Leonidas or Ischolas); in order to conceive of the generosity implied by polygamy, it is necessary to recall the most lofty female figures of the Bible (Leah, Rachel, Sarah), as well as those of Antiquity (Livia, Stratonice). The finest gold tradition has to offer is used to forge a halo for the cannibals.

—Poetics: two "songs," one a war song, the other a love song, corroborate the analysis with a beauty that does not come from the body, but, conscious and creative, is that of the poem.[21] Song is born of ethical passion. That beautiful body of the savage is only there to make room, at the moment of death, for beautiful words. It ends up in a poem, a new *Mythos*. In this way the Fable—Saying—returns, initiating a rebeginning of history; but it is truthful, veracious, it is present, and it will speak to us.

This cannibalistic fable is no longer of the order of discourse. It does not belong to a class of statements (true or false). It is a *speech-act*. It transmits nothing and is not transmitted: one performs the act, or it does not happen. Therefore, it does not behave as a legend or narrative. It is not detachable from a particular place (it is a "special knowledge"), from a dialogic challenge (in the face of the enemy) or from a loss that constitutes its price (depossession). However, faithful speech arises at its place of utterance at the very moment it loses what sustains it. The epiphany of the savage body is only a necessary medi-ation that ensures the passage from the statement (an interpretable discourse that is transportable from place to place, and is deceptive wherever it goes) to utter-ance (an act that is rooted in the courage of saying, and is truthful by virtue of that fact). The half-animal, half-divine utterance of the beautiful body, once it has replaced the mobile, lying statement, is exchanged for the human, mortal mode of utterance of the poem, which is a challenge of and dedication to the other.

Through the death of the warrior or the service of the wife, the body becomes a poem. The song symbolizes the entire social body. The warrior's song trans-forms his devoured body into the genealogical memory of his group, and into a communion with the ancestors through the mediation of the enemy: you are going to be eating "your own flesh." The song, the spirit of the group, ex-presses what lies beyond the "own" [*le propre*], which it puts back into com-mon circulation. The lover's song transforms the adder (serpent of division?)

into a "cordon" that knots the ties of blood ("my sister" and I) to those of love ("my love" and I); it makes a "picture" (the snake's coloring) into the gift of speech which is transmitted from blood relation to marriage. Poetic saying thus articulates the differences it posits.

But does not this detour into the New World reconnect with a medieval model that was then in the process of disappearing? The order of saying (the *oratores*) was gaining the upper hand against the order of the warriors (the *bellatores*) and that of the workers (the *laboratores*). In the order of saying, speech and weaponry coincided in "honor," to which service had to be rendered through a nourishing transformation of things; and struggle obeyed the symbolic rules of a code of honor which restricted it to the closed field of "battle," forbidding it to invade the space of society in the "barbarian," modern form of total war.[22] Everything was linked together under the sign of a symbolic discourse, the sacrament of a society's spiritual self-presence. . . . Swallowed up like Atlantis, this medieval society—which was in part dreamed—reappears with the savages, in that organic multiplicity tied together by a Word [*une parole*].

In fact, if the old model is recognizable in the new world, and if, as always, its slow historical disappearance creates an empty place where a theory of the present takes up residence, then there is, in the passage from the medieval world to the cannibal, a loss of content and a move away form the truth of the world (something *said*) toward the courage to support one's word (a *saying*)—a move from a *dogmatism* founded upon a true discourse to an *ethic* which produces the heroic poem. It is as if, in the birth of a new history on the shores of another world, man had to take control of divine enunciation [*élocution*] himself, and pay the price of his "glory" in pain. There is no longer any "extraordinary" and presumptuous assurance (like that of the priests and prophets) of *detaining a truth* that is "beyond our ken"; what there is instead is the duty to *keep one's word* in a "triumphant loss."

From Speech to Discourse, or Montaigne's Writing

Montaigne's voyage—like that of Alcofrybas Nasier (an anagram of François Rabelais) in Pantagruel's mouth, the New World where a simple fellow reveals to the tourist the strange familiarity of an unknown land[23]—circulates in the space of cannibalistic orality, and he uses what he finds there to authorize a new discourse, in the old world. That discourse culminates in a return, hinted at several times in the letter of the text: "to return to my subject," "to return to our story," etc. If, in the final analysis, the "subject" consists of knowing *where* among us there can arise a writing different from the "false inventions" and proliferation of deception in the West, then the return to "our story" is effected *with* the savages, through the arrival of their word among us and through the credibility it provides for writing that is based on the model it offers.

Their word, a distant beginning as "wild" as a new and natural fruit, gradually draws closer to the place of production of the text that "cites" it: first to cross the ocean are the songs from over there; then comes the interview granted by the speakers in Rouen; finally, there are the responses addressed to the author himself. In Rouen, they express their surprise (they think *we're* savages?) at the *physical* disorder of French society: adult men taking orders from a child; "half" of the people going hungry and allowing the other "half" to wallow in wealth. Their "king" or "captain" tells Montaigne that his "superior position" gives him the privilege of "marching foremost in times of war," and, in peace, of "passing quite comfortably" on paths cleared for him through the underbrush. On the one hand, their speech, a critique of the injustice that divides our social body, judges us. On the other hand, as something groundbreaking and organizing, pathfinding in its own space, it precedes us, moving, passing on. It is always ahead of us, and always escapes us.

As a matter of fact, a blank in memory (like the one that causes the "forgetting" of the island's name in Thomas More's *Utopia*)[24] or the thickness of the "interpreter" keeps the text permanently behind the word it cites and follows. More exactly, that speech only appears in the text in a fragmented, wounded state. It is present within it as a "ruin." The undone body was the precondition of the speech it sustained up to the moment of death; in the same way, this undone speech, split apart by forgetting and interpretation, "altered" in dialogic combat, is the precondition of the writing it in turn supports. That speech makes writing possible by sinking into it. It induces it. But the written discourse which cites the speech of the other is not, cannot be, the discourse of the other. On the contrary, this discourse, in writing the Fable that authorizes it, alters it. If speech induces the text to write, it does it by means of paying the price, just as the warrior's body must repay the speech of the challenge and the poem with his death. It is this death of speech that authorizes the writing that arises, the poetic challenge.

Does this law apply to Montaigne's writing itself? Yes. The textual *corpus* also undergoes a defection in order that something other may speak through it. It must be altered by a dissemination in order for its speaker or "author" to mark his place in it. A "ruin" within the work—a multiple work that is never *there*—conditions the manifestations of the otherly speech which sym-bolizes the text, from outside the text, and brings up the fore like a cannibal in the woods; its name is "I." In the same way as the savage body, the scriptural corpus is condemned to a "triumphant loss" allowing the saying of the "I."

The closing remark of the essay concerns both the speech of the cannibal and that of Montaigne. An impatient, final irony: the text suddenly turns its attention toward its readers, potential figures of the everywhere dreaded enemy, the interpreter.[25] This is similar to the gaze in the paintings of Hieronymus Bosch which, from the background, follows the onlooker and challenges him. "All this is not too bad—but what's the use? They don't wear breeches."

Montaigne repeats the comment in his "Apology for Raymond Sebond": "I once saw among us some men brought by sea from a far country. Because we did not understand their language at all, and because their ways, moreover, and their bearing and their clothes were totally remote from ours, which of us did not consider them savages and brutes?" (II, 12, 343). He who does not understand the language only sees the clothes: the interpreter. He does not recognize that the undone body says the *other*. Thus a swarm of "commentaries" replace the misunderstood author (III, 13). What Montaigne perceived about the savage body, which is a *speaking* body more than a *visible* one—will his readers *hear* and understand it when they *see*, or read, the beautiful textual body that is sustained and shattered by his authorial speech? This question is haunted by mourning: La Boétie, the only true listener, is no longer. So the text will be forever menaced by the exegete, who only knows how to identify a body and perceive breeches.

Finally, the saying that induces writing and the ear that knows how to listen designate the same place, the other.[26] The cannibal (who speaks) and La Boétie (who listens) are metaphors for each other. One is near, one is far, both are absent—both are other. The text, then, is not only based upon the approach of a Word that is always lacking; it also postulates a pre-existing reader who is missing in the text, but authorizes it. The text is produced in relation to this missed present, this speaking, hearing other. Writing arises from the separation that makes this presence the inaccessible other of the text, and the author himself (the "I") a multiple, iconoclastic passer-by in his own fragmented work. The savage ethic of speech opens the way for a Western ethic of writing—a writing sustained by the impossible Word at work within the text. If one cannot be a cannibal, there is still the option of lost-body writing.

Chapter 6
Mystic Speech

A Locus of Speech

The mysticism of the sixteenth and seventeenth centuries proliferated in proximity to a loss. It is a historical trope for that loss. It renders the absence that multiplies the productions of desire readable. At the dawn of modernity, an end and a beginning—a departure—are thus marked. The literature of mysticism provides a path for those who "ask the way to get lost. No one knows." It teaches "how not to return."[1]

But the mysticism of that age is connected as much to the collective history of a transition as it is to inaugural "wanderings."[2] It is the story of the Christian "Occident." It came in, it seems, with the setting sun, but vanished before morning, announcing a day it never knew; the "retreat of mystics" coincides with the dawning of the century of the Enlightenment. The project of a radical Christianity was formed against a backdrop of decadence and "corruption" in a world that was falling apart and in need of repair. It borrowed the vocabulary of the Reformation, applying it to a biographical context: schism, wounds, etc. The end of a world was the experience sought by every spiritual poet. Their daring and luminous paths streaked a night from which they were later extracted by a piety greedy for mystic traces; they inscribed themselves on its black page, and it is there we must relearn how to read them.

The texts of mysticism use the word "night" to describe their global situation, but they also apply it more particularly to ways of experiencing that situation as an existential question. The texts are tales of "passions" *of* and *in* history. The different mystic trends, confronted with hidden truths, opaque authorities, and divided or ailing institutions, did not basically set out to pioneer new systems of knowledge, topographies, or complementary or substitutive powers; rather, they defined a different *treatment* of the Christian tradition. The ways of the mystics were accused (with good reason) of being "new." Prisoners of circumstance ("another shall bind you"), yet grounded in their faith in a Beginning that still comes in the present, the mystics established a "style" in the form of *practices* defining a *modus loquendi* and/or a *modus agendi*. What is essential, then, is not a body of doctrines (which was on the contrary the effect of their practices, and, especially, the product of later theological interpretations), but the epistemic foundation of a domain within which specific procedures are followed: a new space, with new mechanisms. At the heart of the debate pitting the "theologians" or spiritual "examiners" of the age against the mystics, the theorists of the literature see either "mystical statements" ("figures of speech," "turns" of phrase, ways of "turning" words around[3]) or "maxims" (rules of thought or action specific to the "saints," or mystics). The mystics' reinterpretation of the tradition is characterized by a set of procedures allowing a new treatment of language—of all contemporary language, not only the area delimited by theological knowledge or the corpus of patristic and scriptural works. It is ways of acting that guide the creation of a body of mystical writings.

We find, on the one hand, in the context of a degenerating tradition darkened by time, an effort to go beyond; and on the other hand, a progression from a cosmos of divine messages (or "mysteries") to be understood, to itinerant practices which trace in language the indeterminate path of a mode of writing: these two features characterize the modernity of the works which for over two centuries were called "mystic" by those who produced them and theorized about them. They suggest a way of entering those aging texts and surveying the movement of their modes of writing against the background of today's issues.

One last prefatory question: can we postulate, behind the document transmitted to us, the existence of a fixed referent (a fundamental experience or reality), the presence of which would be the test of a properly mystical text? All of these writings display a passion for what *is*,[4] for the world as it "exists," for the thing itself (*das Ding*)—in other words, a passion for what is its own authority and depends on no outside guarantee. They are beaches offered to the swelling sea; their goal is to disappear into what they disclose, like a Turner landscape dissolved in air and light. An ab-solute (un-bound), in the mode of pain, pleasure, and a "letting-be" attitude (Meister Eckhart's *gelâzenheit*), inhabits the torture, ecstasy, or sacri-fice of a language that can *say* that ab-solute, endlessly, only by erasing itself. But what name or identity can be attached to this "thing," independent of the always localized labor of letting it come? The other that organizes the text is not the (t)exterior [*un hors-texte*]. It is not an (imaginary) object distinguishable from the movement by which it (*Es*) is traced. To set it apart, in isolation from the texts that exhaust themselves in the effort to say it, would be to exorcize it by furnishing it with a place of its own and a proper name; it would be to identify it with the residue of already constituted systems of rationality, or to equate the question asked under the figure of the limit with a particular religious representation (one excluded from all of the fields of science, or fetishized as the substitute for a lack).[5] It would be tantamount to positing, behind the documents, the presence of a what-ever, an ineffability that could be twisted to any end, a "night in which all cats are black."

In the beginning, it is best to limit oneself to the consideration of what goes on in texts whose status is labeled "mystic," instead of wielding a ready-made definition (whether ideological or imaginary) of what it is that was inscribed in those texts by an operation of writing. The issues immediately at hand are the formal aspects of the discourse and the tracing movement (the roaming, *Wandern*) of the writing: the first circumscribes a locus, and the second displays a "style," a "walk" or gait, in Virgil's sense when he says, "her walk reveals the goddess."[6]

My purpose here is to pinpoint the locus established by mystic speech, leaving for the future a possible analysis of its walk, or the mystic "procedures" which produce endless narrativity. Only then will we have gained access to these writings, which found the subject on its own dissolution ("aphanisis") in that unreadable something other written in its body.

At the dawn of modernity, then, a new literary and epistemological "form" appears with texts labeled "mystic" in order to distinguish them from other past or contemporary texts (theological treatises, biblical commentaries, etc.). The problem is not to determine whether an exegetical treatise by Gregory of Nyssa, for example, is a product of the same experience as a discourse later termed "mystic," or whether both are constructed following roughly analogous rhetorical processes; it is, rather, to understand what happens inside the field delimited by a *proper name* ("mystic"), in which an operation regulated by an applicable set of *rules* is undertaken. A corpus can be considered the effect of this relation between a name (which symbolizes a circumscription) and rules (which specify a mode of production), even if, as is often the case, the name is used to add different or earlier productions to the constellation of texts it isolates (in the sixteenth and seventeenth centuries, already existing writings were termed "mystic," and a mystic tradition was fabricated), and even if the rules of "mystic" construction were already structuring texts well in advance of their group designation (it is often noted that procedures deemed "mystic" in modern times are regrouped under other labels in earlier or contemporary documents). At the outset of the analysis, we thus find, in the system of differentiation of discursive formations, the isolation of a "mystic" unity articulating a new space of knowledge.[7] The right to exercise language *otherwise* is objectified in a set of circumscriptions and procedures.

We could well ask ourselves what confluence of disciplines, beginning in the thirteenth century, made possible the configuration within which mysticism took definite shape, or what displacements, beginning at the end of the seventeenth century, caused mysticism to be dispersed into other formations. We would need to follow the tradition back to its initiators, Meister Eckhart (1260–1327) and, a half century earlier, Hadewijch of Anvers,[8] in order to understand the gradual constitution of the mystic formation; we would also have to identify the stages marking the transition to other genres, beginning with Mme. Guyon (1648–1717), Fénelon (1651–1715), or Arnold (1666–1714). However, since its historical boundaries are in constant flux, it seemed preferable to begin in the middle and study the field of mysticism at the height of its formalization—from Saint Teresa (1515–1582) to Angelus Silesius (the pseudonym of Johann Scheffler, 1624–1677). At this point, its modes of functioning are more legible, allowing us to define its *place*; a regressive history of its development and a study of its later incarnations are then made possible.

If we envision the procedures of this mystic writing, if we "interpret" that writing (in the musical sense) as a different mode of utterance, we are treating it as a past apart from us, rather than pretending that we are in the same place it is. Such an approach involves an attempt to repeat its movements ourselves, to follow, though at a distance, in the footsteps of its workings; it means refusing to equate this thing, which transformed graphs into hieroglyphs as it passed, with an object of knowledge. We must remain within a certain experience of writing, and observe a modesty that is respectful of distances. These guidelines, adopted in the textual suburbs, soon teach the way to get lost (even if it is only the way to lose a form of knowledge); following them may lead us, by the sound of its streets, to the city transformed into sea. A genre of literature would thus have revealed a part of what constructs it: the power to induce a departure.

A Site: the Tradition Humiliated

Mystic literature belongs first of all to a certain topography. In modern Europe, it has its privileged places: certain regions, social categories, group types, forms of labor, or, even more to the point, certain concrete modes of monetary relations (begging, communal holdings, trade, etc.), of sexual experiences (celibacy, widowhood, etc.), and power relations (allegiances to benefactors, ecclesiastical and political affiliations, etc.). We must first of all ask what constants can be extracted from the data furnished by the few analyses which depart from the "ahistorical" slumber of studies on mysticism.[9] I will summarize some of the relevant information regarding the mystics' place, in particular, their social origins and situations.

During the sixteenth and seventeenth centuries the mystics were for the most part from regions of social categories which were in socio-economic recession, disadvantaged by change, marginalized by progress, or destroyed by war. The memory of past abundance survived in these conditions of impoverishment, but since the doors of social responsibility were closed, ambitions were redirected toward the open spaces of utopia, dream, and writing. Lucien Goldmann tried to explain the Jansenist spirituality of Port-Royal by the situation of its authors, who were members of the *noblesse de robe*, a class which was in the process of losing its former powers.[10] The case was similar (though this is actually not an explanation) for other French mystics of the same period. Many were connected through family ties to the decadence of the petty nobility of the southwest provinces, the misery of the country squires, the devaluation of parliamentary "offices," or, most of all, "to an entire stratum composed of the middle aristocracy, rich in vitality and spiritual needs, but of reduced social service or utility."[11] The same thing applies for the difficulties experienced earlier in the century by compromised Leaguers (such as the Acarie family) or émigrés (such as the Englishman Benoit of Canfeld). Among the religious hermits, we find the same geography of affiliations (minus the parliamentarians).[12] Aside from a few mystics on the road to social promotion (such as René d'Argenson, who was an intendant[13]), the majority of them up to the time of Marguerite-Marie Alacoque[14] belonged to social milieux or "factions" in full retreat. Mysticism seems to emerge on beaches uncovered by the receding tide.

In sixteenth-century Spain, Saint Teresa belonged to a *hidalguía* (noble class) that had lost its duties and holdings;[15] Saint John of the Cross, a nurse in the hospitals of Salamanca, came from a ruined and fallen aristocratic class, etc. But ethnic distinctions, *la raza*, counted more than position in the social hierarchy. The "new Christians," or converted Jews, in whose features their contemporaries saw only the mask of the Excluded, remained close in many ways to the Jewish tradition (the tradition of the *gespaltete Seelen*, divided souls, whose cleaved lives[16] created a hidden interiority); they were prominent in the ranks of the *alumbrados* (illuminati), whose greatest figures number among them (Melchor, the Cazallas, the Ortiz', etc., and many *beatas*).[17] Barred from certain Orders (such as the Hieronymites and Benedictines), suspected by the Dominicans, these "scorned ones" went on to become great spiritual leaders among the Franciscans (Diego de Estella), the Augustinians (Luis de León), the Jesuits (Lainez, Polanco), and the Carmelites (Saint Teresa's grandfather had himself converted to Judaism and was forced to abjure in 1485[18]). From John of Ávila (who turned the University of Baeva into a sanctuary for the "new Christians") to Molinos, a strange alliance linked "mystic" speech and "im-

Social classes.
Displaced aristocracy

pure" blood. In fact, their position midway between two religious traditions, one repressed and internalized, the other public but weighed down by success, allowed the new Christians to become the major initiators of a new mode of discourse freed from dogmatic redundancy—just as in the nineteenth century the widespread adoption of German culture by Jews led to theoretical innovation and exceptional intellectual productivity, the results of differences maintained in the use of a common language.

Interesting

In Germany, seventeenth-century mysticism was similarly a product of an impoverished rural aristocracy (J. J. von Tschech, A. von Frankenberg, Friedrich von Spee, Catharina von Greiffenberg, Angelus Silesius; Danial Czepko, by virtue of his work circle, could be included in this group), or of small-scale urban craftsmen (Jacob Boehme, Quirinus Kuhlmann, Johann Georg Gichtel, J. C. Gifftheil, etc.): in other words, they came from the classes most negatively affected by the progress made by other social categories (in particular, the urban bourgeoisie).[19] The decline of their classes allowed for greater independence from religious authorities, and was accompanied by a refusal of the new order. In addition, Silesia, the privileged land of the mystics (Boehme, Frankenberg, Czepko, Silesius), was the province in the eastern part of the Holy Roman Empire hardest hit by the Thirty Years' War (with losses of 60–70 percent); it was also burdened with the social deterioration of its peasantry, economic competition from Poland and Kurland, and the alienation of its political rights under Charles VI. Sects and schools of theosophy and mysticism abounded in this land forsaken by history.

This topography, which can neither be systematized nor generalized,[20] has already pinpointed areas of particular instability or forms of social disinheritance. In a society based upon an ideology of stability, changing one's "station" in life is never good, and a lowering in social or family status is considered degeneration. Such a fall is an open wound in a social order that is viewed as a struggle against constant deterioration in relation to family origins. It constitutes an inability to protect the heritage against the inroads of time. The tradition is going away and turning into a past connection. That is what these groups, haunted by the certainty of extinction, experienced more deeply than any others. At the extremes, they vacillated between ecstasy and revolt—*mysticism and dissent*.[21] The privileges they "held," handed down from preceding generations, started to fall away, leaving them alone, without inherited property, with no assurances for the future, reduced to a present wed to death.[22] Contrary to what some have said, the dangers of the present were not dispelled by any expectations of future security or any past acquest; the present, for them, was the restricted scene upon which the drama of their doom was enacted, inscribed in facts (a law) and the possibility of a new beginning (a faith). They had nothing left but present exile.

If the mystics were locked within the confines of a "nothing" that could also be an "origin," it is because they were trapped there by a *radical* situation to which they responded with utmost seriousness.[23] In their texts, this can be seen not only in the connection their innovative truth always has to pain, but, more explicitly, in the social figures that dominate their discourse—the madman, the child, the illiterate.[24] An analogous situation today would be if the down-and-outs of our society, the fixed-income elderly or alien workers, were the eponymous heroes of knowledge.[25]

In the minds of the religious believers of the sixteenth and seventeenth centuries, a second state of affairs was inseparable from the foregoing situation—the humiliation of the Christian tradition. They were experiencing, in their shattered Christendom, another fundamental decline: that of the institutions of meaning. They were experiencing the disintegration of a sacred world. In other words, they were leading lives of exile, hounded from their land by the defilements of history. *Super flumina Babylonis*: the theme of mourning, disconsolate despite the intoxication of new aspirations, was endlessly repeated. Here again, referential permanence is lacking. The Churches and the Scriptures were considered equally corrupt.[26] Sullied by time, they obscure the Word whose presence they should be. Of course, they still mark its place, but only in the form of "ruins"—a word which haunted the writings of reformists. They also indicate the places where one should await, beginning *now*, the birth of God. God must be distinguished from His signs, which are subject to deterioration, whereas He, being already dead, is free from the erosion of time. Birth and death—the two poles of the mystics' evangelical meditations. They do not reject the ruins around them. They remain in them; they go to them. In a symbolic gesture, Saint Ignatius of Loyola, Saint Teresa of Ávila and many others wished to enter a "corrupt" order, not out of any taste for decadence, but because those disorganized places represented in their minds the state of contemporary Christianity and, like the cave of rejection at Bethlehem, were *where* they were to seek a repetition of a founding surprise. More generally, their *solidarity* with the collective, historically based suffering—which was demanded by circumstances but also desired and sought after as a test of truth—indicates the place of mystic "agony," a "wound" inseparable from the social ill.[27]

This religious and social experience should be seen in connection with the movement that led "spiritual" scholars and theologians to seek witness among people far below them in social status—maidservants, cowherds, villagers, etc.[28] Real or fictional, these men's stories tell of pilgrimages toward a different kind of "illumination." Conventional scholars formed scientific islands providing the basis for a reshaping of the world scene. Meanwhile, those "spiritual" intellectuals who converted to the "barbarians," on the other hand, were expressing the insufficiency of their knowledge in the face of a disaster in the system of reference; perhaps they also attest to a betrayal on the part of the *docti*. They subscribed wholesale to the dictum that consoled Ockham: *promissum Christi per parvulos baptizatos posse salvari.*[29] Like Cardinal Bérulle climbing up to a maidservant's garret, these Magi go among the "little people" to hear that which still speaks. A field of knowledge takes leave of its textual "authorities" to turn to the exegesis of "wild" voices. Innumerable biographies of poor "girls" or "enlightened illiterates" were produced, and constitute an important part of the spiritual literature of the time. In these writings, a tradition, humiliated after having functioned as the court of reason, awaits and receives from its other the certitudes that escape it.

The Discourse on Utterance

To gain a perspective on the process which slowly replaced a divided Christianity with national *political* units, breaking down the social organization of universal belief into sects, "retreats," and "*spiritual*" communities, it is necessary to take a more general view that includes a recognition of the socio-political instability of the age and the fragmentation of its frames of reference. As a matter of fact, the "Machiavellian Moment"[30] and the "mystic invasion"[31] coincide. The project of constructing an order amid the contingencies of history (the problem of the reason of State) and the quest to discern in our earthly, fallen language the now inaudible Word of God (the problem of the spiritual subject) arose simultaneously from the dissociation of cosmic language and the Divine Speaker. In addition, these two complementary restoration projects have recourse to the same "ecclesial" heritage of a unifying whole, although they express it in henceforth specialized modes: for one, the reason of State, for the other, the "community of saints." The ambition to totalize also inspired the dream of encyclopedic knowledge, philosophical Neoplatonism, metaphysical poetry, urban utopianism, etc. In each of these cases, though, its action was limited to a particular sphere.

Becoming separate from one another was not an aim of these various projects. It was, on the contrary, a necessity imposed by the disorder around them, from which they were obliged to distinguish themselves in order to mark the place of a new beginning. A multitude of microcosms appear, as reductions and replacements for the previous dismembered macrocosm. Two biblical images obsess them—the mythic image of paradise lost, and the eschatological or apocalyptic image of the New Jerusalem.[32] From this point of view, rational (political or scientific) production and irrational (spiritual or poetic) ones are inspired by the same utopian vision, the goal of which is a "great instauration"; though *compartmentalized* in various sectors (the division of the world is the fundamental experience of the age), this shared vision centers all of these recapitulatory attempts on a *unitary* reference: a common origin of history, a general law of the heavenly bodies, and a sacral hierarchy of power, of which the king remains the symbol.[33] The mystics, too, were responding to the desire to "reduce all to one";[34] that desire continued to underlie their "experimental" inquiries long after the ebb of Neoplatonism. Like other sciences, even more so, the "science of the saints" is confronted by the necessity of reconciling a central contradiction: between the *particularity* of the place it delimits (the subject) and the *universality* it strives for (the absolute). Perhaps it is defined by this very tension, which is played out in the opposition between *all* and *nothing*, or between "*notizia*" ("universal and vague") and "understanding" [*l'entendement*] (which can only know the particular). Thus it does not outlast the great recapitulatory project whose last philosophical representative is the *mathesis universalis* and the ecumenical work of Leibniz—until it makes a comeback, outside religion, in nineteenth-century romantic Germany, with Hölderlin and Hegel. Mysticism is the anti-Babel. It is the search for a common language, after language has been shattered. It is the invention of a "language of the angels" because that of man has been disseminated.[35]

Speaking-hearing[36]—such is the problem circumscribing the particular locus at which the universal project of the "saints" develops. The objects of the mystics' discourse have the status of symptoms; essentially, they are prayer (from meditation to contemplation) and the "spiritual" relation (in the form of communal exchanges and "spiritual guidance"). "Communication" (communications from God or those established among the saints) is everywhere a void to be filled, and forms the focal point of mystical accounts and treatises. They are writings produced from this lack. The rupture, ambiguity, and falsity that plurality spreads throughout the world creates the need to restore a *dialogue*. This *colloquium* would take place under the sign of the *Spirit* ("el que habla," the speaker, as St. John of the Cross phrases it[37]), since the "letter" no longer allows it. How can one *hear*, through signs transformed into things, that which flows from a unique and divine *will to speak*? How can this desire in search of a *thou* cross through a language that betrays it by sending the addressee a different message, or by replacing the statement of an idea with utterance by an "I"? "It is a difficult and troublesome thing for a soul not to understand [*entender*] itself or to find none who understand it":[38] like *The Ascent of Mount Carmel*, all mystic texts are born of this "trouble," this distress in expectation of a dialogue. They reach their highest point with the poem driving away any messenger who is not *thou*:

> Acaba de entregarte ya de vero
> No quieras enviarme
> De hoy más ya mensajero
> Que no saben decirme lo que quiero.[39]

In the work of Angelus Silesius, this corresponds to the "invocating drive" which casts aside the opaque positivity of the Holy Writ as a "nothing," and reclaims the "essential"—*thy* Word, in *me*:

> Die Schrift ist Schrift, sonst nichts. Mein Trost
>   ist Wesenheit,
> Und das Gott in mir spricht das Wort der Ewigkeit.[40]

Of course, the *invocatio* has long been the first moment of religious knowledge. It is the initial step in St. Anselm's *Proslogion*, and the field in which a noetic, then a rationality of faith, develop. But from this time onward, the *invocatio* and the *auditio fidei* become isolated from the Christian scriptural corpus, which recedes and is read and experienced "from a distance," and turned into the object either of logical treatment by scholastic theology or historical treatment by positive theology;[41] from language, from which the nominalists' God has been "unbound" (by his *voluntas ab-soluta*) and which he no longer guarantees; and from the cosmos, which becomes infinitely diversified and ceases to be a network of analogies referring to a single referent and speaker.[42] *Invocatio* and *auditio fidei* define something "essential" that is no longer a step on an itinerary of learning, but has been set outside the realm of knowledge. The act of *utterance* becomes separated from the objective organization of statements. And it lends mysticism its formal characteristics—it is defined by the establishment of a place (the "*I*") and by transactions (*spirit*); that is, by the necessary relation between the subject and messages. The term "experience" connotes this relation. Contemporaneous to the act of creation, outside an unreadable history, "utopian" space having provided a new faculty of reason a no-place in which to exercise its ability to create a world as text[43]—a mystic space is constituted, outside the fields of knowledge. It is there that the labor of writing which is given birth through the animation of language by the desire of the other takes place.

This new space does not initially add another domain to the configuration of theological disciplines. Only later, beginning at the end of the seventeenth century, after the texts had allowed the questioning that produced them to be forgotten, were these writings transformed into an "applied" (or "practical") science of theological "speculation."[44] The distancing that constitutes the no-place of allocution on the margins of objective contents does indeed involve a distinction between theory and practice; but the issue is how, or if, one can put into practice a language that is free in theory. In other words, if one can: address *to* God (*tratar con Dios*) the statements that concern Him; be in inter-course (*conversar*), *from thee* to *me*, with the Other or with others; hear and understand (*Audi, filia*) those statements considered inspired.[45] The tradition's ancient cosmological account is set on a new foundation, built upon a few strategic points: the present ability to speak (the *speech-act* in the here and now); the *I* that addresses a *thou* (the allocutionary relation[46]); the *conventions* to be established between the speaker and the allocutor[47] (the presuppositions and contracts of discourse); and the linguistic manifestation of the *allocutionary act* (the basis of the privilege accorded "indexes," i.e., the pragmatic or subjective elements of language, in mystic texts). These points fall within the province of utterance.[48] Moreover, the "experience" by which mystic writings define themselves has as its essential elements the *ego*, the "center of utterance," and the *present*, the "source of time," the "presence in the world that the act of utterance alone makes possible."[49]

For mysticism, unlike theology, it is not a matter of constructing a particular, coherent set of statements organized according to "truth" criteria; and, unlike theosophy, there is no interest in letting the violent order of the world reveal itself in the form of a general account (which makes personal experience irrelevant), but it is a matter of dealing with ordinary language (not the technical sectors) from an inquiry that questions the possibility of transforming that language into a network of allocutions and present alliances. A double cleavage. The initial division spearates the *said* (what has been or is stated) from the *saying* (the act of speaking [*l'acte de se parler*]).[50] The second, produced by "spiritual" labor, cuts into the density of the world to make of it a *dialogic* discourse: *I* and *thou* seeking one another in the thickness of the same language:

> ¿A donde te escondiste
> Amado y me dejaste con gemido?[51]

I and *thou*: two terms whose difference, regained and maintained, will be lost in the relation that posits them.

A certain number of mechanisms necessarily follow. Analogous to the linguistic signs of utterance, these terms do not refer to an object or entity (they are not referential or denominative), but to the agency of discourse itself. "I" is an "empty"[52] form that simply announces the speaker. It is a "siteless site" related to the fragility of social position or the uncertainty of institutional referents. The question addressed is not one of "competence." It targets the *exercise* of language, performance, and thus, in the strictest sense, the "reestablishment of language within the context of discourse."[53] Of the elements in mystic texts related to utterance, I will cite only three—decisive—examples. They concern the precondition of discourse (a division that establishes contractual relations), the status of discourse (a locus where the Spirit speaks), and the figuration of discourse as a content (an image of the "I"). In these three modes—conventions to be established, a place of locution to circumscribe, and a representation on which to base a narrative—the relation of a traditional language to the possibility of its being spoken is renewed. More fundamentally still, what is renewed is the relation between the signifier and the constitution of the subject: do we exist to speak to the other, or be spoken by him?

A Contract ("Volo"), a Subject ("I"), a Figure (the Island)

The first of the three modes outlined above is the effort to determine a course of action to make "utterance contracts" possible once again. Since it was no longer possible to presuppose the same cosmos that was experienced in times past as a (linguistic) encounter between the Divine Speaker and His faithful respondents, it was necessary to *produce* the conventions needed to circumscribe the places where one can "hear" [*entendre*] and where one can "come to an understanding with " others [*s'entendre*]. An essential sector of mystic thought attempts to explain and obtain the conditions allowing one to "speak to" [*parler à*] or "speak with" [*se parler*].[54] It is necessary to compile a "circumstantial" range of possibilities. Mystics are engaged in a politics of utterance—they are comparable to lawyers who make the most complete list possible of the situations and addresses apt to lead a proceeding to a "felicitous"[55] conclusion. This kind of "politics," like contemporary rhetoric,[56] sets forth operational rules determining the relational usage of a language that has become uncertain of the real. It *reconstructs*, where the *ontological* relation between words and things has come undone, *loci* of *social* communication. Of course, this is not dictated by a political "will to persuade," but has to do instead with a spiritual "will to hear" (a distinction which is not all that clear). In any case, a multiplication of "methods" produces and guarantees certain kinds of exchange, such as, in the example of St. Teresa, the community or *compañía*, the relation to authority or "spiritual guidance," and prayer or the "*colloquium*" with God. Other practices construct places of utterance ("foundations" or "retreats").

The establishment of these dialogic spaces is accomplished under the auspices of an essential, fundamental rule which has the status of their condition of possibility. It has the form of an exclusive stricture (*only*): the relation tolerates *only* people who are unshakably resolved. Everything hinges on a *volo*, without which there would be no speech. This prerequisite designates the summoned addressee: "I *only* address those who . . . ," says the mystic. Or, "God *only* speaks to those who . . . " Everywhere, from St. John of the Cross to Surin, this is a necessary "convention." It operates a closure: it delimits in language a path of circulation and a circumscription. It is the opposite of apologetic or predictive discourse based on the convention (for it is one also) of according statements an autonomous status allowing them to cross boundaries between groups. The threshold created by this stricture is expressed in a performative verb: *volo*. "Do not say 'I would' . . . but say 'I will,' " cautions Meister Eckhart.[57] Three and a half centuries later, Surin also summons his interlocutor to take "the first step": "a resolve to refuse nothing to God," effective "immediately,''[58] even though Surin, like Eckhart, affirms that the "will to do" is not the same as the "ability to do." This *volo* does not imply any particular object; it is at the same time *nihil volo* ("I want *nothing*") and "I only want *God*" (that is, "God must will for me").[59] In other words, "it is necessary to give form to the desire,"[60] a desire "tied to nothing."

With this founding act, the subject enters a retreat, it goes where the world's objects are absent. The subject is born of an exile and a disappearance. The "I" is "formed"—by its act of willing *nothing* or by (forever) *being incapable of doing* what it wills—as a "desire" bound only to the supposed desire of a Deity. It is created by the state of being nothing but the affirmation of a will. Aside from what it can do or be, it also functions as a linguistic convention; for by centering on "God," it sticks to a religious language in its very focus. It completes a contract with the interlocutor which goes beyond the uncertain range of particular statements to make a general affirmation: "I place my stakes in language," or "you can be certain that my desire awaits you in words." That is the assurance every addressee is given. It is what, in the vocabulary of the time, was termed "intention" or, in Surin, the "formal aspect" of communication. In this respect, the *volo* manifests and founds what no longer comes naturally—a contract of language which, because it has no property, takes the form of the lack and the desire of the other.

Corresponding to the establishment by a *volo* of a "convention" among addressees that functions to set them apart from non-addressees, there is a need on the part of the addresser (or the author) to found the place at which he speaks. The mystic text does not rely on statements authorized elsewhere, which it might repeat/comment in the name of the very institution that "uttered" them. It does, however, presuppose a "command" (like the one St. Teresa obeys by writing the *Libro de la Vida*[61]), a request (for example, Anne of Jesus' to St. John of the Cross to write his commentary, the *Cántico*[62]), or an apostolic mission (Surin, Angelus Silesius); but these "authorizations" resolve only one question, To whom should I write? and not that other, more fundamental question, Where should I write? That is the question the organization of every mystic text strives to answer: the truth value of the discourse does not depend on the truth value of its propositions, but on the fact of its being in the very place at which the Speaker speaks (the Spirit, "el que habla"). The texts always define themselves as being entirely a product of inspiration, though that inspiration may operate in very different modes. In every case, though, divine utterance is both what founds the text, and what it must make manifest. That is why the text is destabilized: it is at the same time *beside* the authorized institution, but outside it and *in* what authorizes that institution, i.e., the Word of God. In such a discourse, which claims to speak on behalf of the Holy Spirit and attempts to impose that convention on the addressee, a particular assertion is at work, affirming that what is said in this *place*, different from the one of magisterium language, is the *same* as what is said in the tradition, or else that these two places amount to the same.

Right from its Introït (Prologue, Preface, or Introduction), the text indicates its status by assigning its contracting parties their reciprocal places. A topography of personal pronouns suffices to effect this distribution of positions: an example is the Preface to Surin's *Science expérimentale*.[63] A commonplace (the text begins with the words, "one can take two paths to knowledge . . . ") lays out from the very start the disjunction around which the text is organized: *either* "faith" (the "common path") *or* "experience" ("for the few"). On one side, there is "knowledge by hearsay," originating with the "preaching of the Apostles"—that's *"us,"* all of us. The other side is defined by quotations in Latin from the New Testament, "quod vidimus, quod audivimus, quod manus nostrae contractaverunt . . . annuntiamus vobis"—that's *"them,"* the Apostles who, from a distance, contrast their *nos* to the *vobis* that "we" are. This opening places the author and reader on the same footing ("we"), based on a likelihood ("One can . . . ") and something already well known (that there is a present *we* opposed to a past *they*). The second paragraph shifts the scene and actualizes it. The Ancients' "experience" becomes contemporary ("In our own age," "in the middle of France") and the Apostles' experience ("them") becomes "our," although it remains reserved for the few and is always termed "extraordinary." The same passage functions as a transition. Switching back to French, it makes the speaker's "we" coincide with the Apostles' "we" ("we can also volunteer these words: that which we have seen . . . "), thus attributing to the author the "experience" and "extraordinary things" that justified the Apostles' writing ("that is why we have taken pen in hand"). Another "we" has appeared, in league with the Apostles, apart from the readers. A third action then strengthens the assent the "you" (readers) give the "we" (author), by making it hinge on "the faith *you* have in the words of the prophets" and "to which *we* are committed through our adherence to the Catholic religion." This knot ties "you" ("attentive" readers) to "we" (the author of "this discourse") by using the collective *we* ("you" plus "we") of shared belief. Then, gradually extracted from the initial "one" by a series of displacements, set apart from "all those to whom *we* speak in this book," there finally appears the "I" who "would like to do a service for eternity." In apostolic utterance, a subtle gradation of personal pronouns gives the "I" the right to address its readers. This convention puts the "I" *in the place* of the Apostles; the "I" speaks the language of the *other*. After this has been accomplished, it is possible to constitute a "science . . . of the things of the other life"—a heterology. But an "experimental" one, uttered by the "I" in *the present*, far removed from the common faith that has been subjugated by authority, in other words, by a "memory" which articulates the other of *the past*.

The presence of the subject as a speaker in the text he constructs is not a new thing. It dates from the twelfth century, with the troubadours and Dante.[64] What is impoortant here is the fact that the "I" in this case plays the role of a "shifter."[65] On the one hand, it confirms the "objectivity of the text," since the author (the subject of the utterance), the narrator (of the text), and the actor (the hero of the story) are bound together in a single "I," and since the "I" is by convention identical to a proper name. Thanks to this "referential pact," it bolsters the traditional syntagm with new reliability (saying "I believe that . . ." assumes that the subordinate proposition is not, or is no longer, self-evident). On the other hand, it designates both the reason for and the content of the discourse: *why* one writes and *what* one writes. In this way, it compensates for the lack of an ecclesial mission. The need to give personal witness intervenes when Church predication loses its value, when the delegating, missionary institution loses its credibility or neglects its duties. The "I" replaces the world as speaker (and the institution that is supposed to make it speak).

This accounts for the success enjoyed in the sixteenth century by autobiographies of spiritual leaders (but also of poets and memorialists), a trend that continued with Defoe's *Robinson Crusoe* and Rousseau's *Confessions*.[66] The autobiographical *I* is the (empty) space in which the discourse of subjectivity and individuality is constructed. It is defined on the basis of a signifier as a (proper) name,[67] ab-solute, un-bound from the world which no longer supports it, and as the reciprocal term of God, ab-solute, un-bound from the world He no longer supported as his language. This the *mythos* (that which founds speech) our civilization substitutes for the discourse of the cosmos; it is a "full" discourse spoken/produced by its speaker.

In this autobiographical literature, the *I* is both figurative and a figure, a symbolic representation. The figure, the third and last element to be discussed, is not utterative, except disguised as an image. It is, rather, an organizing factor. It marks *in* the text the *empty* place (empty of world) where the *other* speaks, following a process the discourse describes by *recounting its own production*. The opening chapter of St. Teresa's *Interior Castle*[68] illustrates the imaginary, formal schema that is common to so many mystics. Since she "could find nothing to say and had no idea how to begin," she beseeched "Our Lord today that He would speak through me": this discourse is *nothing* if it is not the *other* speaking (a position similar to Surin's). The scriptural experience of letting the other write is not an affair of theory, but takes place "today." But where will the other come from, in what space? At this point a "foundation" "offers itself." It is analogous to the dreams (*sueños*) from which St. Teresa's writing constantly departs. It is fiction, a nothing that causes one to speak and write, but it is also something "there is no point in fatiguing ourselves over by attempting to understand" or verify. It is not something true, it is only a thing of beauty (*hermosura*): "a castle made of a single diamond or of very clear crystal." Like Duchamp's "glass," it is a transparent, finite space that has no place of its own, yet includes "many dwellings." The models of the celestial Jerusalem (an apocalyptic image), of "paradise" (and image of the origin), and of "Heaven" (a cosmological image) become miniaturized and combine in a translucent gem where "He takes His delights."[69] Such is the "soul of the just." This beautiful object immediately unites opposites: it combines unity and a plurality of "dwellings" (*Moradas* [translated in English as "mansions]) which permit an itinerary to be drawn up; it is a strict delimitation[70] of a space one must "enter when one is in it already," a place where one dwells without dwelling there—and whose center is also exteriority (God). The coinciding of these opposites organizes the entire discursive formation devoted to the "interior castle" where, as Carmelite addressees are told, despite "how strictly cloistered you are," "you will take your delight" (*deleitaros*), "for you can enter it and walk about in it at any time without asking leave from your superiors."[71] That is exactly what St. Teresa does.

To what does this dream refer—this dream that opens up for her a free space in which to write (walk about), a space she can enter without permission (*sin licencia*), where she can find so many "treats" (*regalos*)? The subject, the garden of the other,[72] expresses itself in dreams. As with so many of the "palaces of love," retreats or mystic castles of her time—and also Van Helmont's [73] and Kepler's [74] *Somnium*—(the dream is the device utterance uses to provide, in the text, a figure for itself that answers the question, "quaenam in me esset Egoitas" (Van Helmont). There is a triple relation of the "I" to an imaginary *nothing*, an isolated (and atopic) locus outlined by the dream, and a *pleasure* [*jouissance*] which comes to the subject from the other. The subject is compared to "a person holding the candle in his hand, who is soon to die a death that he longs for; and in agony . . . is rejoicing with ineffable joy"—an erotic agony, "a glorious folly," a "heavenly madness" (*un glorioso desatino, una celestial locura*).[75]

It is in this place that St. Teresa's *Life* is written, as a journey to the center. It is a journey whose itinerary combines the normality of an *order* imposed from without, by history ("commands," missions, a series of institutional and rational dependencies), and the *gaps* created in it by irruptions of "folly" (coming from within, from the other, in the form of fictions, dreams, and apparitions). It is built out of this mixture. *Libro de la Vida*: St. Teresa's title already expresses the tension that makes her in-between place a mystic trace. The task of writing consists for her in "ordering," it consists of a chronological and didactic progression, a teaching through prayer requested by "them." But in spite of that, her "life" goes the way of dreams (*sueños*) and "follies" (*desatinos*), "surprises" that "lead her astray" and "ravish" her; it is a nostalgia (*tristezza*) that comes of not being unbound yet, of not being hidden at last by that elsewhere and other given only in fiction; it is to "die from not dying." It is also a nostalgia for an internal transparence that is impossible to achieve within existing relations, even religious ones. That nostalgia led Teresa to construct two transitory avatars of the "castle"—the book and the convent, her two consolations, her two strategies. The *book*: because it articulates dreams and desire in the common language and because that labor of articulation creates a poetic place. The *community* (or *buena compañía*): because it produces a shared speech (the *conversación*) among those who desire, and who agree on a common *volo*. The text (*libro*) and the convent (*fundación*) combine in the "constitution," the contract founding an island of utterance.

This island rising up from the world's black ocean recurs elsewhere as the imaginary schema of the "healthy body."[76] Later, it sets the stage for the development of the novel of the subject. But, little by little, it is turned inside out like a glove. The island, constituted as the space of the subject (with its "fortress" in the middle) and as a place to build, occurs in the modern myth, *Robinson Crusoe*—but now it is filled not with "delights," but with *labor*, not beatific transformation, but *production*. The island becomes a piece of *private* property whose boundaries are threatened by the trace of the other and the mad, "fluttering thoughts"[77] it engenders: thus writing of the other does not cause a disappropriation and a "glorious folly." The economic subject replaces the mystic subject; the factory island replaces the monastic island. In both cases, the island is the same empty stage, but with different operations inscribed upon it—transformational in one case, productive in the other. It grants the delightful "permission" to construct a biographical or autobiographical novel (or to let it be constructed) by a narrativizing of the *I*. Beginning with a proper name (biography) of the "I" (autobiography), the narrative gradually fills in the initial form with predicates, by means of a series of sequences: the scene is populated. This narrativity constitutes the original theological discourse, as seen from its relation to utterance.[78] But it is necessary, in the continuity of the dream, to read (or hear?) what is inscribed fundamentally in the place of the poem.

The Beginning, or the Poem

One may legitimately ask whether the psychological person, far from expressing itself in the personal pronoun, is not rather "an effect of utterance."[79] However that may be, it remains to be known *who* or *what* says "I." Is the "I" a fiction of the other, which offers itself in its place? St. Teresa, when discussing the crystal-castle that is the soul, speaks of a disappearance (ecstasy) or death that constitutes the subject as *pleasure* [*jouissance*] in the other. "I is an other"—that is the secret told by the mystic long before the poetic experience of Rimbaud, Rilke, or Nietzsche.[80] In a different mode, Angelus Silesius, in his role as the subject of a poetic work, expects his creation to be the "son" (or "daughter") of the word of the Other.[81] At the heart of mystic writing, there is something other that comes without reason: the poem and, secondarily, the dream. A "there is"—"es gibst," it gives (Heidegger)—is the beginning.

"Poetry is not born, it gives birth."[82] An approaching strangeness arrives, with an inevitability it founds and names at the same time; there is nothing outside it (not even meaning, for it comes from beyond) to confirm or authorize it. The poet, merely the utterer of this founding act of nomination, bends to its inevitability. He "belongs to that for which it is necessary." He makes way for the "event of the advent,"[83] of which time is *robbed*.

> A stranger it comes
> To us, that quickening word,
> The voice that moulds and makes human.[84]

The poem does what it says; it itself creates what it makes space for. But like the musician in Bosch's *Garden of Earthly Delights*, who is caught in his harp, his arms outstretched as though dead or passed out, played by the song that sends him into ecstasy, insane from being imprisoned in his instrument, that is, in the body of the voice of the other—the poet, too, is *robbed* by that excess which names but remains unnamable. In St. John of the Cross, the little pastor (*pastorcico*) blessed by love climbs a tree, where he dies, inscribing the lover's "trouble" in its branches with his open arms:

> se ha encumbrado
> sobre un árbol do abrío sus brazos bellos
> y muerto se ha quedado asido de ellos
> el pecho del amor muy lastimado.[85]

This kind of poetry is not what the mystics say they "write," a term reserved for commentaries or treatises. It writes itself. It was for a long time, up to St. Teresa, called "the music of the angel"—an angel which "gives body to the advent of a measure."[86] It arrives *before* the hour of labor, "at the time of the rising dawn."[87] The "música callada," silent music,[88] comes first. But from where? Kant spoke of the "rhapsodic beginning of thought." Here, the poem engenders the possibility of existing (as other or otherwise). It begins. But even the beginning has a beginning. Dante recounts that "my tongue moved of its own accord," and his verse arose like a musical air; he decided "to keep these words in mind and use them as a beginning" for a poem yet to come, but which was already there waiting.[89] St. John of the Cross says that sometimes God would give him the words to his poems, and sometimes he would look for them,[90] laboring to follow the track of the "given words." Therefore, he makes a distinction between the "canciones" and his commentary (or "declaración"), which is, strictly speaking, the only thing he writes. While all writing is a demand for love, the "dichos de amor" in particular partake of an unexpected, unexplainable "abundance and impetuousness." Without reason, the *too much* of a "plenitude" overflows the space in which it reveals itself. "What is explainable in it" (*declara*) is only the *least* of it, or the effect it produces in a particular field (of language, of exchanges, of questions), that is, in a mode of writing giving form to one of the possible "meanings" generated by the poem.[91] For Surin also, the poem that comes

> I want to run through the world
> And live the life of a lost child[92]

is not something wholly apart from prose. Instead—born in the "dungeon" in Bordeaux where this "madman" was imprisoned, just as St. John's *Cántico* was born in a prison in Toledo—it appears inside prose, breaking it down into fragments around which text proliferates.

Where, then, is the poem? Where, by itself, without explanation, does it obtain the power "to produce love and affection in the soul"?[93] In what sense is it mystical? These three questions are answered in the writing of St. John of the Cross.

For him, the "canciones" are of such "breadth and plenty" (*archura y copia*) that they "touch (*toca*: burn and penetrate) everything."[94] An excess of fire, occurring at every possible turn in history. This *abundancia* is best guaranteed and most readable in the Scriptures, but it is not more real or efficient there than it is in the poem. *The same* abundance "touches" the poet today as touched the inspired writers of antiquity. There is certainly not the same Church recognition of both, but they share *the same* "impotence" to make that understood, except by using "strange figures and similitudes." Thus, the poem comes at the same place at which the Scriptures speak (more exactly, it is the place where what is said in the Scriptures can "be heard" [s'entendre]), but it does not enjoy the same status. It has not been granted a Church alliance, so even if there are no internal differences, in order to interpret (*declarar*) the poem in the Church, in order to teach and comment on it, it is nevertheless necessary for it to be "confirmed" by the "authority of the Divine Scriptures."[95]

It is in the form of interpretation in a didactic situation that discourse is committed to memory, that historical or institutional alterity. The poem as such does not depend on it any more than that other space, the castle or "garden of delights" St. Teresa's readers may "walk about in at any time without asking leave" of their superiors. The poem has a radical autonomy. Did not St. Ignatius of Loyola, speaking in the third person of his own visions, those unwritten poems, say that "if there were no Scriptures to teach us these matters of the faith, he would be resolved to die for them, only because of what he had seen"?[96] His is a more ambiguous statement, since it presupposes that what he "saw" and the "truths" of the faith are the same. For St. John of the Cross, on the other hand, the Christian exegesis of a poem or vision is an effect of writing and didactics, and is just one of the traces and one of the "meanings" made possible by the "given words."

These "canciones," which are in principle separable from their "declaración" (even though the evolution of the commentary is undoubtedly associated with revisions of the *Cántico*[97]), in addition seem like a love poem. Religious allusions are absent in their content: all proper names and references have been purged, undermining the "Christian" realist illusion. This indication of what makes the poem poetic refers to the form of the "canciones," or more precisely, to their phonetic body. Here, an organization of (erotic) *meaning* serves as the support for an organization of (musical) *sounds*.[98] The *Cántico* is written in the tradition of the *cantar en romance*; using the rhythm of the *lira stanza* (strophes of five verses, two with eleven feet, three with seven), it abounds in rich rhyme patterns, internal assonance and phonic repetitions, all within a structure transferring the words, pronouns, and verbs of the one (*thee*) to the other (*me*): a music of echoes and minor images in which the *Amado* is doubled, bursts, and retrieves himself in the gaze and advent of the other[99]—but which other? Saussure's anagram rule and Ruwet's rule of parallelism—both of which establish the primacy of the signifier over the signified—here seem to be confirmed by the play of nouns ("wound," "quest," etc.), which shift freely from one position to the other, thus destroying the stability of the characters to whom they are attached.

The poem—a cadenced repetition, "generative palilogy,"[100] subtle glossolalia[101]—does not stop at deconstructing meaning and making it music: it is what allows the very production of meaning. The "taste for echoes" awakened by the poem leads one "to seek a semantic connection between elements nothing binds together semantically";[102] it makes possible the indefinite prolongation of this semantical research as an echo effect. It says nothing. It permits saying. For that reason, it is a true "beginning." It is a liberating space, where yesterday's readers—but "we" also—can find speech. The "canciones" did not lay down a meaning once and for all; they created a place of origin for "love effects."

In what sense is this "convulsive beauty," which is "erotic—veiled, exploding—stable, magical—circumstantial,"[103] also mystical? If the musical secret of its efficacy is not answer enough, one could advance some tentative hypothesis: it is possible that the "mystical" character of the poem is located at the meeting point of the poetic and the religious; it could simply be the walk of the "goddess" as she crosses (and leaves) the Christian realm. What would be mystical, then, is the disappearance of the actors (the lover and the loved one, God and man) whereas the transactions between them prevail: "God and I are one in the transaction."[104] The "canciones" inscribe the movement of these transformations of action and agony in the very words and characters they deprive both of meaning and a place to be. Mystical also would be the relation of the poem to the religious tradition whose statements it presupposes, but uses in order to make them say the absence of what they designate. It is by taking words seriously, a life and death game in the body of language, that the secret of what they give is torn from them—and, as St. John of the Cross says in relation to the "holy doctors," to do that is to make them confess the secret of their "impotence," of what they cannot "give." One more thing, perhaps, is mystical: the establishment of a space where change serves as a foundation and saying loss is an other beginning. Because it is always *less* than what *comes* through it and allows a genesis, the mystic poem is connected to the *nothing* that opens the future, the time *to come*, and, more precisely, to that single work, "Yahweh," which forever makes possible the self-naming of that which induces departure.[105]

Chapter 7
Surin's Melancholy

Every biography organizes vestiges into a coherent picture. It frames a fiction. But rather than recounting a mystical, pathological "case history" from the Classical Age, I would prefer to present a collage of disconnected facts and fragments of writing, a portrait in pieces. Jean-Joseph Surin made his appearance on the seventeenth century scene like Dubuffet's Hourloupe, bearing the "title" of madman—"that fine posy on his hat, which no one would ever want."[1]

Surin was born in Bordeaux in 1600 and died there sixty-five years later. His family, originally of the merchant class, had moved up to join the *noblesse de robe*. His father, an honest and able member of the Bordeaux parliament, achieved modest success, only to find it undermined by a painful, unavowed recognition of its insignificance. His mother, on the other hand, became active and invaded the public domain. She was ubiquitous—philanthropist, church-goer, frondeur, political figure. She became in the end a Carmelite nun—a most privileged position to have in the Counter-Reformation urban world. When Surin, more than sixty years old, emerged from his imprisonment in despair to find unexpected happiness, he could only compare his joy to an experience he had at the age of eight: to avoid the plague, he had been sent to spend the autumn in the country, and was "left *alone* with a governess." In this time long past, spent in a "wonderful place," "in fear of no one," far from his mother, he had seen the open spaces of "freedom."[2] A younger sister named Jeanne, a Carmelite amazon who died at thirty-five "with the odor of sanctity," seems to have been Pascal's Jacqueline to sad-eyed d'Artagnan, that Don Quixote of mysticism who joined the Jesuits but was soon after rejected, then praised by the Jansenists, an incongruous "madman of the Lord" amid the celebrated Colleges of the Society of Jesus.

Surin, a brilliant intellectual, wanted nothing to do with humanist "reason," which conceals vanity beneath its efficacity. "Pangs," migraines, paralyses, periods during which he was unable to read—various languages of existential "despair"—interrupted his studies and early endeavors. Nevertheless, he was sent to Loudun in December of 1634, after Urbain Grandier, a parish priest accused of sorcery, had been burned at the stake.[3] The pyre had failed to close the curtain on the theater of demonic possession. Since they had already tried fire, they called in the holy invalid. His task was to exorcize and heal Jeanne des Anges, the principal figure among the possessed. Surin knew that he was not a saintly person, but one exiled from salvation. For three years following, he expressed his anguish in the spectacular language of a diabolical struggle against God. To save the possessed, he offered to assume her burden of aliena-tion. Kierkegaard was later to analyze this "satisfaction in suffering," in partic-ular, the melancholic satisfaction he says he found in "turning all the scorn and mistreatment of the crowd on me."[4] They performed a positional chiasmus on the public stage of Loudun: the exorcist became the possessed. The discovery of the body of the other (Jeanne des Anges); the dramatization of the body's otherness. In the end, they accompanied him from Loudun to be locked away in the infirmary of the Bordeaux College. He was practically incapable of talk-ing, writing, walking, or controlling his "extravagances."

"They gave me a brother to take care of me and act as my supervisor. . . . Although he was a man of good enough character, my great extravagances would annoy him. . . . One day . . . he became so impatient . . . that he took a large, knotted cudgel and repeatedly hit me with it on the head. It is a wonder he did not fracture my skull. I knew he was going to beat me, and never-theless I did nothing to let him know my frame of mind. He also delivered at various times several blows to my face, enough to leave it marked all over with marks and black contusions. People who saw me asked what had happened. I said they were old war wounds. . . . "[5]

In addition to his "ridiculous actions," Surin had "the thought" that he was "already condemned and rejected by God." That, for him, was something quite different from madness:

"This image will seem like only a hollow thought to others, like a dream my mind made up, because the natural, common sense upon which our faith is built bolsters us to such a degree against these things of the other life that, as soon as a man says he is damned, the others judge that it is only madness. But mad-ness is ordinarily in the ideas someone conceives, and even more naturally it is something like hypochondriacs have. They are all the same: one will say he is an idiot, another will say he is a cardinal. These ideas are legitimately held to be mad. But what Father [Surin] said was not like that."⁶ Surin quotes mystics to prove his point: "This is not madness, but extreme suffering in the spirit."

The distinction Surin makes between "extravagances" and "suffering" does not exclude their coexistence. All it does is to distinguish the "thought" of being damned from a mad "idea." According to seventeenth century conceptions, an individual with melancholic or hypochondriacal madness persistently combines an *image* (an "idea" or "dream" which is in itself neither true nor false) with an affirmative *judgment* ("I am" the thing I imagine or dream).⁷ The madness consists in the tenacity of the judgment and the logical conclusions the melancholic draws from it. But with the conviction of being damned, something quite different is at play; it concerns consciousness itself, consciousness as something *excluded from the real*, thrown outside it, kept at a distance, a stranger to the world of the signified. Or, in the language of religion, something set out on the doorstep of the real, of God, abandoned and rejected by Him. Of course, existing as refuse in this way, living in a fallen state, still allows the subject to retreat into an "interior" where knowledge of the world grows as one's own being falls into decay. In the unfolding of "Melancholia," which during the Renaissance was a characteristic of genius, the totalization of the observed coincides with the nothingness of the observer. At this extreme, what is in question is the very discourse which consciousness produces—a discourse hounded from the real, absolute, unbound, and reduced to being *nothing* in *all* that it speaks of. From this point of view, the thought of damnation is the elucidation and agony of the exclusion from which the subject's faculty of speech originated. Thus Surin writes, "in his consciousness he did not judge it mad to believe he was damned."⁸ The "thought" of damnation is less the object of his affirmation and certainty than its motivation. It produces the "belief" rather than being produced by it: it is what puts consciousness in the position of not being being, and thus—since the Supreme Being is a Will—of being deliberately excommunicated by it.

But as long as consciousness is alive, in an animate body, it still inhabits, illegally, the land from which it was driven. It is disobeying the "order of God" which excluded it. "I also believed that this law of God was hurrying me to present myself in hell. I had such an impetuous wish to kill myself that anytime I came upon a well as I was going along the road I would run four or five steps to hurl myself into it. . . . When I was at rest, in my room or in my bed, I would always be thinking of ways of getting out and throwing myself into the water, or into a well, or out the window, so that the justice of God would be done. I often went during the night and stood by the windows facing the street, wanting my body to be found the next morning on the paving stones. . . . I would get up during the night to get knives to cut my throat. . . . At least a hundred times I went from my room to the sacristy to hang myself behind the tabernacle of the Blessed Sacrament, and my joy would be to be found there hanging."[9] Whose eye would experience this joy when it gazed upon the body from which Surin had been exiled?

The transition from wish to action took place on May 17, 1645, at Saint-Macaire, a small residence perched high atop the banks of the Garonne River. He had been taken there by the Jesuits of Bordeaux so he would be "removed from the world's view." On that day, "as he entered (his room), he saw that the window was open. He went up to it and, after considering the precipice, for which he had such a furious instinctive attraction, he withdrew to the middle of the room, still facing the window. There, he lost all consciousness and suddenly, as though asleep and unable to see what he was doing, he hurled himself out the window and was thrown to the ground thirty feet from the base of the wall, right at the water's edge, clad in his robe, with slippers on his feet and his cap on his head. The popular account is that he fell on the rocks and rolled to the river's edge, prevented from falling into the water by a small willow that became wedged between his legs. When he fell, he broke his thigh bone, high up near the hip joint."[10]

The poems Surin wrote during this period of his confinement were inspired by the act of "hurling oneself":

> I want to run through the world,
> And live the life of a lost child;
> I have caught the humor of a vagabond soul,
> After scattering all my goods,
> It is one to me whether I live or I die,
> All that I ask is for love to remain with me.[11]

The poem adopts the form of a travel account or legend, with progressive stages "testing" the caliber of the hero and illustrating his qualities. But here the triumphs have turned into losses; stanza by stanza, the "I" (in this case the hero) is gradually divested of the physical, intellectual, and moral attributes each successive episode is supposed to confer upon him. The story, instead of showering the main character with predicates, strips them away; the hero is hollowed out. The poem moves toward the "fortunate shipwreck" that constitutes the subject—separated from all predicates—through a process in which every possible good is lost or rejected. The narration turns the "I" into an empty space, which the last stanza then fills with a worthy name, the signifier of the other—the name of Jesus:

> My only remaining wish is to imitate the madness
> of Jesus, who one day on the cross,
> For his pleasure, lost both his honor and his life,
> Relinquishing all to save his love.

It is one to me whether I live or I die,
All that I ask is for love to remain with me.[12]

The "pleasure" of losing (oneself) is perhaps what initiated the process, marked by alternating periods of exaltation and depression, which allowed Surin slowly to regain his faculties, beginning in 1647–1648. In 1655, he was still persuaded that he was damned and "expelled from all good"; but it was in that year that the encounter he credits with his "cure" took place. Without lecturing, the priest who came to take his confession "told me that he had great compassion for me, but that he had to tell me his secret: 'I am not,' he said, 'a man who has revelations or puts much faith in instincts. Nevertheless, I must tell you that I have often had the impression, coming neither from my imagination nor from my own senses, that before you die our Lord will have the mercy to let you see that you are mistaken . . . and I hope that you die in peace.' These words had a strong impression on me." After the priest left, "I pondered whether it was actually possible that our Lord could have mercy on me. . . . Then I heard in my heart these vital words pronounced by our Lord . . . : 'Yes, it is possible!' These words, spoken inside me, gave my soul life and revived it."[13] A mutual alteration, an "impression" made by one person on another, thus forms a crack in the system: "Maybe I am not damned."[14]

It was the year before (1654) that Surin, unable to write, dictated to a cooperative friend who came to visit him at the infirmary his most celebrated work, the *Catéchisme spirituel*. It comprises three volumes, all of which he composed in his head while awaiting the precious sessions his scribe would grant him. He emerges from his "dungeon." "If it is a question of transmitting words of love on your behalf, I will go, O my King, with the golden trumpet and stand in the center of the public square. . . . "[15] This "expansion" was following the preceding "narrowing." In 1655, in solitude, he wrote (again in his head) four volumes of the *Dialogues spirituels*. One day when his friend was late for their writing session he felt "a heated desire to produce my thoughts," and "out of impatience, I picked up the pen and acted as though I were going to write. I had written next to nothing in over eighteen years. But in this heated state, it happened that two or three pages were written, though the letters were so confused they hardly seemed human. After that, I continued to write every day for a month."[16] His hand begins to move across the paper. The "interior" finds an "outlet" allowing it to escape its confinement. The excluded becomes embodied and appears on the outside.

His texts went into circulation at the same time as their author began to stir. The *Catéchisme spirituel* was published in 1657. The distribution of his letters and manuscript writings proceeded at too fast a pace for the liking of the Jesuit "party," which was troubled by their popularity. They traveled to parts foreign or hostile to Surin's home institution: to Jansenist circles, for example (they were fond of his evangelical philosophy preaching withdrawal from the world seductive), and even to China. Hobbling along with the mark of despair branded on his haunch, Surin would thenceforth speak, write, and work in suspicion, though with a feeling of "peace" bringing the child's intense but transitory joys back to an aging man to stay. "These are not the only things that can make a man take pen in hand, or negotiate and speak; it can come about from pure joy. . . . Divine love has its serious uses, in war or peace; it has its tasks and many worthy occupations calling the friends of God and his faithful servants. But beyond that, it has its games, its comedies, its fine pleasures, its beautiful promenades, its fires answering to the artificial fires of principle. It has its music and songs of the mind. It has its balls, its dances. . . . "[17]

Throughout this period, from December 1634 to February 1665, there developed an astonishing body of "correspondence" between Surin and Jeanne des Anges. Jeanne des Anges, the star of the possessed of Loudun, had gone on to become a prophetess heading a spiritual network, and even became a necromancer who was consulted in the name of the angel and departed souls who spoke to her. Even though Surin had misgivings about her "setting up shop" with her Angel and running "something akin to an agency for finding out what to do,"[18] she was still "the only person in whom I have enough confidence to tell . . . my deepest thoughts."[19] Her death marks the end of a language: "I will never communicate with anyone like I did with her."[20] An exchange of bodies at Loudun (one possessed person took the place of the other) had led to an interchange of words; that exchange is what made it possible for the other to wound/open Surin's solitary "interior," creating, by means of this bodily alteration, the possibility of a dialogue.

The Signifier, or the Body in Excess

Two scenes described in *Science expérimentale* allow us to clarify the status of the body and of the signifier. In the first, "a love-filled attraction of the heart" draws the patient to his window to view from above the procession of the Blessed Sacrament through the streets of Bordeaux. This scopic drive is thwarted by the "deep terror" and "fright" Surin feels the moment he "lays eyes" on the love object: it "seemed to me that an operation occurred in my mind, functioning as intellectual vision, in which I thought I saw Jesus Christ in the Eucharist, in the form of an armed man throwing thunderbolts at me." The "attraction" that "makes one look" meets an angry gaze which strikes it with lightning.[21] The tangible object within the field of love suddenly becomes a Viewer who, rising up from the back of the picture (as in certain paintings), towers above the onlooker, and in a fury transforms him into something *seen*.[22] Then Surin "falls" and flees, "saving myself from the presence of this terrible God." The "pre-existence of a gaze"[23] surprises him and turns the famished voyeur (he was devouring the procession with his eyes) into the object excluded from the view of the Other, whose autonomy is represented by those eyes armed with anger.

"Intellectual vision" refers to a thought ("I thought I saw"). An act of knowing and/or a hallucination discloses, in the seen, the opposite of what was expected. Thus, in fantasy, things prove to be the *authors* of operations of which they are normally believed to be the objects. A troubling instability intervenes mid-way between the expectation that frames what one sees and the thought (or "operation of the mind") that allows the object to become the subject of an action again (prompting it to burst out of its frame)—between *seeing* (which dominates things) and the *impression of seeing* (which gives things the magical ability to act as a subject, imposing relations of power on another subject). This instability, in fact, brings the epistemology of the Classical Age into focus—it was caught between the world of sorcery and the objectified world. What is seeing? Surin stresses the "terrible" exteriority of the Other. He stands by what he *thinks* he saw.

The experience in the second scene, which was often repeated (as was the first), seems to be the opposite of the previous one: it involves the certitude ("without error") of an internalization of exteriority through the sense of taste. Surin, speaking of his sensation of the bread and wine of the Eucharist, says that "although it is totally contrary to what the scholastics and philosophers say . . . my tongue senses God and tastes God just as it tastes a grape or apricot or melon." He detects the "bodily taste" of "a being who is obviously none other than God"—not qualities, but the "substance" of God.[24] This "feeling," which he experienced only when he was ill, establishes an opposition between sight and taste. The being he sees rejects him and strikes him with lightning; the being he tastes is inside him and "restores" him. These "delights," "treats," and "tasty morsels" do not just place in question the exaltations which follow the melancholic's depressive episodes; they have the force of something "extraordinary," "supernatural," or ecstatic. This sensation, like the drug addict's, pulls Surin out of himself through the touch of the other. It is thus the reverse of the first scene, where he is left to himself, rejected by the other. The same break separating the being-there of the body from the signifier of the other is reproduced, once in the register of sight (the organ of the distant) and once in the register of taste (the organ of the near). Everything points to the conclusion that the difference between the two scenes lies in the fact that with sight the separation involves an exteriority to the other, while with taste it is a question of an exteriority to self.

Surin's sense of taste is also an eroticism of the tongue; it extends to tactile perceptions. He speaks of "a sensation of taste and of the internal membranes of the palate and stomach." He is not referring to the act of eating, which occupies an important place in the Christian conception of the Eucharist; he is therefore not referring to a social, symbolic (ecclesial) *rite* securing its participants' alliance with God, but to a subjective act of *knowing* which parallels the rite (and can be substituted for it), gives *certitude*, and is *erotic* in form. This experience of the mouth and mucous membranes gives the communion a guarantee similar to the one, in Descartes, which the blindman's touch provides the uncertain perception of the sighted. The fact that these intimate palpations and "touches" reveal the "divine being" as something "potable," like a kind of elixir or *hypocras*,[25] is in keeping with the view, widely held, in the first half of the seventeenth century (including Descartes[26]), that the universe was malleable and fluid, composed of "liquors." Also characteristic is that the "internal membranes" constitute, within the body, beaches touched by fluidity. The interior, also, has shores "touched" by a distant sea. The body, like the world itself in Jules Verne (in *Journey to the Center of the Earth*), is hollow. It is a cave inhabited by the "snares of the belly" (Groddeck). The entire body is a "mouth." It has internal shorelines that "kiss," in delicious undulations, the approaches of the other.[27] The problem is that there exists—and this is what is essential for Surin—something which does not deceive.

The theological discourse of the seventeenth century sheds light on the form and the function of this certitude. I will mention one fundamental characteristic. Ockham, the modernist, the *Inceptor* as he was called, pioneered the notion, which gained general currency in theologians' opinion, that divine power is foreign to any theological or metaphysical system of rationality. One day, God may will salvation and, the next, the annihilation of an entire nation. Our reason has no stable connection with his decisions. Even as he declared that the "prose of the world"—that is, the readability of the world as a meaningful discourse—had fallen into ruin, the Inceptor could already pinpoint its historical consequences (or causes): the proliferation of singular and absurd experiences, and the reenforcement of institutional and dogmatic powers. The majority of mystics dwell in the vicinity of those ruins. Coupled with this nominalism are a variety of sensual and/or spiritual empirical systems (only the singular is recognized) and, on the other hand, the "positive" theologies developing the "ideas" of authorized texts (biblical, conciliar, or patristic) with the goal of preserving all of their content, even though nothing in that content could aid in finding in the truth.

From a logical point of view, Ockham's central formulation, the *potentia absoluta*, combines two propositions that are in themselves incompatible: 1) meaning exists; 2) it is unthinkable. This power, unbound (ab-solute) from all knowing and veridiction, is still held to be "God," but now nothing more than that can be said about it. God has ceased to be a signified, becoming purely a signifier, the mark of a truth henceforth absent from discourse, the graph to which any force troubling the order of our reason can be ascribed, the mechanism that catapults our conceptions and experiences beyond their normal bounds. Basically, Surin takes this logic to its extreme, while the politics of institutions and positive systems of knowledge—which are for him irrelevant—compensate for its effect.

For anyone seeking interior certitude, all that remains, in the absence of truth, is the relation between *force* and the *singular*. Just as damnation was the existential enactment of the "potentia absoluta"—a way of being expelled from God's reason while at the same time maintaining one's exteriority in the form of a will—singular and erotic knowing which "restores" being is the only outlet left open for Surin by the system he leads to its final conclusions. The more singular, or "extraordinary," it is, the more convincing it is, to the extent that the "touch" imprints a force reason cannot know. All knowledge is erotic—due to the terrifying, or delicious, change that turns the body itself into an incomprehensible [*méconnaissable*] realm, rendered unreadable by the intervention of the unknown. This mad experience is not unconnected to the sensible theory, current at Port-Royal from Barcos to Sacy, which held that "darkness" and "disorders" are the mark of the Spirit in the biblical text, the index of a poetic energy that agitates discourse by emotionally moving the reader.[28] For Port-Royal, the text is the place of this meaningless thing that frightens or seduces by its "touching"; for Surin it is the body.

It should be added that Surin's madness, whether it adopts the figure of damnation or that of taste, has the final effect of emphasizing the body itself. With an input of too little or too much meaning, the body produces a surplus. Excluded or caressed, its position is outside absolute will. The excess of hate or love which exiles Surin, first from the other, then from himself, renders the relation to the body ex-orbitant by diminishing or destroying the *locus proprius* [*le propre*]. An ecstasy constitutes the "I" by the loss of the ego—it is an "I" carried to incandescence, in-finite, because the other is not a particular, but only the signifier of a forever unlocalizable, in-finite exteriority. In other words, the impossibility of a limited meaning, or the rejection of a circumscribed appropriation, valorizes the emptied *place* where the certitude of being excluded or altered by the other arises—the certitude of being not-thee and not-me, endlessly. The "I" is certified by its own alienation.

Damnation can also be interpreted in terms of the distinction between statements and the act of utterance. It is the exile of the speaker from the realm of verisimilitude, from the system of statements transmitted as true (or false). Damnation places the speaking subject outside language, for no other reason than that an absolute will wills it so, and not in accordance with a just command. Damnation is itself a part of what organizes mystic discourse on the basis of this bracketing, this ob-scene hole or excommunication. Essentially, for the mystic (and this also applies to prophets and men of inspiration), the problem is not so much to know whether the statements that have been handed down are true or false (and thus subject to the human judgment that sorts them out), but rather to know *if* someone is addressing someone else through them, and if so, *who* it is that is speaking. These two strategic questions treated in mystic literature also take the form of demonstratives: orison (prayer) and "spiritual guidance" (the dialogue between master and student, and more generally, between believers). In other words, the mystic asks: Does God address man, and vice versa? and, Is there an utterative contract among believers? Those questions concern the speech act. To St. John of the Cross, the Spirit is "el que habla," the speaker;[29] utterance is what is actuated in language, or out of language, in any case as distinct from it. In this mystic region, all that matters is *invocatio, auditio, conversar, tratar con Dios*, etc.[30]

Damnation exaggerates the break that established the distinction between statement and utterance. It places the entire body of statements between brackets, as something irrelevant, and only retains the (interrupted) relation between the two interlocutors. All that remains is the encounter of two incomprehensibly opposed subjects, or, what comes to the same thing, of two subjects tied together by a dark fury which remains for them the trace of a lost common language. The two of them are all that is left, and they are only held together by what divides them—the "anger" of one and the "hate" the other feels for Jesus, who was God's "favorite."[31] A fight to the death, in which the Strong (God) prevails over the weak (Surin) and arbitrarily favors a third (Jesus). At about the same time that Surin was writing, Jacob Boehme (1575–1624), although not personally a casualty of this war, identified its battleground as God himself: in the Beginning, was Will-Desire, the shadowy rage of the Father against the disobedient Son amidst a circulation of Death (the Spirit).[32] God creates himself out of anger, or pure difference, the Absolute. His mute battle against another— a struggle lacking a Logos—is thus what engenders Him.

If instead of fighting the Father's fury the son admits defeat, then he is in the position of being damned: this is the case with Surin, except that he continues to mark his difference with the "hate" and "horrible jealousies" that "so naturally" come "from himself." Surin, like Boehme, presents the blind and instinctive rebellion of a son to his father, but his outlandish struggle runs counter to the discourse of reason, which demands subservience to the incomprehensible decrees of the Absolute. Thus Surin becomes the other of the Other.

On the Name and Writing

The name, then, is what organizes the entire experience, and mystic writing follows from it. We will discuss first the status, then the functioning, of the name. With damnation—the "impossible hypothesis" which, up to Fénelon, was approached in the context of "pure" and disinterested love ("suppose I am damned, I would love Him no less")—the name of God is placed in the position of being *unthinkable* and *authorizing* at one and the same time. It is all the more authorizing precisely because it is itself authorized by no reason or system of thought. Therefore, it is not the experience that guarantees the existence of God: God, on the contrary, guarantees the experience.[33] The name is authorized by nothing. For that reason, its status is *poetic*—if Edmond Jabès is correct in saying that poetry is what nothing authorizes.

It is important to add, however, that the status of the name protects a transmitted position. It maintains the authority of the religious institution and, more radically, preserves an indefinite reserve of meaning precisely at the point where it ceases to be thinkable. With the aid of this name, the meaningless can always be overcome, for there is, there must be, somewhere (God) some meaning from which we are excluded or which escapes us. That is where the "shrewdness" of which Julia Kristeva speaks comes in. Perhaps the problem is not that there exists, lodged in language, an index of something that does not deceive (there is no thought or discourse that does not find it necessary to postulate one, if only by assigning that role to writing itself). The problem is rather that the index (the word "God") is located exactly where a system of thought defining an order was articulated. The problem is that the authorizing name remains where thought was. It remains engraved there, on the ruins of an order of discourse. As a consequence, this unthinkable relic of a system of thought is in constant danger of being fetishized as the substitute for a loss and/or absence: "I know, I know, but still . . . "[34]

In the mystic experience, the name has two functions. In order to clarify the distinction between them, I will draw examples (admittedly in too summary a fashion) from St. John of the Cross and Surin, even though their writing also evinces the interconnections between the two operations. In the first, the name of God constantly reintroduces something other around the borders of every system of knowledge and every pleasure [*jouissance*]. It is a mechanism of exteriority, an "open sesame" working inside meaning, moving outward in relation to all cognitive or affective states. It is a principle of travel. Something akin to the Lover's repetition of the phrase he addresses to the Shulamite in the *Song of Solomon* (2.17): "flee away"—*Leave*. Likewise, the *Ascent of Mount Carmel* sends the hierarchical order of systems of knowledge and pleasures on an endless voyage, entirely by the force of a "something else again": "This is not it. There is something other." "God" is a tool of dissuasion in every place, a *password*. It makes things pass. It dis-places; it is a "short word . . . of one syllable," "the shortest possible word" (*God* or *Love*, "choose which you like, or perhaps some other"); it is an operative signifier, a part functioning as the *lapsus* or *raptus* the *Cloud of Unknowing* recommends for use.[35]

For Surin also, God is first a password; but another, sometimes ex-orbitant, function of the name is more noticeable in his writing than in St. John of the

Cross'. The name has the power to *construct a body*. It embodies. This second function has doubtless been at the principle of Christian tradition from the beginning. Unlike Judaism, Christianity founded a discourse (the evangelical *Logos*) which offers "consolation" for the loss of the body. The Name replaces the body. The Pentecost, the birth of a message that is not bound to a place, was substituted for the lost being-there of Jesus. It established a lost-body discourse. But then it was necessary for the Name to construct a world: it had to create a Bible (a corpus, a totalization), a Church (a social body of meaning), and an ontology (a universal administration of being). The progression was from the *Name*—arising out of the *nothing* which the body had become—to *writing*, which was in turn destined to redefine and constitute *history*. Leaving aside these generalizations on the Christian paradigm, the sixteenth and seventeenth century mystics, and particularly Surin, seem to represent a variation on the paradigm, transposed to the individual level. The name given to the child is the demonstrative for his body to be constructed. As in Surin's poem on the lost child, a series of deductions is necessary to deprive being-there of its attributes, in order for a name to occupy its emptied place and create a body in and of itself [*un corps propre*]. There are thus three steps in this schema: a *body in excess* (destined to pass away), a *Name* (a "nothing" that authorizes, a "fable" that incites speech), and an *added discourse* (a body that is produced, a body of writing).

This body inferred from a name evokes the body Schreber modeled on the name he had received—*Luder*, whore and putrefaction. President Schreber produced a female, disseminated body for himself, a body that engendered and proliferated uninterruptedly until it became a world. It created itself to fit its name. It became its name incarnate, *Luder*.[36] This act of nomination gave him an identity that was all the more strict and totalizing due to the fact that the tiniest crack in that feminine cosmology built upon the name would precipitate a disaster, the "end of the world." Surin also identified with the name that turned him into one of the "damned" (the Word took on body). He lent performative force to that label (the word did what it named): he threw the lost object that he was out the window. But with him, there is always an exteriority maintained by the name of the other (God), which creates an unbridgeable gap. By virtue of a "loss" that is sometimes the fact of "despair," other times "for His pleasure," Surin has to *be*, in turn, he who is *called* "damned" (the rejected son) and he who is *called* the "Chosen One" (Jesus); this vacillation does not change the fact that he is overpowered by a deictic or demonstrative element (it could be any proper name) that is directed at or designates him. That is where the function of the name as a password enters in.

This brings us back to the question of writing, in relation to the poem. We can discern in mystic writing the intersection of the two functions of the name outlined above. In its capacity as something that effects a passage, the name traces in language the principle of its exile, and this work of the "something else again" is as interminable as language itself. We are never done passing on, as long as we have the force. As in the previously cited poem, writing is the result of this "race," which is ever a "loss," because no step along the way is *it*. If we designate the stages of "loss," as A_1, A_2, . . . A_i, etc., and if we use Ω to designate, not any term of the series, but that in the *name* of which the passage from A_i to A_{i+1}, etc. is made, and that which outside the series allows that passage, we then have the following formula to express each stage:

$$A_i = \text{not } \Omega$$

There is no possibility of finding a resting point at A_{i+1} or at A_{i+2}, etc. Each time, "this is not it." That means that:

$$A_{i+1} = \text{not } A_{i+2}$$

This state is therefore non-identical to itself. It is undermined without its knowing it by a send-back to some other. Using the categories of the *Logique* of Port-Royal, we could also say that every "substantive or absolute term" in some way becomes adjectival, transformed into a "mode of being" or a "modified thing," by virtue of its relation to an "absolute."[37] This "absolute" does not "subsist by itself,"[38] it is off-stage. It is a name. It is not something that "remains" (like a substance) or "holds together" (like a symbol), but something that induces a departure. Mystic writing is this adjectivation of language. It narrativizes an endless exodus of discourse. It is the discourse of the drift of discourse effected by stylistic procedures (metaphor, oxymoron, etc.), and its focal point is the *neither . . . nor*. Thus we have the following "song" written by Surin:

> Felicitous death, felicitous tomb,
> Of this lover in love absorbed,
> Who now sees neither grace nor nature
> But only the abyss into which he has fallen,
> It is one to me whether I live or I die . . . [39]

Language becomes "mystical" when it is transformed into a "manner of speaking" (*modus loquendi* is what the mystics called it)—this comes across in the *Logique* of Port-Royal, where words meant to signify a "manner" are termed "adjectives." It is the endless, multifold adjective of a single substantive, which is none other than a passing name, a "demonstrative" signifier, the "short" operative word that impels and inspires the writing/experience of the *Cloud of Unknowing*.

In this way, the name is embodied. It becomes writing. It finds a place where the labor of loss produces a *locus proprius* [*un propre*] and builds itself a being-there. This no longer constitutes a suicide, a called for extermination, but the positivity of a discourse: first the poem, then the dictated treatises, then the exodus of the hand moving across the paper. An "outlet," as Surin called it—not the one that consists in going out the window, but the one that creates the possibility of space and passage. A *work of the name* is thus composed, a body and a symbolic place for the question of the subject. When he reaches this point, Surin should be able to walk again, which is in fact what happened. Towns will now be the page upon which he inscribes the labor of the name—where it is produced in the form of displacements, metaphorizations, or transports of those dogmatized places, as adjectivations of those substantialized languages. From this perspective, writing is simultaneously the opening of passageways and the construction of a body.

On Mad Love and Laughter

Love is indeed at the heart of Surin's poetry (even if we disregard the "note to the Reader" which serves as a preface to the 1731 edition of the *Cantiques spirituels*; it is not by Surin's hand, but represents a move to bring his "Spiritual Airs" back to the fold and canonize them as "expressions of piety"). On one level, to love is to die of pleasure, it is a "mad" linkage between "loss" and "pleasure." Thus Jesus, in Surin's song,

> For his pleasure, lost both his honor and his life
> Relinquishing all to save his love.

But the form of this "wild" love is "neither one nor the other: neither grace nor nature," "neither the ocean deep nor the shore," neither the "depth" of paradise nor the "hollow" of Hell, etc. "Neither one nor the other" is the logical opposite of "both," but that is what it surreptitiously turns into. In any case, it is the negative mode characterizing the place from which positivity is excluded. The *neither . . . nor* constitutes an interspace, a *zwischenraum*, the converse equivalent of a position that overcomes difference. It is a return to the one ("it is one to me . . . "), a mystic move if ever there was one; but the *one* is not totalizing or substantial. It appears in the mode of a shift, as something *extra* (an excess) or *added* (a passage) that constitutes a hole ("abyss") in experience and has no other possible positive formulation than the *neither . . . nor*, which is to say, the form of the neutral, or *indifference*:

> At all evil, I now only laugh.
> I am free from fear and desire.
> If the best or the worst is required,
> I defer to whomever would choose.
> It is one to me whether I live or I die.
> All that I ask is for love to remain with me.

Perhaps Surin's *laugh* is equivalent to the "pleasure of being Thine." "I now only laugh at it." This hardly seems Christian: in Christianity, the "wicked" laugh, but he who laughs last laughs best. The Greek gods laugh. But for Surin the laugh is the work of the other in the language of positive systems—or of the name. It restores the ineliminable distance between the other and all "good" or "evil." It is at the same time the movement of love and the movement of loss.

Part III
Nineteenth-Century Exoticisms

Chapter 8
The Beauty of the Dead:
Nisard
Written in collaboration with Dominique Julia
and Jacques Revel

*No one agrees voluntarily to be buried alive, and the splendor of
the tomb does nothing to make the sojourn more wholesome.*

—Charles Nisard

"Popular culture" presupposes an unavowed operation.[1] Before being studied,
it had to be censored. Only after its danger had been eliminated did it become
an object of interest. The birth of studies devoted to street literature (the inaugural book is Nisard's, published in 1854) is tied to the social censorship of their
object. They developed out of "a sensible plan" conceived by the police. At the
origin of this scientific curiosity, a political repression: the elimination of booklets judged "subversive" or "immoral." This is only *one* aspect of the problem,
but it raises a question of more general concern.

In the Beginning, a Death

The studies devoted to this form of literature were made possible by the act of
removing it from the people's reach and reserving it for the use of scholars and
amateurs. Therefore it is not at all surprising that street literature is judged by

Copyright © Christian Bourgois. This chapter was originally published as "La beauté du mort"
(Chapter 3), in *La culture au pluriel*, 2nd ed., series 10/18 (Paris: U.G.E., 1980), pp. 49–80, and
is reprinted with permission of Christian Bourgois.

these groups to be "disappearing," that they then go about preserving ruins, or that they see in it the tranquility of something preceding history, the horizon of nature, or paradise lost. Scientific interest no longer understands that, in searching out *popular* literature or culture, it is repeating its origins, and is thus attempting to elude the *people*.

Its results and methods, however, betray its origin; and the censorship of 1852 is only one specific case, as we will see later on. Numerous recent works wax long on the topic, but they are ignorant of what constituted the place their discourse holds. Nisard, for his part, knew quite well. He even gloried in that place—the position of "under-secretary" in the Ministry of Police. "When Mr. Charles de Maupas, the Minister of Police, realized what a disastrous influence was being exerted on everyone's minds by this mass of books, which street hawkers had been distributing up to that time with near impunity in every corner of France, he conceived and executed the sensible plan of establishing a permanent commission to examine the books (November 30, 1852), and had the kindness to notify me and allow me to participate, under the title of under-secretary. This gave me the opportunity to collect these booklets, and study them with the most scrupulous attention."[2]

This statement was made after the republican days of February and June 1848, and after the restoration of the Empire in 1852. What had been subjugated could now be made an "object" of science.

An old reflex. Soriano has shown that it had a part to play during the Fronde, from 1647–1653, when the language of the "riff-raff," painstakingly introduced into their burlesque poems by the Perrault brothers, was *turned into* an object of derision and simultaneously served to ridicule the "classics." On the one hand, this Trojan horse served as a tool in polemics against the "ancients": a quarrel among *docti*, like today's dispute between classical and modern schools of thought. But then, as the popular uprisings of the Fronde spread, this popular reserve, which had been useful at a certain point, turned terrifying. The Perrault brothers therefore began to treat it with more distance, with irony and hostility, and increasingly so as their allegiance to Mazarin grew. The "humorousness" and "curiosity" of this kind of speech corresponds in the work of these imperiled members of the upper middle-class with the triumph of *order* assured by the Cardinal. Burlesque is a measure of the people's defeat; their culture is all the more "curious" the less they are to be feared.[3]

This system is still functioning, although in different modes, and in the very works that today inspire opinions opposite to those of the past. Before, they were conservative, passionately and explicitly so; Nisard is an example. In recent years, especially since 1960, scholarship in the service of popular culture has been of Marxist inspiration, or at least "populist" in spirit. It has taken its place in the development of "social history," in full swing for thirty years now. It also sketches the utopia of a new political relation between the masses and the elite.[4] But does the scientific *operation* it undertakes now obey different laws than it did in times past? On the contrary, it still seems to be dominated by the mechanisms of age-old excommunications. "The sociology of 'popular culture,' " said Mühlmann, "begins with the secularism of the heretics."[5] That very same process of elimination has been prolonged. Knowledge remains linked to the power that authorizes it.

The question, then, is not one of ideologies, or of options, but that of the relations of an object and its associated scientific methods to the society that sanctions them. And if the procedures of science are not innocent, if their objectives depend on a political structure, then the discourse of science itself should acknowledge the function allotted it by society: to conceal what it claims to show. What this means is that a simple improvement in methods, or a reversal of conviction, will not change what that scientific operation does to popular culture. It needs to take political action.

A look at its history will shed some additional light on the present renewal in the study of popular culture.

The Birth of Exoticism (the Eighteenth Century)

How did this internal exoticism come about, this gaze which assumes the oppression of the very reality it objectifies and idealizes? Two periods are particularly revealing in this context: the end of the eighteenth century and the years from 1850 to 1890. The liberal, enlightened aristocracy of the end of the eighteenth century developed a passion for the "popular." But this rusticophilia, so evident in the novels of Louvet and Rétif, had a flipside of fear: fear of the city, which was seen as dangerous and corrupt because the traditional hierarchies become blurred there. This motivated a return to the primal purity of the countryside, the symbol of time-honored virtues. And that domestic savage, the French peasant—the thickness of history here replaces geographical distance—had the advantage of being *at the same time civilized* by Christian morals: closeness to nature, coupled with centuries of Christian morality, produced the "faithful subjects, both docile and laborious,"[6] who could be seen in action, for example, each June 8th at Salancy, in Picardy, when a village virgin ("rosière") was crowned for chastity:

"Salancy, Heaven's select, if ever the history of Virtue is written, your festival shall be famed among its glories. There, it shall be said, good and wise citizens live in a state of simplicity worthy of the first Age. There, far from false necessities, hard-working hands provide frugal fare for vigorous bodies. There, chaste wives make the days of their honest husbands happy ones. There, the only dowry a girl brings the man who seeks her hand is her sageness, sweetness and the glory of having merited the Rose. There, finally, under a wise Pastor, industrious people, following gentle laws, peacefully fulfill their duties as Christians and as citizens.

"Festival of the Rose, institution sanctified by wisdom and honor! August solemnity, where the most simple prize is awarded to the innocence most pure!"[7]

The vogue for "rosière" celebrations, which began in the 1770s, represents a return toward the people, whose words had been silenced, to domesticate them more completely.[8] The idealization of the "popular" is made all the easier if it takes the form of a monologue. The people may not speak, but they can sing. The fashion for popular songs—Dame Poitrine performed the song *Malbrough s'en va-t-en guerre* before the court of Louis XVI in 1781, and Beaumarchais three years later had the page Cherub sing the same song in *Le mariage de Figaro*—is one more sign of this confiscation of a lost treasure. It is precisely the pleasure provided by the "popular" halo of these "natural" melodies that formed the foundation for an elitist conception of culture.[9] The emotion derives from the very distance that separates the auditor from the presumed composer.

But the attitude thus outlined was not confined to the more or less masochistic aristocracy. It was shared by the members of the Constituent Assembly. An indication of their preoccupations can be seen in the investigation into the various patois of France launched in August 1790 by the Abbot Grégoire, the head priest of Embermesnil; it culminated in his famous report, issued in Pririal, Year II, *Sur la nécessité et les moyens d'anéantir les patois et d'universaliser l'usage de la langue française.*[10] What is important here is less the information presented —which the historian can and should draw upon to aid in analyzing popular culture—than the express intention of the investigator and his corresepondents. That intent is *both* to *collect* ("Do you have works, printed or manuscript, old or modern, in patois? . . . Is it possible to get hold of them easily?"[11]) and to *reduce* ("What would be the religious and political significance of the total destruction of this patois? . . . Do the people of the countryside have many prejudices, and of what kind? . . . Are they more enlightened than they were twenty years ago?"). The majority of the responses (which were for the most part from the bourgeoisie, from men in the legal profession or parish priests) came out in favor of eliminating all patois. The reason most frequently cited in favor of the universalization of the French language was the destruction of the hated feudal system, which it was thought would be perpetuated by the survival of local identities. But are not these enlightened urbanites, without even realizing it, the new standardbearers for the old education campaign organized by the Church since the Catholic Counter-Reformation? National unity—like the recuperation of the heretic attempted earlier—was to come about through education, in other words through the elimination of the resistance caused by *ignorance*. Of course, this raised some concerns for the "purity" of rustic morals; but as one writer who voiced this concern pointed out, the patois had *already* been condemned:

"The morality of our good forefathers was as simple as their patois, which seemed made to express simplicity and good-naturedness. For this reason, they perhaps should have been allowed to keep their simple and natural virtues, before this baneful change was brought about; but now ignorance in league with corruption will be the worst of all evils."[12]

We are once again forced to the conclusion: the ethnologist and the archaeologist arrive at the moment a culture has lost its means of self-defense. As Grégoire himself stated in his report to the Convention: "Familiarity with the dialects can shed light on several monuments of the Middle Ages. . . . Almost every idiom has works which enjoy a certain reputation. Already, the Arts Commission has in its directives recommended that these printed or manuscript monuments be collected; we must look for pearls even in the dung-hill of Ennius."[13]

Charles Nisard (1854)

The period from 1850 to 1890 marks the second stage in the development of this castrating cult of the people, now constituted as an object of "science." Once again, it is necessary to look at the subjacent postulates of "folklore studies." It is at the very same time that street literature is pursued with the utmost vigor that the scholars turn their attention with glee to popular books and contents. The Minister of the Interior, in an implementation order for the law of July 27, 1849, on newspapers, wrote to the prefects: "The most common feature of the papers they are now endeavoring to circulate, which are given the most popular form, is that they divide society into two classes, the rich and the poor, that they represent the former as tyrants, the latter as victims, that they incite the envy and hatred of one against the other, and that they are thus preparing, in our society so needful of unity and fraternity, all the elements of a civil war."[14]

Concerns such as these led, on November 30, 1852, to the creation by the Ministry of Police of a "Commission for the Examination of Chapbooks." It was not enough to keep tabs on the hawkers; it was necessary to control, by means of taxes and stamps, the content of the works distributed. It had to be verified that they were not contrary to "order, morality, and religion." But it is to Charles Nisard, who as we noted above headed this commission, that we owe the first *Histoire des livres populaires et de la littérature de colportage*.[15] In the preface to the first edition, the author openly announces his intentions with disarming naiveté: "It was my estimation that if, in the interests of those easily seduced, as are the workers and the inhabitants of the countryside, the Commission could not neglect to prohibit the sale of three-quarters of these books, this prohibition did not apply to those who could stand the test of evil readings, that is to say scholars, bibliophiles, collectors and even those who are simply curious about eccentric literature. I therefore believed I was doing something all of these people would appreciate by assembling these booklets under a unified point of view, and by saving them *en masse* from the shipwreck in which they were separately going to perish.''[16]

Thus the people are *children* whose original purity it is befitting to preserve by guarding them against evil readings. But the enlightened amateur could reserve a space on the ''curiosa'' shelf of his library for the folklorists' collections, just as the aristocrats used to bind almanacs with their coat of arms on the cover. The collector's interest is a correlate of the repression used to exorcize the revolutionary danger which, as the days of June 1848 had demonstrated, was still very close, lying dormant.

The Heyday of Folklore (the Third Republic)

The first wave of folklore studies came twenty-five years later, at the start of the Third Republic. It drew upon a rural world that the railroad and compulsory military service (let alone the mass media) had not yet brought into contact with the town: it would undergo a sudden transformation after the First World War. The concern for folklore was not, however, without its ulterior motives: its intent was to situate, reconnect, guarantee. What it was interested in was almost the opposite of censorship: reasoned integration. Popular culture was thus defined as a patrimony, in accordance with a two-pronged grid that was both historical (the intrapolation of themes guarantees a historical commonality) and geographical (their general presence throughout a certain space bears witness to the cohesiveness of that space). Genealogy and comparative studies arose to support the existence of a unified French repertory, through which the *French mentality* is expressed. Thus secured, the popular domain ceased to be the disquieting world Nisard worked so hard to exorcize and confine less than a quarter century before. Folklore ensured the cultural assimilation of a henceforth reassuring museum: ''Listening to our country songs would not be without profit to musicians and poets. They would better understand, by listening to them, that the secret of charming and stirring emotion does not lie in the search for bizarre resonances and expressions, but in the precision of the tones and the sincerity of the inspiration. . . . '' So declares a journal which in the same breath denies that colonial ethnology has any interest and concludes by reminding its readers to ''remain French, that above all else.''[17]

The interest in the popular is ambiguous in another way. The connotations of the word ''popular'' in the folklore journals of the time are revealing: the popular is associated with what is natural, true, naive, spontaneous, and childlike. Often, folkloric zeal goes hand in hand with federalist concerns whose political significance is obvious. It is no mere coincidence that ''popular'' was from this time forward invariably identified with the peasant. The culture of the elites, the elites themselves, were threatened from other quarters: the laboring or dangerous classes of the cities, especially Paris, presented a new kind of menace. G. Paris made no effort to hide this fact; in a solemn address at the Sorbonne, he defined popular art as: "All that is produced or preserved among the people, far from the influence of the urban centers."[18] Pressure for the restoration of provincial life under the auspices of a well-composed medieval-ism; the demand for a social renewal that would put the peasant back in the worker and celebrate the primitive virtues of the land;[19] the longing for a return to aesthetic sources in a reaction against "questionable sophistication and intel-lectual misconceptions": so many themes which prefigure those of the National Revolution—Vichy, that other golden age of tradition and folklore. But for the moment, they are only evidence of the existence of a populism of the powerful, a political faction in search of a new alliance. Its echo can be heard in this curi-ously contemporary flight of oratory, which nevertheless smacks of Déroulède: "Yes, let us go to the workers and peasants. Better yet, if we can, let us become peasants and workers ourselves, let us join in their festivals. Let us bring those whom intolerance and oblivion have murdered back to life. Let us create new celebrations."[20] Bourgeois France—one big country fair? One good turn de-serves another.

The people. Spontaneous, naive. The child, again. But not the vaguely menacing and brutal child they used to want to mutilate: the prodigal son returns from afar bedecked with the allurements of exoticism. And he shares its distance also. For Georges Vicaire, "tradition, a world of unexpurgated sensations," should teach us about "the soul of the peasant, so obscure, so difficult to pene-trate."[21] The people are another Japan; their taste for music must be reculti-vated. They are a river; their waters should quench the thirst.[22] And, of course, they are a woman who should be revealed as what she is: "In summary, every creation of the human spirit must, in order to attain perfection, pass through three stages: first, the near-spontaneous conception of an ideal in the popular imagination, in other words Tradition and Unconsciousness; then, the reasoned organization of this ideal in a work of genius, in other words Consciousness and Art; and finally, the incarnation of the ideal in reality, in other words Social Progress. . . . A man of genius always has, and must have, a sentimental and nervous unconscious, like a woman; but he has in addition, and always must have, a clear-sighted and dominating virility. . . . "[23] A homage to dialectical rape? In any event, it is an almost undisguised admission of an age-old violence, which now oscillates between voyeurism and pedagogy. Almost anything is possible here. The mildly contemptuous liberalism of certain groups indicates precisely that "the new mind holds no one in contempt; in nature, in humanity, it finds nothing uninteresting."[24] The people, in the final analysis, are the noble savage: the reservation and the museum can now replace cultural confinement.

The gaze of the *docti* can present itself as neutral, and—why not?—even kindly. The most secret violence of the first folklore wave was to have camouflaged its violence. That brings us up to the present day.

The Myth of the Lost Origin

What is the "popular"? Marcel Maget, in his study on "*popular* and *people*," speaks of the "impossibility of a definition" and of "logical aporia." He adds and multiplies criteria, which his analysis attributes to others, ad infinitum, to the point of vertigo.[25] Is history more successful when inquiring into the popular literature of the *ancien régime*? It is doubtful that it is, despite the testimony of some remarkable studies by Robert Mandrou, Geneviève Bollème, Marc Soriano, etc.[26] In this outpouring of scholarly works, popular literature still does not say its true name.

Like other authors—more clearly than others—Soriano distinguishes two kinds of literature termed popular, "writings destined for the use of the people" and "genuinely popular works." However, the texts themselves (the tales written by the Perrault brothers, of course, but also almanacs, as Bollème shows) were written by professional *authors*.[27] What they display, then, is the mentality of the *docti*. But did not these specialists, these learned ones, adapt their writing to the tastes of their audience? To put it another way, is the "popular" to be sought on the side of its *readers*? Most likely not, in spite of the widespread circulation of almanacs under the *ancien régime* (72,000 copies for Colombat's almanacs, 150,000–200,000 for the others combined). In 1780, France still had an illiteracy rate of 60 percent (it was 80 percent in 1685); the almanacs ended up in middle-class homes—M. Chartier made that observation,[28] and many archives have confirmed it. The booklets of the eighteenth century thus seem to have the same role as our contemporary pocketbooks: they reached a larger number of readers, but apparently did so without passing beyond the boundaries of the well-off middle classes.[29]

Where, then, is the "genuinely popular" to be found? Some see it in the hidden treasure of the oral tradition, the "primitive" and "natural" source of written literature. Others postulate a cultural unity, but one that is stretched along a line of movement in which the literature of the elite is the harbinger of global evolutions. There exist a number of explanatory systems.

According to Bollème, the literature of the elite under the *ancien régime* degenerated into a "popular" culture elaborated by specialist writers, but had the transitory function of inspiring in the people a need for knowledge and happiness. Once it had fulfilled this role, the almanac no longer had a reason for being; it became "obsolete, outmoded," for the people then began to speak the language of the ordinary philosophy, "a combination of good living, science, the search and taste for the truth, the desire for happiness, and efforts toward virtue.''[30] But for Bollème, all that could function because *there was already*, among the people, a ''taste'' for knowledge and for ''being educated''[31] that the almanacs merely awoke from its slumber. This ''taste,'' which was equivalent to a ''need'' or basic nature, was brought to the light of day by the stimulus of the almanacs, which at first portrayed the people as the dwelling place of a poor God, where an internal wisdom was independently transmitted. But in the final analysis, must we not conclude that the hidden God was none other than that ''taste'' or ''need'' itself, that sun which the bugles of the *docti* summoned from the night?

With Soriano, the scenario seems reversed. According to him, popular literature is itself ''ancient,'' with roots at the origins of history; it was sustained by an oral tradition which emerged in classical literature. It gradually began to appear in works by the learned, even though, like the Perrault brothers, they had no ''particular sympathy for the toiling masses'' and thought they were using the tradition. Soriano's hypothesis is the opposite of Bollème's, in that he sees a movement rising up from the depths of popular tradition and reaching into classical works, not one descending from the literature of the elite to become a stimulating vulgarization.

This upward motion is fueled by ''fundamental needs'' and ''profound aspirations,'' of which popular expresion is the first manifestation.[32] It is the natural ''origin'' for literary history. In Soriano's viewpoint, this ''origin'' is not totally invisible, nor is it reducible to an evocation of popular aspirations. ''Authentic'' expression in popular art is closer to the origin than are the works of the learned. The search for the origin thus takes the form of research into ''primitive'' texts. His textual method, which is remarkable in its own right, assumes that these *primitive* texts are characterized by an ''effective, nervous and sober style.'' In this way, it becomes possible to fix a hierarchical order of the various versions of the same folktale and to pinpoint what is ''genuinely popular'' in the literature of the elites. ''Sobriety,'' conciseness, vigor, the presence of these traits coupled with a fundamental genius allows one to say *where* the ''primitive'' is.

Of course, this theoretical construction is based upon precisely what it claims to prove. It presupposes that the popular is the *beginning* of literature and the *infancy* of culture; that the purity of a social origin lies buried in history; that there is a primitive genius that is always compromised by literature, and always has to be preserved or recaptured; and finally, that the popular tradition articulates the depths of nature (''profound aspirations'') and the perfections of art (sobriety, vivacity, narrative efficacity). Applying a little psychoanalysis, it would be easy to see in this the repression of the origin and the return of the repressed in the language of repression itself.

What is striking about these analyses is not, as Maget has said, the ''aporia'' resulting from the way in which the terms of the problem are posed, but the weight attached to the problem: find the lost origin. Whatever its scientific treatment, this fascination with the lost object sweeps the methods in use up into the swirl of its internal contradiction. It entraps them in its own impossibility.

The purpose of our examination of the studies we have mentioned is not to belittle the admittedly considerable contributions they have made, but rather to highlight the semi-obsessional pressure that this question of the origin exerts on them. The very concept of "popular culture" is at stake.

What, then, casts this pall? How was this form constituted, which only seems to enter into the studies as something evanescent and ungraspable? As early as Henri Marrou's fine and penetrating "Introduction à la chanson populaire française," it has been said that, in the last instance, "the folksong owes its distinctive character to the popular halo it has in our eyes."[33] What then is the meaning of this phantom that designates the origin and at the same time conceals it, this "halo" that reveals while "covering over"?

At this point, there is a hypothesis that demands attention, even if it does not account for everything: these studies of popular culture take as their object *their own* origin. They pursue across the surface of texts, before their eyes, what is actually their own condition of possibility—the elimination of a popular menace. It is not surprising that this object of interest appears in the figure of a lost origin: the fiction of an as yet unfound reality preserves traces of the political action at its basis. Scientific literature makes the act that gave rise to it function as a mythic representation. It is thus incapable of introducing into the discourse, as an object or result of rigorous procedures, the inaugural act which constituted a topic of interest by effacing a reality. And, doubtless, it will never resolve its internal contradictions as long as this founding deed is "forgotten" or denied.

Learned Readings of Popular Themes

Once again, this time on the level of thematic analysis and interpretation, we are confronted with the ambiguity of the object *popular culture*. This ambiguity is evidenced by the existence of opposing formulations of the problem of the origin, which nevertheless have much in common. The first step is the inventory; it is useful and necessary, but that does not say that it can stand on its own. Bollème and Mandrou have made inventories—open-ended ones—in which they catalogue the essential themes they found in the almanacs and the booklets of the Bibliothèque Bleue: "By exploring the major themes, the presences and absences, in the repertory of the Bibliothèque Bleue, we gain access, to a large extent, to the themes of popular French culture itself under the *ancien régime*. . . . "[34] That is all fine and good. But there is an assumption here that the themes presenting themselves as relevant, and the "meaningful elements" thus catalogued, are actually what they make themselves out to be. This brings us back to the classic and annoying problem created for historians and other specialists as well by the self-assertive modesty of the folklorist, from the Aarne-Thompson classifications to Van Gennep's *Manuel*: though solidly entrenched in a proclaimed positivity, in the refusal to interpret and conclude, are not these inventories the ultimate ruse, interpretation's revenge? Today we know enough to realize that no one is pure.

This leads to two questions: from what position do the historians of popular culture speak? And what object do they constitute as a result of that position? It is not without relevance to note that the notions they use to form their inventory grid are all borrowed from the categories of knowledge (it is the case in Bollème's works), or, in a more general sense, from the same learned culture whose popular pole ("an unknown, forgotten cultural level") Mandrou wishes to manifest.[35] The terms *fairy tale, supernatural, pagan,* and *scientific* and *occult* sciences define less the content of a popular culture than the historian's gaze itself. Bollème finds in the almanacs of the eighteenth century a "reorientation toward the real, the actual, the human": to what real, to what history, to what humanity does this reorientation lead? Is not this refusal of duration—rather than a characteristic proper to the cultural heritage under study, as it is claimed to be[36]—in fact learned culture's present recognition of its own essential temporality and, in the end, a stunned avowal of its other? And the uncertainty about the boundaries of the popular domain, about its homogeneity over against the profound and always reinforced unity of the culture of the elites—does it not signify that the popular domain has yet to exist, because it is impossible for us to speak of it without annihilating it? Mandrou writes that "inconsistencies are part of the vision of the world propagated by the Bibliothèque Bleue for over two centuries."[37] Paradoxically, these are the very same terms employed by the old censors. But these inconsistencies are in reality the flipside of our inability to recapture the coherence of a cultural totality: so here are our primitives. The result—and this is the most serious objection—is that the object that has been classified, resituated, and rendered reassuring in this way is disqualified.

The Popular in Social History

But there is more. The problems of the inventory approach are closely related to the problems of thematic interpretation, and first to those arising from the very status of interpretation. What do the texts brought to light in this way say, what can they say? The thematic study of popular literature is presented in these works as the manifestation of something else, upon which it claims to be based: the *popular.* Nothing is more revealing in this context than Soriano's summary chapter on the peasant masses and folklore at the end of the seventeenth century.[38] He jeopardizes the very possibility of a social history of culture by magnifying the scope of the problems addressed: to serve as a historical backdrop for his study, he offers a cursory evocation of the "somber seventeenth century," some generalizations about the social tensions within the French peasantry (revolts) and on their supposed ideological derivation (witchcraft), and allusions to the world of belief and superstition borrowed from recent authors. "It is," says Soriano, "within this context that folklore must be placed, that is, within the totality of the artistic manifestations of the peasantry: dances, ceremonies, songs, and of course folktales."[39] Aside from the point that the identity between "artist" and "popular" is not self-evident, it is easy to see that Soriano's definition of popular culture is wholly tautological: anything that directly "*reflects*" the historical situation of the people under the *ancien régime* is "popular." The task, then, consists in extracting the themes of social history out of cultural history. We are caught in a system of endless interpretation and cross-referencing. Inventiveness is stunted, becoming merely recognition, and the corpus is turned into a catalogue of citations. Neither folklore nor history gain by this.

In what way does cultural expression function in relation to its insertion in society? If it is true that what we designate as popular culture perfused all aspects of peasant life in the seventeenth century, then into what dreams, what myths was it organized?[40] In response to a question raised by Le Roy Ladurie, Soriano wishes to reconstitute the grid governing Perrault's borrowings from the repertory of folklore; this is, in fact, a key question regarding the *Contes*.[41] But how can he presume that the problem of the repertory itself has been solved since this repertory was also composed after a grid? It is not in any way astonishing that the themes, that is to say, the *popular* itself, fluctuate between positivist social description ("the social content of the folktales") and allusions to the ungraspable content of a deceptively self-evident domain. Quite symptomatically, Soriano strays from the problem of popular culture's modes of coherence and functioning, moving instead toward genealogical research into primitive texts. The presence, out there, of popular culture is presupposed at each stage of the process for which it stands as guarantor. Therefore, it is always elsewhere; in the end, it is nothing.

Various remarks here and there do, however, give us a glimpse of what a thematic analysis could be. Mandrou and Bollème, more attentive historians working on neighboring corpuses, observe that books and almanacs manifest a crack in the hardened representation they present of society, a representation imposed from above: the function of the shepherd—by profession a social marginal, the subject and object of nature whose simplicity is governed by evangelical certitude, whose innocence simultaneously guarantees the holiday and harbors violence—could well reveal, incidentally, the other's gaze upon a society built on silence and the exclusion of the other.

Elsewhere, Bollème makes the remark that "Catholicism is the religion of the poor people" and that the God of the almanacs is the "God of the poor": this evangelical theme is a commonplace with a rich past, and undoubtedly an even richer future; in spite of the cliché, it is tempting to regard the poor as a social group striving to make its truth heard (which means, first of all, to position itself within truth) through its allegorical participation in the sufferings of the Gospel. It is all the more tempting when the author notes the apparently paradoxical importance of religious language in the (otherwise secularized) almanacs of the eighteenth century.[42] However, this could be seen, just as easily as a sign of growing popular religiosity, as the retreat of popular culture into the only language still available for its expression after the triumph of reason, which desires to negate it. The language of religion would then be the last recourse of a culture that could no longer find expression, that was being forced to fall silent or mask itself so a different cultural order could be heard. This takes us to the root of the problem: popular culture can only be grasped in the process of vanishing because, whether we like it or not, our knowledge requires us to cease hearing it, to no longer know how to discuss it.

Finally, beyond the question of methods and contents, beyond what it says, the measure of a work is what it keeps silent. And we must say that the scientific studies—and undoubtedly the works they highlight—include vast and strange expanses of silence. These blank spots outline a geography of the *forgotten*. They trace the negative silhouette of the problematics displayed black on white in scholarly books.

A Geography of the Eliminated

Confining ourselves to a quick sketch of this geography, there are three regions which seem to be absent in the studies, though in different ways: the child, sexuality, and violence.

The Child

The child, absent? It seems paradoxical to say so when these works have as their very leitmotif the combination "the child and the people." They often proceed, moreover, from children's literature to popular literature. Literature for children, literature emanating from the origins of humanity, pedagogical literature: all of these themes favor an assimilation of the people and children, and suggest the meaning of such a move. But they make what is *said* about the child all the more symptomatic; the child is a figure which serves as an allegory for what these writers *think* about the people.

Soriano has masterfully demonstrated that the problem of the father is one of the keys to the work of Perrault. Doubtless, it would be justified to expand this thesis into a much more general hypothesis, and to extend its scope to include a great many folktales and legends. But is it certain that, as Soriano believes, this fact must be interpreted to indicate a "death" or effacement of the father? He sees it as proof that a generation was born without fathers or "elders,'' was left to its own devices, and was educated solely by the books that were proper to it. Children's literature would be the substitute for the presence of the father.

There are many indications leading to the opposite conclusion. First, there are very few children in the literature discussed. On the contrary, in the mirror of the texts allegedly destined for children, it is adults who create an image of themselves, as they dream they are. They offer themselves their own legend through the intermediary of the image of adults presented to children. The question may be asked as to whether this also applies for the members of the middle classes, who repeat and idealize themselves in the image of themselves they claim to proffer the ''good people.'' If that were the case, it would be less surprising that the lesser nobility and the bourgeoisie found such delight in reading this literature, supposing they constituted the majority of its market. In the same way, adults would buy the folktales designed to please themselves ostensibly to ''please their children.'' Self-satisfaction, which is also a tautology of adults, would in that case simply have children as its pretext, its means, and its guarantee.

More than that, when the child does appear, he has the knowledge and virtues of the adult. The "little witch," the "little magician," etc.,[43] or the "wise three-year-old"[44] knows as much as any adult, and more. Is such a child in opposition to adults? No, he follows in the footsteps of his predecessors, only precociously. Thus he confirms that there are not in fact two ways of wisdom or two moral orders, but that that of the parents will remain that of the children, of the future, forever. The ''naturalness'' of the child rejoins the parents' saying; it corroborates it much more than it threatens it. The child's spontaneity is one thing adults are supposed to lack, but this divergence is a ruse that only increases adults' confidence in their knowledge.

The authors of this children's literature—the ''fathers'' of the booklets—reconfirm, in reference to the ''nature'' of children, their own conceptions and aspirations, which they need to route through the other in order to increase their recognition. Children ''no longer have fathers,'' and do not experience the father's violence, for the very simple reason that they themselves, in the literature treating them, have been turned into the repetition and image of the father. A certain power speaks in them, through them, without having to admit its presence. But it was soon to show itself for what it was, when the ''new pedagogy'' claimed to know, as an object, the child's ''nature,'' and thus posited in advance the ''instincts'' and ''needs'' it wished to develop.[45]

''Children'' writes Maget, ''are the repository of a culture that perpetuates itself on the fringes of adult culture, of which it represents an altered form.''[46] *That* is what children are, as refashioned by ethnological studies. Their ''culture'' is presented as something altered to prevent it from seeming different from that of adults. It was necessary to ''alter'' it in order to adjust it to the dreams of the adult and to place it under the sign of the *"Civilized,"*[47] or the *Mirrors of Virtue*. In the process, two of its fundamental characteristics were expunged: sexuality and violence.

Sexuality

Was not the same thing done to the people, to make them conform to the self-image that ethnographical or "populist" exoticism purposed to provide for the adult, for man, and the bourgeoisie? There is nothing quite so fine "as the crude and rude honesty of the craftsman," writes the journal *Le Français* (August 1868) in relation to a popular booklet, *La Malice des grandes filles*. "Woe to he who muddies the clarity of these waters." The censorship commission will be the "guardian angel" protecting the innocence of the people from "impure photographs."

Nisard, as always the St. John Chrysostom of this science, has much to say on the topic. For example, when discussing the sexual knowledge of children, he goes into raptures over the "idiocies" he finds in the *Catéchisme des amants, par demandes et réponses, où sont enseignés les principales maximes de l'amour et le devoir d'un véritable amant* (Tours, 1838), which alludes to the "age at which one can begin making love, which is fourteen for boys and twelve for girls."[48] His knowledge of peasant and child mores is wanting.

Adults have a need for the "innocence" they attribute to children (which has been demystified by, for example, Gaignebet's studies on nursery rhymes).[49] The adult denies whatever contradicts his dream. This is a characteristic reflex, whose role in the elimination of sexuality and violence is deserving of more in-depth analysis. However, we will content ourselves with identifying two more blank spots.

A striking thing about the studies we are discussing is the silence that reigns on the subject of sexuality. Soriano recounts the strange story of the fate of *Sleeping Beauty*: a princely adolescent was substituted for the married man who had previously been her lover, and she only makes love to him while she is unconscious, after falling into magical slumber, and she GIVES BIRTH in that state.[50]

Can we not regard this tale as an allegory of what happens in some of the studies devoted to popular culture? Sexual knowledge and realtions fall into magical slumber. They enter the unconscious of scholarly literature. From Nisard to Bollème, they are hardly mentioned, except to cry "unrealistic!"

Violence

"Dangerous classes," threatening demands—they never make an appearance in this *literature*. Before they can appear, Soriano, for example, finds it necessary to leave the literary domain, switching over to *history* (especially in his article in *Annales*) for an analysis of the literature's *function* and social place.

The texts' articulation with a certain political history is, however, fundamental. It is the only thing capable of explaining how a particular *gaze* was constituted.

The same "forgetting" occurs with peasant revolts, regionalist claims, autonomist conflicts—in short, violence. Mandrou has emphasized how, beginning with the eighteenth century, popular literature has played the role of an alibi, and has functioned to alienate the people, whom it "distracts" and represents.[51] The same goes for the nineteenth century: the folklorists erase the wars of the peasantry; all that remains of the peasant is his "dark soul." The only trace of the rebellions in the provinces to be found in the writings of the "Traditionist" Society is an allusion to "the deep reservoirs where the blood and tears of the people lie" (1887). The popular uprisings appear only indirectly in scholarly studies, in the form of a piteous object to be "preserved": "obliterated or marred French traditions."

Is it possible to be Breton? asks Morvan-Lebesque. No, answers the scientific literature, except as an "obliterated" or nostalgic object. But history shows that violence was erased from literature by an earlier violence. The dates speak for themselves. The Perrault brothers' "burlesque" (1653) came after the suppression of the political uprisings. The interest in patois evidenced by Grégoire's correspondents (1790–1792) accompanied and presupposed the political effacement of regionalist movements by "patriotism." Nisard's studies on chapbooks (1854) were made possible by the defeat of the republican and socialist movements of 1848 and by the restoration of the Empire in 1852. The elimination of violence from the study of localisms and popular "culture" is explained by a political violence. What allowed these lost paradises to be handed over to the scholars was in every instance the victory of a certain power.

We cannot reproach a literature for grafting itself upon a prior violence (for that is always the case); but we can reproach it for not admitting it.

Science and Politics: An Inquiry

Wherever we turn, we come across the same problems that ethnologists—from Lévi-Strauss' *Tristes tropiques* to Jaulin's *Paix Blanche*—have learned to confront in the context of a praxis that is more directly concrete and political, and more decipherable, than the historian's. For now, we should take stock of the lessons to be learned from the recent, important books we have too glibly and too lengthily criticized here. They have the not inconsiderable merit of having invented a topic, with all its ambiguities. Also, of having undertaken an enormous, groundbreaking labor opening a number of possible paths of study. The most classical of these, and perhaps the most difficult owing to the rarity of significant documents, is the path of a sociology of culture, of its production, diffusion, and circulation: this is, if one wishes, an outside approach to a mode of coherence, one that is necessary but still insufficient. The other path consists of an internal critique of that same coherence; it could take advantage of tools as diverse (and problematical) as linguistic analysis, the formalization of narratives schematized according to type,[52] textual method, the analysis of conceptual representations, etc. However, these are only approaches whose primary role is to define an ambition, and thus an object to be invented.

The historian's goal, and the ethnologist's, is to outline the functioning of a cultural aggregate, to make its laws visible, to hear its silences, to structure a landscape that is nothing if it is not more than a simple reflection. But it would be wrong to think that these tools are neutral, or their gaze inert: nothing gives itself up, everything has to be seized, and the same interpretive violence can either create or destroy. The most ambitious of our studies, the most audacious, is also the least historical, the one that most surely misses its object in claiming to subject it to the converging lines of fire of a series of different inquiries (literary, folkloric, linguistic, historical, psychoanalytic, etc.). Soriano announces that he "willingly accepts the label of eclecticism."[53] But an eclecticism that claims to subject the same object to so many inquiries, as if each one did not constitute, in its specificity, a new object whose *distance* from the others, not its proximate similitude, is its constitutive basis—is not such an eclecticism one of indifference, is it not illusory? The danger does not lie in "simultaneously" using "methods reputed to be unreconcilable"—which the author denies having done—but in using them in the same way without drawing any benefit from their differences. In this sense, what is most instructive is the near-autobiographical architecture of the book, in which we may attempt to read how the inquiry "led" its author on.[54] All things considered, Soriano's study informs us less about popular culture itself than about what it means for a progressive academic to speak of popular culture today. This brings us back to a ubiquitous problem we must try to answer: *Where does one speak? What can be said?* But also, in the end: Where do *we* speak? This makes the problem directly political, because it makes an issue of the social—in other words, primarily repressive—function of learned culture.

It goes without saying that it is our own place which, through our critique of Soriano, we have set ourselves the task of defining. Where are we, outside of learned culture? Or, if you like: does popular culture exist outside of the act that suppresses it? So much is clear: our aggressiveness postulates—perhaps less directly but just as assuredly as our authors' self-confident progressivism—a kind of political and social linkage in which the relation of popular culture to learned culture could be other than one of simple hierarchization, where it could be a type of cultural democracy; this utopia is only the countertype of the violence we practice. If we reject the distinction elite/people, which the works we have been discussing accepted without difficulty from the very outset, we cannot ignore the fact that it is impossible for a *written* act (ours), an ambition, to suppress the history of a repression, to seriously purport to found a new kind of relation: the last ruse of knowledge is to reserve for itself the role of political prophesy. Is it even possible to conceive of a new organization in the heart of culture that would not go hand in hand with a change in the relation of social forces?

This is precisely what historians—it is, after all, *our* place—can demonstrate to the literary analysts of culture. It is a function of the historian to flush the literary analysts out of their alleged position as pure spectators by showing them that social mechanisms of selections, critique, and repression are everywhere present, by reminding them that it is violence that invariably founds a system of knowledge. Because of this, history is the privileged place where the gaze becomes unsettled, even if it is only that. It would be vain, however, to expect an emancipation of cultures, a finally liberated outpouring, an unchained spontaneity to result from a political critique, as was the ambiguous hope of the first folklorists. The history of the old divisions teaches us that not one among them is neutral, that any organization presupposes a repression. What is uncertain is simply whether this repression must always function according to a hierarchical social distribution of cultures. Only active political experience can teach us what it could be—if we know how to read that experience. It is not out of place to call this to mind at a time when pressing questions about political and cultural action are being raised.

What remains is to set the limits of the inquiry itself. Any anthropology articulates culture and nature in accordance with the static, majority order of the gaze and of knowledge. Political invention can propose new articulations which take account of the dynamics of repression. It is not a question of predicting or willing this new order, which is the political act itself, something like the flipside of history. The political act is capable of contesting all of culture and placing all of its divisions in question. However, a new culture presupposes yet another repression, even if it founds a new order of political participation. Language is lodged in this ambiguity, between what it implies and what it says outright. From the political event, science itself receives its objects and its form, but not its status; science is not reducible to the political event. Doubtless, there must always be a death for there to be speech; but speech expresses the absence or the lack of that death, and indicating what made speech possible at any given moment does not explain all there is to explain about it. Sustained by the corpse whose trace it carries, aimed at the inexistence it promises but never delivers, speech remains the riddle of the Sphinx. It maintains, between the actions it symbolizes, the problematical space of an inquiry.

Chapter 9
Writing the Sea:
Jules Verne

According to the terms of the contract drafted by the publisher J.-P. Hetzel on October 18, 1877, Gabriel Marcel, a geographer in the service of the National Library, is "charged with assembling the documents and texts necessary for the publication of Jules Verne's book, *Les Grands Voyages et les Grands Voyageurs*, already begun"; Verne is to "revise" this preparatory work and "modify it to make it his own." The publisher at 18 rue Jacob, an old friend and advisor of Verne's (who was one of his successful authors, along with George Sand, Victor Hugo, etc.), agreed to pay 5,000 francs to the signatory for each of the three uncompleted volumes of *Les Grands Voyages*; of that sum, 750 francs were to be forwarded to Marcel.[1] A very unequal allotment. It brought to mind what Verne himself considered the scandalous difference between the "reward" received by Bougainville at the close of his journeys (1766–1769), and that of his first mate, Guyot-Duclos; the former was "showered with honors" while the latter was merely promoted to the rank of ship's captain.[2] The price of the signature, one of the themes of the work, is marked from the very outset. The name pays. The publication contract seems to duplicate—as its shadow, as the conditions of its production—the book in which heroic explorers go about filling the great, empty expanses of the map of the world with names.

That same month, October 1877, Hetzel advanced the author the amount owed for the three upcoming volumes. "I must say," Verne wrote in response,

Copyright © Michel de Certeau. This chapter first appeared as "Écrire la mer" (Preface), in *Les grands navigateurs du XVIII siècle* by Jules Verne (Paris: Ramsay, 1977), pp. i–xix.

"that the present (it is just that, what you have given me for the continuation of *Les Grands Voyages*) was something of an inducement for this folly."[3] The "folly" was the purchase, after the favorable advice of Paul Verne, Jules' brother and an officer in the French Navy, of the steam-powered yacht Saint-Michel III, for the price of 55,000 francs; it had an acceleration power of 25 horsepower, cruising power of 100, and could lodge fourteen people (including six crew members). Under the command of Captain Ollive, the steamship was to take Verne to Algeria (1878), Scotland (1879), Copenhagen (1880), etc. The author of *Les Grands Navigateurs du XVIIIe siècle* wrote sections of his books at sea: he simultaneously wrote upon the immense page of the sea, and transformed the striations of his European voyages into global writings. His practice consisted in establishing relations between the machine and the sea through the mediation of writing. It found its motto in the project devised in 1880 for a four-volume work entitled *La Conquête scientifique et industrielle du globe*. The project was never completed, but it is already present in the *Histoire générale des grands voyages et des grands voyageurs*, whose sequel it was to be, and of which *Les Grands Navigateurs du XVIIIe siècle* (published by Hetzel and Cie in 1879 in the "Library of Education and Recreation") was a part.

Library Navigation

"To go back to the sources themselves and take only what comes from absolutely original documents": this project, outlined in the Foreword, in fact specifies Gabriel Marcel's task. But it also designates the corpus Verne received from him, which he was to "make his own" under the terms of the contract agreed to in 1877: that corpus consisted of an anthology of selected pieces, prepared in advance, thus already constituted as a fiction of the eighteenth century. The book is the result of these two distinct and coordinated operations: Marcel's *collection* and Verne's *treatment* of it. It is a modification effected within the museum created by the employee of the National Library. Navigation is first of all a labor of displacement, alteration and construction undertaken in a space that has been "invented" by another from extracts of *Voyages, Discoveries, Histories, Diaries*, and *Accounts* dating from the eighteenth century. A library circumscribes the field within which these travels are elaborated and unfold.

In much the same way, there is a library located at the center of the Nautilus in *20,000 Leagues Under the Sea*, and it is what organizes Captain Nemo's expeditions. It reproduces, moreover, the library that belonged to Hertzel, who was an adventurer in the realm of politics, then publishing.[4] This cavern of industrious, selective memory can be taken as the myth for the laboratory in which *Voyages Extraordinaires* was invented. It is a novelistic figure expressing the place and the mode of production of all of Verne's novels. As in the case of *Robinson Crusoe*,[5] the received representation delimits the emplacement of

Verne, the narrator accompanying the subject, Marcel, in the archives

the new treatment that transforms it. Far from presupposing a reality that tells its story in the documents, *Les Grands Voyages* presents "discoveries" made on the basis of and within a certain memory. It is a book that is closer to Borges' "fictions" than to Michelet's "resurrections." Verne's travels are fictions inscribed upon fictions of travel. In short, his is an "art of memory"[6] made up of the thousand and one ways of composing a simulacrum with relics.

Thus, the work's relation to its "sources" and the "originals" is not governed by the search for an origin, nature or truth that would be there *before* and *behind* the documents. What gradually fills the world's voids with words, multiplies and details representations (geographical maps, historical enactments, etc.), and thus "conquers" space by marking it with meanings, is a component of and force within history. From this point of view, the series *Les Grands Navigateurs* is not an exception within Verne's work; it is not a study in historical geography that should be isolated from the adventure stories. The only exceptional thing about it is that it makes the general process of fabrication visible: the interlinkage of the imaginary and the collection, in other words the labor of fiction within the library. That invention haunts the "sources" is everywhere indicated by the citations, from the moment one opens the book. It is the law of the other in the narrative. The text is induced by these fragments (broken mirrors deforming the past they represent), but it displaces and transforms them in the fiction it generates by manipulating them.

This doubling, the play of one on the other, corresponds, moreover, to the literary shift which in each novel places the narrator *beside* the traveler and *in his space*. Just as the scholar Aronnax (who narrates *20,000 Leagues Under the Sea*) writes of the voyage of the other (Captain Nemo) who receives and detains him in his submarine; just as Axel (the narrator of *Journey to the Center of the Earth*) is a guest and prisoner on the expedition of his terrible uncle, Lidenbrock, and also its witness—so too Verne himself recounts Gabriel Marcel's discoveries in the cavernous depths of the National Library. More than that, in both of these novels the voyage of the other (Nemo, Lidenbrock) is a continuation of other voyages, older ones, to which the writing bears witness: Nemo's library is at the principle of *20,000 Leagues Under the Sea*, and Humboldt is in that library (his portrait closes the gallery of *Les Grands Navigateurs*); the cryptogram of Arne Saknussemm, a sixteenth century alchemist and explorer (the first period treated in the *Histoire générale des grands voyages et des grands voyageurs*), opens *Journey to the Center of the Earth*. In the beginning, there is a graph which envelops a lost-past voyage, and whose secret the novel unfurls in a new variation. The "historical novel,"[7] *Les Grands Voyageurs*, follows the same schema. It begins with the travel act of Gabriel Marcel, the act of "going back to the sources themselves"—old books, the National Library—that is, to earlier texts relating yet earlier voyages. Like shelves in a library, the narrative stacks up strata in which the same travel adventure undergoes an inversion, now appearing in the form of documents that are traversed, now appearing in the form of lands and seas that are navigated: the narrator writes beside the traveler, who follows a text, which in turn traces other voyages. If we read this longitudinally, we have the accompanying chart:

NARRATOR ◄──	EXPLORER ◄──	EARLY ◄── NARRATOR	EARLIER TRAVELER
Arronax	Nemo	Library	19th Century
Axal	Lidenbrock	Cryptogram	16th Century
Jules Verne	Gabriel Marcel	National Library	18th Century

In fact, the stages by which the text represents its own production become inverted and coil in successive transformations from written to physical spaces, and vice versa:

In addition, these unfurlings in the form of voyages and retractions into writing must be seen superimposed one on top of the other: the text, in this indefinite stratification, offers the gaze a structure *"en abyme."* Like so many depths, crevices, craters and abysses haunting Verne's imaginary, and which he sees from above, descends into or rises up out of, the narrative displays a multiplication of trajectories, which unfurl an earlier writing in space, and of documents, which bury the past beneath displacements of location. But all of this occurs in the same place, in a book, or rather in a collection of books, each of which, due to its particular geography, is different from the preceding one, in other words stands *beside* the other, yet nevertheless repeats the same depth-effect by placing itself *above* or *below* the other. To navigate is to descend into or rise up out of this abyss of the library, to which the voyages of the reader respond in echo.

Transferences and Relics

Jules Verne's *Histoire* is constructed in the field of the other, inside the corpus constituted by Gabriel Marcel. But at the same time, it conceals that corpus. The narrative only reveals relics—citations—of the body it effaces as it erects itself upon it. The narrative's appearance makes the place of its production disappear;

We become authors by recovering Marcel's "voyages"

it makes this place its secret, the invisible condition of possibility of its own emergence. All that remains in the final work of the corpus provided by the librarian are scattered pieces, flotsam and jetsam: a fragmented body. The novel arises from it, and we, as readers, can in turn become its author. We can do so by trying to find the corpus lost in the text, by raising up relics until the absent body is reached, revealing the phantom, by creating a simulacrum of the library that framed Verne's work, by mapping in this way Gabriel Marcel's voyages in the National Library.

What do we find, if not the same labor of production and effacement, only at an earlier stage? Marcel, also, in replacing the eighteenth century authors with the anthology he presents to Verne, fragments them and makes them disappear. His selection cuts apart into (choice) pieces the works he uses to fabricate a corpus. The slender publications we have by him put numerous, solid sources on display with the intention of presenting an "overview of the question," in other words a didactic picture of the situation: examples are his article of 1873 on New Caledonia,[8] and his 1883 analysis of the "first French explorations of the coast of Africa."[9] Of course, this research, which remains at the level of printed material and does not descend as far down as the manuscript under-layers, once again only gives us a side view—and perhaps isolated edited fragments—of the corpus reposing beneath the work of Verne. But there is already a style in evidence. Marcel carries out on his sources a labor analogous to Verne's on his corpus. Between the two, there is a duplication of procedures which reveals works by fragmenting them, and thus by making them disappear. Fictions replace bodies.

The data that garnish *Les Grands Navigateurs* suggest an indefinite reproduction of this process. For example, there are numerous, even impressive references to early cartography. Besides the classics (Cassini, etc.), mention is made of the maps of Bellin,[10] Buache,[11] G. Delisle,[12] "Pietergos,"[13] Sanson,[14] Van Keulen,[15] etc. Verne's navigators move within a history of cartography.[16] But the author's blunders, or the typographer's,[17] and especially the implantation of these references within citations from early explorers, preclude the hypothesis of a direct connection between the text we have before us and these venerable documents. The allusions to sixteenth and seventeenth century cartographers, and even to those of the eighteenth century, only surface in the narrative caught within fragments from eighteenth century authors, who moreover refer to them, more often than not, in order to criticize them. These are not, therefore, elements which belong to Marcel's corpus, but remnants set within remnants, signs of the labor of fragmentation and utilization performed by the chroniclers of the eighteenth century upon an earlier corpus, or, as the text says about one of them, upon "the diary manuscripts he had in his possession."

The fragments of Marcel's shattered mirror which survive in Verne are studded with slivers of mirror from an older stratum of source processing. These

Why chasms? from stratification?

in turn manifest an analogous operation performed upon their own sources. The representation of absent texts (their conversion into relics) is thus repeated on each textual level embedded within the final text. The definitive work is made up of this relic-filled stratification. It is the product of this stratification, and manifests the gradual disappearance of what it displays in a piecemeal fashion. This perspective-effect opens pathways within the text along which—like the sea routes opened by the vessels of the explorers—the reality it brings to the surface, in order to make visible, recedes and vanishes. A strange space of memory: it is on the move, *Mobilis in mobili*[18]; it is a place of comings (it is returning) and goings (it is departing), of descents and surfacings. The narrative's object is only shown in the process of being engulfed by the narrative.

This movement does not only take place in the semi-vertical depth of the citations which play upon one another. It is traversed by adjacent currents, by lateral annexations of information. The *Histoire* accidentally cites contemporary "scholarly communications," such as that of Jules Garnier, which was "inserted," Verne writes, "in the November 1869 issue of the *Bulletin de la Société de géographie*."[19] The surreptitious signature of the scholar beneath the narrator's name: that instigator, eliminated from the text, returns to the author's place through a "slip" by the author, who says *too much* for it to be *he*. But what is significant is rather that a detail from a contemporary source makes an appearance, suddenly cutting across the stage upon which pasts interpenetrate one another.

An irruption of the actual? No. The out-of-place element is also an effect of the relic, or its absence. It comes in a note about the disappearance of La Pérouse on the Vaniko Islands (1788): the search for traces of him continued throughout the nineteenth century. Following the voyages of Marchand, Entrecasteaux, and Kermadec, those of Dillon, Dumont, d'Urville, and Benier to New Hebrides circle the void created by this great tombless death. The contemporary scientific allusion—and observation made on the *occasion* of an expedition toward the unspecified place of catastrophe, a proliferation of knowledge around the missing—appears in the gaps left in the old texts, where a paucity of data prevents the dead from being located on the map or in language. So recourse is taken in the present labor of the institution (the Société de Géographie), whose memory works tirelessly on as long as the absent has yet to receive a name or a place of rest, as long as a representation has yet to fill the void. Thus the scholarly institution adds only a codicil here and there to the testamentary perusal of old *Accounts*,[20] which cover the space of the seas with relics and transform unknown regions into languages spelled out by the missing.

Names and a Map

Although Verne's text creates chasm effects in its accumulation of sources, its aim, on the contrary, is to fill in the gaps of maritime geography with "great

[handwritten annotations at top: "why is the world empty until it's created/desurrounded/already filled in" "oh. Ocean is Void."]

explorers," to make a map using these proper names, and to *make space into a language*. Essentially, Verne's explorers are name-givers; they contribute to the world's genesis through nomination. The leitmotif of the history: "we gave them the name *Labyrinth* because we had to make several tries to find our way out"; the three islands "received the name *Baumann*"; "we call it *Pitcairn*"; "Bougainville could not refrain from giving it a new name"; etc. The explorations semanticize the voids of the universe. Their durations, accidents, episodes, and trials metamorphose into words which fill the indefinite expanses of the sea: "the Island of Vexation," "the Frigid Isles," "Arid Island," "the Island of Appropriation," "Betrayal Harbour," "Desolation Island," "the Recreation Islands," etc. The voyages write the Pacific's great white page: graphs of journeys and words (fragments) from histories traced on maps.

An episode from *l'Île mystérieuse* provides the model for this nominative activity which generates meaning, multiplies semantic units scattered like islands, and slowly saturates the seas. It is its myth. It is necessary to quote this scene from the novel, which recounts the founding deed that is reproduced and disseminated throughout the entire history of the great explorers. Once upon a time, on an unknown island (analogous to the one Daniel Defoe chose for Robinson Crusoe, the solitary castaway) there were six men, who came out of nowhere. One day, they climb to the island's highest summit, and begin to name. A solemn moment, and a triumphant one, which occurs in the narrative at the precise moment they decide, as the engineer Cyrus Smith puts it, "to no longer look upon ourselves as castaways, but rather as colonists who have come for the purpose of colonizing":

> "Friends," responded the engineer, "I think it would be good to give this island a name, and also the points, promontories and waterways we see before our eyes."
>
> " . . . In the future, it would simplify the instructions we may have to give or follow."
>
> " . . . Let us give them names like Robinson Crusoe's, whose story Harbert has often read to me: 'Providence Bay,' 'Sperm Whale Promontory,' 'The Cape of Vain Hope'! . . . "
>
> "Or instead," responded Harbert, "names like Smith, Spilett, Nab! . . . "[21]
>
> "My name?" cried Nab, exhibiting his sparkling white teeth.
>
> "Why not?" replied Pencroft. " 'Port Nab' would do quite well! And 'Point Gédéon' . . . "
>
> "I would prefer names taken from our country," responded the reporter, "so they would remind us of America."
>
> "Yes, for the most important ones," Cyrus Smith said, "for the names of the bays and waters, I would agree to that gladly. For example, let us give that large bay to the east the name 'Bay of the Union,' and let us call that wide indentation to the south 'Washington

Bay,' and the mountain we are standing on 'Mount Franklin,' and the lake below us 'Lake Grant.' My friends, nothing could be better. These names will remind us of our country and of the great citizens who have honored it. But for the rivers, gulfs, points and promontories we see from the top of this mountain, let us instead choose denominations that recall their particular configurations. That way they will be engraved in our minds better, and will be more practical at the same time. The shape of the island is unusual enough that we should have no difficulty imagining names suggested by their forms. As for the waterways we are not familiar with, the various parts of the forest we will explore later, the inlets we will subsequently discover, let us baptize them as they present themselves to us. What do you think, my friends?''

The engineer's proposal was unanimously accepted by his companions. The island lay before their eyes like an unfolded map, and all they had to do was give a name to each of its concave and convex edges, and to each of its land features. Gédéon Spilett inscribed them as they went along, and the geographical nomenclature of the island was definitively adopted.[22]

To "baptize" with words designating the avatars of a hunt, a network of associates, national figures, dream images; to catch the island up in the net of these names of belonging; to turn the island into the "unfolded map" of a memory that inscribes itself; to turn it into the manipulable page one can read and where one can be read: that is "to colonize." The *Histoire* proceeds by multiplying this primitive scene. But in *L'Île mystérieuse*, as in *Les Grands Navigateurs*, the meaning of this production of space as language is that it provides a ground for scientific and industrious activity. It makes future operations possible. The representation constructed through nomination does not express things, it allows a labor to be undertaken. In Verne, it is a condition of possibility, not a result. It is an act which initiates progress, not a portrait of a piece of land or the product of an appropriation. The image lies at the basis of a science, as the decision that generates it. The navigational colonization inaugurates an operativity by providing it with a place of its own: the map, which replaces beings, "calls" them to the linguistic network which situates them in advance in a field of human history.[23]

Undoubtedly, the indefinite act of naming, of circumscribing and delimiting units, of thus dragging oneself out of maritime indeterminacy, is also the narrative path followed by a relation to maternal indifferentiation. The ocean is an always present primordiality. It envelops. Names must be carved out of it relentlessly (islands, submarines, "floating apparatuses"), outlets for meaning must be engineered in it, the dotted lines of a paternal symbolic system must be inscribed upon it, one must attempt to *leave*, to be born, to walk. Navigations in a primal cavern, where one must mark out names and places. Voyages simultaneously within and without. Professor Lidenbrock, embarking *upon* the sea

Naming in order to act,
In order to act,
Fend off primordial void-ness.

that lies *beneath* the earth—an archaic, liquid vastness in the belly of the world—performed the exorcism which consists in naming. According to his nephew Axel, "upon leaving" a small, natural port in that interior ocean, "my uncle, who was quite attached to his geographical nomenclature, wanted to give it a name, my name. . . . "[24] The orphan's name, imposed by the uncle on the mother earth, is itself a "port," it limits and demarcates, it borders upon unnamed depths.

Nomination, whose victories the explorers' histories recount, is thus struck with ambivalence. It functions as an interspace between linguistic conquest and confinement in oceanic primordiality. The "scientific progress" whose "discoveries" it marks does not simply figure as an extension. Its advance is encircled, haunted, even momentarily engulfed by the indeterminate element through which it progresses, just as ships, *mobiles in mobili*, are borne, menaced and sometimes swallowed by the great sea that they write.

Verne, in addition, suggests that there is a frenzy in naming: "the mania, then in fashion, for imposing new vocables on every location one visited." *Mania*: a madness. A rush to perform the rite of exorcism, a pioneering rush to found, but also the feverish affixing of *more* or *too many* words "of their own" [*mots "propres"*] by explorers who travel in their predecessors' language. The symbolic act of making history by calling things is repeated on islets and shores that have already been named several times. These heroes, martyrs of departure who brave the unknown, enter a space of words. They move within the text of others. But they still must re-perform the civilizing act. Even after it has ceased to be justified by any scientific relevance, this "baptism" must be endlessly recelebrated on every beach. It is a rite which repeats the act of genesis of the Occidental map. It is important because it reproduces the origin of all knowing, not just because it produces a surplus of knowledge. In itself, nomination "makes sense" (*sacer-facere*): it is the sacrifice.

The Circular Exodus

Around the World in Eighty Days, Verne's success of 1873, has many descendants, beginning in 1874 with a piece by D'Ennery.[25] This encircling of the earth is the figure-type of a kind of itinerary of knowledge. It defines the perfect observation process. The encyclopaedic ambition follows a trajectory which returns to its point of departure. Science is circled, just like the earth. The organizing framework is not the medieval one of ascension, nor that of the dictionary, which prevailed during the eighteenth century. The order of knowledge takes the form of a circular voyage. *Le Tour du Monde. Nouvelles géographiques*: the title of this bulletin, which became an eight-page weekly in 1891, is an echo of Verne's work,[26] but it also recapitulates the content of his *Histoire* recounting a series of "circumnavigations."

This series of circuits organizes *Les Grands Navigateurs* according to relations between the circle and the straight line. On the one hand, these trips around the world one by one return to the same: they pass by the same capes and the same islands, and come back to their European point of origin (English, French, Spanish). But the supplementary information and articles they bring back pile up in the laboratories and museums where new expeditions are planned. Linear progress only occurs at the point where the knowledge is stockpiled:

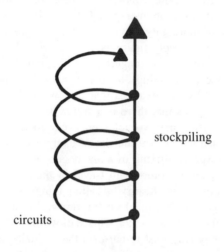

stockpiling

circuits

This linear progress has as its equivalent, at the same (Occidental) point, the history that is capable of serializing "circumnavigations." Narrativity organizes, as an expansion of *our* knowledge, the successive voyages which return one after another to the narrative's place of production.

the
narrative

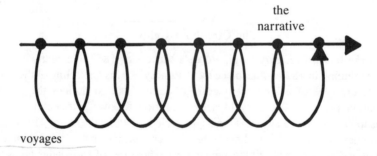

voyages

The narrative, as the Occidental capitalization of observations collected by explorers, forms a line of circles. As Verne constantly emphasizes, the success of this cumulative narrative operation is made possible by the technical knowledge of the explorer and by the presence on board of teams of scientists. In this way, the voyage gradually eliminates the losses: everything must be observed, and everything that is *seen* in faraway places must be able to be *known* in London or in Paris. There must be no "remainder" marking the exteriority of the voyage in relation to the narrative, allowing an elsewhere outside the place of return to escape. Thus, the narrative exposes its own condition of possibility when it recounts how knowledge progresses aboard ship. The voyagers are placed in hierarchical order according to their success in avoiding losing things along the way, thus depriving the narrative of something. James Cook, for example, is "classed well above the French explorer" Bougainville, who "embellishes" and does not know how to "faithfully represent things." The work ends with Alexander von Humboldt, "the perfect model of the voyager" (these are the last words of the book), which is to say that he is an explorer who "reports" everything with precision and closes the distance separating the voyage and the narrative. The history can come to a close with Humboldt because in him the narrator coincides with the voyager. The circle is perfect, with no remainder.

On the other hand, it is true that "Verne's work is no more than a long meditation, or reverie, on the straight line. . . . Title: the adventures of the straight line."[27] A will to rigor must uniformly impose itself upon disparities of circumstance and location, it must triumph over diversions, going straight to the target as fast as possible. Like Phileas Fogg, the hero of *Around the World in Eighty Days*, the good navigator takes the shortest and quickest route to the unknown entity to be located, then back to London or Paris to report the information. The narrative itself cuts out digressions and chooses the documents that get most directly to the point. In the typology of Verne's fictional characters, as in his classifications of eighteenth century explorers, the priority accorded the straight line is translated into a preference for the British over the French (who are always a little "fanciful," and prone to geographical and literary detours[28]), until the German, Humboldt, takes over. In the last analysis, the journey could be described in the same terms as Fogg: "this gentleman . . . did not travel, he described a circumference."[29] Its ideal would be the train, a steam engine which, in Verne, traverses vast expanses "cleaved by the line of its tracks."[30]

But the straight line forms a circle. By virtue of its very straightness, it circles the earth, it completes a circuit around it. There is another machine that symbolizes this paradoxical power: the watch. Verne, a pioneer in technological history, paid special attention to watch-making and devoted some important pages to it.[31] Moreover, he compares Fogg to a "chronometer." The clock reconciles the circle and the straight line, and it is what has, since the time of Cook, made precision and exploration possible. In fact, it is its model: the clock, a celibatory machine that remains autonomous "despite the conditions of the sea and differences of temperature," impervious to all alteration, inviolable, allows the "reduction" of ship time to the time at the port of embarkation; it allows each

clock

celibatory voyage distracted by Feminine Tahiti

moment of circumnavigation to be tied to the referential time of departure; and it is the rotation of the chronometer that allows for the measuring, control, and rectification of any drift in space.

Must we recognize in the watch, which travels without ever leaving the point of departure or being altered, the semi-eponymous figure of the bachelor explorers (homologues of Nemo, Robur, Lidenbrock, Herr Schultze, Doctor Ox, Zacharius, etc.), of the voyages without women,[32] of islands inhabited solely by men—in short, of the myth of the celibatory machine? The explorations of the eighteenth century tended to orbit like the shell fired from Professor Schultze's canon in *Les 500 millions de la Begum*—a solitary shell, thrown into orbit by an excess of speed, trapped in endless circumnavigation, never again to fall to earth.

This is actually not the case. The narrative creates stop-off points. It brakes the rotation of the clock by multiplying descriptions of landscapes and customs. The necessity and urgency of geographic discovery (what Verne calls the "labor") is suspended by narrative stopovers (designated "depictions"). History is a combination of "labor" and "depictions." Island stays provide a counterpoint to the law of the watch. There is even, in the heart of the Pacific, a point of delay and tarrying, a paradisiac transgression of work, a pleasure place, an "enchanting picture," as Verne writes: Tahiti. Six times the explorers' history stops off there.[33] The warrior's repose, the place where Captain Cook observed Venus' passage, Bougainville's "New Cytherea," located at the other end of the earth, this Fortunate Isle covered with gardens crossed by silvery brooks is inhabited by a people full of health and vigor who are ruled by a queen (Oberoa), are free of religious superstitions and whose only concern is to please; they offer their women to the sailors, welcome the Western strangers with banana branches and see them off with tears. A feminine place? In any case, a meeting place of alliances. From there and nowhere else comes the native, that *other* introduced into the fellowship of the explorers. Through the native, the reality of the elsewhere causes the voyage to drift, it diverts it, anchoring it in a dreamland. The circle is not perfect. Fiction cuts across it. That exodus transformed into "circulation" remains open to "embellishments" and interlacing with the other.

The International of Discovery

Jules Verne has a politics.[34] It comes out in the praises sung for "philanthropy," which consists in "regarding every man as a brother," and reveals in the conduct of certain of the explorers premonitory signs of the rights of man and the National Convention's emancipation of Blacks. The criticism of the "*ancien régime*, where everything was arbitrary," and the "indignation" toward the "facility" with which colonizers everywhere "destroy without motive or need"

what's with this ending?

and "abuse their power," the irony expressed, for example in relation to Carteret, by "the ridiculous ceremony of claiming the country (New Britain) in the name of George III"—all of these traits comprise the political flipside of a history in which patriotism itself ("our geographers," etc.) is overshadowed by an International of courage and competition. *Les Grands Navigateurs* is something like the "Olympic Games." Verne is its prose Pindar. He makes himself the Michelet of the sporting conquests of maritime spaces. Even though the teams are national, the events produce "rivals," proving the superiority of the English or French.

In addition to this "sports" epic, history is divided by a major opposition. It squares two rivals off against each other. Bougainville and Cook. Here, the division is as much social as scientific. A secret hostility surrounds, in the text, the French aristocrat, whose abilities and brilliant career annoy Verne. The hero is James Cook, the son of a farmhand from Morton, a child of the people who methodically organized his campaigns, a pioneer of contemporary knowledge, killed in Hawaii in a solitary battle to prevent a massacre. The narrative unfolds around him and erects at its center a monument to his memory. The explorers' International quietly becomes an arena of class struggle.

Thus the conqueror-sage who, like Roggewein, is "greeted like a god" in eighteenth-century history, is not just anybody. No one could forget that after re-reading Verne's "apotheosis" of the explorer. He based it on a text of Bouguer's; in his account of a French expedition to Peru (1736), at the outset of his work, he traces, in the "glory" of Mount Tabor, the Discoverer's epiphany, the immense shadow of the pioneer.

> A cloud, which had engulfed us and was now dissipating, permitted us to see the sun, rising and radiant. The cloud moved to the other side. It was but thirty paces away, when each of us saw his own shadow projected above, and only his own, for the cloud did not offer a unified surface. The distance was small enough for us to distinguish every part of the shadow; we could see the arms, the legs, the head; but what surprised us was that this last-named part was adorned with a glory or aureole formed of three or four small, concentric coronas, very bright in color, each with the same varieties as the rainbow, red on the outside. The spaces between these circles were equal; the last circle was the dimmest; and finally, far in the distance, we saw a great, white circle surrounding it all. It was like a kind of apotheosis for the viewer.

Chapter 10
The Theater of the *Quiproquo*:
Alexandre Dumas

"O great secrets, meticulously concealed in the mysteries of history, how small you are when the chronicler's hand reveals you to the eyes of the public, naked and unveiled!"[1] So the great state secrets inhabiting the edifice of official history are simply imaginary. If we look behind the façade, we see the heroes "with their clothes off"; we see their passions and "private habits"[2] and hear the murmur of little secrets—"the true causes of the wars that have stained the world with blood since the time of the Trojan War."[3] If it is true that "not one historian managed to be historical,"[4] it is because they have confused the real with crowd-impressing appearances.

Alexandre Dumas, a regular at court, knew too much about the "ceremonial gowns" history drapes over the shoulders of its actors in order to give itself an air of majesty: the effect is only a function of distance and secret. So he takes a look behind the scenes. He shows the back-hall "dramas" and "comedies." It is in the back hall that is to be found the truth told by the past and present chroniclers of whom Dumas—always the tireless ferreter, the inexhaustible traveler and questioner—is so fond. That is where verisimilitude resides; and it must be reconstructed after official knowledge has orchestrated its forgetting. By inverting history in this way, he sets it back on its feet, he presents its underside, he demystifies and democratizes it, transforming it into an everyday thing whose secrets can be openly read—those comic and pathetic secrets composed of *quiproquos* and surprises that everyone sees, and in which everyone can recognize himself. Welcome to the *Historical Theater*, the stage built at huge expense by the architect Dedreux and christened in February 1847 with the performance of *La Reine Margot*.⁵ Ladies and gentlemen, come this way and you will see history for one, for all, a history recounting both the proximity of the past and the foreignness of your private life, or the present as a metaphor for a somewhere else.

Does not this displaced history have the form of a dream? Like Freud's *Moses and Monotheism*,⁶ it is a "historical novel," or the effect on another, theatrical scene, of rhetorical diversions, synecdoches, asyndetons, metonymies and anamorphoses of the past-present. It is a *fiction*, if what is understood by that is a discourse which traces the outline of the divided place of its own production; or, if one prefers, a representation that is marked—or better yet, tattooed like a body—by the obscure law that haunts that place and organizes the practices that function there. What is produced (*fingere*) on Dumas' stage is effectively determined by two archaeologies of its present, one of which is historical, the other genealogical. Two forms of the same law: the first is the *ancien régime* (the "old regime"); and the other is the individual's relation to his parents.

In Dumas, the *ancien régime* plays the same role "primitives" were to play a half century later, from Freud to Durkheim: it is the region of the origin, which must be redone, rewritten and re-presented. In 1850, the society of the *ancien régime* not only had the characteristic, by its proximity in time, of something "uncanny," or disquietingly familiar (the spatial proximity of colonization would later endow primitive man with the same attribute); it was also the world from which the nineteenth century had distanced itself, declaring it dead. It was the part of the present from which the Revolution had broken away and rejected as "old," so its own birth could belong to a different history. This break is both the condition of possibility and the effect of a beginning. But the "old" returns. It forbids one to feel at home in the new age. The actual remains engaged in a "fantasy" debate with this phantom, which continues to haunt it. The *ancien régime* is the ghost of Hamlet's father.⁷ The presence of the lost one. The obsessional shadow of what history assassinated. As in a dream, this shade stalks the theatrical and novelistic stages of the time (Vigny, Hugo, Dumas, Delavigne, etc.).

But the "Historical Theater" of Alexandre Dumas exorcizes the "old" that appropriates the place of the present, by multiplying its apparitions, by recounting it in its own way. It tears it to pieces, fragmenting it in individual plays; it acts it out; little by little, it reconquers it, like the scientific imaginary of ethnology did to the primitive world; it expresses new fantasies, desires, and conflicts using shades drawn from the parental world, the disappearance of which is "uncertain." That is what re-presenting is.⁸ Dis-quieting corpses return to the grave if they become the lexicon of the living. The world of yesteryear is summoned to recount *our* history: that is what ensures that it "cannot harm us," that it "presents no danger."⁹ The birth of a new century is thus inscribed in the space of the preceding one. The "Historical Theater" transforms the multiform text, which nevertheless continues to dictate its law. It tricks the past; it comes up on it from behind and turns it around. It "unclothes" this all-too-close foreignness, stripping it of its threatening solemnity, and "assimilating" it into the nineteenth century. Cannibalism by detour. A second death: first there was a revolutionary murder, then the ghost undergoes a theatrical turn-about. The *ancien régime* becomes a legend—no longer that injunctive legend hovering above the present like a phantom and "citing" it, but a legend that can be turned into the object of citations, or a collection of relics with which to construct the fable (*fari*: that which speaks) of the actual. In this theater of historical operations the *voice* of the past is transformed into *images* presented to the public. The specter that once owned the night is replaced by an unlimited array of mirrors reflecting the day that has dawned. The memory which "re-morses" [*remord*]¹⁰ the new century becomes its imaginary museum.

The success of this operation is never certain. It must be endlessly rebegun. Dumas' curiosity and inventiveness are a result of this uncertainty, and it shows in his novels: daring always goes hand in hand with the theme of the "lost cause."¹¹ But which cause is lost? It has to be that of the *author* in relation to *his double*. The works themselves are an indication that this is indeed the case: they double one another. Division (which is here, as in Freud, *Zweifel*, doubt, internal division) does not just break the unity of the discourse "held" successively or simultaneously by the characters in the novels or plays; it even affects the author's position (the nominal center where the fictional unity of the work is produced), appearing there in the form of shared credit between Dumas and any one of his many *alter egos* (Danzats, Fiorentino, Lockroy, Meurice, and especially Maquet, who in 1856 and 1858 claimed his rights as co-author of eighteen of the most celebrated novels published under the name of Dumas). This division is clearly marked in the plays: "By Alexandre Dumas and Auguste Maquet." The place of the author is occupied by one *and* the other, and neither has a place of his "own" [*un lieu propre*]. Often, one of the authors will be given the "public" name and costume, but behind it, in the back hall, there is still the "private" work of another, presented by the theatrical text for the eyes of the public. But then *who* appears in the play? Does Dumas himself know which author's role he is acting out? To what extent is he the re-presentation of that foreign intimacy? His theater is, precisely, the production of the no-place of the author, the comic or tragic confession of the property owner who is in fact only a renter, or someone in debt, living in a "borrowed home" that is—as the "title implies—metaphorical."¹² This theatrical truth, with no place of its own [*sans propre*], can only re-produce itself in perpetual displacement, and Dumas' biography is just one more re-enactment of it.

Dumas' theatrical creations cannot be separated from the *Chroniques* and the *Histoires*, which provide them a space and a lexicon. His plays only very rarely construct a space that is fictional (that is to say, imaginary) or poetic (not authorized by a system of referentiality). On the contrary, they bend to the demands of history, or to the law of the other. They inscribe themselves in the text of others. They insinuate themselves into the work of past authors, who define and occupy Dumas' place as much as he colonizes theirs. The literary content of his work thus repeats the question of the relation of the nineteenth century to the *ancien régime*: who has taken whose place? A *quiproquo* structure. Who masks whom? Who is the "author"? Dumas' stage is haunted by the other. And that is what makes it truly "historical."

In this context, mention should be made of characters who are "historical theaters" in themselves, or enactments of doubling. They are characters in whom a strange power has taken over the functioning of the subject: Balsamo, alias Cagliostro, the Count of Monte-Cristo, the mysterious Doctor, etc. What these eponymous heroes display is not so much an excess of *knowledge* as a *force* that comes to them from somewhere else, and whose foreignness of origin is repeated in the effects that flow from it; the landlord (not really the owner) of this force does not himself have the power to see or know, but can *induce* his interlocutors *to see* or *know* or *say* the truth. These characters can exercise the power they receive from the other only through others still. A strange power of transference—which is also metaphorical. It links truth to a force-effect in the gap between the other and others; a medium maintains the break between them and assures the transmission. This is fundamentally the same as the power of the historian, who induces the dead he visits to speak their (or the) truth—in short, the power of a Michelet. And, in fact, the medium, or hypnotist, must put his subjects to "sleep" in order for them to see and speak. Only then do the "little secrets" determining the greatness of history appear, "naked and unveiled."

Dumas' *Urbain Grandier*—a work which is itself double[13]—contains a particularly revealing variant of this haunted character. The play re-presents the celebrated case of possession at Loudun (Poitou), which lasted from 1632 to 1640, and in the course of which Urbain Grandier, a parish priest, was unjustly burned at the stake on charges of witchcraft.[14] The literary development of this story began with the pamphlets and gazettes of the seventeenth century, continued with Vigny's *Cinq-Mars*, *La Sorcière* by Michelet, Aldous Huxley's *The Devils of Loudun*, and has passed down to the present day in the form of such productions as a Swedish novel (*Dreams of Fire and Roses*, 1949) by Johnson, a Polish film by Kawalerowicz (*Mother Jeanne of the Angels*, 1960), Penderecki's German opera (*The Devils of Loudun*, 1969), and an English film (*The Devils*, 1972) by Russell. The extent of the tradition is in no way surprising, because possession places identity in question; as the hold of the other (god, spirit, devil, or angel) over the subject, it theatricalizes doubling: who is possessed by whom? Dumas, in contrast to the interpretations of "unbelievers," does indeed present Grandier as a sorcerer: "a power was given to me," he declares. But he transposes possession from the cosmological scene (in which humanity is divided in a war between Satan and God) to a psychological scene (the gift of a hypnotizer). There is thus a movement "from myth to fiction" through the internalization of the conflict and the double.[15] Private life, the reality of history, becomes the theater of the *quiproquo*.

If the gift is henceforth in the service of truth, and no longer a Satanic rebellion, and if, on the other hand, it necessitates Grandier's death at the hands of the defenders of order, it is because history and truth are no longer in agreement and one or the other is constantly gaining the upper hand. This is a reversal of the old system, where the triumph of truth, the presupposition of the cosmos, doomed history to the role of a heretic or something altogether irrelevant. By assassinating the witness who receives the foreign power to make truth be spoken—in short, by assassinating the poet—Dumas dramatizes the social repression of the double.[16] He preserves a kind of "possession" that can only lead to failure. He recounts the impossibility of *and* the search for ecstasy, as well as the impossibility of and search for a place of one's own. He oscillates in the space between—between the inaccessible and an altered "own"[le propre altéré]. His theater is "historical" because it is the enactment of the *Zwischenraum*.

Corresponding to this incertitude of identity—the doubling of the subject, the division of the author, the alteration of every place—are the "private" secrets that disrupt the genealogical order. Dumas once invoked "Oedipus, who kills his father, marries his mother, and has children by her, who are simultaneously his sons, grandsons and brothers."[17] Who is the father and who is the son? That is the question asked by Dumas' historical theater as a whole. "Alexandre Dumas" is itself the name of both the father and the son: this doubled proper name receives the Oedipal function that makes the son the mother's husband, and the husband the son of his wife.

The confusion of generations, the transgression of sexual prohibitions—these are the true secrets, naked and unveiled, brought before the eyes of the public by the theater of Dumas. For example, in *Urbain Grandier*, the Countess of Albizzi is a mother in love with her son, to whom she sacrifices her daughter; Jeanne de Laubardemont's father is in love with her, and she calls Grandier, whom she in turn loves, "my father"; the nuns in the convent perform sapphic dances, and Grandier has a homophilic affection for his brother Daniel. The private is the secret space of drift. Love relations, revolutionary movement beneath the surface of the socio-political order, cross the barriers of sexuality in the name of an instability which makes every place the possibility and the presence of its other. No public prohibition can stop them. It is the dark reign of non-distinction, a kind of "matter" that never makes it into the analytical taxonomies of social "form," a silent hemorrhaging of public life by an uncontrollable individual mobility.

Along with this proliferation of vanishing points (which so fascinates Dumas) comes a time-serpent, which is perhaps akin to that of the sleep provoked by the hypnotizer, a sleep ignorant of differences of place: it is the time of loss and "caressing," not the time of order estranging the past from the present. It is a time which makes the difference between *one* and the *other* disappear; a time that is created by the fiction of Alexandre Dumas as the utopia of pleasure and the no-place of the individual. His Urbain Grandier suggests this with an adroit comparison: "Time is a serpent which bites those who do not know how to use it, and caresses those who know how to profit by it."

Chapter 11
The Arts of Dying:
Celibatory Machines

On this fringe of a fable torn in two.

—Yves Bonnefoy, *Dans le leurre du seuil*

Todesarten: Theoretical Fictions

Ingeborg Bachmann, in 1966, introduced her book *Malina* as a "cycle" treating the "different ways of dying." *Todesarten*. A return to the ("popular") literature of the *Art of Dying*? But now the circle of the text is closed. And what is imprisoned in language has become the agent of a *Grenzübertritt* (a move past the boundary) that is never more than a game of chess—fictions of prisons and fictions of escape, a painted window, a pane of glass/mirror—where the evidence of what can neither be said nor "found" is at play. There are no gaps and tears but written ones. Comedies of laying bare, machinery of torture, "automaton accounts" stripped of meaning, faces broken down into cogwheels. With the appearance of "celibatory machines," a fantasy realm without precedent (except in the relation between the artifact and death) goes into action. It is on the order of myth, not only by virtue of the founding break it marks at the turn of this century, but also because of the no-place of the event/advent which figures in it in "different ways"—an entrance and/or exit.

Freud, in the *Interpretation of Dreams*, constructs (*bauen*) a celibatory machine which is not displayed in Michel Carrouges' collection.[1] But by its nature and date it certainly belongs in the series.[2] It is an "apparatus" (*Apparat*) that is built around an internal difference and is composed of interconnected "systems" (*Système*) functioning in such a way that *it is inscribed* and accumulates within (mnemic traces), in such a way that it circulates—forward during the day and backward at night (a *rücklaufigen Weg* and a *regredientes Rückschreiten*)—and in such a way that it transforms energy (*die Energieumsetzungen im Innern Apparats*). Meticulously constructed, this fantasy "mechanics" explains which elements of the Eliminated (masculine/feminine) return to the "scene of the dream" (*der Schauplatz der Traüme*). Freud calls it a "theoretical fiction," *theoritische Fiktion*.[3]

That name is well suited for the entire series, if it is true that fiction is written in the language of a rejected land and a dispossessed body,[4] with all the trappings of a fatal exile or an impossible exodus. Fiction is the solitary machine which engineers the Eros of death. It is a comedy of mourning in the tomb of the Absent (masculine/feminine). A debt inseparable from rejection. But the "torture" remains literary. Wounding, wracking, killing the body on a veiled/violated page, it only textually breaks the closure of the text. A scriptural celibacy, organized by its imaginary other. The breakdown (de-fection) of characters falling to pieces—gears and springs. Of characters painted on the pane, where they meld with the objects behind the glass/window, or with the reflection of the spectator before the glass/mirror.[5] It traces, still scripturally, the *limit of writing* and the cleavage that disseminates the subject despite the minimal promise of fusion this transparence provides.

Of course, only an eroticism is able to set the apparatus in motion (*den Apparat in Bewegung zu bringen*), but eroticisms are directed toward a (something) other which will never be *here* (or is driven away from this space by a challenge issued by dispossession), and which renders obsessive the (narcissistic) gaze of the voyeur surprised by his Double as he moves among the things offered/rejected in the glass/mirror. The graph painted on Duchamp's glass is the legend of the illusion that transforms into a sex/image the point on the transparent wall at which the celibate (male/female) stands.[6]

This is most certainly an antimysticism. An anti-"realism" also. The time is over when the "real" seemed to enter the text and writing seemed to make love with social violence. Verism was on the side of the simulacrum, a theater of verisimilitude. After Zola came Jarry and Roussel and Duchamp and Kafka: theoretical fictions of the impossible other, of writing abandoned to its circular movement, to its solitary erection/constructions. Backward motion (*Regression*) toward the "place" (*Lokalität*) inside the machine where an inaccessible law— which the text mimics by enacting its own death—is imprinted (*Aufdruck*) and leaves its trace (*Spur*). Writing, an exquisite cadaver, gets no respect anymore:

it is only the illusory sacrament of the real, the space of the laugh and/or blasphemy which is not one. It deploys only the ironic, meticulous labor of mourning, which draws entrances and exits on the translucent wall. *Todesarten*.

For more than four centuries in the West, writing has been the substitute for myth, and—from *Robinson Crusoe* to *Moses and Monotheism*—it was the subject of "novels" playing the part of myths. It is a praxis. Up until the twentieth century, writing had the triple privilege: of establishing a field of its "own" [*un champ propre*] standing apart from the spellbound world—the *blank page*; of building upon it, through cumulative (written) trajectories, a domain of knowledge elaborated on the basis of a tradition, or with reference to nature, in contrast to both of which it appeared as unknowledge—the *text*; and finally, of being able to *make* history, from its base in a space where a will stocked its acquisitions and outlined a "model"—a *capitalist, productive* mode of writing. It was the action/myth of a society capable of transforming itself into a blank page upon which it could write the story of its own genesis, and relate that story to what the society was separating from (as *knowledge*) without losing the referent (since it *used* it). A machine *par excellence*, in turn pedagogical, entrepreneurial, urbanist, scientific, and revolutionary.

But then that "blank" space becomes laden with unclean and ob-scene images (after becoming glass or fiction, the written page is changed by what it excludes). The text, closed in upon itself, loses the referent that authorized it, and is no longer anything more than *der Schauplatz der Traüme*; utility is inverted, becoming "sterile gratuitousness," repeating the *coitus interruptus* of the bachelor Don Juan, or the solitary production of the bride's "widower," left with nothing other than itself, with no reproduction but symbolizing reproduction, with no foreign land, without a woman and without nature. Writing proliferates in the vicinity of the break that vibrates in the nothing of the work. It is an "island/inscription," a *Locus solus*, a "penal colony," a dream inhabited by the unreadability to which, or of which, it thinks it "speaks." It is this baring of the scriptural myth—an act of derision—that makes the celibatory machine blasphemous. It challenges the principle of Occidental ambition. With its traps and machinations, it undermines the *simulacrum* of being that comprised the (now unveiled) secret/sacred aspect of a Bible transformed by four centuries of bourgeois writing into the gospel of the domination of things by the letter and the cipher.

A wound, no longer hidden behind the painting, but inscribed at its center, breaks the text into two fragments held together with safety pins.[7] A fable torn in two. It is the equivalent of the bar separating *La Mariée* into two sections, or of the pane of glass itself. Theoretical fiction points to the site of writing. Which is what brought up the problem addressed by Duchamp: "The Preconditions of a Language."

The Writing Machine

The language in question has "antimystical" preconditions. "Antimystical" is an approximation connoting first of all one of the celibatory machines' modes of functioning in the environment from which they emerged at the beginning of the century: a surrounding tendency was to locate the mystical in literature. But celibatory fictions also pass back over the graphs of mystic language. In a kind of makeshift clock repair, they isolate these precious parts, disseminate them in another space, "set them going" in backward motion (the *Regression* of the dream) and reverse their usage. Thus in Roussel, the biblical words *Mané, Thécel, Pharès*[8] become by association *manette, aisselle, phare* (lever, armpit, beacon), the verbal constellation around which Fogar's activities organize themselves.[9]

This procedure is not totally new. It is, in fact, one of the characteristics of a specifically mystic mode of rhetoric. Even as early as Angelus Silesius, the *terms* preserved by the mystic tradition serve as the *place* where a labor, taking as its raw material the accepted semantic objects, is undertaken and enables him to produce enactments of dialogues with God.[10] Closer to celibatory machines, biblical words in the work of Bloy function as nuclei/images which generate histories; they provide him with a dictionary he uses to turn narrative into the art of circumstantiating quotations.[11] For Bloy, the mystic or biblical lexicon is the verbal raw material for *phonetic* derivations: procedures which change the semantic usage of words without altering the substance of the sounds, thus effecting a shift of meaning beneath the same phonetic material, generate the possibility of icon *effects* or fantasy narratives.

The mystic repertory is still recognizable in Bloy, even after having passed through an entire series of linguistic operations and imaginary displacements: the island, the castle, the cave, the wall, lightning, the arrow or needle, the fish, the sea, the other land (*Wonderland*), but also nakedness, flagellation, the crown of thorns, hanging, the crucifixion, the tomb, etc. More important than these resurgences themselves, however, is the literary *praxis* that produces the reusages; it is a direct descendant of the one that oversaw the production of "mystic phrases"[12] in the seventeenth century, and, according to that period's theorists of mysticism, constitutes its very definition. For them, the generative principle is a "way of (mis)treating" the accepted language. Mystic discourse is a *modus loquendi*. It is the outcome of an entire set of operations on and in the shared social text. It is an *artifact* (a production) created by the labor of putting language *to death*.

This labor of "wounding" acts upon *semantic* formations. It infiltrates an order of discourse. It plays on *meanings*, throwing them off balance through the systematic use of oxymoron and catachresis, everywhere applying the science of "mystic incision and anatomy" with a "sharp knife," taking the "liberty" of employing "imperfect, improper and dissimilar terms," "vicious in its excesses"; and also through the systematic practice of "stooping to indecent similes," "carrying oneself to holy excess as though mad or deranged"; and through an "immodesty" whose goal is not to generate a surplus of meaning, but on the contrary to induce a de-fection of meaning in order to demonstrate the existence of an "off-stage" (ob-scene) in language, and in order to create fade-out points everywhere.[13] Anamorphosis—torturous anamorphosis. Therefore, a double thematic of *laying bare* (not an "uncovering" of truth in the Greek sense, but a stripping down and demystification of the semantic order) and *torture* is essential to this labor. Of course, its first manifest appearance is in the form of "the experience" recounted in biographical discourse (for example, St. Teresa's love wound). It thus marks in narrative (in "fiction") the process by which narrative is constructed. The defoliation of meaning and torture are not just what is said in the discourse. They define its mode of production. A *modus loquendi*: a speaking machine.

This seventeenth century rhetorical mode has its own conditions of possibility. For one, a *semanticized universe* is presupposed by the erosion it effects. In addition, an *accredited place*, established by "ecstasy" (an "exile"), allows (mystic) utterance to substitute itself for (theological) statements by claiming to stand, by virtue of its self-dispossession, at the very place where the (meaningless) Spirit speaks. Finally, a *referential vocabulary*—itself the object of metaphorical displacements—is nevertheless the instrument, handed down by the religious tradition, that is used to authorize the torture operation. These conditions taken together lend torture and the referent the support of a truth that *is not*, and never could be, identical to what is said, but is instead postulated by the labor of the negative, which spies it in the interspace between the body and language. That interspace is the place where feelings injuring the body and paradoxes damaging the discourse have their immaterial meeting point.

By the twentieth century, all of these postulates of the religious *episteme* of the seventeenth century had disappeared. Although they abandon the hypothesis that there is one, traditional, semantic system (meaning is everywhere) and that there is spiritual legitimacy (a proper place from which to speak)—in other words, though they have finally freed themselves from the need for an institution concealing a truth somewhere in its dark recesses (mysticism arose in relation to a religion)—celibatory machines nevertheless practice both the art of laying bare and torture. Theirs, however, is a *linguistic* rather than semantic labor. It can no longer take recourse in "truth." In the seventeenth century the location of the truth was doubtless uncertain, but its existence was never in doubt. In the twentieth, the play is on words, through a system of phonetic drift (Roussel's "phonic cabbalah"[14]) which allows the production of a narrative or painting. The only "authorities" are verbal. The torture thus takes place in the slender thickness of language—a pane of glass, a wall—without the assumption that a non-localizable reality enters in. The text stands alone. It is the only referential "body." It is a substitute (*Ersatz*), kept at a distance (*Locus solus*), of both the speaking subject and the maternal body: one is the absent author (it authorizes nothing); the other is "tread upon" by a writing which is separated from it.[15] The celibatory machine is not a *modus loquendi*, but a *modus scribendi*. A writing machine.

Similarly, since laying bare occurs in relation to an impossible incest, the fading away of the "land" that guarantees language appears both in the form of blasphemies directed against the woman/mother [*mère*] and dreams of the sea [*mer*]. With Hadewijch of Anvers, Catherine of Sienna, Catherine of Genoa, St. Teresa of Ávila, Marie de l'Incarnation, Madame Guyon, Antoinette Bourignon, etc., the *mother* is dominant in mystic discourse, which is "born of woman," the product of a matrilineal descent, infused by what Luce Irigaray calls the "mystical."[16] Its exegete, however, was the clergyman, the male adherent of mystic discourse who expected to receive through its feminine alteration, not his power, which remained as it was, but the ability to produce and "speak." The machine is the narrative of the *celibate*, in relation to the impossible *mère* (*mer*), to the female hanged man, to the bride stripped bare. An irreparable break is here at the principle of the artifact.

In modern times, laying bare and torture no longer enter in *before* the loss; they no longer inhabit a land from which negative effects functioning on behalf of the truth can be extracted. They come *after*, in the solitude of a discourse discoursing with itself. Although derision and torture remain the mainsprings of narrative, they no longer depend on a belief that it is possible to gear into something "unsayable." The only roaming that takes place is within oneself, in the form of homophonous drifts, obscene metaphors, puns traversing the stratified meaning of a given sound, slips of the tongue—in short, the turns of phrase circumscribed by language. Plays on words, involving "good" words or bad, using "any abstract word, which is to say any word that does not have a concrete reference" (Duchamp).

Laying Bare and Torture

Although there are many analogies between the old and the new functioning of these two procedures (laying bare and torture), the distance separating them remains considerable.

Laying bare in the old sense came about only after one had been dressed in costume by and for the theater of the world. Whatever disparaging of history it accomplished it did by itself, by working from *within* the "illusion" it was fighting, an illusion from which it would never emerge until the moment of death. "Not naked, not clothed, but stripped bare," said Angelus Silesius: not a primitive innocence regained, but its deconstruction through the agency of a necessary social construct—a privative solemnity [*sérieux*] within positivity and deceit. The only way to make truth out of error. it necessitated sending all costumes to the "graveyard of liveries and uniforms"; it was a descent into disorder, madness, and obscenity. The tradition continued right up to Bataille, in his *Méthode de méditation*, which followed the *Nouvelle théologie mystique*: "I think like a girl takes off her dress. At its most extreme point, thought is immodesty, obscenity itself."[17] Mysticism, also, returns to the body, touched and emotionally moved—to that shadowy paradise of a reality which is no longer located in language, and which eyes no longer see.

Finally, since visual experiences are never certain (they were the form of experience least trusted and most supervised in the seventeenth century), laying bare was provided with "eyewitnesses"—God and/or his official representatives—in the hope of *letting them see* what the subject can neither see nor designate. The denuded body knows not what it says. It presupposes a reader by whom it allows itself to be read like a hieroglyph that is indecipherable in itself. (This was soon to become the province of the invalid or madman, transformed into the eye of wisdom.) The (auto)biographical text of the body laid bare—like the text of the critical editions of the same period, stripped of the coverings of time—is offered for the hermeneutical reading practice of an other, present or yet to come. It awaits a foreign exegesis, which is a probability that remains unknown; for there does not, in fact, exist a *mathesis universalis*.

But the probability of an eyewitness is not enough. It is necessary for the body to be *written* by the other, engraved, pierced, or, more precisely, transverberated [*transverbéré*]. It is necessary for the outline of the unreadable signifier to be traced in it. The proof of its inscription will be proportional to the wound it leaves, because its truth can no longer be read. Beginning with the Franciscan stigmata, inscription on the body—tattooing and torture—constitutes a proof more than it makes sense. The inscription remains an unknown graph (though it is known by its unknown author). Thus, pain is the only guarantee of the good fortune of being written. And the indecipherability of the signature imprinted by the wound is, precisely, the trademark left by the Stranger when he annexes the body to the realm of the real that lies outside all thought. This genesis remakes the mystic in the image of God; the more unknown the process remains, the more confident it is. Thanks to the lucky wound made by an unintelligible glyph.[18]

Torture replaces pen and page (the writing of progressive accumulation and diffusion in unchanged form) with the sword and the body—a writing of loss progressing toward the point where death becomes a "fortunate shipwreck" (Surin). Everything flows toward this endpoint of inversion, because the de-fection of thought by the body, and the de-fection of the body by death, line the way to the real. The present inversion is only the negative labor of what is to come. Certitude—driven to pain and spelled out in that antilanguage—finds an outlet in the end. The mystic rushes toward that terminal point, exhausting all that he has as fast as he can. "Dying from not dying."

It is here that the most significant difference emerges. For the mystics, death is "effacement" in the "real" life. In preparation for it, life in the present is gradually stripped of all luster, by adopting the preliminary form of anonymity in daily life—"common life"[19] is what they called this laborious prefiguaration of the final disappropriation. The situation with celibatory machines is different. Death, for them, does not herald the real. It is its collapse. A fall into nothingness. Therefore death, that ecstatic torture, functions only in a *literary* mode, in a game with the other that causes it—that is, with the *life* of the author: a meaningful but unavowable life in interaction with a meaning-less but published text. As long as an individual (the subject) keeps on writing, he is not dead; in fact he is in fine shape, only unpresentable. He authorizes nothing. He lends credibility to no system of verisimilitude. He is just *there*, as the condition of possibility for his other, the text. What dies, then, is not the author, but a validating mode of utterance buttressed by a promise of immortality made to the subject. Since the certitude of an end with *no exit* leaves nothing to prepare for, *there is only the text*. The bride the mystics expected in death will never come, *tremenda et fascinenda*, to reestablish or found an order or truth of life. This final torture is missing, and the simple stop replacing it crowds all death into language, which is tolerated (but no longer supported) by a present life devoted to mineralization. The machine ceases to evangelize an alterity whose witness it claims to be. Its only end is an end in itself. It is a game. A *fable: without power*.

It is not surprising that in this space from which utterance is absent representation is always organized by the clock. Time kills. Duration is thus repressed by celibatory machines, every bit as much as the subject or intuition. Of this stalled ("broken") clock that is the text, the caption of the *Machine à Peindre* (Painting Machine) declares that "the end of the World will not stop its activities." The game of the solitary is unaffected by that which kills. It is already "dead" (no longer a "still life" [*nature morte*], but a still machine). It is something immobile. Not a speech-act, but a statement, a sentence without a referent, and with no need of one.

In effect, laying bare exorcizes the bride, who is transformed into an insect on display behind glass, into the Milky Way, into a nereid illusion in the reflection of an island/aquarium. Narrative rejects this iridescent multitude of the other, this phantasm woman, every bit as much as it rejects the author's life. The female apparition outside the window of the train must be conquered by the wheels of the five celibate cyclists in the 10,000 mile race. Rendered unreal—in other words laid bare—she becomes an excuse to produce without her.

The text is therefore constructed by henceforth auto-matic tortures, in the closed space where a (solitary) labor is undertaken on a detail that stands out, as in a dream. The *sueño* (dream) for St. Teresa was a part of *life*, and created the constant deviations of "follies" (*desatinos*), which *writing* was charged with "putting back in order" through the production of a controlled madness—the *Libro de la Vida*, an institution *wedding* reason and imagination. But the writing machine functions within the dream, or at least within the systematically sought-after continuity of the oneiric procedures Freud was analyzing during the same period. It adopts and artificially "cultivates" the "mechanisms" that make it so that *it is written* [*ça s'écrit*] in the dream, in front of "eyewitnesses" who only multiply the position of the dreamer. It supervises nothing (in whose name would it do that?). It interprets nothing (in the name of what referential discourse would it do that?). It has no outside with which to unite. The celibatory machine constitutes an autonomous *praxis*, with no censorship or regulation for it to wed; it has no subject who would claim to capitalize on its labor. It is the torture of language by language in the self-propelling game of its own mockery and production. It is a machine that has taken yesterday's driver and made him today's spectator. A working administration through which *it circulates* with no thought to an author or responsible official. In the words of Duchamp, a "*torture morte*." But why is the body—torn by the harrow that writes the Law—in the heart of the machine? The officer in Kafka's *Penal Colony*, commenting on the marks made by the needles on the body of the victim, says to the observer: "You have *seen* how difficult it is to decipher the script with one's *eyes*; but our man deciphers it with his *wounds*." After the torture victim vomits, the final hour arrives: "how we all absorbed the look of transfiguration on the face of the sufferer!" Then, the "corpse falls at the last into the pit with an incomprehensibly gentle wafting motion."[20] The same theme is also found in Duchamp, Roussel, and Jarry. A quote from Jarry's *Doctor Faustroll*: "Like a musical score, all arts and sciences were inscribed in the curvature of the limbs of the ultrasexagenarian ephebe and prophesied the infinite process of their perfection." An ancient law: *pete ferro corpus*, "pierce me with the sword."[21]

But now the transfiguring torture is demanded by no one, and has no author. It is self-subsistent. Therefore, it is now only seen, not suffered—the opposite of the mystic wound (which is experienced but not read). This reversal is marked in narrative: it is written [*ça s'écrit*] on the body, but "at a distance"; it is only *read* by Kafka's reader. Writing is not used for the purpose of imitation, nor is it destined to be inscribed in the real, exercising a power of words over the real. The observer can gaze at it, but does not practice it. If he takes the place of the victim, like the officer in the *Penal Colony*, others can find in him "no sign of the promised redemption." He dies, and that's all. It is no longer possible to play Christ. When real death loses its meaning, the crucifix becomes nothing more than an image. The only tortured body is the text. Reciprocally, once the relevance of the subject is lost, the imprintable body can be nothing more than a text.

The body of the letter is also the letter purloined from its former owner. What is written is no longer tied to the viewer by the blind pain that used to guarantee its intimate workings. It is unbound, ab-solute, like an unavowable history. The living subject enjoys the *leisure of seeing* the machinery. He is the humorist who witnesses, from the outside, a torture that is neither ''his'' nor that of the other, but an excess enclosed in a transparent mirror. The celibate—like Borges' television viewer (*Esse est percipi*), who watches a story he does not author, but which is actually fabricated on the picture screen—makes love with the glass behind which his altered body appears.

But the glass shines, that multifaceted apologue: it is atheist, since it posits the absolute of the limit; it is anarchic in its opposition to the political discourse of realism; it denounces the society of the spectacle.

The Male Divide

The paradox is that this stalled machine produces. For one thing, like the dream in Freud, it reverses the direction of the movement going from the system of perception to the system of motility: *regression*. It is removed from time, from the body and from the woman. It is also taken from God's reach (''Do not touch: Artwork.''). But it is still a theology (a discourse of the male, of the unique, of the same: a henology) that excludes the mystical (an altered feminine discourse: a heterology).[22] A cipher, alone.

Yet it produces effects. Despite the ironic, meticulously outlined directions for use that accompany it to detail its functioning, the represented machine is not intended to work. However, it has the strange power of rearranging the practices of he who merely reads it; it alters our way of transforming texts by reading them, it modifies the field of culture within which it moves, becoming the instrument of our analyses. It leads to the discovery of other celibatory machines, of other functionings of the celibatory machine. Where does it get this ''mythic'' energy, whose source it will not disclose, causing its lack to become the object of an obsession? What engine is hidden in its seeming transparence?

The fact that it produces according to a principle that is hidden from sight, the fact that it ''compels belief'' through the agency of something it obscures— not by virtue of its thickness, but with the translucence of glass, with the total visibility of a drawing, in its clarity of detail—brings us back to an old question. What gives a machinery of contestation the power to ''produce believers''? The problem of the institution. The mechanism of censure operating in the minute multiplicity of a code exploits its capacity to ''get subjects going.''[23] Thus thirteenth-century canon law, the exemplary institution in the eyes of Pierre Legendre, had to conceal/disclose the source of its energy. It functioned as the monstrance of the blind spot of a filiation, as an authorizing authorization, which gave it the power of making itself loved.

Language is likewise an institution, as is the celibatory machine, to the extent that it constitutes a closed language and a practice (of reading, not of speaking). The celibatory machine, though, has no need to disclose something hidden. A refusal of the title, "son of," is the very principle of this construct featuring the Separate, the celibate and readable god. There is nothing hidden because *exteriority* takes its place. The recognition of an absolute *outside* dispenses with the need to introduce *into* the text a concealed/disclosed allusion to an authority that would make it believable.

Mysticism presupposed the internal perception by an ego of its exteriority,[24] in other words, it had to quote the other in the text. The celibatory machine keeps the other outside of itself. *Fortgehen ohne Rückschau.*[25] The very exactness of its details (each part is a "well arranged item") emphasizes their separation from one another, within systems themselves carefully distinguished. No confusion intervenes to make us forget about difference. The apparatus shines like a blade. It has the cleanliness of a suicide which *makes way* for the world's alterity, with no compensation.

Having put an end to the *coincidatio oppositorum*, and having washed its hands of any "consolation" overcoming difference, the machine's essential characteristic is that it is male. It behaves as such at its place of production. It confesses (or flaunts, whichever you like) its relation to its limit, the limit of being masculine and nothing but. The celibate of the machine, in effect, returns to the fundamental, structuring form of difference—sexuality—and refuses to exercise any masculine power of expressing the feminine in speech [*dire la femme*]. A cutting refusal, made exactly at the time when the impossibility of becoming, through pain, the writing of an other (feminine) causes the ambitions formerly invested in death to flow back toward the erotic.

In setting its limit, the celibatory apparatus is also refusing to express the feminine in writing [*écrire la femme*]. It does not make use of the power of a masculine narrative to bring the feminine to expression [*faire parler le feminin*]. Despite everything the apparatus inherited from alchemy, a central figure in that ancient tradition seems to get frayed in the new machinery[26]: the androgyne, the perennial virile ambition to play both roles, not one after the other as in transvestism, but in a double-space permitting everything which exceeds "his" limit to be reduced to the same.

Undoubtedly, it is as difficult to discuss the sex of a discourse as it is to discuss the sex of an angel: these two apparatuses of circulation and/or drift of meaning—one linguistic, the other cosmological—constantly avoid determinations as to their place, by means of the *quiproquo* (who has taken whose place?). The celibatory machine's narrative or painting defines itself as *having a sex*; by virtue of the break creating its "angelic" transparency, or its "conventional coloring," it can induce a wide variety of effects based on what it places outside of itself, or the body/woman/subject. Its engine is this "other," repressed with so much precision—and therefore, first and foremost, the reader. We have seen how a certain number of characteristics confirm this rejection of the other, beginning with the refusal to use the power of recapitulating (the man and the woman) in ("human") representation. This makes its discourse antimagical, areligious, and nonsymbolic: it does not play on the ability of words to get things going; rather than link together, it cuts apart; and finally, it deprives itself of any means of filling in the deficiency of the concept and concealing its gaps through the production of potential "sym-bols."[27] This practice of division gives the textual artifact the energy of what it methodically eliminates. It is the male divide that gives it its power—the violence of a writing whose eroticism increases with its *loss* of power (religious, cosmological, or political) over the other.

Part IV
Others' Histories

Chapter 12
The Black Sun of Language: Foucault

Michel Foucault's book, *The Order of Things*,[1] sold out within a month after it first appeared—or so goes the advertising legend. The work, though long and difficult, numbers among those outward signs of culture the trained eye should find on prominent display in every private library, alongside the art books. Have *you* read it? One's social and intellectual standing depends on the response. But there are those who say that success, let alone faddishness, is a sure sign of a superficial or outmoded work.

First of all, Foucault is far from "boring." In fact, he is brilliant (a little too brilliant). His writing sparkles with incisive formulations. He is amusing. Stimulating. Dazzling. His erudition confounds us; his skill compels assent; his art seduces. Yet something in us resists. Or rather, the initial charm gives way to a kind of second-degree assent, a complicity that remains after we have taken a step back from the first flush of bewitchment, but whose basis we would be hard-pressed to explain.

However, a different kind of conviction takes shape in the historian's mind once he has recognized the sleight-of-hand element of the work—after he has had a chance to discuss both the information Foucault presents (which, after all, owes so much to Jacques Roger's book, *Les sciences de la vie dans la pensée*

Copyright © Michel de Certeau. This chapter first appeared as "Les sciences humaines et la mort de l'homme," in *Études*, 326 (March 1969), pp. 344–360, and was later published as "Le noir soleil du langage: Michel Foucault" (Chapter 5), in *L'absent de l'histoire* (Paris: Mame, 1973), pp. 115–132.

française du XVIIIe siècle[2]) and the virtuosity of a dialectic which seemingly stops at nothing. A question arises which leads to an inquiry essential to all contemporary thought. It is less a formulated question than the premonition of one. The dazzle and, at times, preciosity of the style combine with the minute dexterity of the analysis to produce an obscurity in which both author and reader fade from view: the work itself seems to illustrate the opposition it so often underlines between "surface effects" and the hidden "ground" they ceaselessly signify and conceal. This relation between the content and the form of the book is what arouses in the reader a sympathy without certitude which leads him, paradoxically, to wonder: what is it saying that is essential?

The Black Sun of Language

So what is it about? It is not Foucault's first book. In *The Order of Things* he elaborates upon a method already set forth and illustrated in two works, to my mind far superior: *Histoire de la folie à l'âge classique*[3] and *Naissance de la clinique*.[4] He also returns to themes present in numerous other studies—in his book, *Raymond Roussel*, in his articles on Maurice Blanchot, Jules Verne, etc. His breadth of learning as a historian, philosopher, and literary critic caters to a curiosity at once imperious, scrutinizing, and insatiable. With a hurried step, sometimes too quickly, this voyager tours the various zones of culture and periods of thought in search of a Reason that would account for the inorganic multiplicity of the ascertainable. With an ironic wave of the hand, he dismisses the naive certitudes of evolutionism, which believes it can finally grasp a reality that had always lain within reach beneath the illusions of yesteryear. He has nothing but contempt for the postulate of continuous progress, that touching self-justification of a present-day lucidity which all of history ought to prophesy. And not without reason.

Beneath thoughts, he discerns an "epistemological foundation" which *makes them possible*. Between the many institutions, experiences, and doctrines of an age, he detects a coherence which, though not explicit, is nonetheless the condition and organizing principle of a culture. There is, therefore, order. But this "Reason" is a ground that escapes the notice of the very people whose ideas and exchanges it provides the foundation for. No one can express in words that which gives everyone the power to speak. There *is* order, but only in the form of what one does not know, in the mode of what is "different" in relation to consciousness. The Same (the homogeneity of order) appears as otherness (the heterogeneity of the unconscious, or rather of the implicit).

To this first rift, we must add a second: analysis can uncover a beginning and an end to this language that speaks unbeknown to the voices that pronounce it. After having ensured the "positivity" of a historical period, the "foundation" suddenly crumbles to make way for another ground, a new "system of possibility" which reorganizes the floating world of words and concepts and implies, with its mix of vestiges and invention, an entirely different "epistemological field" (*episteme*). Over time, and in the density of its own time, each *episteme* is made up of the heterogeneous: what it does not know about itself (its own grounding); what it can no longer know about other *epistemei* (after the disappearance of the "foundations" they imply); what will be lost forever of its own objects of knowledge (which are constituted by a "structure of perception"). Things are defined by a network of words, and they give way when it does. Order emerges from disorder only in the form of the equivocal. Reason, *rediscovered* in its underlying coherence, is always being *lost* because it is forever inseparable from an illusion. In Foucault's books, reason dies and is simultaneously reborn.

Thus, what is presented here is a philosophy as well as a method. Although it is useful to distinguish them for purposes of exposition, the two are inseparable. Doubtless, when he undertakes "a structural study which attempts to decipher the conditions of history itself in the density of the historic" (*NC*, p. XV), Foucault is inaugurating a new criticism ("a strange discourse, I admit" [*NC*, p. XI; Eng., p. XV]). It is a criticism which aims to detect and define the successive alliances formed between words and things, the "structures" which delineate one by one, over time, the spaces of perception, and thus the tacit (though determining) combinations of saying and seeing, of language and the real, which are implied in the processes of thought and practice.

A criticism of this nature unfolds within the very field of the human sciences it relativizes, and makes use of their technical tools. So however new and cardinally important (and arguable) it may be, it does not carry within itself the means for its own justification, at least not now. The method remains the signifier of a signified that is impossible to put into words. The moment it demystifies the "positivism" of science or the "objectivity" of things by defining the cultural shifts which "created" them, it opens onto the nocturnal underside of reality, as if the fabric of words and things held within its net the secret of its own ungraspable negation. The combinatory system of saying and seeing has as its underside, or as what fundamentally determines it, "an essential void" (*OT*, p. 16), the unassimilable truth of the modes of structural coherence. Since it shifts and slips away, the ground beneath scientific or philosophical certitudes bears witness to an internal rift—never locatable, the rift is perceptible only in that illusion forever hidden and avowed by the temporary organization of languages prior to all conscious thought.

Histoire de la folie recalls that dreams and madness had become, for the German romantics, the horizon of something "essential." In their time, unreason foreshadowed this "essential" something through lyric pathos or the literature of the absurd. For Foucault, unreason is no longer the outer limit of reason: it is its truth. It is the black sun imprisoned in language, burning unbeknown to it—it is what revealed to him, as it did to Roussel, "the untiring journey through the domain common to both language and being, the observation of the play in which things and words mark their presence yet are absent from themselves, expose and mask themselves."[5] But to speak of unreason is still to give negativity the title of stranger; it is to locate it "elsewhere." That takes us off the track again. In fact (at the stage represented by *Naissance de la clinique* and *The Order of Things*), this *other* is an *internal* truth: death. Thus all of Foucault's works revolve around the sentence which, like a motto, opens *Naissance de la clinique*: "This book is about space, about language, and about death" (*NC*, p. V; Eng., p. IV). Language and the epistemological spaces of perception constantly refer to the inscription above the door: "Here, it is a question of death." An absence, which is perhaps meaning, has been trailed and is overtaken where we would least expect to find it—in rationality itself.

What is serious about this way of thinking is the impossibility of separating its spectral analysis of cultural history from its awakening to that obscure ray of light diffracted in it. Its philosophical discourse announces an "anxiety of language," taken in the most physical and fundamental sense—an uncertainty which rises up from the subterranean shifting to infiltrate the coherency of our certitudes. The affirmations proper to a culture are delivered over to this uncertainty and opened to questioning. All discourse finds its law in death, "the innocent, good earth beneath the lawn of words" (*NC*, p. 199).

In order to place Foucault's thought in context, we must first take note of the general subject matter of his work, which presents itself as the history of ideas in Western Europe over the last four hundred years—and as its renewal. His thought is new, and still in search of itself: it is imperialist, but does not really succeed in defining its ambitions or conquests; it is often imprecise exactly where it is most incisive.[6] It must also be said that critics proceed with care over this still unsteady ground, even if they cover it with praise as they go. This is doubtless due both to the importance of the questions raised and the way in which they are presented. Rather than discussing Foucault's historical analysis, I shall focus on several of these questions of method and foundation.

From Commentary to "Structural Analysis"

Foucault's work seems to be the result of an irritation or a weariness with the monotony of commentary. The historian of ideas seems capable of nothing else. Commentary "questions discourse as to what it says and intended to do" (*NC*, p. XII). It always supposes that there is "a necessary, unformulated remainder of thought that language has left in the shade" (*NC*, p. XII; Eng., p. XVI) and, inversely, that what has been formulated carries within it a content that has not yet been thought (ibid.). In a constant play between the excess of thought over language and the excess of language over thought, commentary "translates" into new formulations the "remainder" of the signified or the "residue" latent in the signifier. It is an infinite task, since what one claims to find is always pre-given in that unlimited reserve of "intentions" buried beneath words, in that inexhaustible capital of words richer than the thoughts that assembled them. Is that not the principle behind any history of science, philosophy of history, or theological exegesis? They know in advance the reality they "discover" hidden in a mythological or naive language from the past. They endow the expressions *or* the ideas of the past with a richness that shatters their shared articulation, untying the knot of the signifier and signified. What is essential in this is the relation to the commentator: the hidden treasure of the past is measured against the thoughts of the interpreter; what is implicit in one is defined by what is explicit in the other.

Foucault proposes substituting for commentary a different kind of activity: "a structural analysis of the signified that would evade the fate of commentary by leaving the signified and signifier in their original adequation" (*NC*, p. XIII). Understanding a proposition will no longer be equated with an exegesis that reduces the relation between text and commentator to a tautology. On the basis of a historical "adequation" between language and thought (an adequation which defines the text), the explanation will bring to light the relations which articulate the proposition "upon the other real or possible statements which are contemporary to it" and which place it in opposition to other propositions "in the linear series of time" (*NC*, p. XII; Eng., p. XVI).

Instead of identifying a thought with other thoughts—whether earlier ("influences") or later (our own)—instead of supposing a mental continuum over which a range of *resemblances* is spread and which authorizes our making explicit the unformulated or unthought, interpretation will take *difference* as the element of its theoretical rigor and the principle of the distinctions it makes. In keeping with this theoretical rigor, meanings must be grasped in terms of *relations* (and no longer as something hidden-and-seen); for propositions, texts, or institutions, as for the words of a language, the value accorded each element is determined and can be explained only by the relations into which it enters. What must be rediscovered is the overall *organization* of meaning which has determined specific meanings, and to which the elements of those meanings refer in referring to each other. Thus, a "reason" becomes apparent which is in fact a mode of being signified by a system of words. An order appears—the order of "structures."

What gives criticism the possibility of theoretical rigor is therefore this principle of making radical distinctions. The analysis of relations and interferences allows one to affirm (as, for example, Foucault does in relation to the institutions and ideas concerning madness in the eighteenth century) that "this system of contradictions refers to a hidden coherence" (*HF*, p. 624). The analysis then takes the form of a "historical structure" (the "structure of the experience a culture can make of madness,'' *HF*, p. 478, n. 1), and the coherence it discovers can be held to constitute within history a homogeneous but limited block. There are regions of coherence, with sudden shifts from one to another.

The classic historical concept of *periodicity* is here expanded into a notion of *discontinuity* between mental blocks. This displacement can itself be related to the global situation of consciousness, which has undergone a reversal in the past fifty years. Not long ago, the concept of periodicity was elaborated within the context of a progressive development whose successive stages tended to confirm the self-confidence of the terminal position. The starting point was a present certainty from whose peak could be seen to approach a truth which had been gradually extracted from the errors and illusions once covering it, but was now definitively known. Today, Foucault's thought is developing in a climate of co-existence among heterogeneous cultures, or among irreducible experiences isolated by the primitive symbolizations of the subject (the role of ethnology and psychoanalysis is of capital importance here, cf. *OT*, pp. 373–386). He is therefore led to uncover, beneath the continuity of history, a discontinuity more radical still than the evident heteronomy that lies beneath the fictional homogeneity of our own time. His lucid awareness of the ambiguities of universal monoculture, or totally affective communication, focuses his attention upon the equivocal nature of historical continuity. At one and the same time, the brutal novelty of the present is recognized and constituted as a source of anxiety: behind it lies the abyss of difference. The rifts of time now forbid contemporary thought from believing it holds the truth of what preceded it; it no longer has this peace of mind or recourse. It therefore faces a new risk, with no guarantee. The heterogeneous is for each culture the sign of its own fragility, as well as of its specific mode of coherence. Each cultural system implies a wager affecting all of its members, though none among them is responsible for it. Along with ''a mode of being of order,'' it defines a form of confrontation with death.[7]

''A mode of being of order'': the phraseology is Foucault's (cf. *OT*, p. XXI). What are we to understand by that? What is the status of these ''historical structures''? In *The Order of Things* Foucault does not define them. He limits himself to writing an ''account'' (*OT*, p. XXII) of them, as an ethnologist would set out to do for a faraway culture. But his description has to provide some indication of what he is analyzing. He offers the reader ''an inquiry whose aim is to rediscover *on what basis* knowledge and theory became possible'' (*OT*, p. XXI). ''What I am attempting to bring to light is the epistemological field, the *episteme* in which knowledge, envisaged apart from all criteria having reference to its rational value or to its objective forms, grounds its positivity and thereby manifests a history which is not that of its growing perfection, but rather that of its conditions of possibility'' (*OT*, p. XXII).

To understand the problem and Foucault's object of study, we must return to his initial observation. It is one of surprise. At the opening of his book, a passage by Borges expresses what this astonishment was for Foucault, and what it will be for others. The passage cites "a certain Chinese encyclopaedia" in which it is written that "animals are divided into: a) belonging to the Emperor, b) embalmed, c) tame, d) suckling pigs, e) sirens, f) fabulous, g) stray dogs, h) included in the present classification, i) frenzied, j) innumerable, k) drawn with a fine camelhair brush, l) *et cetera*, m) having just broken the water pitcher, n) that from a long way off look like flies" (*OT*, p. XV). "In the wonderment of this taxonomy," adds Foucault, "the thing we apprehend in one great leap, the thing that, by means of a fable, is demonstrated as the exotic charm of another system of thought, is the limitation of our own, the stark impossibility of thinking *that*" (ibid.).

A hint, and nothing more. It does, however, evoke the reference to another order, another "modality of order," as what baffles and fascinates us. The aberrant is the first signal of another world; but if it stimulates a curiosity eager to escape from its own problematic, it still does so from a desire to grasp "the fundamental codes" of a *different* culture and to rediscover, after the initial surprise, a principle of order. Heteronomy is at the same time the stimulus and what is inadmissible. It is a wound in rationalism. There are thus two stages to the process: first, the apprehension of a *system* that is *different*; second, the need for a reciprocal localization of systems held to be "different modes of being of order."

The marginal refers to an essential structure, to a "table" or "*tabula*" (*OT*, p. XVII) upon which are inscribed and coordinated analogies and oppositions unthinkable for us. The rare exception, an institution, or a theory, implies, like the tip of an iceberg, a coherence that is not on the same level as ideas and words, but lies "beneath" them. It invites us to wonder "on what 'table,' " according to what grid of identities, similitudes, analogies are arranged "so many different and similar things" that lie outside our view (*OT*, p. XIX). This applies equally to the confinement of the insane and the seventeenth-century conception of grammar.

When we have perceived that in the past sciences were constituted, experiences reflected, rationalities formed as a function of a "historical *a priori*" different from our own, when we affirm that "the order on the basis of which we think today does not have the same mode of bieng as that of the Classical Thinkers" (*OT*, p. XXII), we ourselves are changed by that discovery. Our relation to others, modified by our realization of this process of cultural leveling, transforms our relation to ourselves. The ground of our certainty is shaken when it is revealed that we can no longer *think* a thought from the past.

The surprise that places our *a priori* in question is expressed in the "account" by an effort to locate the rifts on the basis of the systems which slip away or originate at these frontiers. Foucault's dating scheme is hardly original: the passage from the sixteenth to the seventeenth century, the end of the eighteenth century, the middle of the twentieth century. But it carries a weight of its own because of the project the feeling of surprise sidetracks. For a system of thought concerned with identifying a *coherence*, the rift presents itself as an *event*, but "an event rising up from below": more fundamental than the continuity evident in the "surface movement" is a "sudden" change (Foucault emphasizes the suddenness), which may be a "minuscule but absolutely essential displacement" that "topples the whole of Western thought" (*OT*, p. 238). Thus, "within the space of a few years a culture sometimes ceases to think as it had been thinking up till then and begins to think other things in a new way" (*OT*, p. 50). Something essential happens which has identifiable premonitory signs and consequences, but which in the last analysis remains unexplainable,[8] "an erosion from outside" (*OT*, p. 50). A change marks the end of one "system of simultaneity" and the beginning of another. The same words and the same ideas are often reused, but they no longer have the same meaning, they are no longer thought and organized in the same way. It is upon this "fact" that the project of an all-encompassing and unitary interpretation runs aground.

The Discontinuities of Reason

The cracks which form in cultures, in the end breaking them apart, are located on the same "level" as the "system of simultaneity" that analysis identifies as organizing the multiplicity of cultural signs. A problem arises: what is the nature of this "level," said to be that of the "ground" or "epistemological foundation"? What validity does it have? All we have to go on is the manner in which structures arise in Foucault's account. The fact that the "level" at which they are found is defined by a method, or that Foucault's account also narrates a research process, is glossed over. There is a reciprocity between his analytic technique and its ordering of facts, which is necessarily scaled to instruments supplied by a system of interpretation. Thus, the gaps of history are located precisely where the historian's structuralist interpretation comes to a standstill.

The fact that Foucault fails to account for the interference between his method and his results—or rather, that the problem is deferred until a "later work"—is what causes the reader's unease. But at the same time as we rue this omission on so central a point—one which undoubtedly would have led Foucault to situate *himself* in history on the basis of his particular reading of the historical avatars of reason—we must recognize, as previously stated, that his work nevertheless raises the issue at every turn. It reasserts itself here. The question of *dating*, long classified among the givens of historical inquiry, becomes an epistemological problem. It takes on two equivalent forms: Why do these changes in the constitutive order of a culture occur? Why are there standstills in the unfolding of the interpretation? Of course, at the point where his chronological account takes on philosophical dimensions the reader might wonder whether Foucault is simply going to borrow the historians' old clothes, tailored to the specifications of those whose methods he so rightly criticizes, and then act as though they were the body of history. But the analyses in *Histoire de la folie* and *Naissance de la clinique* support his case well; they demonstrate with remarkable precision how the meat of reality is wrapped up with the adornments of dating.

Reason is thus placed in question by its own history. A heterogeneity breaks apart its self-identity; reason manifests itself in the succession of "modes of being" of order, which does not define a progression, but is on the contrary discontinuous. If Foucault could define what a "ground" *is*, he would be able to invoke an encompassing whole and thereby surmount the heteronomy of historical "reasons" with an appeal to a reason that embraced them all.[9] But that is exactly what he holds to be impossible. He can therefore only produce an "account" in which the problem of order and the problem of method are raised in identical terms. Within the confines of a *technical* rigor (call it the history of ideas, in spite of Foucault), he formulates a philosophical question that is today "fundamental" (a favorite term of his): the possibility of truth. There is no philosophy and, *a fortiori*, no faith which a problematic such as his fails to touch, and perhaps (but this is what is at issue), circumvent.

The Ambiguities of Continuity: "Archaealogy"

Foucault's analysis is too penetrating not to find continuity in the metamorphoses and restructurings characterizing each epistemological period. The subtitle of *The Order of Things* ("An Archaeology of the Human Sciences") already announces the movement which, according to the book, propelled Western thought of the Classical Age toward the formation of the human sciences, by way of three models proper to the nineteenth century, namely biology, economy, and philology—the roots of psychology, sociology, and linguistics. This same movement is behind today's challenge of these sciences by history, ethnology, and psychoanalysis. Primitive scenes, in the psychoanalytic sense of the term, lurk within and determine these developments. Beneath the cultural displacements there persist original wounds and organizing impulses, still perceptible in thoughts that have forgotten them.

Evolution, then, does indeed constitute a "sequence." In a Pascalian twist, Foucault brings continuity to light precisely where a rupture had appeared, just as before he pointed to a discontinuity breaking into the homogeneity of the development of science. But this continuity is indissociable from the equivocal; it is what persists unbeknown to consciousness, in the mode of deception. The vestiges of various kinds disclosed by analysis take the form of an illusion.

On one level, we have a surface permanence which, despite shiftings of ground, keeps words, concepts, or symbolic themes the same. A simple example: the "madman" is spoken of in the sixteenth, eighteenth, and nineteenth centuries, but actually "it is not a question of the *same* malady" (*HF*, p. 259) in any two of them. The same thing applies to theological exegesis as it does to medicine. The same words do not designate the same things. Ideas, themes, classifications float from one mental universe to another, but at each passage they are affected by structures which reorganize them and endow them with a new meaning. The same mental objects "function" differently.

There is a kind of permanence that has an inverse form. In the history of ideas, new concepts arise which seem to announce a different structure. In reality, they are soft categories that do not determine their content, but only cover it: concepts capable of embracing contradictory terms, floating signifiers in which past fears and perspectives persist. Thus the fear which in the sixteenth century exiled the madman in an effort to avoid diabolical contagion, in the eighteenth century adopts medical terminology and resurfaces in the form of precautions against the contaminated air of the hospitals (*HF*, p. 431; Eng., p. 204). More generally, each historical region of the *episteme* is the locus of a restructuring demanded (but no longer organized) by the structures of the preceding age. Foucault demonstrates this in the case of psychoanalysis, for example. The family, at the end of the eighteenth century, overwhelmed that age's miners of the mind, and found as its mythic antithesis the social "milieu" (the corruptor of nature). This set the stage for the attack against the father, which Freud considered the destiny of all Western culture (and perhaps of all civilization), whereas in language he saw only a sediment collected in consciousness in the course of the preceding century. He detects and unearths in words what had recently been deposited in them "by a myth of disalienation in patriarchal purity, and by a truly alienating situation in an asylum constituted in the family mode" (*HF*, pp. 588–589; Eng., p. 253). Guilt also resurfaces in Freudian language, but only because it was embedded there by the replacement of constraint with the technique of *confession* in the philanthropic asylums of the latter part of the eighteenth century (*HF*, pp. 596–597). In the same way, the valorization of the doctor-patient pairing (which also dates from the eighteenth century) and the concentration of therapeutic assistance in the person of the doctor cleared the way, unbeknown to its inventors, both for Freud's demystification of all the other asylum structures and the reinforcement (forgetful of its origins) of the place accorded the analyst, who, concealed behind the patient's back, judges, gratifies, and frustrates him, becoming, according to Foucault, at the same time the "key" and the "alienating figure" of the therapeutic relation (*HF*, pp. 608–612; Eng., pp. 273–278).

Contrary to the original intentions behind the invention of a given formula— which are forgotten by those who later represent that formula in a different way—continuity is ruled by the ambiguous. There is a real continuity between the age of hermeneutics (sixteenth century), the age of "representation" (seventeenth-eighteenth centuries), the age of positivism, or the objectification of the "inside" (nineteenth century), and the present age, but it is lived in the mode of misinterpretation. The issue is not the relation of illusion to truth (as the mythology of progress would have us believe), because the deception is mutual. It is the relation of other to other. The ambiguity proper to the exchanges between cultures, or related to their succession, does not nullify the reality of the connections, but rather specifies their nature. Ambiguity of communication is related to an "anxiety" that intertwines the continuity of history and the discontinuity of its systems: difference.

It is in fact difference which carves the isolating gaps into the homogeneity of language and which, conversely, opens in each system the paths to another. The internal instability of cycles and the ambiguity of their connections do not constitute two problems. Rather, it is in these two forms—the relation to other and the relation to self—that a single unending confrontation agitates history; it can be read in the ruptures that topple systems, and in the modes of coherence that tend to repress internal changes. There is both continuity *and* discontinuity, and both are deceptive, because each epistemological age, with its own "mode of being of order," carries *within itself* an alterity every representation attempts to absorb by objectifying. None will ever succeed in halting its obscure workings, or in staving off its fatal venom.

Outside Thought

Those who cling to continuity think they can escape death by taking refuge in the fiction of a permanence that is real. Those who box themselves inside the solid walls of the discontinuous systems believe they can keep death an external problem, confined to the absurd event that brings an end to a particular order; they avoid the problem posed by the system of order itself, a problem which first appears in the image of the internal "limit." For the sixteenth century, it was the other world, either divine or demonic; for the seventeenth, "non-being," bestial or imaginary; for the nineteenth, the "inside" dimension (the past, force, dreams).

Internal finitude struggles against the structurings that try to overcome it, and provides the arena for the defense of the same, or self-identity. Alterity always reappears, and in a fundamental way, in the very nature of language. A truth is spoken by the organization of a culture, but it escapes its own collaborators. Certain relations predetermine subjects and cause them to signify something other than what they think they say or can say. To be spoken without knowing it is to be caught dead unawares; it is to proclaim death, believing all the while it is conquered; it is to bear witness to the opposite of what one affirms. Such is the law the historian discovers as soon as he is forced to distinguish language from unconscious intentions. "The presence of the law," says Foucault in his article on Blanchot, "is its dissimulation."[10] Alienation is not simply the germinal stage of a culture, but its internal norm, as well as the relativizing of all individual consciousness. The self-evidence of the "I am" is thus endangered by its own language, that is, by "that outside where the speaking subject vanishes" (*PD*, p. 525). The truth of all thought is outside thought.

As for "outside thought," "one may assume that it was born of that tradition of mystic thinking which, from the time of Pseudo-Denis, has prowled the borderlands of Christianity; perhaps it has survived over the past millennium or so in the various forms of negative theology" (*PD*, p. 526). This occasional reference indicates the kind of problem Foucault sets out to interpret. The problem was brought to light, he says, when "Sade ceased to allow anything to speak other than the nudity of desire, as a law without a law of the world" (*PD*, p. 526): sadism, "a cultural fact of enormous dimension which arose precisely at the close of the eighteenth century," is tied to the era when "unreason, confined for over a century and reduced to silence, reappears, no longer as an image of the world, no longer as *figura*, but as language and desire" (*HF*, p. 437; Eng., p. 210).

Death only appears within the cohesive web of reason as the position of man in language, or as the evolution of languages. It is not a historical phenomenon, not an individual fact, and is therefore not localizable. Neither is the wild claim of an author who would like to burst through the doors of reflexive philosophy, smash the languid furnishings of consciousness, and plant his black flag there. It is not the end of man that Foucault proclaims, but of the conception of man that believed it had solved, by means of the positivism of the "human sciences" (that "refusal of negative thought," *HF*, p. 233), the ever-lingering problem of death. Because every system's downfall is the illusion of having triumphed over difference, the question today is posed in terms of this alienation in language every bit as much (it is, after all, the same thing) as it is in terms of the "successive systemic collapses." "The fact that we are already, before the least of our words, governed and paralysed by language" (*OT*, p. 298) is what leads the quest toward "that region where death prowls" (*OT*, p. 383), toward the kind of literature in which the law of discourse and "the absolute dispersion of man" (*OT*, p. 385) coincide.

Thus, it is in his discussions of literary works that Foucault most clearly reveals the radical absence that "lies beneath the sign it produces in order to enable one to approach it as though it were possible to rejoin it" (*PD*, p. 531). It speaks in the "I." Not only, as Mallarmé thought, and as the new literature reiterates, is the word "the manifest inexistence of what it designates," but the being of language is the visible effacement of the speaker. A forever nonobjectifiable expectation is directed toward the nothing that inhabits it, and "the object that would come to fill it could do nothing but efface it" (*PD*, p. 544). Long before those who speak, language is already waiting for Godot.

Open Questions

Not long ago, in the comic vein of his memorable adventures, Felix the Cat was depicted in a situation analogous to the one we are describing. He is walking at a fast pace, then suddenly notices, at the same time as the viewer, that the ground has gone out from under him: he had left the edge of the cliff he was following a while before. *Only then* does he fall into the void. Perhaps this image expresses the problem and the perception to which Foucault's book bears witness.

The fall is that second moment of realization: the ground upon which we believed we walked and thought has vanished. It plunges reflection back to the necessity of "letting-speak" what is spoken in man, without giving credence to consciousness or to the objects created by any particular configuration of knowledge. A new universe of thought opens up. It may come in the form of a catastrophe, but just for those who only know how to walk on the old "epistemological foundation." Before, the "I" occupied the "king's seat" in the network of representations, but now language takes the privileged position in saying its truth; before, the ego was held to be the invisible center of the known world, but now it is repositioned in perceptual relations and figures only as one term among many within an underlying, fundamental combinatory apparatus; before, continuity was the safeguard and also the *a priori* of a system, but now discontinuity is the jump-off point of any new risk or problem.

Foucault exhibits the eagerness of a Dr. Strangelove in expressing this sudden change. He announces the new era with analyses that are sure to endure, but he leaves many of the questions he raises hanging. Will the prophet of this new *episteme* also be its philosopher? Who is he to know what no one else knows, what so many thinkers have "forgotten" or have yet to realize about their own thought? He acts as though he were omnipresent (since all the heteronomies of history constitute the only account his thought will relate), but he is also absent (since he has designated his own place nowhere in that story). His work sets out to say the truth of language systems, but that truth is tied to no limit, and therefore to no engagement on the author's part. The ruptures within and between language systems are in the end bridged by the lucidity of his universal gaze. In other words, he speaks of the death that founds all language without really confronting the death within his own discourse; in fact, his approach may be a way of avoiding it.

We may thus ask ourselves two questions regarding Foucault. First, what history does he recount? On this, the historians have the floor; they can confirm that his is a reading of history that sifts through the real, decides itself what is significant, and takes refuge in the "density" of history when the surface resists his treatment.[11] Second, the philosophic determination of the status of his discourse, the clarification of the relation between his particularity and his project (who is speaking? from where?), and the elaboration of the concepts he uses (foundation, ground, positivity, etc.), mark the spot where that magnificent "account" should transform into philosophy.[12]

His work is an open book, of capital importance but uncertain, demystifying but mythic still. Will Mephistopheles become Faust? For now, he fascinates some, annoys others, invites contradictory interpretations, all because he evoked, "below the level of representation, an immense expanse of shade which we are now attempting to recover, as far as we can, in our discourse, in our freedom, in our thought. But our thought is so brief, our freedom so enslaved, our discourse so repetitive, that we must face the fact that that expanse of shade below is really a bottomless sea" (OT, p. 211).

Chapter 13
Micro-techniques and Panoptic Discourse:
A Quid pro Quo

In his *Discipline and Punish*,[1] Michel Foucault examines the organization of penal, academic, and medical "surveillance" at the beginning of the nineteenth century. He multiplies synonyms and evocations in an attempt to approximate proper nouns for what are the silent agents of his story (as if these escaped verbal identity): "apparatus," "instrumentations," "techniques," "mechanisms," "machineries," and so on. This very uncertainty and terminological instability is already suggestive. Yet the basic story the book has to tell—that of an enormous quid pro quo or socio-historical deal—postulates a fundamental dichotomy between ideologies and technical procedures, and charts their respective evolutions and intersections. In fact, what Foucault analyzes is a chiasmus: how the place occupied by humanitarian and reformist projects at the end of the eighteenth century is then "colonized" or "vampirized" by those disciplinary procedures that have since increasingly organized the social realm itself. This mystery story narrates a plot of substituted corpses, the sort of game of substitution that would have pleased Freud.

As always, for Foucault, the drama is played out between two forces whose relationship to one another is inverted by the ruse of history. On the one hand, there is the ideology of the Enlightenment, with its revolutionary approach to the matter of penal justice. The reformist projects of the eighteenth century aim essentially at doing away with the "ordeal" of the *ancien régime*, with its bloody ritualization of hand-to-hand combat intended to dramatize the triumph of royalty over criminals whose crimes had particular symbolic value. Such projects involved the equalization of penalties, their gradation according to the crime, and their educational value both for the criminals and for society itself.

In actual fact, however, disciplinary procedures evolved in the army and in the schools rapidly come to prevail over the vast and complex judicial apparatus elaborated by the eighteenth-century Enlightenment, and the new techniques are refined and applied without recourse to any overt ideology: the development of a cellular grid (whether for students, soldiers, workers, criminals, or sick people) transforms space itself into an instrument that can be used to discipline, to program, and to keep under observation any social group. In such procedures, the refinement of technology and the attention to minute detail triumph over theory and result in the universalization of a single, uniform manner of punishment—prison itself—which undermines the revolutionary institutions of the Enlightenment from within and everywhere substitutes the penitentiary for penal justice.

Foucault thus separates two heterogeneous systems. He describes the triumph of a political technology of the body over an elaborated system of doctrine. Yet he does not stop here: in his description of the institution and of the triumphant proliferation of this particular "minor instrumentality"—the penal grid—he also tries to elucidate the workings of this type of opaque power, which is the property of no individual subject, which has no privileged locus, no superiors, and no inferiors, which is neither repressive nor dogmatic in its action, and whose efficacity is quasi-autonomous and functions through its capacity to distribute, classify, analyze, and give spatial individuality to any given object. A perfect machinery. Through a series of clinical—and splendidly "panoptical"—tableaux, Foucault attempts to name and classify the "methodological rules," the "functional conditions," the "techniques" and "processes," the distinct "operations" and "mechanisms," "principles" and "elements" that would constitute something like a "microphysics of power." His text is thus an exhibition of their secrets, an exhibit that has a dual function: 1) to diagram a particular stratum of non-verbal practices and 2) to found a discourse *about* those practices.

Nature and Analysis of the Micro-techniques

How are such practices to be described? In a characteristic strategy of indirection, Foucault isolates *the gesture that organizes discursive space*—not, as in *Madness and Civilization*, the epistemological and social gesture of confining an outcast in order to create the space of reason itself, but rather a minute gesture, everywhere reproduced, by which visible space is partitioned in order to subject its inhabitants to surveillance. The procedures that repeat, amplify, and perfect this gesture organize in turn that discourse which comes to be called the "human sciences" or *Geisteswissenschaften*. Thus, in Foucault's view, eighteenth-century procedures that constitute a *non-verbal gesture* have been privileged (for historical and social reasons) and have then been articulated through the discourse of contemporary social sciences.

The novel perspectives[2] opened up by this analysis might also have been prolonged into a whole stylistics, a whole method for analyzing the non-verbal gesture that organizes the text of thought itself. But that is not my purpose here. Rather, I wish to raise several questions relating to these practices.

First Question: In his archaeology of the human sciences—Foucault's explicit project since *The Order of Things*—and in his search for that common "matrix"—the "technology of power"—which could be found to organize both the penal code (the punishment of human beings) and the human sciences (the knowledge of human beings), Foucault is led to make a *selective choice* from among the totality of procedures that form the fabric of social activity in the eighteenth and nineteenth centuries. He begins with a proliferating system examined in its *present status* (essentially our contemporary scientific or juridical technology), and moves backward to the past. It is a surgical operation. It consists in *isolating* the cancerous growth from the social body as a whole, and thereby in *explaining* its contemporary dynamic by way of its *genesis* in the two preceding centuries. Drawing on an immense mass of historiographic materials (penal, military, academic, medical), this method disengages the optical and panoptical procedures which can increasingly be found to proliferate within our society, thereby identifying the disguised indices of an apparatus whose structure gradually becomes more precise, complex, and determinate within the density of the social fabric or body as a whole.

This remarkable historiographic "operation" raises two distinct questions at one and the same time: on the one hand, the decisive role of *technological procedures* and apparatuses in the organization of a society; on the other, the exceptional development or privileged status of *one particular* category (i.e., the panoptical) among such apparatuses. We must therefore now ask:

a) How do we explain the *privileged development* of the particular series constituted by Foucault's panoptical apparatuses? It is perhaps not so surprising, when we recall that optical epistemology is fundamental since the sixteenth century in the elaboration of modern sciences, arts, and philosophy. In this case, the panoptical machinery is only a historical effect of this technical scientific and philosophical optical tradition. It does not constitute the victory of anything new, but the victory of a past, the *triumph of an old system* over a new, liberal, and revolutionary utopia. A past model of organization is coming back and "colonizing" the revolutionary projects of a new time. This return of the past suggests a Freudian story.

b) What happened to all the *other* series of procedures that, in their unnoticed itineraries, failed to give rise either to a specific discursive configuration or to a technological systematization? There are many other procedures besides pan-optical ones. These might well be looked on as *an immense reserve* containing the seeds or the traces of alternate developments.

It is, in any case, impossible to reduce the functioning of a whole society to a single, dominant type of procedure. Recent studies (such as that of Serge Mos-covici on urban organization,[3] and Pierre Legendre on the medieval juridical apparatus[4]) have revealed other kinds of technological apparatuses, which know an analogous interplay with ideology, and prevail for a time before falling back into the storehouse of social procedures as a whole, at which point other appara-tuses replace them in their function of "informing" a whole system.

From this point of view, then, a society would be composed of certain prac-tices which, selectively developed and externalized, organize its normative insti-tutions alongside innumerable other practices. The latter, having remained "minor," do not organize discourse itself but merely persist, preserving the premises or the remnants of institutional or scientific hypotheses that differ from one society to another. But all these procedures present the double characteristic underscored by Foucault of being able to organize both space and language in dominant or subordinate ways.

Second Question: It is the final formation or "full" form—in this instance the whole contemporary technology of surveillance and discipline—which serves as the point of departure for Foucault's archaeology: the impressive coherence of the practices he selects is thereby explained. But can we really assume that all procedures in themselves had this coherence? A priori, no. The exceptional and even cancerous development of panoptical procedures would seem to be indistinguishable from their *historic role* as a weapon against hetero-geneous practices and as a means of controlling the latter. Thus, their coherence is the effect of a particular historic success, and not a characteristic of all tech-nological practices. Thus, behind the "monotheism" of the dominant panoptical procedures, we might suspect the existence and survival of a "polytheism" of concealed or *disseminated practices*, dominated but not obliterated by the his-torical triumph of one of their number.

Third Question: What is the status of a particular apparatus when it has become the organizing principle of a technology of power? What is the effect upon it of that process whereby it has been isolated from the rest, privileged, and transformed into a dominant? What new kind of relation does it maintain with the dispersed ensemble of other procedures when it has at length been insti-tutionalized as a penitentiary and scientific system? It might well be that an appa-ratus privileged in this fashion could lose that efficacity which, according to Foucault, it originally owed its own mute and minuscule technical advances. On emerging from that obscure stratum where Foucault locates the determining mechanisms of society, it might well find itself in the position of an institution itself imperceptibly colonized by other, still more silent procedures. Indeed, this system of discipline and surveillance, which was formed in the nineteenth century on the basis of preexisting procedures, is today in the process of being "vampirized" by still other ones which we have to unveil.

Fourth Question: Can we go still further? As they have evolved, the apparatuses of surveillance have themselves become the object of elucidation and a part of the very language of our rationality. Is this not a sign that they have ceased to determine discursive institutions? They now belong to our ideology. The organizing apparatuses the discourse can explain would no longer fill that silent role which is their definition for Foucault. At that point (unless we are to suppose that, by analyzing the practices from which it is itself derived, *Discipline and Punish* surmounts its own basic distinction between "ideologies" and "procedures"), we have to ask what apparatus determines Foucault's discourse in turn, an underlying apparatus which by definition escapes an ideological elucidation.

By showing, in a single case, the heterogeneous and equivocal relations between apparatuses and ideologies, Foucault has constituted a new object of historical study: that zone in which technological procedures have specific effects of power, obey logical dynamisms which are specific to them, and produce fundamental turnings aside in the juridical and scientific institutions. But we do not yet know what to make of other, equally infinitesimal procedures that have remained unprivileged by history yet which continue to flourish in the interstices of the institutional technologies. This is most particularly the case of procedures that lack the essential precondition indicated by Foucault, namely the possession of a locus or specific space of their own on which the panoptical machinery can function. Such techniques, which are just as operative though without locus, are rhetorical "tactics." I suggest that these secretly reorganize Foucault's discourse, colonize his "panoptical" text, and transform it into a "trompe-l'oeil."

Micro-techniques to Produce a Panoptical Fiction

When theory, instead of being a discourse upon other preexistant discourses, ventures into non- or pre-verbal domains in which there are only practices without any accompanying discourse, certain problems arise. There is a sudden shift, and the usually reliable foundation of language is missing. The theoretical operation suddenly finds itself at the limits of its normal terrain, like a car at the edge of a cliff. Beyond, nothing but the sea. Foucault works on this cliff when he attempts to invent a discourse that can speak of non-discursive practices.

But we may consider the micro-techniques as building the theory, instead of being its object. The question no longer concerns the procedures organizing social surveillance and discipline, but the procedures producing Foucault's text itself. In fact, the micro-techniques provide not only the content of the discourse but also the process of its construction.

Recipes to Produce a Theory

As in cooking, here we find subtle "recipes" to get theories of practices. Yet in the same way that a cooking recipe is punctuated with a certain number of action imperatives (blend, baste, bake, etc.), so also the theoretical operation can be summed up in two steps: extract, and then turn over; first the "ethnological" isolation of some practices for obtaining a scientific "object," then the logical inversion of this obscure object into an enlightening center of the theory.

The first step is a "découpe": it isolates a design of some practices from a seamless web, in order to constitute these practices as a distinct and *separate* corpus, a *coherent* whole, which is nonetheless *alien* to the place in which theory is produced. It is the case for Foucault's panoptical procedures, isolated from a multitude of other practices. By this way, they receive an ethnological form. Meanwhile, the particular genre thereby isolated is taken to be the metonymy of the whole species: a part, observable because it has been circumscribed, is used to represent the undefinable totality of practices in general. To be sure, this isolation is used to make sense out of the specific dynamics of a given technology. Yet it is an ethnological and metonymic "découpage."

In the second step, the unity thus isolated is reversed. What was obscure, unspoken, and culturally alien becomes the very element that throws light on the theory and upon which the discourse is founded. In Foucault, procedures embodied in the surveillance systems at school, in the army, or in hospitals, micro-apparatuses without discursive legitimacy techniques utterly foreign to the *Aufklärung*, all become the very ordering principle that makes sense of our own society just as they provide the rationale of our "human sciences." Because of them, and in them, as in a mirror, Foucault sees everything and is able to elucidate everything. They allow his discourse itself to be theoretically panoptical in its turn. This strange operation consists in transforming secret and aphasic practices into the central axis of a theoretical discourse, and making this nocturnal corpus over into a mirror in which the decisive reason of our contemporary history shines forth.

This very "tactic" marks his history as belonging to the same species of practices he analyzes. Foucault, of course, already studies the determination of discourse by procedures in the case of the "human sciences." His own analysis, however, betrays an apparatus analogous to those whose functioning it was able to reveal. But it would be interesting, in regard to a theory of these micro-techniques, to consider the differences between the panoptical procedures Foucault has told us about and the twin gesture of his own narrative, which consists in isolating a foreign body of procedures and inverting its obscure content into a spotlight.

An Art of Making Panoptical Fictions

In this way, Foucault's theory is also part of the art of "scoring." It does not escape its object, that is, the micro-procedures. It is an effect and a network of these procedures themselves. It is a narrative, a theoretical narrative, which obeys rules analogous to those panoptic procedures. There is no epistemological and hierarchical break between the theoretical text and the micro-techniques. Such a continuity constitutes the philosophical novelty of Foucault's work.

This kind of "art" is easy to see at work. It is an art of telling: suspense, extraordinary quotations, ellipses of quantitative series, metonymical samples, etc. A complete rhetorical apparatus is used for seducing and convincing an audience. It also is an art of seizing the opportunity and of making a hit, by crossing old texts and contemporary conjunctures. Foucault has specified himself as a "reader." His reading is a poaching. Hunting through the forests of history and through our present plains, Foucault traps strange things which he discovers in a past literature and uses these for disturbing our fragile present securities. He has an almost magic power for pointing at surprising confessions in historical documents as well as in contemporary ones, for gathering both these past and present curiosities into a system, and for transforming these revelations of non-verbal practices determining our political and epistemological institutions into convincing evidence. His rhetorical art, creating an obviousness that reverses our obvious convictions, is the literary gesture of a certain way of acting. His immense erudition is not the principal reason for his effectiveness, but rather this art of speaking which is also an art of thinking.

His manner of using a panoptical discourse as a mask for tactical interventions within our epistemological fields is particularly remarkable. He practices an art of "scoring" by means of historical fictions. *Discipline and Punish* draws on subtle procedures for "manipulating" erudite exhibitions. It is a calculated alternation between three variants of optical figures: representational tableaux (exemplary narratives),[5] analytic tableaux (lists of ideological "rules" or "principles" relating to a single phenomenon),[6] and figurative tableaux (seventeenth–nineteenth century engravings and photographs).[7] This system combines three sorts of shop-windows: case-study narratives, theoretical distinctions, and past images. It only pretends to show and not to explain how a machinery worked: it makes this opaque process visible and transparent by staging it in three different panoptical settings. Organizing a rhetoric of clarity—or "écriture de la clarté"—it produces an effect of self-evidence in the public. But this theater of clarity is a ruse. It systematically displaces the fields in which Foucault successively intervenes. It is a subversive operation, hidden by and within a limpid discourse, a Trojan horse, a panoptical fiction, using clarity for introducing an otherness into our "epistemè." Taken for granted, the panoptical space of our contemporary scientific language is consciously and craftily reorganized by heterogeneous micro-techniques. It is colonized and vampirized, but voluntarily colonized by procedures that obey contrary rules.

This way of thinking cannot have a discourse of its own, because it amounts essentially to a practice of non-locus. The optical space is the frame of an internal transformation due to its rhetorical reemployment. It becomes a façade, the theoretical ruse of a narrative. While the book analyzes the transformation of Enlightenment ideologies by a panoptical machinery, its writing is a subversion of our contemporary panoptical conceptions by the rhetorical techniques of a narrative.

On a first level, Foucault's theoretical text is still organized by the panoptical procedures it elucidates. But on a second level, this panoptical discourse is only a stage where a narrative machinery reverses our triumphant panoptical epistemology. Thus, there is in Foucault's book an internal tension between his historical thesis (the triumph of a panoptical system) and his own way of writing (the subversion of a panoptical discourse). The analysis pretending to efface itself behind an erudition and behind a set of taxonomies it busily manipulates is like a ballet dancer disguised as a librarian. And so, a Nietzschean laughter meanwhile runs through the historian's text.

Two short propositions may be an introduction to a debate, and may take the place of a conclusion:

1) Procedures are not merely the objects of a theory. They organize the very construction of theory itself. Far from being external to theory, or from staying on its doorstep, Foucault's procedures provide *a field of operations within which theory is itself produced*. With Foucault we get another way of building a theory, a theory which is the literary gesture of those procedures themselves.

2) In order to clarify the relationship of theory with those procedures that produce it as well with those that are its objects of study, the most relevant way would be a *storytelling discourse*. Foucault writes that he does nothing but tell stories ("récits"). Stories slowly appear as a work of displacements, relating to a logic of metonymy. Is it not then time to recognize the theoretical legitimacy of narrative, which is then to be looked upon not as some ineradicable remnant (or a remnant still to be eradicated) but rather as a necessary form for a theory of practices? In this hypothesis, *a narrative theory would be indissociable from any theory of practices*, for it would be its precondition as well as its production.

Chapter 14
The Laugh of Michel Foucault

A few years ago, at Belo Horizonte, in the course of a speaking tour of Brazil, Michel Foucault was once again questioned about his place: "So, then, in what capacity do you speak? What is your specialty? Where are you coming from?" This identity request struck him to the quick. It sought to grasp his secret as a man of passage.[1] It had provoked, in *The Archaeology of Knowledge*, an irritated retort, singular in tone, and in which the movement that produced the work suddenly shone forth:

> No, no, I'm not where you are lying in wait for me, but over here, laughing at you.
>
> What, do you imagine that I would take so much trouble and so much pleasure in writing, do you think that I would keep so persistently to my task, if I were not preparing—with a rather shaky hand—a labyrinth into which I can venture, in which I can move my discourse, opening up underground passages, forcing it to go far from itself, finding overhangs that reduce and deform its itinerary, in which I can lose myself and appear at last to eyes that I will never have to meet again. I am no doubt not the only one who writes in order to have no face. Do not ask who I am and do not ask me to remain the same: leave it to our bureaucrats and our police to see that our papers are in order. At least spare us their morality when we write.[2]

A live voice that still eludes the tomb of the text.

To be classified the prisoner of a place and qualifications, to wear the stripes of authority which procure for the faithful their official entry into a discipline, to be pigeonholed within a hierarchy of domains of knowledge [*savoir*] and of positions, thus finally to be "established"—that, for Foucault, was the very figure of death. "No, no." Identity freezes the gesture of thinking. It pays homage to an order. To think, on the contrary, is to pass through; it is to question that order, to marvel that it exists, to wonder what made it possible, to seek, in passing over its landscape, traces of the movement that formed it, to discover in these histories supposedly laid to rest "how and to what extent it would be possible to think otherwise."[3] That is how Foucault responded to his questioners at Belo Horizonte, but in words that were better adapted to the subtleties of the Brazilian scene and that designated his philosophical style: "Who am I? A reader."

From Poitiers, where he was born (1926), to the Salpêtrière Hospital, where he finally fell (June 25, 1984), his trajectories crisscrossed domains of knowledge and countries. He visited books just as he went around Paris on bicycle, around San Francisco or Tokyo, with exact and vigilant attention, poised to catch, at the turn of a page or a street, the spark of some strangeness lurking there unnoticed. All these marks of otherness, whether "minuscule lapses"[4] or enormous confessions, were for him citations of an unthought. They are there, he would say, quite readable, but unread because they take the expected and the codified by surprise. When he discovered them he would roll with laughter. Sometimes an irrepressible laugh like the one he mentions apropos a text by Borges, which "when read shatters all the familiar landmarks of thought—our thought, the thought that is of our age and our geography—breaking up all the ordered surfaces and all the planes with which we are accustomed to tame the wild profusion of beings."[5] This, he says, is the "birthplace" of the book *The Order of Things*. His other works seem to have the same origin: bouts of surprise (in the same way there are bouts of fever), the sudden jubilatory, semi-ecstatic forms of "astonishment" or "wonder" which have been, from Aristotle to Wittgenstein, the inaugurators of philosophical activity. Something that exceeds the thinkable and opens the possibility of "thinking otherwise" bursts in through comical, incongruous, or paradoxical half-openings of discourse. The philosopher, overtaken by laughter, seized by an irony of things equivalent to an illumination, is not the author but the witness of these flashes traversing and transgressing the gridding of discourses effected by established systems of reason. Nor has he prepared in advance a place to keep his finds. These are the events of a thought yet to come. This surprising inventiveness of words and things, this intellectual experience of a disappropriation that opens possibilities, is what Foucault marks with a laugh. It is his philosophical signature on the irony of history.

Hence his complicity with the great detectors of the surprises of language and the chance events of thought, from the Sophists down to Roussel or Magritte. But his practice of astonishment constantly provides new departures for the relentlessness, in turn imperious and fragile, meticulous, irritable, always tenacious, with which he seeks to elucidate this "other dimension of discourse" revealed to him through chance encounters. It even gives the tone of a Western to his archival and analytical work aimed at unraveling the truth games that are first signaled by paradoxical spotlights. Try as he may, the care he puts into controlling, classifying, distinguishing, and comparing his readerly finds is incapable of stilling the tremble of awakening that betrays in his texts his manner of discovery. His works, then, combine the laugh of invention with the concern for exactitude, even if the proportions vary, and even if, over the years, the exactitude gradually wins out over the laugh, either (perhaps) because of the allergy his style (more than his theses) provoked among the practitioners of well-established scientific systems, or because his surgical passion for lucidity developed, becoming in his last two books an ascetic clarity, stripped even of its lively virtuosity. Leaving aside this evolution, and the polemics tied to his *oeuvre* as to his shadow, what is important in his work is first of all this exceptional exercise of astonishment, transformed into an assiduous practice of the "births" of thought and of history.[6]

His "stories," as he called them, recount how new problematics appear and become established. They often take the form of surprises, as in detective novels. For example, the progressive liberalization and diversification of criminal law over the course of the eighteenth century is interrupted, reversed, "cannibalized" by the proliferation of military and pedagogical procedures of surveillance, which impose the panoptic system of the prison everywhere—a development one did not expect.[7] You presume that power is identifiable with the appropriation of isolatable, hierarchical, and legal apparatuses? No, it is the expansion of anonymous mechanisms that "normalize" the social space as they move across institutions and legality.[8] You presume that a bourgeois morality made sex a secret to be hidden away? No, the techniques of confession transformed sex into a tireless producer of discourses and truths.[9] Thus, from book to book, the analysis pinpoints these turnabouts, which, disturbing the constituted domains of knowledge, even the most authoritative (even Marx, even Freud), generate new ways of thinking. Whatever the discussions to which this analysis gives rise, the analysis itself is based not on the personal ideas of an author but on that which history itself makes visible. It is not Mr. Foucault who is making fun of domains of knowledge and predictions, or pre-visions; it is history that is laughing at them. It plays tricks on the teleologists who take themselves to be the lieutenants of meaning. A meaninglessness of history, a mocking and nocturnal god, ridicules the schoolmasters' authority and withdraws from Foucault himself the moralistic or pedagogical role of being an "intellectual" who is always on top of things. The lucidity comes from an attentiveness, always mobile, always surprised, to what events show us without our knowing it.

To this attentiveness which joins philosophy (the analysis of conditions and implications) with history (events and systems), we must add an odd, yet ever-present aspect of the *oeuvre*: its visual character. These works are studded with tables and illustrations. The text is also cadenced by scenes and figures. *Madness and Civilization* opens with the image of the ship of fools;[10] *The Order of Things*, with Velasquez's "Las Meninas";[11] *Discipline and Punish*, with the narrative of the torture of Damiens,[12] and so on. Is this by chance? Or is it to solicit the reader? But each book presents a scansion of images on the basis of which develops the intricate work of distinguishing the book's conditions of possibility and formal implications. Actually, these images institute the text. They cadence it like successive solicitations of Foucault himself. He recognizes in them the scenes of a difference, the black suns of "theories" beginning to show. Forgotten systems of reason stir in these mirrors. On the level of the paragraph or phrase, quotes function in the same way; each of them is embedded there like a fragment of a mirror, having the value not of a proof but of an astonishment—a sparkle of other. The entire discourse proceeds in this fashion from vision to vision. The step that marks the rhythm of the discourse's forward march, in which that march finds support and from which it receives its impulse, is a visual moment. The analysis is constantly using it as a point of departure in order to make explicit, in the form of lists (1st, 2nd, 3rd, 4th . . .) and taxonomical tables that still pertain to the visual, the elements put into play by the iconic or narrative image. This surprise-image therefore plays a role, in turn heuristic and recapitulative, analogous to that of the geometrical figure under the gaze of the mathematician: like a right-angled triangle, it brings together at a glance the possible or already demonstrated properties developed by a series of theorems.

This optical style may seem strange. Did not Foucault find the panoptic machine to be at the very heart of the system of surveillance that spread from the prison to all the social disciplines by means of a multiplication of techniques allowing one to "see without being seen"?[13] Moreover, he exhumed and pursued, following them into the most peaceful regions of knowledge, all the procedures that are based on confession and productive of truth, in order to pinpoint the technology by means of which visibility transforms space into an operator of power. In fact, the visible becomes for him the arena of the new stakes of power and knowledge. Already a major locus for Merleau-Ponty, the visible constitutes for Foucault the contemporary theater of our fundamental options. It is here that a use of space for policing purposes is confronted by a vigilance attuned to what else happens there. Mustered on this terrain of our epistemological wars, the work of philosophy opposes the systems that subject space to surveillance with paradoxes that chance encounters produce in it; it opposes the panoptic leveling with discontinuities revealed in thought by chance. Two practices of space clash in the field of visibility, the one ordered by discipline, the other based on astonishment. With this combat, reminiscent of those of the Greek gods in their heaven, is effected the "reversal" of the technologies of "seeing without being seen" into aesthetics of ethical existence.

By exhuming the implications of aleatory events, Foucault invented the loci of new problematics. With each of his books, he offers a hitherto undrawn map of the possibility of "thinking otherwise." He is that "new cartographer" that Gilles Deleuze depicted with such friendly acuity.[14] These maps present tools proportioned to different issues. Among themselves, they do not form a system, but a series of "Essays" [including the sense of "tries"], always having to do with that "curiosity"—that astonishment—" which allows one to get away from oneself."[15] They thus compose a "plurality of possible positions and functions."[16] This heterogeneity appears not only between the regions that they describe (the birth of a system of reason on the basis of a new treatment of madness, the differentiation of domains of knowledge within the same epistemological configuration, the determination of historiography by the hierarchical place of its production, the nature of disciplinary power, the reversal of a sexual ethic relating to boys into a heterosexual ethic), but still more fundamentally between the problematics put into play (the instituting break, the various modalizations of the same framework of postulates, the silent logic of techniques, the constitution of sexuality as a moral activity, and so on). It is a question of "discontinuous practices,"[17] born of inventions that arise from chance encounters. The event that is elicited by the "wild profusion of beings" adds to each carefully constructed map another possibility. None of these maps defines a destiny or truth of thought. These successive places are not linked by the progress of an Idea that would gradually formulate itself, but by a common *way* of thinking. They answer to the laughs of history. They attest to the necessity of inscribing these chance happenings one after another in our domains of knowledge; they do not undertake, by homogenizing all the discourses, to return their dazzling discontinuities to the shadows. Rarely has philosophical astonishment been treated in a manner so mindful of its possible developments and respectful of its surprises.

Political activity has the same style. It does not appropriate for itself a meaning of history. It does not constitute a strategy, much less a doctrine. It responds to events with the same kind of faithfulness described above in relation to the fortuities of the text. It keeps to the events with the same rigorous constancy and precision, with a view to bringing out the implications of the unthought that breaks through the grid of the established order and accepted disciplines. The chance occurrences of political and social current events, the condition of inmates in French prisons, the Iranian revolution, the repression in Poland, and so many other singular encounters elicited in Foucault the kind of astonishment that generates action. These interventions were not guaranteed success—and were not offered ideologically, from somewhere above the fray—anymore than his maps were. They did not shield themselves from the process of chance that engendered them. Rather, their point of departure was a movement whose ethical character, as Kant was already saying, has to do neither with what seems possible nor with the law of facts. The political gesture is also an ''Essay,'' undertaken with as much lucidity as it can have, and relating to the discoveries made possible by a semi-journalistic ''curiosity'' attentive to the avatars of the times and of people. Thus Foucault's philosophical inventiveness, that founder of discursivities, traces its path once again, this time in the social field, with the same indefatigable expectation of a history that is other.

Chapter 15
History:
Science and Fiction

My analysis of historiography must be situated in the context of a question too broad to be treated fully here, namely the antinomy between ethics and what, for lack of a better word, I will call dogmatism. Ethics is articulated through effective operations, and it defines a distance between what is and what ought to be. This distance designates a space where we have something to do. On the other hand, dogmatism is authorized by a reality that it claims to represent and in the name of this reality, it imposes laws. Historiography functions midway between these two poles: but whenever it attempts to break away from ethics, it returns toward dogmatism.

This antinomy between ethics and dogmatism plays an essential role in the history of sciences, especially in the concerns of the social sciences. The organization of a scientific knowledge that took shape during the seventeenth and eighteenth centuries supposed a change in the fundamental postulate of medieval societies: the religious or metaphysical aim of stating the truth of beings according to God's will was replaced by the ethical task of creating or making history [*faire l'histoire*]. However both ambitions were concerned ultimately with establishing a certain order.

Today, this search for a prevailing order has been superseded by the social imperative to produce a more humane world. Now, value is assigned to every human being according to his actions, his function within a historical economy

Copyright © Michel de Certeau. This chapter is reprinted from *Social Science as Moral Inquiry*, ed. R. Bellah et al. (New York: Columbia University Press, 1983), pp. 125–152.

that is directed by the law of progress, rather than according to his position within a system of absolutes. Differentiated and limited disciplines, which organize operations within coherent frameworks, define theoretical hypotheses, specific objects of knowledge, and scopes of investigations. The social sciences born in modern times form a set of institutions that express ethical postulates through technical operations. For a long period, these special institutions organized "new crusades" of a technical nature to perform ethical tasks; they contrast to other institutions which speak in the name of "reality" and use a dogmatic way of making believe.

However, a new "dogmatism" has appeared, one that has replaced the historical linkage of ethical obligation and technical ability. The scientific establishment has been gradually separating itself from its ethical goals, which for a long time had motivated and directed its technical operations. It has slowly been losing its foundation in social operativity and transforming its products into representations of a reality in which everyone must believe. I call this dogmatizing tendency "the institution of the real." It consists of the construction of representations into laws imposed by the states of things. Through this process, ethical tasks are replaced by what is supposed to be the expression of reality. A touchstone is the concept of "fiction."

1. Fiction

"Fiction" is a perilous word, much like its correlative, "science." Having discussed the fictive aspects of historical discourse elsewhere,[1] I should like here only to specify, in the form of a preliminary note, four possible ways in which fiction operates in the historian's discourse.

1.1 Fiction and History

Western historiography struggles against fiction. This internecine strife between history and storytelling is very old. Like an old family quarrel, positions and opinions are often fixed. In its struggle against genealogical storytelling, the myths and legends of the collective memory, and the meanderings of the oral tradition, historiography establishes a certain distance between itself and common assertion and belief; it locates itself in this difference, which gives it the accreditation of erudition because it is separated from ordinary discourse.

Not that it speaks the truth; never has the historian pretended to do that! Rather, with his apparatus for the critical reading of documents, the scholar effaces error from the "fables" of the past. The territory that he occupies is acquired through a diagnosis of the false. He hollows out a place for his discipline in the terrain of received tradition. In this way, installed in the midst of a given society's stratified and interconnected modes of narrative (that is to say, all that this society tells or told of itself), he spends his time in pursuing the false rather than in the construction of the true, as though truth could be produced only by means of determining error. His work is oriented toward the negative, or, to borrow a more appropriate term from Popper, toward "falsification."[2] From this viewpoint, "fiction" is that which the historiographer constitutes as erroneous; thereby, he delimits his proper territory.

1.2 Fiction and Reality

At the level of analytic procedures (the examination and comparison of documents), as at the level of interpretations (the products of the historiographical operation), the technical discourse capable of determining the errors characteristic of fiction has come to be authorized to speak in the name of the "real." By distinguishing between the two discourses—the one scientific, the other fictive—according to its own criteria, historiography credits itself with having a special relationship to the "real" because its contrary is posited as "false."

This reciprocal determination operates elsewhere as well, although by other means and with other aims. It involves a double displacement, which renders a concept plausible or true by pointing to an error and, at the same time, by enforcing belief in something real through a denunciation of the false. The assumption is made that what is not held to be false must be real. Thus, for example, in the past, arguments against "false" gods were used to induce belief in a true God. The process repeats itself today in contemporary historiography: by demonstrating the presence of errors, discourse must pass off as "real" whatever is placed in opposition to the errors. Even though this is logically questionable, it works, and it fools people. Consequently, fiction is deported to the land of the unreal, but the discourse that is armed with the technical "know-how" to discern errors is given the supplementary privilege of prepresenting something "real." Debates about the reliability of literature as opposed to history illustrate this division.

1.3 Fiction and Science

Through a rather logical reversal, fiction may have the same position in the realm of science. In place of the metaphysician's and theologian's discourse, which once deciphered the order of all things and the will of their author, a slow revolution constitutive of our "modernity" has substituted writings ("écritures" or scientific languages) capable of establishing coherences that could produce an order, a progress, a history. Detached from their epiphanic function of representing things, these "formal" languages in their various applications give rise to scenarios whose relevance no longer depends on what they express but on what they render possible. These scenarios constitute a new species of fiction, scientific artifacts, which are not judged in terms of reality—which they are said to lack—but in terms of the possibilities they generate for producing or transforming reality. The "fiction" is not the photographing of the lunar space mission but what anticipated and organized it.

Historiography also utilizes fictions of this type when it constructs systems of correlation among unities defined as distinct and stable—for example, when it investigates the past, but applies hypotheses and scientific rules of the present; or in the case of historical econometrics, when it analyzes the probable consequences of counterfactual hypotheses (for example, the fate of slavery if the Civil War had not taken place).[3] However, historians are no less suspicious of this particular ficition cum scientific artifact. They accuse it of "destroying" historiography, as the debates over econometrics have demonstrated. Their resistance appeals once again to that method which, while supporting itself by "facts," reveals errors. But, again, the method is founded on the relationship that historians' discourse is presumed to have with the "real." In fiction, even of this kind, historians struggle against a lack of referentiality, an injury to "realist" discourse, a break in the marriage they suppose exists between words and things.

1.4 Fiction and "Univocity"

Fiction is accused, finally, of not being a "univocal" discourse or, to put it another way, of lacking scientific "univocity." In effect, fiction plays on the stratification of meaning: it narrates one thing in order to tell something else; it delineates itself in a language from which it continuously draws effects of meaning that cannot be circumscribed or checked. In contrast to an artificial language which is "univocal" in principle, fiction has no proper place of its own. It is "metaphoric"; it moves elusively in the domain of the other. Knowledge is insecure when dealing with the problem of fiction; consequently, its effort consists in analysis (of a sort) that reduces or translates the elusive language of fiction into stable and easily combined elements. From this point of view, fiction violates one of the rules of scientificity. It is a witch whom knowledge must labor to hold and to identify through its exorcizing. It no longer bears the mark of the false, of the unreal, or of the artificial. It is only a drifting meaning. It is the siren from whom the historian must defend himself, like Ulysses tied to the mast.

In fact, however, despite the quid pro quo of its different statutes, fiction, in any of its modalities—mythic, literary, scientific, or metaphorical—is a discourse that "informs" the "real" without pretending either to represent it or to credit itself with the capacity for such a representation. In this way, it is fundamentally opposed to a historiography that is always attached to an ambition to speak the "real." This ambition contains the trace of a primitive global representation of the world. It is a mythic structure whose opaque presence haunts our scientific, historical discipline. In any case, it remains essential.

This then is the obscure center around which revolve a number of considerations that I should like to introduce concerning the interplay of science and fiction. I shall break these down into three propositions as follows: 1) the "real" produced by historiography is also the orthodox legend of the institution of history; 2) scientific apparatus—for example, computer technology—also have a certain fictive quality in the work of historians; and 3) considering the relationship of discourse to that which produces it, that is, a relationship with a professional institution and with a scientific methodology, one can regard historiography as something of a mix of science and fiction or as a field of knowledge where questions of time and tense regain a central importance.

2. The Epic of the Institution

In general, every story that relates what is happening or what has happened constitutes something real to the extent that it pretends to be the representation of a past reality. It takes on authority by passing itself off as the witness of what is or of what has been. It seduces, and it imposes itself, under a title of events; which it pretends to interpret (for example, Nixon's last hours in the White House or the capitalist economy of the Mexican *haciendas*). In effect, every authority bases itself on the notion of the "real," which it is supposed to recount. It is always in the name of the "real" that one produces and moves the faithful. Historiography acquires this power in so far as it presents and interprets the "facts." How can readers resist discourse that tells them what is or what has been? They must agree to the law, which expresses itself in terms of events.

However, the "real" as represented by historiography does not correspond to the "real" that determines its production. It hides behind the picture of a past the present that produces and organizes it. Expressed bluntly, the problem is as follows: a *mise en scène* of a (past) actuality, that is, the historiographical discourse itself, occults the social and technical apparatus of the professional institution that produces it. The operation in question is rather sly: the discourse gives itself credibility in the name of the reality which it is supposed to represent, but this authorized appearance of the "real" serves precisely to camouflage the practice which in fact determines it. Representation thus disguises the praxis that organizes it.

2.1 The Discourse and/of the Institution

The historian's discourse does not escape the constraint of those socioeconomic structures that determine the representations of a society. Indeed, by isolating itself, a specalized social group has attempted to shield this discourse from the

politicization and the commercialization of those daily news stories which recount our contemporary actuality to us. This separation, which sometimes takes
on an official form (a *corps d'état*), sometimes a corporate form (a profession),
enables the circumscribing of more ancient objects (a past), the setting aside of
especially rare materials (that is, archives) and the codifying of procedures by
the profession (that is, techniques). But all this happens as though the general
procedures for making our common "histories" or our everyday news stories
(television, newspapers) had not been eliminated from their laboratories but,
rather, as though they were put to the test there, criticized, and verified by the
historians in their experimental setting. It becomes necessary, therefore, prior
to analyzing the specific techniques proper to scholarly historical research, to
recall what these procedures have in common with the daily production of news
stories by the media. The institutional apparatus of history itself, in supporting
the researches of its members, blinds them to the ordinary practices from which
they pretend to be detached.

Except in marginal cases, erudition is no longer an individual phenomenon.
It is a collective enterprise. For Popper, the scientific community corrects any
effects of the researcher's subjectivity. But this community is also a factory, its
members distributed along assembly lines, subject to budgetary pressures,
hence, dependent on political decisions and bound by the growing constraints
of a sophisticated machinery (archival infrastructures, computers, publishers'
demands, etc.). Its operations are determined by a rather narrow and homogeneous segment of society from which its members are recruited. Its general
orientation is governed by sociocultural assumptions and postulates imposed
through recruitment, through the existing and established fields of research,
through the demands stemming from the personal interests of a boss, through
the modes and fashions of the moment, etc. Moreover, its interior organization
follows a division of labor: it has its bosses, its aristocracy, its "head research
technicians" (often the foremen managing the boss's research), its technicians,
its pieceworkers, and its clerks of all kinds for performing routine mental and
physical labors. I leave aside, for the time being, the psychosociological aspects
of this enterprise, for example, that recently analyzed as "the rhetoric of university respectability" by Jeanine Czubaroff.[4]

The books that are the products of this factory say nothing about how they
are made or so little as to amount to nothing. They conceal their relationship
to this hierarchical, socioeconomic apparatus. For example, does the doctoral
dissertation [*la thèse*] specify its relation to the boss [*le patron*] upon whom the
promotion depends, or to the financial imperatives which the boss himself must
obey, or to the pressures exerted by the profession on the choice of subjects for
investigation and the methods to be employed? It is useless to insist. Yet one
must insist that these determinants do not concern properly scientific imperatives; nor do they result from personal ideologies. But they do concern the

weight of a present historical reality on discourses which speak little of this presence while blithely pretending to represent the "real."

To be sure, this historian's representation has its necessary role in a society or a group. It constantly mends the rents in the fabric that joins past and present. It assures a "meaning," which surmounts the violence and the divisions of time. It creates a theater of references and of common values, which guarantee a sense of unity and a "symbolic" communicability to the group. Finally, as Michelet once said, it is the work of the living in order to "quiet the dead"[5] and to reunite all sorts of separated things and people into the semblance of a unity and a presence that constitutes representation itself. It is a discourse based on conjunction, which fights against all the disjunctions produced by competition, labor, time, and death. But this social task calls precisely for the occultation of everything that would particularize the representation. It leads to an avoidance in the unifying representation of all traces of the division which organizes its production. Thus, the text substitutes a representation of a past for elucidation of present institutional operation that manufactures the historian's text. It puts an appearance of the real (past) in place of the praxis (present) that produces it, thus developing an actual case of quid pro quo.

2.2 From Scholarly Product to the Media: General Historiography

From this viewpoint, scholarly discourse is no longer distinguishable from that prolix and fundamental narrativity that is our everyday historiography. Scholarship is an integral part of the system that organizes by means of "histories" all social communication and everything that makes the present habitable. The book or the professional article, on the one hand, and the magazine or the television news, on the other, are distinguishable from one another only within the same historiographical field which is constituted by the innumerable narratives that recount and interpret events. Of course, the "specialist" in history will persist in denying this compromising solidarity. But the disavowal is in vain. The scholarly side of this historiography forms only a particular species of it, a species that merely employs different techniques but one that is no more "technical" than other closely related species. It too belongs to the widely diffused genus of stories that explain what is happening.

Without ceasing, morning, noon, and night, history, in effect, "tells" its story. It gives privileged position to whatever goes badly (the event is first and foremost an accident, a misfortune, a crisis) because of an urgent need to mend these holes immediately with the thread of a language that makes sense. In a reciprocal fashion, such misfortunes generate stories; they authorize the historian's or newsmaker's tireless production of them. Not very long ago, the "real" bore the figure of a divine secret that justified the endless narrativity of its revelation. Today the "real" continues to allow an indefinite unfolding of the narrative; only now it takes the form of the event, remote or peculiar, which serves as the necessary postulate for the production of our revelatory discourse. This fragmented god never ceases to give rise to a lot of talk. He chatters incessantly—everywhere, in the news, in statistics, in polls, in documents, all of which compensate by means of a conjunctive narrative for the growing disjunction created by the division of labor, by social atomizations, and by professional specialization. These informational discourses furnish a common referent to all those who are otherwise separated. In the name of the "real," they institute a symbol-creating language that generates belief in the process of communication and in what is communicated, thereby forming the tangled web of "our" history.

With regard to this general historiography, I would note three traits common to the entire genus, even though these are likely to be more visible in the species of the "media" and better controlled (or ordered in different modalities) in the "scientific" species.

2.2.1

The representation of historical realities is itself the means by which the real conditions of its own production are camouflaged. The "documentary" fails to show that it is the result, in the first place, of a selective socioeconomic institution and of a technical encoding apparatus—newspapers or television. In it everything happens as though the situation in Afghanistan merely displayed itself through the medium of Dan Rather. In fact, the situation is told to us in a story which is the product of a certain milieu, of a power structure, of contracts between a corporation and its clients, and of the logic of a certain technicality. The clarity and simplicity of the information conceal the complex laws of production that govern its fabrication. It is a sort of *trompe l'oeil*, but different from the *trompe l'oeil* of old in that it no longer furnishes any visible sign of its theatrical nature or of the code whereby it is fabricated. Professional "elucidation" of the past acts in a similar way.

2.2.2

The story which speaks in the name of the real is injunctive. It "signifies" in the way a command is issued. In this context, the event or the problem of the day (this everyday "real") plays the same role as the divinity of old: the priests, the witnesses, or the ministers of current events make them speak in order to command in their name. To be sure, giving voice to the "real" no longer serves to reveal the secret purposes willed by a god. Henceforth, numbers and data take the place of such secrets. Yet the structure remains the same: it consists in endless dictation, in the name of the "real," of what must be said, what must be believed, and what must be done. And what can possibly be opposed to the "facts"? The law, which is given in numbers and in data (that is, in terms fabricated by technicians) but presented as the manifestation of the ultimate authority, the "real," constitutes our new orthodoxy, an immense discourse of the order of things. We know that the same holds true for historiographical literature; many recent analyses show that it has always been a pedagogical discourse, and a normative and militantly nationalist one at that. But in setting forth what must be thought and what must be done, this dogmatic discourse does not have to justify itself because it speaks in the name of the "real."

2.2.3

Furthermore, this storytelling has a pragmatic efficacy. In pretending to recount the real, it manufactures it. It is performative. It renders believable what it says, and it generates appropriate action. In making believers, it produces an active body of practitioners. The news of the day declares: "Anarchists are in your streets; crime is at your door!" The public responds immediately by arming and barricading itself. The news adds: "Reliable indicators show that the criminals are illegal aliens." The public searches out the guilty ones, denounces certain people, and calls for their execution or exile. The media historian's narration devaluates certain practices and assigns privilege to others; it blows conflicts out of proportion; it inflames nationalism and racism; it organizes or disengages certain forms of behavior; and it manages to produce what it says is happening. Jean-Pierre Faye has analyzed this process, apropos of Nazism.[6] We know many other instances where such stories, fabricated in series, made history. The bewitching voices of the narration transform, reorient, and regulate the space of social relations. They exercise an immense power, but a power that eludes control because it presents itself as the only representation of what is happening or of what happened in the past. Professional history operates in an analogous way through the subjects it selects, through the problematics that it privileges, through the documents and the models that it employs. Under the name of science, it too arms and mobilizes a clientele of the faithful. Consequently, the political and economic powers, who often have more foresight than the historians themselves, are always striving to keep historians on their side by flattering them, paying them, directing them, controlling or, if need be, subduing them.

3. Scientificity and History: The Computer

In order to establish its own setting and base of power, discourse binds itself to the institutional structure that legitimates it in the eyes of the public and, at the same time, makes it dependent on the play of social forces. Corporate bodies underwrite the text or the image, providing a guarantee to readers or spectators that it is a discourse of the "real" while, simultaneously, by its internal functioning, the institution articulates the mode of production upon the ensemble of social practices. But there is a reciprocal exchange in the parts played by these two aspects. Representations are authorized to speak in the name of the "real" only if they are successful in obliterating any memory of the conditions under which they were produced. Now, it is again the institution that manages to achieve an amalgam of these contraries. Drawing on common social conflicts, rules, and procedures, the institution constrains the activity of production, and it authorizes the occultation of this process by the very discourse that is produced. Carried out by the professional milieu, these practices can then by hidden by the representation. But is this situation really so paradoxical? After all, the exclusion from the discourse of reference to the conditions that produced it is precisely what actually binds the group (of scholars).

Of course, this practice cannot simply be reduced to everything that makes it be part of the category of general historiography. As a "scientific" practice, it has certain specific characteristics. I shall take as an example the functioning of the computer in the field of professional historiography. The computer opens up the possibility of quantitative, serial analysis of variable relationships among stable units over an extended period of time. For the historian, it is tantamount to discovering the Island of the Blessed. At last he will be able to sever historiography from its compromising relations with rhetoric, with all its metonymic and metaphorical uses of details that are supposed to be the signifying elements of the ensemble and with all its cunning devices of oratory and persuasion. At last he is going to be able to disengage historiography from its dependence on the surrounding culture, out of which prejudgments and expectancies determine in advance certain postulates, units of study, and interpretations. Thanks to the computer, he becomes capable of mastering numbers, of constructing regularities, and of determining periodicities according to correlation curves—three frequent distress points in the strategy of his work. Thus, historiography becomes intoxicated with statistics. Books are now filled with numerical figures, the guarantors of a certain objectivity.

But, alas, it is necessary to disenchant him, though we need not go as far as Jack Douglas or Herbert Simons, who speak of a "rhetoric of numerical figures."[7] A counterpart to the ambition to mathematize historiography is the historicization of that particular kind of mathematics known as statistics. We need to identify the following elements of this mathematical analysis of society: 1) its relationship to the historical conditions that made it possible; 2) the technical reductions that it imposes methodologically and, thus, the relation between what it treats and what it is unable to take into account; and 3) its effective functioning in the field of historiography, that is, the mode in which it is recuperated and assimilated by the very discipline it is supposed to transform. This identification will involve one more way of noting the return of the fictive within a practice that is scientific.

3.1

Nothing seems more extraneous to the avatars through which the historian's discipline has passed than this mathematician's scientificity. In its theorizing practice, mathematics is defined by the capacity of its discourse to determine the rules of its production, to be "consistent" (that is, without contradicition among any of its propositions), "univocal" (that is, without ambiguity), and constraining (precluding by its form any denial of its content). Therefore, its writing has at its disposal a certain autonomy that makes "elegance" the internal principle of its development. Actually, its application to the analysis of society is dependent on circumstances of time and place. Despite the fact that the seventeenth century *Theologia . . . mathematica* by John Craig, with its "rules of evidence,"[8] already put forth the idea of calculating the probabilities of testimony, it was not until the eighteenth century that Condorcet established the foundations of a "social mathematics" and produced a calculus of "probabilities," which he thought could account for the "motives of belief" and, thus, for the practical choices made by individuals who are joined together in society.[9] Only then did the idea of a mathematizable society take shape, the principle and the postulate of all subsequent analyses that take a mathematical approach to social reality.

This "idea" did not just emerge as a matter of course, although the project for a society ruled by reason goes back to Plato's Republic. In order for the "langue des calculs," as Condillac called it,[10] to define the discourse of a social science, it was first necessary that a society be understood as a totality composed of individual units and as an aggregate of their respective wills. Thus, "individualism" was born with modernity itself.[11] It is presupposed by any mathematical treatment of the possible relations among individual units, just as it was the necessary presupposition for the conception of a democratic society. Furthermore, three circumstantial conditions connect this idea with a particular historical conjuncture. First is progress in the techniques of mathematics (the calculus of probabilities, etc.), which cannot be dissociated from the quantitative approach to nature and to the deduction of universal laws that are characteristics of eighteenth century science;[12] then the sociopolitical organization of an administration for rationalizing territory, centralizing information, and furnishing the model for the general management of citizens; and, finally, the establishment of a bourgeois elite ideologically persuaded that its own power and the wealth of the nation would be assured by the rationalization of society.

This triple historical determination, one technical, another sociopolitical, and a third ideological and social, was—and remains—the necessary condition for all statistical operations. In addition is the fact that today scientific progress, a national or international institutional apparatus, and a technocratic milieu combine to support the computer industry.[13] In other words, the mathematization of society does not escape history. On the contrary, it depends on new knowledge and on institutional structures and social formations, the historical implications of which are developed across the entire field of this ahistorical methodology.

3.2

Furthermore, mathematical rigor pays the price of restricting the domain in which it can be employed. Already in Condorcet we find a threefold reduction. In his "social mathematics" Condorcet assumes 1) that one acts according to what one believes, 2) that belief can be reduced to a number of "motives of belief," and 3) that these "motives" are reducible to probabilities. He wants, indeed, to carve out of the real a mathematizable object. Therefore, he leaves out of his calculation an enormous mass of material, that is, the tremendous social and psychological complexities surrounding the choices people make. His "science of strategies" assembles simulacrum. What, finally, did this mathematical genius calculate about the society he pretended to analyze? The price of the rigorous novelty in his method is the transformation of its object of study into a fiction. From the end of the eighteenth century, as Peter Hanns Reill has shown in connection with the emergence of German historicism,[14] the mathematical model was rejected for the sake of evolutionism (which is concurrent with the historicization of linguistics);[15] it was restored in history as well as elsewhere by the macroeconomic structuralism of the twentieth century.

Today only drastic restrictions permit the use of statistics, which is still an elementary form of mathematics, in historical studies. So, from the very outset of the statistical operation, one can retain only so much of the material being studied as is susceptible to arrangement in a linear series; and this kind of data favors, for example, electoral history or the history of urban planning, to the detriment of other histories, which are left to lie fallow or are relegated to amateurs. One must define the units to be treated in such a way that the statistical sign (the numbered object) must never be identified with things or words, in which case historical or semantic variations would compromise the stability of the sign and, thereby, the validity of calculations. In addition to these restrictions necessitated by the "cleaning" of the data are those imposed by the limits of the theoretical instruments themselves. For example, it would be necessary to have access to a "fuzzy logic" capable of treating categories like "a little," "rather," "perhaps," etc., categories that are characteristic of the field of history. However, despite recent research, which sets out from notions of "proximity" or "distance" between objects and introduces "fuzzy" relationships into computational analysis,[16] the computer algorithms continue to be reducible to three or four formulas.

We have all witnessed the elimination of certain material from a historical study because it could not be treated in accordance with the rules imposed by this computational methodology. I could recount the transformations in historical research concerning, for example, the *Etats-Généraux* of 1614 or the *Cahiers de doléance* of 1789, objects finally rejected and placed outside the narrow field of inquiry accessible to the computer. At the elementary level of the analysis and breakdown of material into units, the mathematical operation excluded entire areas of historicity, and for its own good reasons. It creates an immense amount of refuse, rejected by the computer and piled up all around it.

3.3

To the degree that they are honored in the actual practice of the historian, these constraints produce a technical and methodological auditing of sorts. They make some effects of scientificity. To characterize these effects, one might say, in general, that wherever it is introduced into the computation, calculation multiplies hypotheses and enables the falsification of some among them. On the one hand, combinations among the elements that have been isolated will suggest previously unthought of relationships. On the other, the computation of large numbers will prohibit interpretations founded on particular cases or on received ideas. There is, thus, an expansion of what is possible and a determination of what is impossible. Computation proves nothing. It increases the number of legitimate formal relations among abstractly defined elements, and it designates the hypotheses to be rejected on the grounds that they are poorly formulated, unexaminable, or contrary to the results of the analysis.[17]

But this being so, computation ceases to be fundamentally concerned with the "real." It amounts to no more than a managing of formal units. Actual history is, in fact, thrown out of its laboratories. Consequently, the reaction that the computer produces in historians is extremely ambiguous. Simultaneously, they want it and they don't want it. They are at once seduced by it and rebel against it. I do not speak here of theoretical compatibility but of a factual situation. It must have some significance. In examining how it works, we can mark out at least three aspects of the way the computer actually functions in historiographical work.

3.3.1

In distinguishing, as one must, among the computer sciences (where statistics plays a lesser role), probability theory, statistics itself (and applied statistics), and the analysis of data, it could be said that, in general, historians confined themselves to the last sector, the quantitative treatment of data. In the field of history, the computer is used essentially to build new archives. These archives, public or private, duplicate and then eventually replace the older archives. There exist remarkable data banks, such as the Inter-University Consortium for Political and Social Research (ICPSR) of the University of Michigan at Ann Arbor, or the archival banks created in France at the *Archives Nationales* by Remi Matthieu and Ivan Cloulas (which are concerned with the administration of townships in the nineteenth century), and at the *Minutier central* of the Parisian notaries.

This extensive development of computer-assisted historical research is still restricted largely to the archivistic, which is a discipline traditionally taken to be "auxiliary" and distinguished from the interpretive work that the historian reserves as his proper concern. Although in transforming documentation, it also transforms the possibilities of interpretation,[18] the computer is nonetheless lodged within a particular sphere of the historiographical enterprise, at the interior of the pre-established framework that used to protect the autonomy of the historian's hermeneutics. It is permitted only an "auxiliary" place, determined once again by the old model, which would distinguish the assembling of data from the elucidation of meaning and which would order the techniques in a hierarchy. In principle, this pattern of work permits the historian to utilize computation without having to bow to its rules. No doubt it explains why, as Charles Tilly asserts, at the level of intellectual proceedings there have been few epistemological confrontations between mathematical and interpretive operations in the field of historiography so that, despite tensions, porosities, and reciprocal displacements, the field maintains a sort of epistemological bilingualism.[19]

3.3.2

Rather than employing the computer for the sake of the formal operations that it sets in motion, historians use it as a source of more solid and extensive data. The computer appears in their work in its current image of technocratic power. It is introduced into historiography by virtue of a socioeconomic reality rather than by virtue of a system of rules and hypotheses proper to a scientific field. This is the reaction of a historian, not of a mathematician. The computer is inscribed in the historian's discourse as a massive and determinant contemporary fact. By the way, the historian's institution refers to that data-processing power that generates modifications across all the areas of socioeconomic life.

Consequently, each book of history must include a minimal base of statistics, which both guarantees the seriousness of the study and renders homage to the power that reorganizes our productive apparatus. The two gestures, one of conformity to a contemporary technical method and the other of dedication to the reigning authority, are inseparable from each other. They are one and the same.

From this point of view, the tribute that contemporary erudition pays to the computer will be the equivalent of the "Dedication to the Prince" in books of the seventeenth century: a recognition of obligation with respect to the power that overdetermines the rationality of an epoch. Today, the institution of computerized information processing, like the princely and genealogical institution of old, appears in the text under the aegis of a force that is right and takes the lead over the discourse of representation.

In relation to these two successive seats of power, the historian is in the position of being equally near them and yet a foreigner. He is in attendance on the computer just as in the past he was in attendance on the king [*auprès du roi*]. He analyzes and mimics operations that can only be carried out at a distance. He utilizes them, but he is not in command of them. In sum, he does work in history, but he does not make history. He represents it.

3.3.3

On the other hand, his dedication to this scientificity accredits his text. It plays the role of the authoritative citation. Among all the authorities to which the historiographical discourse may refer, it is this one that lends it the utmost legitimacy. In the final analysis, what always accredits the discourse is power because power functions as a guarantee of the "real," in the manner in which gold bullion validates bank notes and paper money. This motive, which draws the representational discourse toward the center of power, is more fundamental than psychological or political motivations. Power today takes on the technocratic form of the computer. Therefore, to cite its operations is, thanks to this "authority," to bestow credibility on the representation. By the tribute it pays the computer, historiography produces the belief that it is not fiction. Its scientific proceedings express once again something unscientific: the homage rendered to the computer sustains an old hope of making historical discourse pass for discourse on the "real."

A corollary to this problematic of compelling belief by citing a source of power is the more general problematic of the "belief" that is bound to a citation of the other. The two are connected, power being the other of the discourse. I shall take as an example the relationship that one particular discipline maintains with another. In my own experience of collaborations between historians and computer scientists, a reciprocal illusion makes each group assume that the other discipline will guarantee what it otherwise lacks—a reference to the "real." From the computer sciences, historians ask to be accredited by a scientific power capable of providing a certain "serious" quality to their discourse. From historiography, the computer scientists, disquieted by the very ease with which they are able to manipulate formal units, require some ballasting for their computations, something of the "concrete" derived from the particulars of the historian's erudition. Each plays the role in the other's field by compensating for the two conditions of all modern scientific research: its limitation, which is the renunciation of totalization, and its nature as an artificial language, which is the renunciation of the possibility of being a discourse of the "real," or of representation.

In order to come into being, a science must resign itself to a loss of both totality and reality. But whatever it has to give up in order to establish itself returns under the figure of the other, from which it continually awaits a guarantee against that lack that is at the origin of all our knowledge. The specter of a totalizing and ontological science reappears in the form of a belief in the other. The reintroduction, which is more or less marginal, of this model of science expresses the refusal of that loss and bereavement that accompanied the break between discourse (writing) and the "real" (presence). It is not surprising that historiography—which is undoubtedly the most ancient of all disciplines and the most haunted by the past—should become a privileged field for the return of this phantom. The use of the computer in the field of historiography cannot be dissociated from what it enables the historian to make others believe, nor from what it presupposes he believes himself. This superabundance (this superstition) of the past plays a part in the way historians employ modern techniques of investigation. So it is that in this very relation to scientificity, to mathematics, to the computer, historiography is "historical"—no longer in the sense that it produces an interpretation of previous epochs but in the sense that it is reproducing and recounting what modern sciences have rejected or lost and constituted as "past"—a finite, separate entity.

4. Science-Fiction, or the Place of Time

This combination may be what constitutes the essence of the historical: a return of the past in the present discourse. In broader terms, this mixture (science and fiction) obscures the neat dichotomy that established modern historiography as a relation between a "present" and a "past" distinct from each other, one being the producer of the discourse and the other being what is represented by it, one the "subject," the other the "object" of a certain knowledge. This object, presumed to be exterior to the work of the laboratory, in fact determines its operations from within.

The presence of this combination is frequently treated as the effect of an archaeology that must be gradually eliminated from any true science or as a "necessary evil" to be tolerated like an incurable malady. But I believe it can also be understood as the index of a peculiar epistemological status and, therefore, of a function and a scientificity to be reckoned with in its own right. If this is the case, then we must bring to light those "shameful" aspects that historiography believes it must keep hidden. The discursive formation which will then appear is an interspace (between science and fiction). It has its own norms and these do not correspond to the usual model which is always being transgressed but which one might like to believe, or to make others believe, it obeys. This science fiction, science and fiction, like other "heterologies," operates at the juncture of scientific discourse and ordinary language, in the same place where the past is conjugated in the present, and where questions that are not amenable to a technical approach reappear in the form of narrative metaphors. In concluding, I would like to specify a number of questions which an elucidation of this mixture of science and fiction must consider.

4.1 A Repoliticization

Our sciences were born with that "modern" historical act that depoliticized research by establishing "disinterested" and "neutral" fields of study supported by scientific institutions. This act of neutralization continues in many instances to be organizing the ideology proclaimed in certain scientific communities. But the further development of what this act made possible has tended to invert its neutralizing effects. Having become actual seats of logistic power, scientific institutions have fitted themselves into the system they serve to rationalize, a system that links them to each other, fixes the direction of their research, and assures their integration into the existing socioeconomic framework. These effects of assimilation naturally weigh most heavily on those disciplines which are the least technologically developed. And this is the case with historiography.

It is therefore necessary today to "repoliticize" the sciences, that is to focus their technical apparatus on the fields of force within which they operate and produce their discourse. This task is preeminently that of the historian. Historiography has always been lodged at the frontier between discourse and power. It is a battlefield for a war between sense and violence. But after having believed for three or four centuries it was possible to dominate and to observe this relation—to situate it outside of knowledge in order to make it an "object" for knowledge and to analyze it under the category of a "past"—we must recognize today that the conflict between discourse and power hangs over historiography itself and at the same time remains an integral part of it. Historical elucidation unfolds under the domination of what it treats. It must make explicit its internal and prevailing relationship to power (as was the case in the past for the relation to the prince). This explication is the only means available to prevent historiography from creating simulacra. Assuming the guise of a scientific autonomy, those simulacra would have the effect of eliminating any serious treatment of the relationship that a language of sense or of communication maintains with a network of forces.

Technically, this "repoliticization" will consist in "historicizing" historiography itself. By a professional reflex, the historian refers any discourse to the socioeconomic or mental conditions that produced it. He needs to apply this kind of analysis to his own discourse in a manner that will make it pertinent to the elucidation of those forces that presently organize representations of the past. His very work will then become a laboratory in which to test how a symbolic system articulates itself in a political one.

4.2 The Coming Back of Time

In this way the epistemology that would differentiate an object from the subject and, consequently, reduce time to the function of classifying objects will be modified. In historiography, the two causalities, that of the object and that of time, are connected. For three centuries maybe the objectification of the past has made of time the unreflected category of a discipline that never ceases to use it as an instrument of classification. In the epistemology that was born with the Enlightenment, the difference between the subject of knowledge and its object is the foundation of what separates the past from the present. Within a socially stratified reality, historiography defined as "past" (that is, as an ensemble of alterities and of "resistances" to be comprehended or rejected) whatever did not belong to the power of producing a present, whether the power is political, social, or scientific. In other words, the "past" is the object from which a mode of production distinguishes itself in order to transform it. Historical acts transform contemporary documents into archives, or make the countryside into a museum of memorable and/or superstitious traditions. Such acts determine an opposition which circumscribes a "past" within a given society: In this way, a drive to produce establishes a relationship with what is not part—with a milieu, from which it cuts itself off; with an environment, which it must conquer; with resistances, which it encounters; etc. Its model is the relationship that a business undertakes with its raw material or with its clients, inside the same economic area. Documents of the "past" are thus connected to a productive apparatus and are treated according to its rules.

In this typical conception of the expansionist "bourgeois" economy, it is striking that time is exterior, is considered "other." Moreover, as in a monetary system, it only appears as a principle of classification in relation to those data which are situated in that exterior, objectified space. Recast in the mold of a taxonomic ordering of things, chronology becomes the alibi of time, a way of making use of time without reflecting on it, a way of banishing from the realm of knowledge the principle of death or of passing (or of metaphor). Time continues to be experienced within the productive process; but, now, transformed from within into a rational series of operations and objectified from without into a metric system of chronological units, this experience has only one language: an ethical language which expresses the imperative to produce.

Perhaps in restoring the ambiguity that characterizes relationships between object and subject or past and present, historiography could return to its traditional task—which is both a philosophical and a technical one—of articulating time as the ambivalence that affects the place from which it speaks and, thus, of reflecting upon the ambiguity of place as the work of time within the space of knowledge itself. For example, the "archaic" structure that transforms the use of the computer into a metaphor while still maintaining its technical function makes evident that essential, temporal experience, which is the impossibility of identifying with a given place. A "past" reappears through the very activity of historiographical production. That the "other" is already there, in place, is the very mode through which time insinuates itself.[20] Time can also return within historiographical thinking by means of a corollary modification concerning the practice and understanding of the object instead of that of place. Thus, "immediate history" can no longer distance itself from its "object," which, in fact, envelops it, controls it, and resituates it in the network of all other "histories." So, too, with "oral history" when it is not content to transcribe and exorcise those voices whose disappearance was formerly the condition of historiography. If the professional applies himself to the task of listening to what he can see or read, he discovers before him interlocutors, who, even if they are not specialists, are themselves subject-producers of histories and partners in a shared discourse. From the subject-object relationship, we pass to a plurality of authors and contracting parties. A hierarchy of knowledges is replaced by a mutual differentiation of subjects. From that moment, the particular place of the relationship that the technician maintains with others introduces a dialectic of all these places, that is, an experience of time.

4.3 Subjects and Affects

That the particularity of the place where discourse is produced is relevant will be naturally more apparent where historiographical discourse treats matters that put the subject-producer of history into question: the history of women, of blacks, of Jews, of cultural minorities, etc. In these fields one can, of course, either maintain that the personal status of the author is a matter of indifference (in relation to the objectivity of his or her work) or that he or she alone authorizes or invalidates the discourse (according to whether he or she is "of it" or not). But this debate requires what has been concealed by an epistemology, namely, the impact of subject-to-subject relationships (women and men, blacks and whites, etc.) on the use of apparently "neutral" techniques and in the organization of discourses that are, perhaps, equally scientific. For example, from the fact of the differentiation of the sexes, must one conclude that a woman produces a different historiography from that of a man? Of course, I do not answer this question, but I do assert that this interrogation puts the place of the subject in question and requires a treatment of it unlike the epistemology that constructed the "truth" of the work on the foundation of the speaker's irrelevance. Questioning the subject of knowledge demands that one rethink the concept of time, if it is true that the subject is constructed as a stratification of heterogeneous moments and that whether the scholar is woman, black, or Basque, it is structured by relations to the other.[21] Time is precisely the impossibility of an identity fixed by a place. Thus begins a reflection on time. The problem of history is inscribed in the place of this subject, which is in itself a play of difference, the historicity of a nonidentity with itself.

This double movement, which, in introducing time, disturbs the security of place and of the object of historiography, also recalls the discourse of affect or of passions. After having been central in analyses of society up until the end of the eighteenth century (through Spinoza, Hume, Locke, and Rousseau), the theory of passions and of interests was slowly eliminated by an objectivist economics, which, in the nineteenth century, replaced it with a rational interpretation of the relations of production, retaining only a residue of the old formulation and, thereby, anchoring the new system in the notion of "needs." After a century of being rejected, the economics of affects came back in the Freudian mode as an economics of the unconscious. With *Totem and Taboo, Civilization and Its Discontents*, and *Moses and Monotheism*, an analysis is presented, necessarily connected with an unconscious, which articulates anew the subject's investments in collective structures. Like ghosts, these affects constitute in themselves a return of the repressed in the order of a socioeconomic reasoning. They make it possible to formulate, in theory or in historiographical practice, questions which have already found expression in the work of Paul Veyne on the historian's desire,[22] of Albert Hirschman on disappointment in economics,[23] of Martin Duberman on the inscribing of the sexual subject in its historical object,[24] and of Régine Robin on the structuration of the historiographical process by the mythic scenes of childhood.[25] Studies of this kind inaugurate a different epistemology from that which defined the place of knowledge in terms of a position "proper" to itself and which measured the authority of the "subject of knowledge" by the elimination of everything concerning the speaker. In making this elimination explicit, historiography returns once again to the particularities of the commonplace, to the reciprocal affects which structure representations, and to the multiple pasts which determine the use of its techniques from within.

4.4 A Scientific Myth as Ethical Discourse

The fact that identities of time, place, subject, and object assumed by classical historiography do not hold, that they have been stirred by forces that trouble them, has been for a long time underscored by the proliferation of fiction. But this is a part of historiography which is held to be shameful and illegitimate—a disreputable family member that the discipline disavows. This is all the more curious when one considers that in the seventeenth century historiography was placed at the opposite extreme; at that time, the generalist historian gloried in practicing the rhetorical genre par excellence.[26] During the space of three centuries, the discipline has passed from one pole to the other. This oscillation is already the symptom of a status. It will be necessary to specify its transformation and, in particular, to analyze the progressive differentiation, which, by the eighteenth century, separated the "sciences" from the domain of "letters"; historiography was found stretched between these two domains to which it was attached by its traditional role of "global" science and of "symbolic" social conjunction. It has remained so, albeit under different guises. But improvements in its technique and the general evolution of knowledge have increasingly led it to camouflage its links, inadmissible to scientific thought, with what had been identified during the same period of time as "literature." This camouflage is precisely what introduces into contemporary historiography the simulacrum that it refuses to be.

In order to grant legitimacy to the fiction that haunts the field of historiography, we must first "recognize" the repressed, which takes the form of "literature," within the discourse that is legitimated as scientific. The ruses that the discourse must employ in its relationship to power in the hope of using that power without serving it, the manifestations of the object as a "fantastic" actor in the very place of the "subject of knowledge," the repetitions and returns of time that are supposed to be irrevocably past, the disguises of passion under the mask of reason, etc.—all concern fiction in the "literary" sense of the term. And fiction is hardly a stranger to the "real." On the contrary, as Jeremy Bentham already noted in the eighteenth century, "fictitious" discourse may be closer to the real than objective discourse.[27] But another logic comes into play here, which is not that of the positive sciences. It began to re-emerge with Freud. Its elucidation will be one of the tasks of historiography. Under this aspect, fiction is recognizable where there is no fixed, "univocal" position proper to itself, that is, where the other insinuates itself in the place of the "subject of knowledge." The central role of rhetoric in the field of historiography is precisely an important symptom of this different logic.

Envisaged then as a "discipline," historiography is a science which lacks the means of being one. Its discourse undertakes to deal with what is most resistant to scientificity (the relation of the social to the event, to violence, to the past, to death), that is, those matters each scientific discipline must eliminate in order to be constituted as a science. But in this tenuous position, historiography seeks to maintain the possibility of a scientific explanation through the textual globalization produced by a narrative synthesis. The "verisimilitude" that characterizes this discourse is its defense of a principle of explanation and of the right to a meaning. The "as if" of its reasoning (the enthymematic style of historiographical demonstration) has the value of a scientific project. It maintains a belief in the intelligibility of things that resist it the most. Thus, historiography juxtaposes elements that are inconsistent and even contradictory and often appears to "explain" them; it is through historiography that scientific models are reconnected with what is missing from them. This relating of systems to what displaces them, or metaphorically transforms them, corresponds as well to the way time appears to us and is experienced by us. From this perspective, historiographical discourse is, in itself, the struggle of reason with time, but of reason which does not renounce what it is as yet incapable of comprehending, a reason which is, in its fundamental workings, *ethical*. Thus it will be, in the vanguard of the sciences as the present fiction of what they are only partially able to achieve. An affirmation of scientificity rules this discourse, which conjoins the explicable with the not yet explicable. What is recounted there is a fiction of science itself.

Continuing to maintain its traditional function of "conjunction," historiography links the cultural, legendary manifestations of a time to what, in these legends, is already controllable, correctible, or prohibited by technical practices. It cannot be identified with its practices, but it is produced by what those practices trace, erase, or confirm in the received language of a given milieu. The traditional model of a global, symbolizing, and legitimating discourse is thus still in evidence here but worked by instruments and controls that belong specifically to the productive apparatus of our society. Furthermore, neither the totalizing narrativity of our culture's legends nor its technical and critical operations can be assumed to be absent or eliminated, except arbitrarily, from what finally results in a representation—the historical book or article. From this point of view, each of these representations, or the mass they form taken together, could be compared to myth if we define myth as a story permeated by social practices—that is, a global discourse articulating practices which it does not talk about but which it must respect, practices that are at once absent from its narrative and yet oversee it. Our technical practices are often as silent, as circumscribed, and as essential as were the initiation rites of the past, but henceforth they are of a scientific nature. It is in relation to these technical practices that historical discourse is elaborated, assuring them as a symbolic legitimacy and at the same time, "respecting" them. They depend on historical discourse for their social articulation, and yet they retain control over it. Thus, historical discourse becomes the one possible myth of a scientific society that rejects myths—the fiction of a social relationship between specified practices and general legends, between techniques that produce and demarcate places in society and legends that propose a symbolical ambiguity as an effect of time. I shall conclude with a formula. The very place established by procedures of control is itself historicized by time, past or future; time is inscribed there as the return of the "other" (a relationship to power, to precedents, or to ambitions), and while "metaphorizing" the discourse of a science, it turns it into the discourse of a social reciprocity and of an ethical project. While place is dogmatic, the coming back of time restores an ethics.

Part V
Conclusion

Chapter 16
The Politics of Silence:
The Long March of the Indians

On the afternoon of July 14th (1973)
the roads leading down to Guambia
began to fill with Indian comrades . . .
The first to arrive came from nearby "resguardos,"[1]
from Jambalo, Pitayo, Quisgo, Totoro,
from Paniquita and neighboring hamlets.
Next came the Inganos and the Kamsa[2]
from Putumayo,
and the representatives of the Narino[3] "parcialidades"
and also the Aruacos of the Sierra Nevada of Santa Marta,[4]
who had travelled four days on foot, by train and by bus
in order not to miss the Gathering.
And later those coming from the West arrived,
and after midnight came the comrades from the East, from Tierradentro,
who had crossed the "paramo."[5]
We already numbered nearly two thousand.
Since it was very cold and our comrades from the warm lands[6]
did not even have a ruana to cover them,
we built eleven fires to warm us.

This is how the majority of us spent the night,
First organizing then warming ourselves,
Some talking, others playing music and singing.
Also, from time to time, we would drink a little coffee to fool our hunger.
Sunday July 15th dawned full of sun,
and we were full of contentment . . . [7]

"Some walked all night," adds the author of this letter addressed "to all Indian comrades." They are walking toward a new morning. No longer ravaged by poverty, as they were when I knew them in Misiones (Argentina); no longer in the throes of the "simultaneously political, social, and mystical crises" that Alfred Métraux revealed in the pilgrimages toward the Land-of-No-Pain, and in the solitary suicides of Indians from Gran Chaco[8]—but resolved to determine the course of their own history. "Recent actions have changed our perspective: more than a reaction against future extinction, today growth and development are our objectives."[9] The goal of the Gatherings of the tribes and the Assemblies of Chiefs is no less than reconquest. Taking shape in fact and consciousness is a *peasant* and *Indian* revolution: it is already stirring the silent depths of Latin America.

Memory, or the Tortured Body

The period of repression, however, is not yet over. On the contrary, as the Indians press for their rights to the land and organize self-managed associations, they are meeting with even stiffer repression. Recent events give proof enough: the destruction of the hamlet of El Cedro, in the Indian zone of Veraguas, at the hands of the Panamanian National Guard (March 15, 1976); the pillaging and burning of the towns of Palenque, Ocosingo and Chinon in Mexico, by government troops who drove out 2,400 inhabitants, abusing and raping many (June 12–13, 1976); the murder and detention of Indians in Merure (Mato Grasso, Brazil) in an effort to prevent the establishment of a reservation for the Bororo Indians, an action taken on behalf of the large property owners of the colonial tradition (July 15, 1976); etc., etc. The list of abuses that made it into the national or international press would be long indeed. But these bloody traces rising to the surface of the telecommunications media tell nothing at all of the *daily reality of the violence*. Imprisonments, arson, and even murder are doubtless less destructive than economic alienation, cultural domination, and social humiliation—they are less dangerous than the overall process of day-to-day *ethnocide*.

"You know," said Russell Means, "Indians have a long memory." They do not forget their fallen heroes and their land under occupation by "foreigners." In their villages, the Indians preserve a painful recognition of four and a half centuries of colonization.[10] Dominated but not vanquished, they keep alive the

memory of what the Europeans have "forgotten"—a continuous series of uprisings and awakenings which have left hardly a trace in the occupiers' historiographical literature.[11] This history of resistance punctuated by cruel repression
is *marked on the Indian's body* as much as it is recorded in transmitted
accounts—or more so. This inscribing of an identity built upon pain is the
equivalent of the indelible *markings* the torture of the initiation ceremony carves
into the flesh of the young.[12] In this sense, "the body is memory." It carries,
in written form, the law of equality and rebelliousness that not only organizes
the group's relation to itself, but also its relation to the occupiers. Among the
Indian ethnic groups of "Latin" America (there are about 200), this *tortured*
body and another body, the *altered earth*, represent a beginning, a rebirth of the
will to *construct* a *political* association. A unity born of hardship and resistance
to hardship is the historical locus, the collective memory of the social body,
where a will that neither confirms nor denies this writing of history originates.
It deciphers the scars on the body proper [*le corps propre*]—or the fallen
"heroes" and "martyrs" who correspond to them in narrative—as the index of
a *history* yet to be made. "Today, at the hour of our awakening, we must be
our own historians."[13]

The relation of the "solar race" to "spilled blood" which "obligates," and
to the lost earth which awaits its "masters," seems to link the political speech
of the Indian directly to the efficacy of *associative* and *rural* strategies. In any
case, ideology is more often than not absent from their demands. In effect, a
common language would only create for the Indian groups a substitute body. It
would finally replace the earth with doctrinal speech; it would efface the feder-
ated ethnic groups by imposing a unitary, all-encompassing discourse. As it
stands, on the contrary, the instituting alliance of each community with a body
and a territory allows the *real* differences between their respective situations to
be maintained. The actions the Indians take are directed less toward the construction of a common ideology than toward the "organization" (a word-
leitmotif) of tactics and operations. In this context, the *political* relevance of the
geo-*graphical* distinctions between separate *places* is echoed, on the level of the
association joining different ethnic groups, in the distribution of places of
power, and in the rejection of centralization that has characterized the internal
functioning of each of these associations.[14] Because of this, the Indian awakening has been *democratic* and *self-managing* in form; it can recognize itself in the
specific traits of its political organization, and in the objectives it draws from
its analyses.

A Political Awakening

What stands out in the Indian Manifestoes are two essential elements, which are
interconnected yet remain distinct: on the one hand, a *political form all their own*

(which necessitates, for example, a refusal to participate in political parties, which are "foreign to our American reality,"[15] as the 1973 Congress of Indians in Paraguay declared); and on the other hand, a *common economic* situation shared by the entire Latin American rural proletariat (indebted, underpaid agricultural or manual workers lacking contracts or guarantees, victimized by exorbitant interest rates on borrowing; over-taxed small-scale producers duped by middlemen who buy their products, or by shopkeepers, etc.). Their close linkage of politics and economics avoids two very common reductions: the assimilation of the "own" [*le propre*] into a cultural identity frozen by the ethnologist (when he does not bring it into being!), isolated from society as a whole, withdrawn from history, and doomed to repeat itself in a quasi-mechanical way; or, the disappearance of political and ethnic specificity in the generality of productive relations and class conflicts. The Indians prefer a *political* third way to either the alibi of *cultural* identity (more or less grandiose and nostalgic) constructed by the science of ethnology, or the loss of self resulting from the (effectively imperialist) domination of *socioeconomic* laws and conflicts imposed by the international market.[16] That third way consists in transforming—following strategies *of their own*—the reality that places them in *solidarity* with the non-Indian peasant movements.

In this way, their specificity is no longer defined by a given, by their past, by a system of representations, an *object* of knowledge (and/or of exploitation), but finds its affirmation in a set of procedures—*a way of doing things*—exercised within an encompassing economic system which creates, among the oppressed, the foundations for revolutionary alliances. "Cultural" specificity thus adopts the form of a *style of action* which can be deployed within the situations created by capitalist imperialism.

Doubtless, this *political* determination of cultural specificity is the result of long historical experience, of a difference that has survived due to the rootedness of the Indian ethnic groups in a particular soil, and of their particular resistance to the seductions of ideology. Three points must be emphasized.

First, the Spanish institution of the *encomienda* in the first colonial age, the privatization and capitalization of the land by its occupants, the resulting demographic collapse of the Indians, the artificial grouping of the remainder of the indigenous population into *reducciones* (the city-factories of the seventeenth century) and the institution of forced Indian labor on large landholdings or in the mines[17]—all of these forms of colonization, and others still, functioned to separate the work force from its means of subsistence. Colonization erected, atop the rubble of the old social systems (which often exhibited the beginnings of "feudal" organization; Incan society is an example[18]), the foundations for a paleo-technical capitalism whose *first proletarians* were the Indians. The already commercial and industrial manipulations that made possible a specifically colonial power and an ethnic separation between dominator and dominated were tested out at a safe distance before they were reproduced and perfected within the colonizing nations themselves, in the form of the division of labor and class struggle. It can be said that the critique of capitalism contained in the recent Indian Declarations originates from that economic system's oldest witnesses, from people who have had more than four centuries' experience with it, from the survivors of the disasters it wrought in their lands—from people for whom the fight for political existence and a lucid analysis of capitalism are inseparable.[19]

Second, if the survivors' resistance has found political expression, it is because—despite the allotment of the best land to the colonizers, despite the spatial reductions and distortions caused by the colonizers' geographic expansion, and the equally significant pressures exerted on Indian lands by small-scale colonial adventurers (the dregs of the dominant system, forced to move one step ahead of it), and finally, despite the (also centrifugal, but opposite) movement forcing the Indians off land too poor to feed them toward employment in other areas as agricultural or unskilled laborers—their communities continued to return periodically to the home village, to claim their rights to the land and to maintain, through this collective alliance on a common *soil*, an anchorage in the *particularity* of a place. The land, serving as a reference point, in addition to preserving local representations and beliefs (often fragmented and hidden beneath the occupiers' system[20]), is also a ballast and defense for the "own" [*le propre*] against any superimposition. It was, and is, a kind of palimpsest: the gringos' writing does not erase the primary text, which remains traced there—illegible to the passersby who have manipulated the areas for four centuries—as a silent sacrament of "maternal forces," the forefathers' tomb, the indelible seal joining the members of the community together in contractual agreement.[21]

The soil "keeps" the Indians' secret, which remains uncompromised despite the alterations to which their Testament, or the Tablet of their collective law— the earth—is subjected. It has always made possible, and continues to make possible, the designation of a *locus proprius* [*licu propre*]. It enables the resistance to avoid being disseminated in the occupiers' power grid, to avoid being captured by the dominating, interpretive systems of discourse (or by the simple inversion of those discourses, a tactic which remains prisoner to their logic). It "maintains" a difference rooted in an affiliation that is opaque and inaccessible to both violent appropriation and learned cooptation. It is the unspoken foundation of affirmations that have *political* meaning to the extent that they are based on a *realization of coming from a "different" place* (different, not opposite) on the part of those whom the omnipresent conquerors dominate.

Finally, the style adopted by the Resistance is related to a particular kind of internal social organization. It has often been emphasized (to the point of becoming one of the "myths" of ethnology itself) that coercive power is absent in Indian communities, except in times of war. "It is the lack of social stratification and authority of power that should be stressed as the distinguishing feature of the political organization of the majority of Indian societies.''[22] The beehive is the metaphor for these egalitarian societies.[23] The point of reference is not a direct rejection of centralizing institutions, but a society lacking a *separate representation* (the leader) of the power which organizes it. The law functions in that society as the *tacit coordination of traditional practices*. The law is the very functioning of the group—an authority that is embedded in practical norms, not set above them. Since the alliance with the land minimizes the role a system of representations can play, and is expressed through gestural relations between the body and the mother earth, the totality of social practices and functions constitutes an order that no singular figure can detach from the group, or make visible to it in such a way as to impose obligations of obedience or offer all of its members supervisory or oversight possibilities. Neither do the Indian ethnic groups, as "societies of the multiple,"[24] give their present-day claims a recapitulatory representation, or an integrating organization (like the one a strategic discourse supposedly capable of coordinating local actions would create), or a central power whose role would be to serve as an umbrella for the local groups. A plurality of communities and practices has remained its structural form. It reproduces, at the level of the association among communities, the type of organization proper to those communities taken individually. Ethnic *difference* is affirmed using a different *political* model—rather than conforming to our model in self-defense against it.

A Revolution: A Federation of Self-Managing Communities

If we summarize the features observable in the Indian Manifestoes, the following model emerges: an associative interweaving of sociopolitical micro-units, each of which is characterized by community self-management of resources (essentially land), in other words, by a range of complementary rights and obligations which have as their object the same commodity, and which are assigned to various holders, none of which is inherently entitled (as either an individual or legal entity) to what we call the right of ownership. Moreover, the model's mode of manifestation in the present circumstances—or, if one prefers, the labor of conscious formulation allowing the political enunciation of the model—follows procedures that are in harmony with the structure under formation: there is a constant return to "on-going consultation with the communities" through a series of local, regional, national, and federal councils. In addition, the positions of the group are under constant review, and are challenged and improved through tours, meetings, consultations, seminars, and direct, oral discussions (preferably over the radio) which keep the organization of the federation in touch with its multiple reality.

As the 1973 Founding Act of the Confederación de Indigenas de Venezuela declared, the Indian communities "propose different social modes with a view to different development alternatives."

At a time when the idea and effectiveness of Western democracy are everywhere undermined by the expansion of cultural and economic technocracy, and are in the process of slowly disintegrating along with what had been that system's condition of possibility (differences between local units and the autonomy of their sociopolitical representations); at a time when micro-experiments and explorations in self-management are attempting to compensate for the evolution toward centralization by recreating the diversity of local democracies[25]—it is the same Indian communities which were oppressed and eclipsed by the Western "democracies" that are now proving to be the only ones capable of offering modes of self-management based on a multi-centennial history. It is as though the opportunity for a sociopolitical renewal of Western societies were emerging along its fringes, precisely where it has been the most oppressive. Out of what Western societies have held in contempt, combatted and believed they had subjugated, there are arising political alternatives and social models which represent, perhaps, the only hope for reversing the massive acceleration and reproduction of totalitarian, homogenizing effects generated by the power structures and technology of the West.

As early as 1971, Georges Balandier, basing his statements on his analyses of African countries, brought attention to the fundamental practical and theoretical innovations taking shape in the so-called "underdeveloped" nations.[26] The search for different models would, he said, center on the very areas where it had been claimed that the "benefits" of colonization had been introduced. Since that time, studies of this kind have appeared, for example, in economics, with the work of Ignacy Sachs on development policies,[27] and in the field of ethnology, with the new "political anthropology" championed by Pierre Clastres.[28] Other examples worthy of mention include investigations into the origins of political power,[29] and studies based on the advances made possible in the Marxist analysis of productive relations by the examination of structures of thought and political power in "primitive" societies.[30]

That is exactly what Francisco Servin, pai-tavytera, said before the Congress of Indians held in Paraguay in October 1974: "We were once the masters of the earth, but since the gringos arrived we have become veritable pariahs. . . .We have the hope that the day will come when they realize that we are their roots and that we must grow together like a great tree with its branches and flowers."[31] That day is dawning. The silhouette of that tree, which in the past has signified revolutions based on the liberty and solidarity of the people, seems to have returned with the Indian awakening and its parallels in Western experiments and explorations. Perhaps an "age of self-management"[32] has been inaugurated by this strange coinciding of phenomena in the societies of Europe and America, and by their different forms of political return.

Only the preservation and deepening of these differences would be in keeping with the project of self-management that is beginning to see the light of day. The political figure of Indian practices therefore cannot serve as an example. It would only be a mystification, an object produced by our discourse, if we transformed it into a utopian model, into the dream solution for all our problems, or into an ideological substitute for the technical difficulties faced by the project of self-management in our societies. The Indians' Declarations specifically oppose this kind of ideological exploitation. They advocate an egalitarian labor of differentiation and cooperation, which applies as much to the relationship of a network of communities to a foreign society as it does to their relations among themselves. This attitude opens horizons and raises questions. A quick enumeration of them also serves as a summary of the reasons in favor of solidarity with the movement to which the Declarations bear witness:

1. The passage from a *micro-politics* (of self-managing communities) to a *macro-politics* (the federation). In our societies, this passage corresponds to an until now unbridgeable gap marked by the integrating structures of the State.

2. The *collective contracts with the earth*, in their dual aspect as economic (rural cooperatives) and ecological (harmony with nature). Western development, because of the favor accorded industrialization and social conflict, has created a "history" for itself in which "nature" only figures as an *object* of labor and the *terrain* of socioeconomic struggles. It has no value other than the negative one of peasant "resistance" to be overcome, of a biological limit always to be transcended, or of traditionalist anchorings to be rejected. Indian proposals for recognition of the earth, the waters, the forests (and also for the teaching of traditional medicine and herbalism in the schools) are just as important as the project of establishing rural cooperatives. A different relation to nature is at issue in both of these approaches.

3. Lastly, *cultural pluralism* is also essential to the self-management perspective. It assigns the schools, placed under the control of the community and of "sages" (*amautas*), the task of teaching the social procedures of rural "cooperativism," of transmitting the necessary agricultural knowledge and the history of relations with the West, and of developing proficiency in both the mother tongue and the national language—in other words, of providing the tools which make it possible to use and symbolize various practices. The dominant culture and the "country schools" established thus far ("a catastrophe") have made these practices hierarchical, devaluing or crushing difference, and thereby depriving democratic undertakings of cultural landmarks and technical means.

A space of exchange and sharing is thus established.[33] Silently. It is accompanied—is it any surprise?—by references to the Great Spirit, but discreet ones, because the "daily recognition of the Unseen and Eternal" is "unspoken": "Each soul must meet the morning sun, the new sweet earth and the Great Silence alone."[34] It is around such silences, the "cornerstones" of the community, that the networks of Indian activities, organizations, and federations are formed. Beyond the borders of these Indian lands, a different kind of silence seems to answer theirs: the militant, but unspectacular, activities of the religious or social organizations which, in Latin America,[35] the United States,[36] Germany,[37] Sweden,[38] Denmark,[39] and many other distant countries, devote themselves to information sharing and active support work. From the time of Bartolomé de Las Casas (1474–1566), the sounds of similar stirrings of solidarity have been heard across the Western world. Readers, you and I stand invited to assist in this work, which is inspired by concern for the other, and is meant to rise to the same beat as the Indian awakening.

Notes

Notes

Chapter 1. Psychoanalysis and Its History

1. *Il re-mord*. A play on words meaning literally, "it bites again," but also suggesting "il re-mort" ("it re-deads," repeats death or brings back the dead) and "le remords" ("remorse").—Tr.

2. Sigmund Freud, "On the History of the Psychoanalytic Movement,"*Standard Edition*, tr. James Strachey (London: Hogarth, 1953–1974), Vol. 14, p. 37.

3. "Fragment of an Analysis of a Case of Hysteria" (the case of "Dora," 1905), *SE*, Vol. 7; "Analysis of a Phobia in a Five-Year-Old Boy" (the case of "Little Hans," 1909), "Notes upon a Case of Obsessional Neurosis" (the "Rat Man," 1909), *SE*, Vol. 10; "Case History of Schreber" (1911), *SE*, Vol. 12; "An Infantile Neurosis," (the "Wolf Man," 1918), *SE*, Vol. 17.

4. Freud, *Moses and Monotheism, SE*, Vol. 23.

5. *Moses, SE*, Vol. 23, p. 130 (*Gesammelte Werke*, Vol. 16, p. 239).

6. "Group Psychology and the Analysis of the Ego," *SE*, Vol. 18, p. 69.

7. *Delusions and Dreams in Jensen's "Gradiva," SE*, Vol. 9.

8. "The Antithetical Meaning of Primal Words," *SE*, Vol. 2, pp. 158–162; *Leonardo da Vinci and Memory of Childhood, SE*, Vol. 2.

9. *Totem and Taboo, SE*, Vol. 13, p. xiii.

10. Ibid., p. 126.

11. Quoted in Roland Barthes, *Michelet* (Paris: Seuil, 1965), p. 92.

12. Theodor Reik, *Ritual. Psychoanalytic Studies* (New York: Farrar, Strauss, 1946), pp. 10–12, 15.

13. "On the History," p. 37.

14. *Papers 1906–1908, SE*, Vol. 9.

15. *Thomas Woodrow Wilson: Twenty-Eighth President of the United States* (Boston: Houghton Mifflin, 1961).

16. "On the History," pp. 44 and 37.

17. This gives the *correspondance* between analysts a special importance. It constitutes a transversal narrativity in relation to the modes of scientific discourse.

18. It has been rightly said that a psychoanalyst is a doctor who is afraid of blood.

19. Leon Trotsky, *Littérature et révolution* (Paris: Juilliard, 1962), pp. 279-283.

20. Cf. V. Schmidt, *Education psychanalytique en Russie* (1924); M. Wulff, "Die Stellung der Psychoanalyse in der Sowjet Union," *Psychoanalytische Bewungung* (1930); Joseph Wortis, *Soviet Psychiatry* (Baltimore: Williams and Wilkins, 1950).

21. Cf. Abram Kardiner, *My Analysis with Freud* (New York: Norton, 1977).

22. Nathan G. Hale, Jr., *Freud and the Americans* (Oxford: Oxford University Press, 1971) and *James Jackson Putnam and Psychoanalysis* (Cambidge, Mass.: Harvard University Press, 1971).

23. Norman O. Brown, *Love's Body* (New York: Random House, 1966).

24. Erik Erikson, *Young Man Luther* (New York: Norton, 1958) and *Gandhi's Truth* (New York: Norton, 1969).

25. John A. Garraty, *The Nature of Biography* (New York: Knopf, 1957); Philip Reiff, *Freud, The Mind of a Moralist* (New York: Viking, 1959); C. Strout, "Ego Psychology and the Historian," in *History and Theory*, Vol. 7 (1969), pp. 281-296, etc.

26. Cf. Lloyd Demause, *The History of Childhood* (New York: Psycho-History Press, 1974); John Demos, *A Little Commonwealth: Family Life in Plymouth Colony* (Oxford: Oxford University Press, 1970).

27. Günter Rohrmoser, *Das Elend der Kristischen Theorie* (Freiburg: Rombach, 1970), p. 20.

28. Wilhelm Reich, *The Mass Psychology of Fascism*, tr. Vincent Carfagno (New York: Farrar, Strauss, 1970).

29. Erich Fromm, *Escape from Freedom* (New York: Farrar and Rinehart, 1941).

30. Herbert Marcuse, *Eros and Civilization* (Boston: Beacon Press, 1966) and "The Obsolescence of the Freudian Conception of Man" in *Five Lectures* (Boston: Beacon, 1970). Cf. Carl and Sylva Grossman, *The Wild Analysts* (New York: Braziller, 1965) and Paul Robinson, *The Freudian Left* (New York: Harper, 1969).

31. Albert Thibaudet, "Psychanalyse et critique," *Nouvelle Revue française* (April 1921); he notes the "curiously nationalist character" of psychology in France (p. 467).

32. George Devereux, *From Anxiety to Method in the Behavioral Sciences* (New York: Humanities Press, 1967); Alain Besaçon, *Le Tsarévitch immolé* (Paris: Plon, 1967).

33. Freud, *Gesammelte Werke* (London: Imago, 1940-1952); *Standard Edition*.

34. There was a Sabbatean saying that "the law is fulfilled by transgression."

35. Gilles Deleuze, in his preface to Félix Guattari, *Psychanalyse et Transversalité* (Paris: Maspero, 1974). See also *Recherches*, no. 21 (1976), "Histoires de la Borde."

36. Immanuel Kant, "What Is Enlightenment? *On History: Immanuel Kant*, ed. Lewis Beck (New York: Library of Liberal Arts, 1963), pp. 3-11.

Chapter 2. The Freudian Novel: History and Literature

1. An example of this split is the separation between "Histories" and "Mémoires" in the field of historical literature in the seventeenth century.

2. Thus, in the nineteenth century, the fantasy novel plays with/undoes the boundary positive sciences established between the real and the imaginary. Cf. Tzvetan Todorov, *The Fantastic: A Structural Approach to a Literary Genre*, tr. Richard Howard (Ithaca: Cornell University Press, 1975).

3. This text follows up two precedent essays: M. de Certeau *L'Ecriture de l'histoire* (Paris: Gallimard, 1975), pp. 289-358 and above, chapter 1, pp. 3-16.

4. "Inkompetent": cf. *Der Mann Moses* in *Gesammelte Werke* (*GW*), Vol. 16, p. 123.

5. *Studien über Hysteria*, *GW*, Vol. I, p. 227; *Studies on Hysteria*, *Standard Edition*, Vol. 2, pp. 160-161.

6. Sigmund Freud, *Delusions and Dreams in Jensen's "Gravida,"* *SE*, Vol. 9.

7. Sigmund Freud—A. Zweig, *Correspondance*, transl. (Paris: Gallimard, 1973), p. 162 (21 février 1936), etc.

8. This is the definition Freud gives to his psychic apparatus, in *The Interpretation of Dreams*, chap. 7.

9. Freud—Zweig, *Correspondance*, p. 75 (8 mai 1932).

10. Jacques Lacan, Séminaire sur "L'ethique de la psychanalyse," 1959–1960.

11. *Studies on Hysteria*, ibid.

12. Aristotle, *Poetics*, II, B, 1449b–1458a (on tragedy) and *Rhetoric*, II, 1450a–1453 (on rhetoric and passions); two texts which Freud's interpretation brings to mind.

13. Cf. Maynard Mack, "The Jacobean Shakespeare: Some Observations on the Construction of the Tragedies," in Alvin B. Kernan, ed., *Modern Shakespearean Criticism* (New York: Harcourt, Brace and World, 1970), pp. 323–350.

14. Georges Dumézil, *Du mythe au roman* (Paris: PUF, 1970).

15. Cf. Claude Imbert, "Stoic Logic and Alexandrian Poetics," in Malcolm Schofield et al., eds., *Doubt and Dogmatism: Studies in Hellenistic Epistemology* (Oxford: Clarendon Press, 1980), pp. 182–216. Concerning these tactics and their relationship to fictive narrative, see M. de Certeau, *The Invention of the Everyday*, tr. Steven Rendall (Berkeley: University of California Press, 1984).

16. Cf. C. B. MacPherson, *The Political Theory of Possessive Individualism* (Oxford: Clarendon Press, 1962); Alan MacFarlane, *The Origins of English Individualism* (Cambridge: Cambridge University Press, 1978); etc.

17. Emmanuel Kant, "What is 'Enlightenment'?" in *Critique of Practical Reason and Other Writings in Moral Philosophy*, tr. Lewis White Beck (Chicago: University of Chicago Press, 1949).

18. Sigmund Freud, *Der Mann Moses*, in *GW*, Vol. 16, pp. 137–138.

19. See Albert O. Hirschmann, *The Passions and the Interest* (Princeton: Princeton University Press, 1977).

20. Sigmund Freud, *Delusions and Dreams*, op. cit.

21. Cf. Ferdinand Alquié, "Le surréalisme et la psychanalyse" in *La Table ronde*, déc. 1956, pp. 145–149.

22. Emile Benveniste, *Problems in General Linguistics*, tr. M. E. Meck (Miami: University of Miami Press, 1971), "On the function of language in the Freudian discovery."

23. Charles Bally, *Traité de stylistique française* (Geneva: Georg & Co., 1951).

24. Cf. Roland Barthes, "L'ancienne rhétorique," in *Communications*, no. 16, 1970, pp. 172–225: on *elocutio*, pp. 217–222.

25. *Geschichtsschreibung*: this is the term used by Freud in *Der Mann Moses* in discussing Hebraic historiography (*GW*, Vol. 16, p. 175) and in other places, for example, in *Leonardo da Vinci* (*GW*, Vol. 8, p. 151ff) to refer to other historiographies.

26. *GW*, Vol. 23, p. 71ff.

27. Friedrich von Schiller, *Die gölter Griechenlands* (1800), final lines of the second poem: "*Was unsterblich im Gesang soll leben / Muss im Leben untergehen.*"

28. Edited by Jean-Pierre Richard, "Mallarmé et le rien, d'après un fragment inédit," in *Revue de l'histoire Littéraire de la France*, Vol. 64, 1964, pp. 633–644.

29. Ibid., p. 644, n. 1.

30. Cf. W. V. Quine and J. S. Ullian, *The Web of Belief*, (New York: Random House, 1970).

31. Philippe Lejeune, *Le pacte autobiographique* (Paris: Seuil, 1975).

240 □ NOTES TO PAGES 35-45

Chapter 3. The Institution of Rot

1. Daniel Paul Schreber, *Memoirs of My Nervous Illness*, tr. I. Macalpine and R. Hunter (London: Dawson and Sons, 1955), pp. 124–125. Translation modified. (*Denkwürdigkeiten eines Nervenkranken* [Leipzig: Oswald Mutze, 1903], pp. 136–137).

2. *Collected Poems of Saint-John Perse* (Princeton: Princeton University Press, 1971), pp. 58–69.

3. Schreber, p. 50 (German, p. 13).

4. See Chapter 5. (For "re-presentation," see Chapter 9, note 8—Tr.).

5. See Michel de Certeau, "La fiction de l'histoire. L'écriture de 'Moïse et le monothéisme,' " in *L'Ecriture de l'histoire* (Paris: Gallimard, 1975), pp. 312–358.

6. Schreber, p. 164 (German, p. 203).

7. Jacques Lacan, *Le Séminaire III: Les psychoses* (Paris: Seuil, 1981), pp. 39–358.

8. Ibid., pp. 71–82.

9. Schreber, p. 77 (German, p. 59).

10. Matthew 23.27. In Greek it is *akatharsia*, in Latin *spurcitia*. In Luke a lawyer comments on the insulting nature of words such as these (11.45).

11. See for example Michel de Certeau, "Le corps folié: Folie et mystique aux XVIe et XVIIe siècles," in Armando Verdiglione, ed., *La folie dans la psychanalyse* (Paris: Payot, 1977), pp. 189–203.

12. There is an abundant literature on the subject. Cf. Amnesty International, *Report on Torture* (London, 1973) and *Torture in Greece* (London, 1977); Jean-Claude Lauret and Raymond Lasierra, *La torture blanche* (Paris: Grasset, 1975); Artur London, *L'Aveu* (Paris: Gallimard, 1968); Bao Ruo-Wang (Jean Pasqualini), *Prisoner of Mao* (New York: Coward, McCann, Geoghan, 1973); Pierre Vidal-Naquet, *Torture: Cancer of Democracy, France and Algeria, 1954-1962*, tr. Barry Richard (Baltimore: Penguin, 1963); etc.

13. Cf. for example Steven E. Ozment, *Mysticism and Dissent* (New Haven: Yale University Press, 1973) for the sixteenth century; for the seventeenth century (and only if the reader makes distinctions between different kinds of experiences that are too closely equated by the author), cf. Leszek Kolakowski, *Chrétiens sans Eglise* (Paris: Gallimard, 1969). Cf. Michel de Certeau, *Politica e Mistica* (Milan: Jaca, 1975).

14. Cf. Pierre Clastres, *Society against the State*, tr. Robert Hurley (New York: Urizen, 1977), pp. 152–160 ("Of Torture in Primitive Societies").

15. Torture victims work not to "forget" their solidarities, like the resister who repeated the names of his comrades to himself while he was being tortured. The victory of torture is to efface the memory of any other name besides *Luder*.

16. Gottfried Benn, *Poèmes*, tr. Pierre Garnier (Paris: Librairie Les Lettres, 1956).

17. For example, Reiner Schürmann, "Trois penseurs du délaissement: Maître Eckhart, Heidegger, Suzuki," *Journal of the History of Philosophy*, Vol. XII (1974), pp. 455–477 and Vol. XIII (1975), pp. 43–59; or Stanislas Breton, "Métaphysique et Mystique chez Maître Eckhart," *Recherches de science religieuse*, Vol. 64 (1976), pp. 161–182.

18. *The Ascent of Mount Carmel*, Book II, chap. 4, in *Complete Works of St. John of the Cross*, Vol. I, E. Allison Peers (London: Burns, Oates and Washbourne, 1934), pp. 73–78. On this text, cf. de Certeau, "Le corps folié," p. 193.

19. Jean Louis Schefer, *L'invention du corps chrétien* (Paris: Galilée, 1975), p. 141.

20. Schreber, p. 75 (German, p. 65).

21. Schreber, p. 278 (German, p. 384).

22. Jacques Lacan, *Ecrits: A Selection*, tr. Alan Sheridan (New York: Norton, 1977), p. 183.

23. Sigmund Freud, *The Case of Schreber*, in *Standard Edition*, tr. James Strachey (London: Hogarth, 1953-1974), Vol. 12, p. 71.

24. Schreber, p. 177 (German, p. 226).

25. Must we recognize as a homologue of this structure the Aristotelian articulation of *form* and *matter*? Matter (ὐλή) is, for Aristotle, at the same time what decomposes, dissolves (rots?), and what stands in opposition to form as a woman to a man. To give form to a certain "matter" (an indeterminacy in defection): the role of the institution?

Chapter 4. Lacan: An Ethics of Speech

1. Jacques Lacan, *Acte de fondation* de l'Ecole Freudienne de Paris, June 21, 1964. The Charters appear in the *Annuaires* published by the Ecole Freudienne de Paris. [I have provided references to available translations of Lacan's works. Unless otherwise noted, all other translations are mine— M.-R. Logan.]

2. Lacan, *Encore: Le Séminaire, Livre XX* (Paris, 1975), p. 9.

3. This declaration, dated January 15, 1980, figures as an epigraph in a special issue of *Libération* (September 11, 1981), the best among a number of periodical issues devoted to Lacan since his death.

4. The figure of Empedocles haunts Lacan's texts at key moments. See, for example, Lacan, *Ecrits: A Selection*, tr. Alan Sheridan (New York, 1977), pp. 102–104.

5. Lacan, "Ethique de la psychanalyse," an unpublished seminar from the academic year 1959–1960.

6. The paths taken by Lacan's thought have been the object of much study and interpretation: see particularly the schema outlined by Jacques-Alain Miller, "Jacques Lacan, 1980–1981," *Ornicar?* (September 9, 1981), pp. 7–8.

7. Lacan, *Télévision* (Paris, 1974), p. 10.

8. Ibid., p. 29.

9. In the *Ecrits: A Selection*, p. 77, Lacan quotes Antoine Tudal: "Between man and the world, there is a wall."

10. Lacan, *Encore*, p. 101.

11. Lacan, "Hommage fait à Marguerite Duras, du Ravissement de Lol V. Stein," *Cahiers M. Renaud et J.-L. Barrault*, 52 (December 1965), p. 9.

12. Lacan, *The Four Fundamental Concepts of Psychoanalysis*, tr. Alan Sheridan (New York, 1978), p. 58.

13. Freud, *Studies on Hysteria*, tr. James Strachey (New York, 1966), p. 299ff. Cf. M. de Certeau, "The Freudian Novel: History and Literature," *Humanities in Society*, 4.2–3 (1981), pp. 121–141.

14. See Freud, *Civilization and Its Discontents*, tr. James Strachey (New York, 1961), p. 22.

15. Lacan, *Ecrits: A Selection*, p. 102.

16. Lacan, "Ecrits 'inspirés': Schizographie," *De la psychose paranoïaque* (Paris, 1975), pp. 365–382.

17. Lacan, "Le Problème du style," ibid., pp. 383–388.

18. See David Steel, "Les Débuts de la psychanalyse dans les lettres françaises, 1914–1922," in *Revue d'histoire littéraire de la France* (1979), pp. 62–89.

19. Lacan, *Ecrits: A Selection*, p. 76.

20. Roman Jakobson, "Closing Statements: Linguistics and Poetics," in T. A. Sebeok, ed., *Style in Language* (New York, 1960), pp. 350–377.

21. Lacan, *Ecrits: A Selection*, pp. 146–178.

22. Lacan, *The Four Fundamental Concepts*, pp. 32–34.

23. Lacan, "Hommage fait à Marguerite Duras," pp. 9–10. Lacan echoes Freud's comment in his analysis of Jensen's *Gradiva*, "The novelist has always gone before the scholar."

24. Marguerite Duras, *Le Ravissement de Lol V. Stein* (Paris, 1976), pp. 106, 187.

25. Lacan, "Hommage fait à Marguerite Duras," p. 10.

26. Ibid., pp. 9, 14.

27. These studies range from Georges Mounin's first analysis to François George's *L'Effet' yau-de-poêle* (Paris, 1979). See especially the semiotic presentation of the "rhetorical games" in J.-B. Fages, *Comprendre Lacan* (Paris, 1971) and the philosophical study of P. Lacoue Labarthe and J.-L. Nancy, *Le Titre de la lettre* (Paris, 1972).

28. In *Communication*, 16 (1970), pp. 219, 223.

29. Thus the rigorous study of Gilbert Hottois, "La Hantise contemporaine du langage: Essai sur la situation philosophique du discours lacanien," in *Confrontations psychiatriques*, 19 (1981), pp. 163–188, evaluates Lacan in the context of linguistic philosophy. As Wittgenstein would have said, "It misses the point."

30. Lacan, *Télévision*, p. 27.

31. Lacan, *The Four Fundamental Concepts*, pp. 136–146; *Télévision*, pp. 28–29.

32. Kant, *Kritik der Urteilskraft*, s 43, in *Werke*, ed. W. Weischedel (Insel-Verlag, 1957), V, pp. 401–402.

33. Lacan, *Les Ecrits techniques de Freud: Le Séminaire, Livre I* (Paris, 1973), p. 88.

34. See Lacan, "The Mirror Stage as Formative of the Function of the I as Revealed in Psychoanalytic Experience," *Ecrits: A Selection*, pp. 1–7.

35. "Le Désir et son interprétation: Séminaire de 1958–1959," TS, pp. 376–577 (lectures from March 4 to April 29, 1959). After Freud's interpretations, Hamlet became a center of "family" interest, with the commentaries of Jones (1910), Rank (1919), and others.

36. *Hamlet*, Act III, Scene iv. Lacan translated this passage in "Le Désir et son interprétation," lecture of March 11, 1959. [See Lacan, "Desire and the Interpretation of Desire in *Hamlet*," tr. J. Hulbert, *Yale French Studies*, 55/56 (1977), pp. 11–52.—M.-R. Logan.]

37. Ibid.

38. Freud, *Moses and Monotheism*, tr. Katherine Jones (New York, 1967), pp. 4–7. See M. de Certeau, *L'Ecriture de l'histoire*, 2nd ed. (Paris, 1978), pp. 337–352.

39. Lacan, *Les Psychoses: Le Séminaire, Livre III* (Paris, 1981), p. 48.

40. Lacan, *The Four Fundamental Concepts*, p. 275.

41. Lacan, *Encore*, pp. 25, 63.

42. Ibid., p. 16.

43. Ibid., p. 44.

44. A recurrent eponym of Lacan; see, for example, Lacan, *Ecrits: A Selection*, p. 98.

45. Lacan, "Ethique de la psychanalyse," Séance XXVII.

46. Lacan, *Télévision*, pp. 28–29.

47. This dedication was corrected in the second edition (1975) of the thesis: "To my brother, the Reverend Father Marc-François Lacan, Benedictine of the Congregation of France." The "Congregation of France" designates the group of Benedictine abbeys subject to the Abbey of Solesmes.

48. See, for example, Dom Jean Leclercq, *Le Désir de Dieu et l'amour des lettres* (Paris, 1957).

49. Lacan, "Ethique de la psychanalyse," Séance XIV.

50. "It is perhaps today, among all the Seminars which ought to be published by someone, the only one which I will revise myself, which I will turn into an essay [*écrit*]," *Encore*, p. 50; see also pp. 9, 54, 65. There are in Lacan's work numerous references to "the ethics of psychoanalysis": see, for example, "Hommage fait á Marguerite Duras," p. 13.

51. See Lacan, "Ethique de la psychanalyse," Séance XXIV; *Ecrits: A Selection*, p. 321.

52. Lacan, "Ethique de la psychanalyse," Séance XI; Lacan calls this request the "vacuole."

53. Ibid., Séance XXVII.

54. Ibid.

55. See note 1 above.

56. Lacan, "Propos sur la causalité psychique," *Ecrits* (Paris, 1966), p. 151.

Chapter 5. Montaigne's "Of Cannibals": The Savage "I"

1. Citations refer to the book and chapter of Montaigne's *Essais*; page numbers, where given, refer to the English translation by Donald Frame, *The Complete Essays of Montaigne* (Stanford: Stanford University Press, 1958). In some cases, the translation has been modified. Quotes with no reference are to the essay, "Of Cannibals," I, 31, pp. 150–159.—Tr.

2. Cf. Michel de Certeau, *L'Invention du quotidien: I. Arts de faire* (Paris: UGE, 1980), chap. 9 ("Récits d'espace").

3. Cf. in particular the works of Yuri Lotman, for example in *Ecole de Tartu: Travaux sur les systèmes de signes* (Brussels: Complexe, 1976).

4. Cf. François Hartog, *Le miroir d'Hérodote: Essais sur la représentation de l'autre* (Paris: Gallimard, 1980).

5. On this structure, cf. Michel de Certeau, *L'Ecriture de l'histoire* (Paris: Gallimard, 1978), pp. 215–248 ("Ethnographie: L'oralité ou l'espace de l'autre: Léry").

6. Cf. Jean de Léry, *Histoire d'un voyage fait en la terre du Brésil*, chap. 20.

7. A nomadism analogous to Montaigne's own. "I do not find myself in the place where I look" (I, 10, 26).

8. Cf. Frances Yates, *The Art of Memory* (Chicago: University of Chicago Press, 1966).

9. Montaigne has the same criticisms of historians as he does of cosmographers; among historians, he also prefers "the simple, who have not the wherewithal to mix in anything of their own" (II, 10, 303). Cf. I, 27; II, 23; III, 8; and Jean Céard, *La nature et les prodiges: L'insolite au XVIe siècle, en France* (Geneva: Droz, 1977), p. 424ff.

10. Cf. for example Urs Bitterli, *Die "Wilden" und die "Zivilisierten": Die europäischuberseeische Begegnung* (Munich: Beck, 1976).

11. *Sauvage* in French means both "savage" and "wild."—Tr.

12. This is a reference to the French version of the game "hunt the slipper" (*le furet*, "ferret"). The players form a circle, with one person standing in the middle. An object is passed around the circle, and the person in the middle has to guess who has the "ferret." As the object circulates, the players cry out *Il court, il court, le furet!* The game is often alluded to by Lacanians in relation to metonymy and the function of the phallus.—Tr.

13. See Michel de Certeau, "L'Illettré éclairé," *Revue d'Ascétique et de Mystique*, Vol. 44 (1968), pp. 369–412.

14. In addition to Lopez de Gomara's *Histoire générale des Indes* (translated into French by Fumée, 1584), mention must be made of Chauvreton's transposition of Benzoni, *Histoire naturelle du nouveau monde* (1579), Osorio's *Histoire du Portugal*, etc.

15. André Thévet, *Les Singularités de la France Antarctique* (1557) and *Cosmographie Universelle* (1575).

16. See note 6 above.

17. See Marcel Bataillon, "Montaigne et les conquérants de l'or," *Studi francesi* (déc. 1959), pp. 353–367.

18. Not to mention sources from the Ancients. Prime among them is the *Odyssey* (Chapters VII–XIII); the Cyclops (which, it seems, Odysseus met on the Lepani Islands, halfway between Italy and Sicily) presents a model of the "savage" (no laws, no trade, cannibalistic, etc.) which is very close to that of the sixteenth-century explorers—and of Montaigne himself. See Roger Dion, *Les anthropophages de l'Odyssée: Cyclopes et Lestrygons* (Paris: Vrin, 1969).

19. Except once, at the beginning of the development: "as my witnesses told me . . ."

20. Cf. Frank Lestringant, "Les représentations du sauvage dans l'iconographie relative aux ouvrages du cosmographe André Thévet," *Bibliothèque d'Humanisme et Renaissance*, Vol. XL (Geneva: Droz, 1978), pp. 583–595.

21. On these two songs (later taken up by Goethe), cf. Luis da Camara Cascudo, "Montaigne et l'indigène du Brésil," *Bulletin de la Société des Amis de Montaigne*, Series 5, no. 14–15 (1975), pp. 89–102, and Marcel Françon, "Note sur les chansons brésiliennes citées par Montaigne," ibid., series 5, no. 16 (1975), pp. 73–75.

22. Cf. Georges Duby, *The Three Orders: Feudal Society Imagined*, tr. Arthur Goldnammer (Chicago: University of Chicago Press, 1982), "Genesis," chap. 4.

23. Rabelais, *Gargantua and Pantagruel* (II, chap. 32): "How Pantagruel Covered the Whole Army with His Tongue, and What the Author Saw in His Mouth."

24. The forgetting of the name, coupled with the cough that makes it inaudible, reproduces in relation to More's text the destruction of several pages of Theophrastus by the monkey. On these alterations of the text, cf. Louis Marin, *Utopiques: Jeux d'espaces* (Paris: Minuit, 1973), p. 226ff.

25. "I have a mortal fear of being taken to be other than I am by those who come to know my name" (III, 51, 643). On interpretation, cf. III, 13: "It is more of a job to interpret the interpretations than to interpret the things" (p. 818).

26. On the problem of the *other* in Montaigne, cf. also the observations of Anthony Wilden in "Montaigne's *Essays* in the Context of Communication," *Modern Language Notes*, Vol. 85, no. 4 (May 1970), pp. 462 and 472–478.

Chapter 6. Mystic Speech

1. Marguerite Duras, *India Song*, tr. Barbara Bray (New York: Grove Press, 1976), p. 21. Also, *Le Vice-Consul* (Paris: Gallimard, 1966), p. 9. The subject is the beggar-woman who finally goes to the Ganges, "where she found the way to get lost" (*Le Vice-Consul*, p. 181).

2. Over the *paths* and *ways* of which so many mystic texts speak travels the wanderer, *Wandersmann*—the title given in 1675 to the work of Angelus Silesius (1657). The connotations include "pilgrim" as well as "wanderer"; the word refers in particular to one who travels by foot.

3. Antoine Furetière, *Dictionnaire universel* (1690). In Pascal we find the same emphasis on the "style of writing," and, in the domain of logic, "ways of turning things over," or "propositions." On Pascal's rhetoric, cf. Pierre Kuentz, "Un discours nommé Montalte," in *Revue de l'Histoire Littéraire de la France*, 71 (1971), pp. 195–206.

4. Cf. Ludwig Wittgenstein, *Tractatus Logico-philosophicus* (London: Routledge and Kegan Paul, 1960), p. 187 (6.44): "It is not *how* things are in the world that is the mystical, but *that* it exists." ("Nicht *wie* die Welt ist, ist das Mystische, sondern *dass* sie ist.")

5. Cf. Ludwig Wittgenstein, *Notebooks 1914–16* (New York: Harper and Row, 1969), p. 51 (25.5.15): "The urge towards the mystical comes of the non-satisfaction of our wishes by science. We *feel* that if all *possible* scientific questions are answered *our problem is still not touched at all*."

6. Virgil, *Aeneid* (I, 405): "Vera incessu patuit dea." This line occurs at the time of her departure.

7. The isolation of this domain of truth is already apparent linguistically with the change in the status of the word "mystic" from an adjective to a noun. See Michel de Certeau, "*Mystique* au XVIIe siècle: Le problème du langage Mystique," in *L'homme devant Dieu. Mélanges de Lubac* (Paris: Aubier, 1964), Vol. 2, pp. 267–281, and Gotthold Müller's comments in "Ueber den Begriff der Mystik," *Neue Zeitschrift f. System Theologie*, 13 (1971), pp. 88–98. It should be kept in mind that in the vocabulary of that time "*mystic*" referred essentially to a way of treating *language*; "*spirituality*" designated the experience. Cf. the two great interpreters, M. Sandaeus, the Dedication to *Pro Theologia mystica clavis* (Cologne: 1640); and Honoré de Sainte-Marie, *Tradition des Pères et des Auteurs ecclésiastiques sur la contemplation* (Paris: 1708), Vol. 2, p. 601ff.

8. See Dom Porion's clarifications regarding the dating of the Poems in Hadewijch d'Anvers, *Ecrits mystiques* (Paris: Seuil, 1954), pp. 26–29.

9. Gerhard Scholem criticizes this "ahistorical" tendency in *On the Kabbalah and Its Symbol-*

ism, tr. Ralph Manheim (New York: Schocken, 1965), p. 5. See also, by the same author, "Mysticisme et société," *Diogène*, 58 (1967), pp. 3–28. Leszek Kolakowski claimed to "treat" mystic ideas and movements "as manifestations of social conflicts" (*Chrétiens sans Eglise* [Paris: Gallimard, 1969], pp. 44–45), but failed to keep his promise. On the relations between mysticism and society, the basic texts are: Ernst Troeltsch, *The Social Teaching of the Christian Churches*, tr. Olive Wyon (New York: Macmillan, 1956), in particular, Vol. II, pp. 729–806, "Mysticism and Spiritual Idealism"; and Ivo Höllhuber, *Sprache Gesellschaft Mystik* (Munich: Reinhardt, 1963)—pages 332–333 contain his three theses on "the connection between language, society and mysticism."

10. Lucien Goldmann, *The Hidden God*, tr. Philip Thody (London: Routledge and Kegan Paul, 1964), esp. p. 103ff.

11. Alphonse Dupront, "Vie et création religieuses dans la France moderne," in *La France et les Français*, (Paris: Gallimard, Pléiade, 1972), p. 535.

12. Jean Sainsaulieu, *Les ermites français* (Paris: Cerf, 1974) pp. 47–93: the old nobility outnumbers the *noblesse de robe* among seventeenth century AnTchorites. Many Leaguers were also old nobility.

13. Michel de Certeau, "Politique et mystique: René d'Argenson," *Revue d'Ascétique et de Mystique*, Vol. 39 (1963), pp. 45–82; also, *Politica e Mistica* (Milan: Jaca Books, 1975), pp. 195–233.

14. Cf. Jacques Le Brun, "Politique et spiritualité: la dévotion au Sacré-Coeur," *Concilium*, no. 69 (1971), pp. 25–36.

15. Cf. Marie du Saint-Sacrement, *Les parents de Sainte Thérèse* (Paris, 1914).

16. Jonas Andries van Praag, *Gespleten zielen* (Groningen: J. B. Wolters, 1948).

17. Cf. Marcel Bataillon, *Erasmo y España* (Mexico City: Fondo de Cultura Económica, 1966), chap. 4; and Antonio Domingues Ortíz, *Los Judeoconversos en España y America* (Madrid: ISTMO, 1971), pp. 149–166. The latter specifies the reasons for this affiliation among the new Christians: they were neophytes freed from rites and secular superstitions; they were distanced from the formalism of the synagogue and were not eager to fall into another formalism; they were members of a hated class attracted to Erasmus' doctrine of the mystic body (so different from the unsophisticated racism underlying the hierarchy based on *limpieza de sangre*); they were readers of the Bible ignorant of scholastic writings, etc. (ibid., p. 160). Cf. by the same author *Las Clases privilegiades en la España del Antiguo Régimen* (Madrid: ISTMO, 1973), chap. 13, "Las órdenes femeninas," pp. 321–336.

18. See Efrén de la Madre de Dios, "Tiempo y vida de Santa Teresa de Jesus," *Obras completas* (Madrid: BAC, 1951), Vol. I, pp. 162–171; Narciso Alonso Cortes, in *Boletín de la Real Academia de España*, 1947; and Gerald Brenan, *Saint John of the Cross* (Cambridge: Cambridge University Press, 1973), pp. 91–95.

19. See Friedrich Lütge, *Deutsche Sozial-und Wirtschaftsgeschichte* (Berlin: Springer, 1966); J. B. Neveux, *Vie spirituelle et vie sociale entre Rhin et Baltique au XVIIe siècle* (Paris: Klincksieck, 1967), pp. 330–359, 503–523, etc; and Bernard Gorceix, "Mystique et société: à propos de la mystique baroque allemande," *Etudes germaniques*, Vol. 28 (1973), pp. 20–28.

20. England is distinguished from the Continent in this respect.

21. Steven E. Ozment, *Mysticism and Dissent: Religious Ideology and Social Protest in the 16th Century* (New Haven: Yale University Press, 1973). This is a remarkable study of "mystical writings in protest against established Christendom," dealing with authors classified by Williams as "revolutionary spiritualists."

22. The present "wed" to death is a general motif. It is found in both sixteenth- and seventeenth-century iconography and literature. Cf. esp. Alberto Tenenti, *La vie et la mort à travers l'art du XVe siècle* (Paris: A. Colin, 1952); Michel Vovelle, *Mourir autrefois* (Paris: Gallimard-Juilliard, 1974); and Philippe Ariès, *Western Attitudes toward Death*, tr. Patricia Ranum (Baltimore: Johns Hopkins Press, 1974).

23. This confinement in a contradictory present is not without similarities to the antinomical situation which, in Brazil, inspires messianic movements, quests for "a third society which is neither the traditional society nor Western society." Maria Isaura de Queiroz, *Réforme et révolution dans les sociétés traditionnelles* (Paris: Anthropos, 1968).

24. See Michel de Certeau, "L'illettré illuminé," *Revue d'Ascétique et de Mystique* 44 (1968), pp. 369–412.

25. In this context, Simone Weil refers to the "idiot of the village . . . who sincerely loves truth." She opposes "genius" to the "talents" that education favors and encourages: "real genius is nothing other than the supernatural virtue of humility in the domain of thought." *Ecrits de Londres et dernières lettres* (Paris: Gallimard, 1957), p. 31.

26. Michel de Certeau, in *Recherches de Science Religieuse* 63 (1975), pp. 243–268.

27. Louis Massignon makes this "solidarity" between social suffering and a "healing pain of salvation" the central point in his study on Al-Hallāj, *La passion de Husayn Ibn Mansûr Hallāj* (Paris: Gallimard, 1975), Vol. 1, pp. 25–28. He quotes Albert Béguin: "The deciphering of history is reserved for certain pained existences."

28. Cf. note 24.

29. *Dialogus*, in M. Goldast, *Monarchia Sancti Romani Imperii* (Frankfort: 1614), Vol. II, p. 506. On Occam's position, cf. Francis Rapp, *L'Eglise et la vie religieuse en Occident à la fin du Moyen Age* (Paris: PUF, 1971), p. 359; and Yves Congar in *Dogmengeschichte* (Freiburg: Herder, 1971), p. 191.

30. John G. A. Pocock, in *The Machiavellian Moment* (Princeton: Princeton University Press, 1975), shows that at a time when the Florentine republic was confronted by its own finitude and irrational events threatening its equilibrium, Machiavelli tried to restore moral as well as political stability, and contrasted "virtue" (a force of character and thought) to "fortune" (chance) and "corruption." Characterized by the presence of a structural relation between the founding principles of a *vivere civile* on the one hand, and the unreadability of Providence and the disorder of the world on the other, this "moment" finds its first expression in sixteenth-century Florence, but recurs in seventeenth-century England in the form of a neo-Machiavellian political economy, and later in the United States. In France (which Pocock does not discuss), it was the middle of the seventeenth century. Etienne Thuau speaks of it in *Raison d'Etat et pensée politique à l'époque de Richelieu* (Paris: A. Colin, 1966).

31. Henri Bremond, *A Literary History of Religious Thought in France* (New York: Macmillan, 1926–36), Vol. 2 ("The Coming of Mysticism: 1590–1620).

32. See Charles Webster, *The Great Instauration: Science, Medicine, and Reform, 1626–1660* (London: Duckworth, 1975), pp. 15–31.

33. This unitary reference recedes further out of this world the more incomprehensible it appears. Past origins, the stars and mystic interiority are probably expressions of this oneness after it has become unreadable in the social experience. This accounts for, in particular, the short-lived but widespread importance of astrology, which assured a connection between the organic movement of the stars and the multiplicity of the visible, between celestial stability and the contingencies of history. Cf. Keith Thomas, *Religion and the Decline of Magic* (London: Penguin, 1973), pp. 335–458. Likewise, there is a general tendency to fall back on the notion of *spiritus*, which is "neither matter nor mind," but "transfuses the universe and transmits the power of the superior beings to the inferior ones." Thus, a *universal* but *"spiritual"* shifter (the Cartesian *Materia subtilis*, the Platonists' *anima mundi*, or the chemists' "universal Spirit") serves as the unitary counterpart of the multiple "objects" distinguished by intellectual analysis. Cf. P. M. Rattansi, "The Social Interpretation of Science in the 17th Century," in P. Mathias, ed., *Science and Society, 1600–1900* (Cambridge: Cambridge University Press, 1972), pp. 1–32.

34. John Wallis, *Truth Tried* (1643), p. 91, quoted by Webster, op. cit., p. 30.

35. On the theme of Babel among modern Spanish mystics, cf. Arno Borst, *Der Turmbau von*

Babel: Geschichte des Meinungen über Ursprung und Vielfalt der Sprachen und Völker (Stuttgart: Hiersemann, 1960), Bd. III, Vol. 1, pp. 1150–1166. On the status of language, cf. Irene Behn, *Spanische Mystik: Darstellung und Deutung* (Düsseldorf: Patmis-Verlag, 1957).

36. *Entendre* is translated variously below as "to hear" or "to understand." Both connotations should be kept in mind in each instance. The archaic Spanish *entender* is similar—Tr.

37. Prologue, *Subida del Monte Carmelo*, in *Vida y obras de San Juan de la Cruz* (Madrid: BAC, 1955), p. 508. (*The Ascent of Mount Carmel*, in *Complete Works of St. John of the Cross*, tr. E. Allison Peers [London: Burns, Oates & Washbourne, 1934], Vol. I, p. 11.) On this *spirit* playing the role of a shifter in the fragmented text of the world, cf. note 33. With the mystics, it is specified as a "speech act" (J. R. Searle) and identified by its "illocutionary" function (J. L. Austin).

38. "No entenderse un alma ni hallar quien la entienda," St. John of the Cross, *Vida y obras*, p. 509 (*Complete Works*, I, p. 13). This is from the passage justifying the writing of the *Subida*; it refers, precisely, to the confusion of the laborers working on the Tower of Babel ("por no entender ellos la lengua . . . ").

39. *Cántico espiritual*, stanza 6, *Vida y obras*, p. 904. "Surrender thou thyself completely. From today do thou send me now no other messenger, for they cannot tell me what I wish" (*Complete Works*, II, p. 51).

40. Angelus Silesius, *Le Pèlerin chérubique*, tr. Eugène Susini (Paris: PUF, 1964), p. 170: "The (Divine) Writing is writing, nothing more. My consolation is essentiality, and that God speaks in me the Word of Eternity."

41. On the tripartition of "theology" into "scholasticism," "positivism," and "mysticism," cf. Michel de Certeau, "*Mystique* au XVIIe siècle."

42. Cf. Alexandre Koyré, *From the Closed World to the Infinite Universe* (Baltimore: Johns Hopkins University Press, 1979), pp. 58–87 ("The New Astronomy Against the New Metaphysics"); and Michel Foucault, *The Order of Things* (New York: Vintage, 1973), pp. 17–45 ("The Prose of the World").

43. This "*produced-producing* fiction," the organization of space as a text, is the no-place (the other of the locus) postulated by utopian thought. See Louis Marin, *Utopiques: jeux d'espaces* (Paris: Minuit, 1973), pp. 15–50.

44. See M. Godinez, *Práctica de la teología mística* (1681), or the Latin translation and commentary by M. I. de La Reguera, *Praxis theologiae mysticae* (1740).

45. "Tratar con Dios" (conversing with God) or the "modo de trato con Dios" is the subject of mystic works such as St. John's *Subida del Monte Carmel* (cf. the Prologue). *Conversar* (communication and dialogue) is at the center of the spirituality of St. Ignatius of Loyola (cf. Michel de Certeau, "L'universalisme ignatien," *Christus*, no. 50 [1966], pp. 173–183, and Dario Restrepo, *Diálogo: Comunión en el espíritu* [Bogota: CIRE, 1975]). John of Ávila's *Audi Filia* (Madrid, 1588) is a Christological poem on "divine speech and conversation": he transforms the command ("listen") into a lyric on illocution.

46. "Illocutionary" (one can also say "allocutionary" or "illocutory") is the term used by J. L. Austin, the pioneer of research on utterance, to designate the act of speaking and discuss what it changes in relationships among interlocutors.

47. "Allocution" is the utterance of a discourse addressed to someone; the "allocutor" the person to whom the discourse is addressed.

48. Cf. Tzvetan Todorov, "Problèmes de l'énonciation," *Langages*, no. 17 (1970), pp. 3–11.

49. Emile Benveniste, Problèmes de linguistique générale (Paris: Gallimard, 1974), Vol. II, p. 83.

50. Rabelais' fable of the "thawed words" is an inverted, "fantasy" figuration of this science of "saying" and doing, or letting "speak." Will these words frozen by the weather become voices again—and if so, addressed by whom, to whom? Cf. Rabelais, *Le quart livre*, chap. 55.

51. St. John of the Cross, *Cántico*, stanza 1 (*Complete Works*, II, p. 31): "Whither hast thou hidden thyself, And hast thou left me, O Beloved, to my sighing?"

52. Benveniste, *Problems in General Linguistics*, Vol. I, tr. Mary Meek (Coral Gables, Fla.: University of Miami Press, 1971), pp. 219, 227, etc.

53. "Discourse" is to be understood here according to Benveniste's definition: "language in so far as it is taken over by the man who is speaking and within the condition of intersubjectivity, which alone makes linguistic communication possible" (*Problems*, p. 230).

54. The most common meaning of *se parler* is to converse with someone else, but taken literally it means "to speak oneself"; similarly, *s'entendre* can mean to hear or understand oneself, to be heard, or to come to an understanding with another.—Tr.

55. Austin, when explaining the performative (for which the relevant criteria are "success" and "failure" and not "truth" and "falsehood"), uses examples drawn for the most part from law. Cf. *How to Do Things with Words* (Cambridge, Mass.: Harvard University Press, 1975). The essential function of sixteenth and seventeenth century law adds historical relevances to his analyses.

56. See Eugenio Garin's important analysis in *Medioevo e Rinascimento* (Rome: Laterza, 1954), pp. 124–149 ("Discussioni sulla retorica").

57. *Meister Eckhart, A Modern Translation*, tr. Raymond Blackney (New York: Harper & Row, 1941), p. 13. Section 10 of the "Talks of Instruction" in the *Treatises* is entitled "The will is capable of anything and virtue lies in the will, if it is just" (p. 12).

58. Jean-Joseph Surin, *Guide spirituel*, ed. Michel de Certeau (Paris: DDB, 1963), pp. 28–31.

59. *Meister Eckhart*, p. 3.

60. Surin, *Correspondance*, ed. Michel de Certeau (Paris: DDB, 1966), p. 974.

61. These are the first words of the Prologue of the *Libro de la Vida*: "Me han mandado y dado larga licencia para que escriva" ("I have been commanded and given full liberty to write"). She compares this command to the one "I wish I had been allowed to" ("Quisiera yo") receive. Santa Teresa de Jesus, *Obras completas* (Madrid: BAC, 1951), p. 595. (*The Life of St. Teresa*, in *The Complete Works of Saint Teresa of Jesus*, tr. B. Allison Peers [New York: Steed and Ward, 1950], Vol. I, p. 9.) Cf. the beginning of the Prologue to the *Moradas* (*The Interior Castle*): "las cosas que me ha mandado la obediencia," "las cosas que me han mando escrivir," *Obras*, p. 339 ("the things which I am commanded to do," what "I was commanded to write," *Complete Works*, III, p. xxi).

62. St. John of the Cross, Prologue, *Cántico espiritual, Vida y Obras*, p. 902: "pues Vuestra Reverencia así lo ha querido" ("since Your Reverence has so desired," *Complete Works*, II, p. 24).

63. Surin, *La Science expérimentale*, ms., Bibliothèque Nationale, Paris, fds fr. 14596, f. 2r.

64. See Paul Zumthor, *Langue, texte, énigme* (Paris: Seuil, 1975), pp. 163–212 ("Le *Je* du poète").

65. The term *shifter* is borrowed from Roman Jakobson and designates a signifier that effects a shift (a passage/articulation) between different isotopics (or codes).

66. See Georg Misch's monumental *Geschichte der Autobiographie* (Frankfurt: G. Schulte-Bulmke, 1969), Vol. IV, part 2 (from the Renaissance to the Eighteenth Century), esp. pp. 657–776. Also, Joan Webber, *The Eloquent "I": Style and Self in Seventeenth Century Prose* (Madison: University of Wisconsin Press, 1968) on the "non-fiction dramas" of the Anglicans and Puritans; Roy Pascal, *Design and Truth in Autobiography* (London: Routledge, 1960); and Philippe Lejeune, *Le pacte autobiographique* (Paris: Seuil, 1975), pp. 49–163 (on Rousseau).

67. Lejeune, pp. 33–35. Note, in the *Confessions* of St. Augustine, the continuity from one to the other—the text of the *I* is gradually inscribed in a commentary on the book of *Genesis*.

68. St. Teresa, *Moradas del Castillo interior*, chap. 1, *Obras*, II, pp. 341–345 (*Complete Works*, II, pp. 201-205.)

69. *El*, unspecified: "He," the Other.

70. The "Seventh Mansions" of the *Interior Castle* places particular emphasis on this point.

71. Conclusion, *Moradas*, p. 494 (*Interior* in *Complete Works*, III, p. 350).

72. "A garden in which the Lord is to take his delight." He "often comes to the garden to take his pleasure" and waters it "with no labor on our part" (*Libro de la Vida*, chap. 11 [*The Life of St. Teresa* in *Complete Works*, I, p. 65]). Cf. also chaps. 12–19). The "comparison" (*comparación*) of the garden guides her entire discussion of the four degrees of prayer.

73. Jean-Baptiste Van Helmont, *Ortus medicinae* (Amsterdam, 1648), "Confessio authoris," p. 12: "Incidi in somnium intellectuale satisque memorabile. Vidi enim animam meam satis exiguam specie humana . . . "

74. Johann Kepler, *Somnium sive Astronomia Lunaris*, in *Opera omnia*, ed. Frisch (Frankfurt, 1871), VIII, pp. 27–123. Cf. also Patricia Kirkwood's translation in John Lear, *Kepler's Dream* (Berkeley: University of California Press, 1965).

75. *Vida*, chap. 16, in *Obras*, I, p. 683 (*Complete Works*, I, p. 96).

76. An entire tradition of medical writing, like Van Helmont, uses a "scientific" representation of the *body* which is based on the same model as the *Interior Castle*. Cf. for example Robert Fludd's *Integrum morborum mysterium, sive medicinae catholicae* (Frankfurt, 1631), tomi primi, tractatus secundus: the frontispiece represents a "castle of health" that could serve as an illustration and "blueprint" (atlas) of St. Teresa's *Moradas*. On imaginary schemas that combine in a single discourse, cf. Gerald Holton, *Thematic Origins of Scientific Thought: Kepler to Einstein* (Cambridge, Mass.: Harvard University Press, 1974).

77. Daniel Defoe, *Robinson Crusoe* (London: Penguin, 1975), p. 162 on the effects of the trace ("print") of a naked foot on the beach: mad thought and "whimsies" come to Crusoe's mind. He is "out of himself," wild, like a madman. The other is related to the dream, or nightmare.

78. Stephen Criter, "The Narrative Quality of Experience," *Journal of the American Academy of Religion*, 39 (1971), pp. 291–311; Stanley Haverwas, "The Self as Story," *Journal of Religious Ethics*, I (1973), pp. 73–85; James McClendon Fr., *Biography as Theology* (New York: Abingdon, 1974); etc.

79. Lejeune, p. 34.

80. On "possessed" utterance, cf. de Certeau, *L'Ecriture de l'Histoire* (Paris: Gallimard, 1975), pp. 249–273. ("Le langage altéré").

81. Cf. the comments of Didier Anzieu: "Creating has as its pre-condition a symbolic filiation with an unknown creator." ("Vers une métapsychologie de la création," *Psychanalyse du génie créateur* [Paris: Dunod, 1974], p. 3).

82. Joë Bousquet, *Mystique* (Paris: Gallimard, 1973), p. 33.

83. Martin Heidegger, *Erlauterungen zu Hölderlins Dichtung* (Frankfurt: Vittorio Klostermann, 1951).

84. Hölderlin, "To the Source of the Danube," tr. Michael Hamburger, in *Hölderlin: Poems and Fragments* (Cambridge: Cambridge University Press, 1980), p. 385.

85. St. John of the Cross, *Poems*, in *Complete Works*, II, p. 453: "Then climbs he / . . . into a tree, with fair arms wide outspread./ And, clinging to that tree forthwith is dead. / For lo! his breast was stricken very sore."

86. Christiane Rabant, "L'enfer des musiciens," *Musique en jeu*, no. 9 (1972), p. 30. Cf. also Reinhard Hammerstein, *Die Musik der Engel* (Bern: Francke, 1962), on the Middle Ages; and Ernst Benz, *Die Vision: Erfahrungsformen und Bilderwelt* (Stuttgart: Klett, 1969), pp. 418–440 ("Die himmlische Musik"), on the relationship between visions and music—the "visionäre Wort" (pp. 413–417) is meditation, like an air which imposes its form.

87. St. John of the Cross, *Cántico espiritual*, stanza 13/14, *Complete Works*, II, p. 87. In Hölderlin, peaceful nomination also comes "before the morning's light" (*Heimkunft*; quoted in Heidegger, *Erlauterungen zu Hölderlins Dichtung*).

88. St. John's "silent music" recalls Jan Van Ruysbroeck's "silent concert" (*The Book of the*

Twelve Béguines, tr. John Francis [London: J. M. Watkins, 1913]). Cf. Helmut Hatzfeld, *Estudios literarios sobre mística española* (Madrid: Gredos, 1955), chap. 2.

89. Dante, *La Vita Nuova*, tr. Mark Musa (Bloomington: Indiana University Press, 1973), p. 32 (Canzone XIX).

90. "Unas veces me las daba Dios, y otras las buscaba yo," quoted in Roger Duvivier, *Le dynamisme existentiel dans la poésie de Jean de la Croix* (Paris: Didier, 1973), p. 127.

91. Prologue, *Cántico, Vida y Obras*, pp. 901-902 (*Complete Works*, II, p. 212).

92. Surin, *Cantiques spirituels* (Bordeaux, 1662), beginning of Song V.

93. St. John of the Cross, Prologue, *Cántico* (*Complete Works*, II, p. 25). One of thousands of examples attesting to the fact that the poem is self-sufficient is Mother Francisca de Jesus' deposition at St. John's beatification proceedings. She recited several couplets from the *Cántico*, which she said make "such an impression on her that she bursts into tears of devotion." The words, which "have such an effect on her," are born of a practice of poetry, not a study of treatises (quoted in Duvivier, p. 90).

94. St. John of the Cross translates a verse from the *Book of Wisdom* (8, 1) in a strongly original way. The *toque*—penetration, burning, absorption—has a "substantial" signification; it is a touching by "the substance of God of the substance of the soul." (See *Llama*, stanza 2, v. 4, n. 21.) For more on the "touch," see Jean Orcibal, *Saint Jean de la Croix et les mystiques rhéno-flamands* (Paris: DDB, 1966), pp. 70-76.

95. Prologue, *Cántico* (*Complete Works*, II, p. 25).

96. *The Autobiography of St. Ignatius Loyola*, tr. Joseph O'Callaghan (New York: Harper & Row, 1974), p. 39.

97. Cf. Duvivier, *Le dynamisme*, p. 34.

98. On this phonetic organization of poetry, see Julia Kristeva, *Semeiotikè: Recherches pour une sémanalyse* (Paris: Seuil, 1969), pp. 246-277 ("Poétique et négativité"); Jean Starobinski, *Words Upon Words: The Anagrams of Ferdinand Saussure*, tr. Olivia Emmet (New Haven: Yale University Press, 1979); Jean Baudrillard's critique of the preceding book in *L'échange symbolique et la mort* (Paris: Gallimard, 1976), pp. 283-308; Roman Jakobson, *Questions de poétique* (Paris: Seuil, 1973); Nicolas Ruwet, "Parallélismes et déviations en poésie," in *Langue, discours, société* (Paris: Seuil, 1975), pp. 307-351; etc.

99. There exists a "doubling of the subjective agency," for example in Lautréament's *Les chants de Maldoror*. See Kristeva, *La révolution du langage poétique* (Paris: Seuil, 1974), pp. 319-329.

100. Baudrillard, *L'échange symbolique*), p. 307. Palilogy: the repetition of the same word.—Tr.

101. See Jakobson's notes on glossolalia (speaking in tongues) in *Selected Writings* (The Hague: Mouton, 1966), Vol. IV, pp. 637-644.

102. Ruwet, "Parallélismes," p. 319.

103. André Breton, *Poésie et autre* (Paris: Club du meilleur livre, 1960), p. 174.

104. Meister Eckhart, Sermon "Justi vivent in aeternum," in *Deutsche Werke* (Stuttgart: W. Kohlhammer, 1936), Vol. I, pp. 114-115.

105. "I AM THAT I AM . . . I AM that hath sent me unto you" (*Exodus* 3.14). Cf. Jean-Louis Schefer, *L'invention du corps chrétien* (Paris: Galilée, 1975), pp. 107-108.

Chapter 7. Surin's Melancholy

1. Surin, *La science expérimentale*, Vol. II, chap. 4. Two sections of that work were included in *Lettres spirituelles*, ed. F. Cavallera (Toulouse: Editions de la Revue d'ascétique et de Mystique, 1928), Vol. II, pp. 1-151. Extracts can also be found in *Correspondance*, ed. Michel de Certeau (Paris: DDB, 1966). Further references to the 1928 edition will be identified by *Lettres*, and to the 1966 edition by *Corr.*, followed by the page number.

2. *Corr.*, p. 1084.

3. Cf. Michel de Certeau, *La possession de Loudun* (Paris: Juilliard-Gallimard, 2nd ed., 1980).

4. Sören Kierkegaard, *Journal* (1849, XI A, 272): "I am not a saintly person, I am a penitent, for whom it can be indescribably suitable to suffer and for whom as a penitent, there is satisfaction in suffering." *Sören Kierkegaard's Journals and Papers*, tr. Howard and Edna Hong (Bloomington: Indiana University Press, 1978), Vol. VI, pt. 2, pp. 144–147 (no. 6389).

5. *Lettres*, p. 28.

6. Ibid., p. 13.

7. This is the case from Paul Zacchias to Ijsbrood van Diemerbroeck. See Michel Foucault, *Madness and Civilization* (New York: Vintage, 1973), pp. 93–97, 101–107.

8. *Lettres*, p. 14.

9. Ibid., pp. 17–18.

10. Ibid., p. 15.

11. Surin, *Cantiques spirituels* (Bordeaux, 1660), Cantique V.

12. Ibid.

13. *Corr.*, pp. 515–516.

14. Cf. a letter dating from April 1658, *Corr.*, p. 604.

15. *Corr.*, p. 502.

16. Ibid., p. 514.

17. Ibid., p. 1561.

18. Ibid., p. 713.

19. Ibid., p. 1098.

20. Ibid., p. 1675.

21. *Lettres*, p. 33.

22. See Jacques Lacan, *The Four Fundamental Concepts of Psychoanalysis* (London: Hogarth, 1977), pp. 74–75, on Merleau-Ponty's *The Visible and the Invisible*.

23. Ibid., p. 72.

24. *Lettres*, p. 96.

25. A sweet wine brewed with cinnamon, cloves, etc. It was an intoxicating drug commonly used in medicine at that time.

26. Cf. Sylvie Romanowski, *L'illusion chez Descartes* (Paris: Klincksieck, 1974), pp. 83–95. Also, the more general reflections of Luce Irigaray in *Ce sexe qui n'en est pas un* (Paris: Editions du Minuit, 1977), pp. 103–116 ("La 'mecanique' des fluides").

27. Later, Surin will speak of the "peace" that is granted after suffering. God "guarantees peace" on the "frontiers." "He puts an abundance of peace into the mouth of that soul." This peace is like a sea which, "with great impatience," comes to "fill the space of the bed God gave him." "This sea comes in, wild and roaring, though tranquil. . . . The sea, in its plenitude, comes to visit the land and kiss the shores God gave it as a limit." Surin, *Questions importantes à la vie spirituelle sur l'Amour de Dieu* (Paris: Téqui, 1930), Vol. III, pt. 2, pp. 116–117.

28. Cf. Michel de Certeau, "L'idée de traduction de la Bible au XVIIe siècle: Sacy et Simon," in *Recherches de science religieuse*, Vol. 66 (1978), pp. 73–92.

29. Prologue, *Subida del Monte Carmelo*, in *Vida y obras de San Juan de la Cruz* (Madrid: BAC, 1955), p. 508 (*Complete Works of St. John of the Cross* [London: Burns, Oates and Washbourne, 1934], Vol. I, p. 11).

30. See chapter 5.

31. *Lettres*, pp. 20–21.

32. Jacob Boehme, *Mysterium Magnum*, chaps. 3, 11, and *De triplici vita hominis*, chaps. 1, 31, and elsewhere. Cf. Pierre Deghaie, "Jacob Boehme, ou de la difficulté du discours sur Dieu," *Recherches de science religieuse*, Vol. 66 (1978).

33. On Schreber, see Jacques Lacan, *Séminaire III: Les Psychoses* (Paris, 1981), pp. 133–145.

34. See O. Mannon, *Clefs pour l'Imaginaire ou l'Autre Scène* (Paris: Seuil, 1969), pp. 9–33.

35. *The Cloud of Unknowing*, tr. Clifton Walters (London: Penguin, 1961), chap. 7, p. 61.

36. See chapter 3.

37. On the "substantive or absolute" and the adjective, see Antoine Arnauld and Pierre Nicole, *The Art of Thinking*, tr. J. Dickoff and P. James (New York: Library of Liberal Arts, 1964), Pt. 1, chap. 2, pp. 38–42.

38. Ibid.

39. Surin, *Cantiques spirituels*, Cantique V.

Chapter 8. The Beauty of the Dead: Nisard

1. Our topic is the *concept* of "popular culture." For the moment, we are leaving aside the entire question of oral literature as it is presently studied by folklorists.

2. Charles Nisard, *Histoire des livres populaires*, 2nd ed. (1864), Vol. I, p. 1.

3. Marc Soriano, "Burlesque et langage populaire de 1647 à 1653: Sur deux poèmes de jeunesse des frères Perrault," *Annales: Économie, société, civilisation* (1969), pp. 949–975.

4. We are employing the terms "the elite," "the masses," "the people," etc., as they are used in the literature.

5. Wilhelm Mühlmann, *Les Messianismes révolutionnaires* (Paris: Gallimard, 1968), p. 218.

6. Relation de la cérémonie de la rose qui s'est faite dans le village de Salancy le 8 juin 1766 (Noyon, 1766). The ceremony was presided over by the Intendant of Picardy, Le Pelletier de Morfontaine, who was accompanied by the Countess of Genlis, the future educator of Louis-Philippe. Is it by chance alone that in the right-thinking literature addressed to the workers of Lille during the Second Empire there reappears *La Rosière de Salancy* by Joseph Chantrel (1867, 120pp.). See Pierre Pierrard, *La vie ouvriere à Lille sous le second Empire* (Paris: Bloud & Gay, 1965), p. 274.

7. *Histoire de la rosière de Salancy ou recueil de pièces tant en prose qu'en vers sur la rosière dont quelques-unes n'ont point encore paru* (Paris: Merigot, 1777), p. 83.

8. In many accounts of "rosière" celebrations dating from the end of the eighteenth century, the people are only a backdrop seen through the compassionate eyes of the courtiers who have made the trip to Arcadia.

9. Cf. even today Henri Davenson, *Le Livre des chansons* (Paris: Club des libraires de France, 1958), p. 20.

10. See *Lettres à Grégoire sur les patois de France, 1790–1794* (Paris: A. Gazier, 1880).

11. The library of the Société de Port-Royal includes a collection of printed pieces written in patois that were sent to Grégoire.

12. *Lettres à Grégoire*, p. 118.

13. Ibid., pp. 300–301.

14. Directive of January 4, 1851, Archives nationales F (18) 555.

15. *Nisard, Histoire des livres populaires*, 2 vols. First edition, 1854; second edition, 1864. Modern edition published in 1968 (Paris, Maisonneuve et Larose).

16. Ibid., 1854 edition, Vol. I, p. iv.

17. *La Tradition nationale* (October 1896), pp. 4–5.

18. Address of March 24, 1895, in *La Tradition en Poitou et Charente* (Paris, 1896), p. vi.

19. Ibid., p. xiv (address by G. Boucher).

20. Ibid., p. xviii.

21. Georges Vicaire, "Nos idées sur le traditionnisme," *Revue des traditions populaires* (1886), no. 7, p. 189.

22. Ibid., pp. 190–191.

23. *La Tradition nationale*, Vol. 1 (1887), pp. 3–4.

24. Ibid., p. 8.

25. In Jean Poirier, ed., *Ethnologie générale* (Paris: Gallimard, Pléiade, 1968), pp. 1279-1304.

26. Robert Mandrou, *De la culture populaire en France aux XVIIe et XVIIIe siècles: La Bibliothèque bleue de Troyes* (Paris: Stock, 1964). Geneviève Bollème, "Littérature populaire et littérature de colportage au XVIIIe siècle," in *Livre et Société dans la France du XVIIIe siècle* (Paris: Mouton, 1965), pp. 61-92; Bollème, *Les Almanachs populaires aux XVIIe et XVIIIe siècles: Essai d'histoire sociale* (Paris: Mouton, 1969). Marc Soriano, *Les Contes de Perrault: Culture savante et traditions populaires* (Paris: Gallimard, 1968), etc.

27. Cf. for example Bollème, "Littérature populaire . . . ," pp. 66-67.

28. R. Chartier, *Revue historique*, Vol. 495 (1970), pp. 193-197.

29. See, for example, Jean-Paul Sartre, "Points de vue: culture de poche et culture de masse," in *Les Temps Modernes*, no. 208 (May 1965).

30. Bollème, *Les Almanachs populaires* . . . , pp. 123-124.

31. Bollème, "Littérature populaire . . . ," pp. 75 and 89.

32. Soriano, *Les Contes* . . . , p. 489.

33. Henri Davenson, *Le Livre des chansons*, p. 21.

34. Mandrou, *De la culture populaire*, p. 21. The "Bibliothèque Bleue" was a series of chapbooks (which owe their name to the inexpensive blue paper used for the binding) published in Troyes from the beginning of the seventeenth century to the end of the nineteenth, and sold in the streets by hawkers. The booklets were for the most part anonymous, and included tales of chivalry, devotional texts, almanacs, astrological texts, and advice books on everything from cooking to medicine.—Tr.

35. The implicit affirmation of a symmetry is in itself revealing about learned culture, which wants to forget, and make others forget, its repressive relation to popular literature.

36. Bollème, "Littérature populaire . . . "

37. Mandrou, *De la culture populaire*, p. 150. There is, however, a fundamental difference: the "incoherence" of which the censors speak represents a moral judgment against what they see as a mental disorder; in Mandrou it designates "that which escapes," something ungraspable.

38. Soriano, *Les Contes* . . . , Part II, chap. 1, pp. 88-98.

39. Soriano, *Les Contes* . . . , p. 95.

40. See the observations of Nicole Belmont in "Les Croyances populaires comme récits mythologiques," *L'Homme*, (April-June 1970), pp. 74-108.

41. Soriano, "Table ronde sur les contes de Perrault," *Annales (E.S.C.)* (May-June 1970), p. 65. This would be, in the beginning, an essential approach to the historical relations between learned culture and popular traditions. Cf. also *Annales (E.S.C)*, Vol. 41 (1969).

42. Bollème, "Littérature populaire . . . ," p. 79.

43. Nisard, *Histoire des livres populaires*, 1864 edition, Vol. I, p. 184.

44. Ibid., Vol. II, p. 15.

45. See Claude Rabant, "L'Illusion pédagogique," in *L'Inconscient*, no. 8, pp. 89-118.

46. Marcel Maget, in *Ethnologie générale*, p. 1283.

47. Nisard, *Histoire des livres populaires*, 1864 edition, Vol. II, pp. 381ff.

48. Ibid., Vol. I, p. 294.

49. Claude Gaignebet, *Le Folklore obscène des enfants français* (Paris: Maisonneuve et Larose, 1974).

50. Soriano, *Les Contes* . . . , pp. 125-130.

51. The booklets from Troyes, Mandrou says, were "an obstacle to the understanding of the social and political conditions of these popular milieux," *De la culture populaire*, p. 163.

52. See Vladimir Propp, *Morphology of the Folktale* (Austin and London: University of Texas Press, 1968).

53. Soriano, "Burlesque . . . ," p. 638.

54. Ibid., p. 636.

Chapter 9. Writing the Sea: Jules Verne

1. Cf. Jean-Jules Verne, *Jules Verne* (Paris: Hachette, 1973), p. 189.

2. Jules Verne, *Les Grands Navigateurs du XVIIIe siècle*, introduction by Michel de Certeau (Paris: Ramsay, 1977), Part I, chap. 2, end.

3. Cited in Jean-Jules Verne, *Jules Verne*, p. 188.

4. Marcel Moré, *Le très curieux Jules Verne* (Paris: Gallimard, 1960), pp. 49–50.

5. Pierre Macherey, *A Theory of Literary Production*, tr. Geoffry Well (London: Routledge, 1978), pp. 240–249.

6. Cf. Frances Yates, *The Art of Memory* (London: Routledge, 1966).

7. This is the term Freud used to define *Moses and Monotheism*. Cf. Michel de Certeau, *L'Ecriture de l'histoire* (Paris: Gallimard, 1975), pp. 312–358 ("La fiction de l'histoire: L'écriture de Moïse et le monothéisme").

8. Gabriel Marcel, *La Nouvelle Calédonie* (Librairie Guillaume, 1873), 31pp., extract from the *Journal des Economistes* (April 1873).

9. Gabriel Marcel, "Les premières navigations françaises à la Côte d'Afrique," *Revue scientifique* (3), III, Vol. 31, no. 8 (Feb. 24, 1883), pp. 234–240.

10. This reference is to Jacques-Nicolas Bellin (1703–1772), and in particular to his *Carte de l'Amérique septentrionale* (Paris, 1755).

11. Philippe Buache (1700–1773); he published *La Carte d'une partie de l'Amérique* (Paris, 1740) and, with "Guillaume de l'Isle" (or Delisle), the *Atlas géographique des Quatre parties du Monde*, revised and enlarged by Dezauche (n.d.).

12. Guillaume Delisle (1675–1726) began publication of his *Atlas nouveau* in 1700.

13. Actually Pieter Goos (1616–1675), engraver and cartographer, who published *De Zee-atlas, ofte Water-weereld* (Amsterdam, 1666).

14. Nicolas Sanson (1600–1667), the first great French cartographer of the period, at first associated with Melchior Tavernier; Sanson's series of *Atlas* began to appear in 1645.

15. Johannes van Keulen (1654–1704), the author of another *Zee-atlas* (Amsterdam, 1681; English version, 1682).

16. On this history of cartography from the sixteenth to the eighteenth century, cf. Leo Bagrow, *History of Cartography*, tr. D. Paisey (Cambridge, Mass.: Harvard University Press, 1964); R. A. Skelton, *Decorative Printed Maps of the 15th to 18th Centuries* (London: Staples, 1952); Joachim G. Leithaüsen, *Mappae Mundi* (Berlin: Safari-Verlag, 1958); etc.

17. For example "Buache" is sometimes "Bluache."

18. *Mobile in the Mobile Element*: Captain Nemo's motto.

19. There is in this *Bulletin* an entire series of notes and clarifications on Cook's voyages (the Society celebrated their centenary in 1879) and on the events surrounding the disappearance of La Pérouse. Cf. also C. Manoir, *Rapports annuels sur les progrès de la géographie, 1867–1892*, 2 vols. (Paris: E. Leroux, 1895, 1896), for example, Vol. II, pp. 230, 685, etc.

20. The ample travel literature Verne cites is rarely accompanied by bibliographical indications, but the references are often easy to recognize. They can be found most easily in Edward Godfrey Cox, *A Reference Guide to the Literature of Travel*, 4 vols. (Seattle: University of Washington Press, 1936–1938) and in Michèle Duchet, *Anthropologie et Histoire au siècle des Lumières* (Paris: Maspero, 1971), pp. 484–519. Some of the references are more elliptical, as for example the allusion to "Crozet," who is actually the Abbot Alexis-Marie Rochon, *Nouveau voyage à la mer du Sud commencé sous les ordres de Monsieur Marion et achevé après la mort de cet officier sous ceux de*

M. le Chevalier Duclesmeur. Cette relation a été rédigée d'après les plans et journaux de M. Crozet. On a joint à ce voyage un extrait de celui de M. de Surville dans les mêmes parages (Paris, 1783). The ponderousness of titles like this accounts for Verne's, or Marcel's, abbreviations. In any event, the aim of this essay is not to provide a critical apparatus for the text, *Les Grands Navigateurs du XVIIe siècle* (this chapter originally appeared as the introduction of the Ramsay edition of *Les Grands Navigateurs*).

21. These are the names of the castaways. Nab is the Black, the servant of the ingenious Cyrus Smith.

22. Jules Verne, *L'Ile mystérieuse* (1874) (Paris: Livre de Poche, 1973), Vol. I, pp. 140–142.

23. "By the very fact that the word *elephant* exists in their language and that the elephant thus enters into their deliberations, men were able to make, with regard to elephants, before even having had contact with one, resolutions far more decisive for pachyderms than anything that has happened in their history. . . . With nothing but the word *elephant*, and the way in which men use it, things happen to elephants that are favorable or unfavorable, auspicious or inauspicious—in any event, catastrophic—even before a bow or rifle has been raised against them." Jacques Lacan, *Séminaire I: Les écrits techniques de Freud* (Paris: Seuil, 1975), p. 201.

24. Jules Verne, *Voyage au centre de la terre* (1864) (Paris: Livre de Poche, 1973), p. 253.

25. On this " 'Tour du monde' affair," as Verne called it, cf. J.-Jules Verne, *Jules Verne*, pp. 177–183.

26. This weekly bulletin, published under the direction of F. Schrader with the collaboration of H. Jaccottet (Paris: Hachette), went from three to eight pages in 1891. Its agenda, detailed that year, bears a strange resemblance to Verne's. The project is to publish summaries or extracts of articles and reports on "physical or political geography, ethnography, and the development of French or foreign colonies." On this formal schema of the Vernian imaginary, cf. also the special number of *Revue des lettres modernes*, no. 456–461 (1976[3]), "Jules Verne. I: Le Tour du Monde," esp. François Raymond, "Tour du monde et tours du texte: procédés verniens, procédés rousselliens," pp. 67–88.

27. Macherey, *A Theory of Literary Production*, p. 207.

28. Cf. Marie-Hélène Huet, *l'Histoire des "Voyages extraordinaires": Essai sur l'oeuvre de Jules Verne* (Paris: Minard, 1973), pp. 41–58.

29. *Le Tour du Monde*, chap. 2, cited in Huet, p. 45.

30. Ibid., chap. 2.

31. In particular, in the Second Part, chap. 1, p. 1: "Les campagnes des montres," on the watches of Le Roy and Berthoud. A topic worthy of attention. Cf. Pierre-Jacques Charliat, *Le temps des grands voiliers*, Vol. 3 of *l'Histoire universelle des explorations* by L.-H. Parias (Paris: Nouvelle Librairie de France, 1955), pp. 185–232 ("La contre-attaque des chronomètres, 1772–1788"), and Michel Serres' analysis of the "modern" watch in *Jouvences sur Jules Verne* (Paris: Minuit, 1974), pp. 162–165.

32. Only Bougainville unknowingly embarks with a woman on board, disguised as a "Mr. Berger"; on top of that, it is only the "natives" of Tahiti who recognize that she is a woman. For Verne, the story of the "first woman to go around the world," as Bougainville called it, could only be a French story, an "embellishment," one more diversion in Bougainville's expedition.

33. It was discovered by Samuel Wallis in 1767; Bougainville stopped there in 1768, and called it "New Cytherea"; Cook disembarked there in 1769 to "observe Venus' passage" in front of the sun; he returned in 1773, 1774 and 1777.

34. See Jean Chesneaux, "Critique sociale et thèmes anarchistes chez Jules Verne," *Le Mouvement social*, no. 56 (June–Sept. 1966), pp. 35–64; "Science, machines et progrès chez Jules Verne," *La Pensée*, no. 133 (May 1967), pp. 62–85; "La pensée politique de Jules Verne," *Cahiers Nationalistes*, no. 249 (Sept. 1967), pp. 274–304; and the republication of these articles in *Une lecture politique de Jules Verne* (Paris: Maspero, 1971).

Chapter 10. The Theater of the *Quiproquo*: Alexandre Dumas

1. Alexandre Dumas, *Les grands hommes en robe de chambre. Henri IV, Louis XIII et Richelieu* (Paris: Calmann-Lévy, 1877), Vol. 2, p. 209.

2. Ibid., Vol. 1, pp. 1-2.

3. Ibid., Vol. 2, p. 209.

4. A phrase from the *Causeries*, quoted in Henri Clouard, *Alexandre Dumas* (Paris: Albin Michel, 1955), p. 269.

5. It was located on the Boulevard du Temple, and was open from 1845 to the end of 1850. Cf. Clouard, pp. 334-338, and *Notice descriptive du "Théâtre Historique,"* with illustrations by Edmond Renard and Henri Valentin (Paris, 1847), 30pp.

6. On the "historical novel" in Freud, cf. Michel de Certeau, *L'écriture de l'histoire* (Paris: Gallimard, 1975), pp. 312-358.

7. Cf. Dumas and P. Meurice, *Hamlet, prince de Danemark* (Paris, 1848). It was performed at the "Historical Theater" on February 3, 1848.

8. *Représenter* in French means "to perform" (a play) as well as "to represent."—Tr.

9. Michelet, *Préface à l'Histoire de France* (Paris: A. Colin, 1962), p. 175: on "the dead" whom he "safely" visits in the tombs. See de Certeau, op. cit., pp. 7-8.

10. *Re-mordre*, cf. chapter 1, note 1.—Tr.

11. Cf. Jeanne Bem, "D'Artagnan, et après: Lecture symbolique et historique de la 'trilogie' de Dumas," *Littérature*, no. 22 (May 1976), pp. 13-29.

12. If it is true, as Du Marsais writes, that the metaphor is the "borrowed home" [*demeure empruntée*] of meaning. Cf. Jacques Derrida, *Marges de la Philosophie* (Paris: Minuit, 1972), p. 302.

13. There was a "dramatic" version (*Urbain Grandier*, "a drama in five acts, with prologue, by Alexandre Dumas and Auguste Maquet, performed for the first time in Paris, at the Historical Theater, March 30, 1850) and a "historical" version (*Les crimes célèbres*, 1839-1840, Vol. 3 of 4 [Paris: A. Lacroix, 1865]). There are also allusions to Urbain Grandier in *Le Collier de la reine* (1849-1850), *Ange Pitou* (1851), etc.

14. Michel de Certeau, *La possession de Loudun* (Paris: Juilliard-Gallimard, 1970).

15. Cf. Georges Dumézil, *From Myth to Fiction*, tr. Derek Cotman (Chicago: University of Chicago Press, 1973).

16. See Anne Ubersfeld's analysis of *Kean* (1836), "Désordre et génie," *Europe*, no. 490-491 (March 1970), pp. 107-119: she discusses how the artist yields to order.

17. Quoted in Maurice Bouvier-Ajam, *Alexandre Dumas ou cent ans après* (Paris, 1972), p. 127.

Chapter 11. The Arts of Dying: Celibatory Machines

1. Michel Carrouges, *Les machines célibataires* (Paris: Alfieri, 1975).

2. Freud, *The Interpretation of Dreams*, chap. 7, in *Standard Edition*, Vols. 4-5 (*Gesammelte Werke*, Vols. 2,3). The date of Freud's *psychischer Apparat* (1900) places it between Jarry's *Les jours et les nuits* (1897) and *Le Surmâle* (1902), well before Duchamp's *La Mariée* (1911-1925) or Kafka's *Penal Coloy* (1914).

3. This expression refers especially to "the fiction of a primitive psychic apparatus" (*SE*, Vol. 5, p. 598).

4. Cf. Michel de Certeau, *L'Ecriture de l'histoire* (Paris: Gallimard, 1975), p. 313ff. ("Ecrire dans la langue de l'autre, ou la fiction").

5. For example, cf. Katherine S. Dreier and Matta Echaurren, "Duchamp's Glass 'La Mariée mise à nu par ses célibataires, même' ['The Bride Undressed by her Bachelors']: An Analytical Re-

flection'' (1944), in *Selected Publications, Société Anonyme*, Vol. 3 (*Monographs and Brochure*) (New York: Arno Press, 1972), on the *painting-glass-mirror* that Duchamp's *La Mariée* appears as in the library of Miss Dreier's country home.

6. Like the inscription on the glass wall surrounding the island of the nereid in Alfred Jarry's *Les jours et les nuits* (1897): "If someone passionately embraces his Double through the glass, a point on the glass comes to life and becomes a sex organ, and being and its image make love across the wall.''

7. *Tu m'* . . . , Marcel Duchamp (1918).

8. These are the Hebrew words traced by a hand of fire on the walls of the palace of Belshazzar. They announce the ruin of Babylon. *Daniel* 5.25.

9. Cf. Raymond Roussel, *How I Wrote Certain of My Books*, tr. C. Foord and R. Hepper (Berkeley: University of California Press, 1967).

10. For example, Angelus Silesius takes the mystical term "shepherd" and pluralizes it with pronouns (*I am, you are*); in this way, a space of dialogue between the personal predicates and the traditional term is created. It should be noted that for him this construction does not depart from presence, but rather calls for it in the form of what *must* be (*müssen*). This is a kind of mystical utopia.

11. Cf. the unpublished dissertation of Bernard Sarrazin on Léon Bloy's interpretation of the Bible (Paris, 1973).

12. In the seventeenth century, a "phrase" was a "manner of expression," a "way of speaking," a "turn" of phrase (Furetière). It was a practice relative to a place, not a statement.

13. The quotes are from Diego de Jesus, *Notes et remarques en trois discours pour donner une facile intelligence des phrases mystiques* . . . (First Discourse), in *Oeuvres du B. P. Jean de la Croix* (Paris, 1641).

14. The same procedure is followed in Duchamp. The "bride" is *also* the name of an insect, the moth; or, "voie lactée" becomes "voile actée" ("Milky Way," "officially announced sail"), "voilette" becomes "violette" ([hat] "veil," "violet"), "nue" becomes "nuée" ("naked" [woman], [storm] "cloud").

15. It was Freud who introduced the link between writing and walking or "treading upon the body of mother earth" ("Inhibitions, Symptoms and Anxiety," in *SE*, Vol. 20, p. 90).

16. Cf. Luce Irigaray, *Speculum* (Paris: Minuit, 1974), pp. 238–252.

17. Georges Bataille, *L'expérience intérieure* (Paris: Gallimard, 1954), p. 216.

18. Strictly speaking, "glyphs" are the signatures (nicks on the ear, brands) marked on cattle by their owners.

19. This is a historical allusion to the Brethren of Common Life during the fifteenth century.

20. Franz Kafka, *The Penal Colony*, tr. Willa and Edwin Muir (New York: Schocken Books, 1976), pp. 204, 209, 210. My emphasis.

21. Tibullus (I.9.21). See Jean-Louis Scheffer, *L'invention du corps chrétien* (Paris: Galilée, 1975), p. 146.

22. Cf. Michel de Certeau, *L'Absent de l'histoire* (Paris: Mame, 1973), pp. 153–180.

23. Pierre Legendre, *L'amour du censeur* (Paris: Seuil, 1973).

24. These are Freud's last words in the *Gesammelte Werke*, Vol. 18, p. 152: "22. VIII. (1938) Mystik die dunkle Selbstwahrnehmung des Reiches ausserhalb des Ichs, des Es.'' ("August 22, 1938—Mysticism is the obscure self-perception of the realm outside the ego, of the id,'' *SE*, Vol. 23, p. 300).

25. Nelly Sachs, *Brasier d'énigmes et autres poèmes* (Paris: Denoël, 1967), pp. 276–277.

26. On this point, not without temerity, I depart from the opinion of Arturo Schwartz.

27. Daniel Sperber's thesis in *Rethinking Symbolism* (tr. Alice Morton [Cambridge: Cambridge University Press, 1975]) is that a "symbol" is anything that marks the deficiency of a concept.

Chapter 12. The Black Sun of Language: Foucault

1. Michel Foucault, *The Order of Things* (New York: Vintage, 1973). (Translation of *Les mots et les choses* [Paris: Gallimard, 1966].) Page references are identified by the abbreviation, *OT*.

2. Jacques Roger, *Les sciences de la vie dans la pensée française du XVIIIe siècle* (Paris: A. Colin, 1963).

3. Michel Foucault, *Histoire de la folie à l'âge classique* (Paris: Plon, 1961). The English translation (*Madness and Civilization* [New York: Vintage, 1973]) is based on an abridged version that omits most of the passages cited in this chapter. Page references are to the French edition (*HF*), with an additional reference to the English translation where possible.—Tr.

4. Michel Foucault, *Naissance de la clinique* (Paris: PUF, 1963). The English translation (*The Birth of the Clinic*, tr. A. M. Sheridan Smith [New York: Vintage, 1975]) is based on the second French edition (1972). Some of the passages cited in this chapter are absent or altered in the second edition. Page references are to the French edition (*NC*), with an additional reference to the English translation where the texts coincide.—Tr.

5. Michel Foucault, *Raymond Roussel* (Paris: Gallimard, 1963), p. 190.

6. *The Archaeology of Knowledge* (New York: Vintage, 1973) is devoted to the methodological problems posed by the "archaeology" of the human sciences (cf. *OT*, p. XII, n. 1).

7. In this respect, Sartrean criticism is unacceptable without modification (cf. *L'Arc*, no. 30, p. 87). "A refusal of history?" Yes, if by that we mean the refusal to explain how history is made, how systems arise. But also no, since each system implies new tasks and risks.

8. But perhaps it is simply that Foucault is unable or cares not to explain it.

9. This unitary reference does appear, however, in the poorly defined notion of "positivity."

10. Michel Foucault, "La Pensée du Dehors," *Critique*, 229 (1966), pp. 523-540. Page references are identified by the abbreviation, *PD*.

11. It should be noted that the religious sciences are nearly absent from his history of "mentalities," though they played a central role, particularly in the establishment of the *episteme* of the "Classical Age."

12. For example, are we not obliged to question the nature of the methodological postulate (an *a priori* for Foucault) according to which the *episteme* is the ahistorical condition of history?

Chapter 13. Micro-techniques and Panoptic Discourse: A Quid pro Quo

1. Michel Foucault, *Discipline and Punish: The Birth of the Prison*, tr. Alan Sheridan (New York: Pantheon, 1977). I quote *Surveiller et punir. Naissance de la prison* (Paris: Gallimard, 1975). For an analysis of Foucault's first works, see chapter 11 of the present volume.

2. See in particular Gilles Deleuze, "Ecrivain, non: un nouveau cartographe," in *Critique*, no. 343 (December 1975), pp. 1207-1227; Cesáreo Morales, "Poder del discurso," in *Historia y sociedad*, no. 8 (1975), pp. 39-48; Hayden White, "Michel Foucault," in *Structuralism and Since*, ed. John Sturrock (Oxford: Oxford University Press, 1979).

3. Serge Moscovici, *Essai sur l'histoire humaine de la nature* (Paris: Flammarion, 1968).

4. Pierre Legendre, *L'amour du censeur. Essai sur l'ordre dogmatique* (Paris: Seuil, 1974).

5. *Surveiller et punir*, pp. 9-13 (Damiens), 197-201 (the plague city), 261-267 (the galley slaves put in irons), 267-269 (the rolling prison, 288 (Vidocq), 296 (Béasse), etc.

6. Ibid., pp. 28 (four general rules), 96-102 (six rules of the punitive semio-technique), 106-116 (six conditions for the functioning of punishment), 143-151 (four techniques of discipline), 159-161 (four procedures for capitalizing individual time), 185 (three mechanisms of examination), 211-217 (three processes of panoptism), 238-251 (three principles of the penitentiary system),

274–275 (seven principles for a good penitentiary organization), 276 (four elements of the "carcéral" system), etc.

7. Ibid., thirty engravings and photographs at the front of the book.

Chapter 14. The Laugh of Michel Foucault

1. [*Passeur*: one who moves people or things across borders or into forbidden zones; ferryman; taken literally, it means "one who passes"—Tr.]

2. *The Archaeology of Knowledge*, tr. A. M. Sheridan Smith (New York: Vintage, 1973), p. 17.

3. *L'usage des plaisirs*, Vol. 2 of *Histoire de la sexualité* (Paris: Gallimard, 1984), p. 15.

4. "The Discourse on Language," [Translation of *L'ordre du discours* (Paris: Gallimard, 1971)], tr. Robert Swyer, in *The Archaeology of Knowledge*, p. 217. [Translation modified.]

5. *The Order of Things* (New York: Vintage, 1973), p. XV. [Translation modified.]

6. See *The Birth of the Clinic*, tr. A. M. Sheridan Smith (New York: Vintage, 1975); *The Birth of the Prison*, the subtitle of *Discipline and Punish* (New York: Vintage, 1979); and so on. Moreover, these two works are, I believe, Foucault's most decisive "interventions."

7. *Discipline and Punish*.

8. Ibid.

9. *The History of Sexuality. Volume I: An Introduction*, tr. Robert Hurley (New York: Pantheon, 1978).

10. *Madness and Civilization*, tr. Richard Howard (New York: Vintage, 1973), chapter 1, pp. 3–37.

11. *The Order of Things*, chapter 1, "Las Meninas," pp. 3–16.

12. *Discipline and Punish*, pp. 3–5.

13. Ibid., part 3, chapter 3, "Panopticism," pp. 195–228.

14. Gilles Deleuze, "Ecrivain non: un nouveau cartographe," *Critique*, Vol. 31, No. 343 (December 1975), pp. 1207–1227.

15. *L'usage des plaisirs*, p. 14.

16. "The Discourse on Language," p. 231. [Translation modified.]

17. Ibid., p. 229. [Translation modified.]

Chapter 15. History: Science and Fiction

1. Michel de Certeau, "La fiction de l'histoire," *L'écriture de l'histoire*, 2nd ed. (Paris: Gallimard, 1978), pp. 312–358.

2. Karl Popper, *The Logic of Scientific Discovery* (London: Hutchinson, 1959).

3. See Ralph Andreano, ed., *La nouvelle histoire économique* (Paris: Gallimard, 1977), p. 258.

4. Jeanine Czubaroff, "Intellectual Respectability: A Rhetorical Problem," *Quarterly Journal of Speech*, 59 (1973), pp. 155–164.

5. Jules Michelet, "L'héroisme de l'esprit" (1869), in *L'Arc*, no. 52, pp. 7–13.

6. Jean-Pierre Faye, *Les langages totalitaires* (Paris: Hermann, 1973).

7. Jack D. Douglas, "The Rhetoric of Science and the Origins of Statistical Social Thought," in *The Phenomenon of Sociology*, ed. Edward A. Tiryakian (New York: Appleton-Century-Crofts, 1969), pp. 44–57; Herbert W. Simons, "Are Scientists Rhetors in Disguise? An Analysis of Discursive Processes Within Scientific Communities," in *Rhetoric in Transition*, ed. Eugene E. White (University Park: Pennsylvania State University Press, 1980), pp. 115–130.

8. John Craig, *Theologiae christianae principia mathematica* (London: 1699). See the Latin

text and a translation of his "rules of historical evidence" in *History and Theory*, Beiheft no. 4, 1964.

9. Condorcet, *Mathématique et société* (Paris: Hermann, 1974).

10. Condillac, *La langue des calculs* (Paris: Charles Hovel, 1798).

11. See C. B. MacPherson, *The Political Theory of Possessive Individualism* (Oxford: Clarendon Press, 1962) and Alan Macfarlane, *The Origins of English Individualism* (Cambridge: Cambridge University Press, 1978).

12. See Morris Kline, *Mathematics in Western Culture* (New York: Oxford University Press, 1972), pp. 190-286.

13. See, for example, "IBM ou l'émergence d'une nouvelle dictature," *Les temps modernes*, no. 351, octobre 1975.

14. See Peter Hanns Reill, *The German Enlightenment and the Rise of Historicism* (Berkeley: University of California Press, 1975), p. 231.

15. See Michel de Certeau, D. Julia, and J. Revel, *Une politique de la langue* (Paris: Gallimard, 1975), chap. 4.

16. See, for example, Charles Corge, *Informatique et démarche de l'esprit* (Paris: Larousse, 1975).

17. On the subject of computer-assisted historical analysis, see Charles Tilly, "Computers in Historical Analysis," *Computers and the Humanities*, 7 (1973), pp. 323-335.

18. See François Furet, "Le quantitatif en histoire," in *Faire de l'histoire*, ed. Jacques Le Goff and Pierre Nora (Paris: Gallimard, 1974), I, pp. 42-61.

19. Tilly, "Computers," pp. 333-334.

20. For a fuller analysis of this problem about the "return" of the past in the present, see chapter 1.

21. The same problem poses itself at the collective level, as is shown, for example, by the difficult relationship that the new black-African historiography, of a nationalist type, maintains with the ethnic plurality of its object-subject. See Bogumil Jewsiewicki, "L'histoire en Afrique et le commerce des idées usagées," *Canadian Journal of African Studies*, 13 (1979), 69-87.

22. Paul Veyne, *Comment on écrit l'histoire* (Paris: Seuil, 1971).

23. Albert O. Hirschman, *The Passions and the Interests: Political Arguments for Capitalism Before Its Triumph* (Princeton, N.J.: Princeton University Press, 1977).

24. Martin Duberman, *Black Mountain: An Exploration in Community* (New York: Dutton, 1973).

25. Régine Robin, *Le cheval blanc de Lénine ou l'histoire autre* (Bruxelles: Complexe, 1979).

26. See Marc Fumaroli, "Les mémoires du XVIIe siècle au carrefour des genres en prose," *XVIIe Siècle*, nos. 94-95, 1971, pp. 7-37; F. Smith Fussner, *The Historical Revolution: English Historical Writing and Thought, 1580-1740* (Westport, Conn.: Greenwood Press, 1962), pp. 299-321.

27. Jeremy Bentham's theory of linguistic fictions and of "incomplete symbols" enables him to analyze the effective operations connected with a logic of "as if." See C. K. Ogden, *Bentham's Theory of Fictions* (London: Kegan Paul, 1932).

Chapter 16. The Politics of Silence: The Long March of the Indians

1. *Resguardos*: reservations set aside for the Indians by the Spanish crown, then by the Republic of Colombia. The *Cabildo* (the Indians' government) distributes land to each family to cultivate, but ownership of the land is communal. The *resguardos* whose names follow are located in the Cauca River Valley.

2. *Kamsa*: Indian groups, tribes.

3. *Narino*: a district in the southern part of the country, bordering on Ecuador.

4. *Santa Marta*: in the northern part of Colombia, between the Coast and Venezuela.

5. The *paramo*: a very cold zone, lying above about 9,700 feet in elevation.

6. Since there are no seasons in Colombia, but the climate varies according to the elevation, people commonly speak of the "warm lands," the "cold lands," and the *paramo*—the three tiers of Colombia.

7. The Gathering of Indians of the Cauca region in Colombia, from the minutes prepared by the Regional Council of the Cauca "as a contribution to our common struggle." The text was published in French in *La Lettre*, no. 188 (April, 1974), pp. 14–15.

8. Alfred Métraux, *Religions et magies indiennes d'Amérique du Sud* (Paris: Gallimard, 1967), esp. chaps. 1 and 6. Cf. Michel de Certeau, "Terres lointaines," *Etudes* (April 1968), pp. 582–590, and *L'Absent de l'Histoire* (Paris: Mame, 1973), pp. 135–150 ("Religion et société: les messianismes").

9. Statement of ANUC and the Regional Council of the Indigenous Peoples of the Cauca, Bogotá, August 31, 1974.

10. Jean-Loup Herbert et. al., *Indianité et lutte de classes* (Paris: UGE, 1972), pp. 227–228.

11. Ibid., pp. 216–217, relates the many acts of resistance and rebellions in Guatemala that have been kept quiet.

12. Cf. Pierre Clastres, *Society Against the State*, tr. Robert Hurley (New York: Urizen, 1977), "Of Torture in Primitive Societies," pp. 148–158 (chapter on initiation ceremonies).

13. Address by Justino Quispe Balboa (Aymarà, Bolivia) before the first Indian Congress of South America, October 13, 1974, in the presence of Paraguayan authorities and observers. Quispe Balboa was 21 years old at the time. DIAL Document no. 196.

14. Cf. Clastres, after many others, *Society Against the State*, chap. 2, pp. 19–37 and chap. 7, pp. 132–141.

15. "American" here designates what preceded colonization.

16. These two "reductions" go together: the fixed, ideological construct ethnology produces as its object, in other words "indigenous" *culture*, reinforces and camouflages the *socioeconomic* loss of autonomy produced by capitalist domination. Knowledge and power combine to impose both the representations and the laws of the Western world upon societies which often end up internalizing both.

17. Cf. Nathan Wachtel, *The Vision of the Vanquished: The Spanish Conquest of Peru Through Indian Eyes, 1530–1570*, tr. Ben and Siân Reynolds Hassocks (New York: Harvester, 1977), pp. 134–211 ("Destructuration"). On the historical effects of the process of destructuration, cf. Sakari Sariola, *Power and Resistance: The Colonial Heritage in Latin America* (Ithaca, N.Y.: Cornell University Press, 1972), pp. 266–292, and especially Stanley and Barbara Stein, *The Colonial Heritage of Latin America* (New York: Oxford University Press, 1970), pp. 28–53, 174–185.

18. Wachtel, *The Vision of the Vanquished*, pp. 61–85.

19. Cf. for example André Gunder Frank's remarkable documentation in *Capitalism and Underdevelopment in Latin America: Historical Studies of Chile and Brazil* (London: Penguin, 1969).

20. Cf. Jacques Monast, *On les croyait chrétiens: les Aymaras* (Paris: Cerf, 1969), and Michel de Certeau, "Le danger de l'insignifiance ou l'évangélisation superficielle," *Spiritus*, no. 44 (1971), pp. 6–90.

21. T. C. McLuhan, ed., *Touch the Earth* (Fargo, N.D.: Touchstone, 1976).

22. Clastres, *Society Against the State*, p. 20.

23. Clastres, *Chronique des indiens Guayaki* (Paris: Plon, 1972), p. 219.

24. This is the definition Pierre Clastres gives "primitive societies." "Entretien avec Pierre Clastres," *L'anti-mythes*, no. 9, p. 5.

25. These "explorations" in *self-management* remain for the most part *utopian*, both mobilizing and mythic, an index of experiments and studies to be undertaken. It is in this respect similar to the

democratic utopias which, in the eighteenth century, prepared the way for the great revolutions of the end of that century and of the following century.

26. Georges Balandier, *Sens et puissance: Les dynamiques sociales* (Paris: PUF, 1971). Cf. also, by the same author, *Anthropo-logiques* (Paris: PUF, 1974).

27. Ignacy Sachs produced an important study, *Le changement technologique comme variable des politiques de développement et l'avenir des rapports entre le tiers monde et les pays industrialisés* (Paris: IREM, 1974). See, by the same author, *La découverte du tiers monde* (Paris: Flammarion, 1970).

28. Cf. the works by Clastres cited above (notes 12, 23, and 24).

29. Jean William Lapierre, *Essai sur le fondement du pouvoir politique* (Aix-en-Provence: Faculté d'Aix-en-Provence, 1968).

30. Maurice Godelier, *Perspectives on Marxist Anthropology*, tr. Robert Brain (New York: Cambridge University Press, 1977).

31. Cf. DIAL Document no. 196.

32. Pierre Rosanvallon, *L'âge de l'autogestion* (Paris: Seuil, 1976).

33. Robert Jaulin, *Gens du soi, gens de l'autre* (Paris: UGE, 1973), p. 377.

34. *Touch the Earth*, p. 36.

35. Cf. for example, for Mexico, *Eco, primer periódico Bicultural Bilingue de Información general en la Zona Mazahua*, Temascalcingo Edo., Mexico. For Brazil, the *Boletim* of the Conselho Indigenista Missioñario (CIMI), Brasilia. For Paraguay, see the publications of the *Coordinación pastoral de la Selva*, Asunción, in *Catequesis Latinoamericana* (esp. the July–Sept. 1974 issue).

36. *Indigena* and *American Friends of Brazil*, Berkeley, California, published *Supysáva: A Documentary Report on the Conditions of Indian Peoples in Brazil* (1974). See also *Akwesasne Notes*, the official publication of the Mohawk Nation of New York.

37. For example, *Gesellschaft für Bedrohte Völker* of Hamburg, which publishes *Pogrom*.

38. See *Syd Amerikansk Chaski*, Stockholm, of which the first issue appeared in June 1976.

39. *The International Work Group for the Indigenous World* (IWGIA), which publishes a remarkable documentation series.

Index

Index

The author of over fifteen books, **Michel de Certeau** works in the fields of history, literary studies, and psychoanalysis. De Certeau was professor of French and comparative literature at the University of California, San Diego, from 1978 until mid-1984, and is now director of studies at the Ecole des Hautes Etudes en Sciences Sociales in Paris. His *Practice of Everyday Life (L'invention du quotidien)* appeared in English translation in 1984.

Brian Massumi is translator of Jean-François Lyotard's *Postmodern Condition* and translator of Jacques Attali's *Noise: The Political Economy of Music*—both volumes in the Theory and History of Literature series.

Wlad Godzich teaches comparative literature at the Université de Montréal and is series co-editor with Jochen Schulte-Sasse.